Bt 4.35

Metternich's Diplomacy
at Its Zenith
1820-1823

Chancellor Prince Klemens Lothar Wenzel von Metternich, around 1820

Published with the permission of Librairie Arthème Fayard, Paris

Metternich's Diplomacy
at Its Zenith
1820 - 1823

by

Paul W. Schroeder

UNIVERSITY OF TEXAS PRESS · AUSTIN

PUBLISHED WITH THE ASSISTANCE OF A GRANT
FROM THE FORD FOUNDATION
UNDER ITS PROGRAM FOR THE SUPPORT OF PUBLICATIONS
IN THE HUMANITIES AND SOCIAL SCIENCES

TO MY WIFE,

whose principal contribution
to this book consisted in
reminding me occasionally
that there are things in life
more important than Metternich.

PREFACE

This work, as the title suggests, is a study of Metternich's diplomacy during the years 1820 to 1823. While I have tried to keep in mind the general European developments of the time, I have not attempted to write a general account of European politics or even of European international relations during this period. The emphasis is entirely upon Austria's foreign policy and upon Metternich's thought and action. This qualification may, I hope, explain and justify the relatively brief space given to certain events, for example, the revolutions in Spain, Portugal, and Greece, and the whole question of the revolutionized Spanish and Portuguese colonies in the New World, as compared to the much greater attention accorded other events, especially the revolution at Naples in 1820. Metternich had little interest in Spain, Portugal, Greece, or the New World, while the Neapolitan Revolution was, I am convinced, the most important concern for him in this period.

For this same reason, I have included considerable discussion of some proposals and plans by Metternich which never reached fruition and therefore had no practical effects, for example, his proposal of an international Act of Guarantee at the Congress of Troppau, his attempts to promote an Italian League analogous to the German Confederation, and his efforts to set up antirevolutionary information centers in Milan and Vienna. To present an adequate picture of Metternich's diplomacy, it is as necessary to discuss his failures and unfulfilled aspirations as his successes and achievements.

The title chosen for this study, "Metternich's Diplomacy at Its Zenith, 1820–1823" is borrowed from Joseph V. Fuller, *Bismarck's Diplomacy at Its Zenith* (Cambridge, Mass.: Harvard University Press, 1922), because the term "zenith" appears to fit this period in

Metternich's diplomacy peculiarly well. While it can undoubtedly be argued that his diplomatic achievements and contributions to history were greater within the years 1813–1815 than at any other time, during this earlier period Metternich did not completely dominate the European stage, but had to share the limelight with Castlereagh, Wellington, Alexander I of Russia, Talleyrand, and Hardenberg. From 1820 to 1823, however, Metternich was clearly the pre-eminent figure in European diplomacy, exercising a control over persons and events which he had never achieved before and would never attain again. This fact, I believe, makes the period a particularly fruitful one in which to study his diplomatic policies and methods.

Since this is an analysis as well as a history of Metternich's diplomacy in this period, I have reached some definite conclusions which are given in detail in the final chapter, but also indicated elsewhere in the study. It would not be surprising if a reader should suppose these to be simply a return to the old liberal view on Metternich without an adequate awareness of the revisions made by more recent Metternich scholarship. The first part of this charge, I would have to confess, is at least in part true, but I would demur as to the second. In fact, I began research on this topic without any fixed views, but with the general supposition that the revisionist views on Metternich, particularly those of his eminent biographer, Heinrich Ritter von Srbik, were probably correct, and that my main task would be to illustrate and amplify them by the evidence I found in this period. I soon came to the conclusion, however, that the task of fitting the material with which I was daily confronted into the interpretation offered by Srbik would have defeated Procrustes, and hence abandoned the attempt and eventually ended up with the conclusions given here.

Most of the materials for this study, and all of the unpublished material, were drawn from the Haus- Hof- und Staatsarchiv in Vienna. While the use of other archives, particularly those in London and Paris, would undoubtedly have helped to shed light on certain points, enough has been published in the way of memoirs, documents, letters, and secondary accounts dealing with the policies of other powers and leaders that I feel confident this omission does not seriously affect the conclusions reached in this study on Metternich.

The reader may benefit from a brief explanation of certain usages followed in the text and footnotes. The great majority of the archival materials cited are drawn from the section Staatskanzlei: Auswärtiges Amt. These words have therefore been omitted from all citations, and the material simply cited according to its nature: Weisungen, Berichte, Varia, etc.; the country it concerns: Russland, Frankreich, etc.; the number of the fascicle in which the document is contained, and the number (if any) of the particular dispatch. When material from other divisions is cited, it is given first according to its full category (e.g., Staatskanzlei: Provinzen: Lombardei-Venezien) and in succeeding instances in shorter form (Provinzen: Lombardei-Venezien).

My use of the terms "Congress" and "Allies" may bear some explanation. Technically, only the Congress of Verona in this period was a congress; the meetings of Troppau and Laibach, lacking full representation of all the powers, were only conferences. Similarly, the only real Allies of which one should speak (apart from the purely nominal Holy Alliance) were the four powers of the Quadruple Alliance—Austria, England, Prussia, and Russia. The informal union of the five great powers, including France, should be called the Concert of Powers or the Concert of Europe, while the special coalition of Austria, Prussia, and Russia set up at Troppau should be called the Eastern powers or the Eastern bloc. In practice, however, the diplomats often referred to the meetings of Troppau and Laibach as congresses, and to the Concert of Powers or the Eastern bloc as "the Allies." For the sake of simplicity I have followed their practice without attempting to maintain any nice distinctions.

Given names have been for the most part kept in the original (exceptions are Russian and Turkish names and names of monarchs). Titles accompanying names, however, have been Anglicized.

For the sake of avoiding confusion, Viscount Castlereagh, who became second Marquess of Londonderry in April 1821, has been referred to throughout the work simply as "Castlereagh." Likewise, his brother, Lord Stewart, who inherited the title after Castlereagh's suicide in August 1822, has been referred to as "Stewart."

All dates, including Russian and Turkish, are given according to the Gregorian calendar. The difference between the New and Old Style calendars at this time was twelve days.

Finally, I would like to express my gratitude to all who have encouraged and assisted me in this project. My special thanks go to the United States Department of State and the United States Educational Commission in Austria for the Fulbright grant under which I was able to do archival research; to Geheimrat Dr. Gebhard Rath, director of the Haus- Hof- und Staatsarchiv in Vienna, for his valuable assistance in making available the materials I needed; to Professor Dr. Heinrich Benedikt, professor of history at the University of Vienna, for some important suggestions on sources and bibliography; and, above all, to Professor R. John Rath, of the University of Texas, who not only encouraged and advised me throughout the project, but also while he was in Vienna directed me to certain valuable archival materials.

PAUL W. SCHROEDER

Concordia Senior College
Fort Wayne, Indiana

CONTENTS

LIST OF MAPS

Metternich's Diplomacy
at Its Zenith
1820-1823

CHAPTER I

METTERNICH'S DIPLOMACY AND
THE CONCERT OF EUROPE,
1815-1820

A vital key to Metternich's diplomacy in the years 1820 to 1823 is the Vienna system established in 1814 and 1815. In these two years the foundation of Austria's foreign policy was laid, and it is hardly an exaggeration to say that from then on, all Metternich's energy and talents as a diplomat went into maintaining and defending this system.

Obviously it is impossible to indicate here, even in brief outline, all the deliberations carried on and the decisions reached by the powers of Europe in those two epoch-making years.[1] It will be

[1] For obvious reasons I have attempted no survey of even all the major secondary works on the Congress of Vienna and its attendant diplomatic events. For the remarks here I have depended on the following works: Charles K. Webster, *The Congress of Vienna, 1814–1815;* Karl Griewank, *Der Wiener Kongress und die neue Ordnung Europas 1814–1815;* Harold G. Nicolson, *The Congress of Vienna: A Study in Allied Unity, 1812–1822;* Edward Vose Gulick, *Europe's Classical Balance of Power: A Case History of the Theory and Practice of One of the Great Concepts of European Statecraft;* Walter Alison Phillips, *The Confederation of Europe: A Study of the European Alliance, 1813–1823, as an Experiment in the International Organization of Peace;* Heinrich Ritter von Srbik, *Metternich: Der Staatsman und der Mensch,* Vol. I, 182–229; and Alfred Stern, *Geschichte Europas seit den Verträgen von 1815 bis zum Frankfurter Frieden von 1871,* Vol. I, 30–41. Other works used include Jacques-Henri Pirenne, *La Sainte-Alliance: Organisation européenne de la paix mondiale,* Vol. I, *Les Traités de Paix, 1814–1815;* Frederick B. Artz, *Reaction and Revolution, 1814–1832,* pp. 110–118; W. P. Cresson, *The Holy Alliance: The European Background of the Monroe Doctrine;* Hans Rieben, *Prinzipiengrundlage und Diplomatie in Metternichs Europapolitik, 1815–1848;* Hans G. Schenk, *The Aftermath of the Napoleonic Wars: The Concert of Europe—An Experiment;* and Wilhelm Schwarz, *Die Heilige Allianz: Tragik eines europäischen Friedensbundes.*

sufficient for our purposes here to say that the Congress of Vienna, along with the treaties of peace and alliance which preceded and followed it, accomplished four major purposes. First, it restored the balance of power in Europe. True, the balance which was restored was no mathematically precise one, a condition impossible to attain. Russia emerged from the Napoleonic wars as easily the strongest of the land powers in Europe, England was supreme on the sea, and Prussia remained visibly weaker than the other great powers. Nevertheless, the peace settlement did revive the eighteenth-century pentarchy of great powers, leaving no one of them strong enough to dominate Europe as France had done for twenty years.

Second, without imposing a vengeful peace upon France, the Allies created barriers against a renewal of French aggression by means of territorial changes and treaties. To prevent France from once again expanding to the Rhine or invading Italy, the Congress united Belgium and Holland into a strong Kingdom of the Netherlands, strengthened Prussia with extensive territories on the Rhine, set up a German Confederation, largely for purposes of defense, and provided for Austrian domination of the Italian peninsula. A still more formidable check on France was the great alliance initiated by the Treaty of Chaumont of March 1, 1814, revived on March 25, 1815, upon Napoleon's return from Elba, and formally renewed at Paris on November 20, 1815. The treaty of November 1815 set up a twenty-year alliance between Austria, Russia, Prussia, and England to guard against any revival of the Bonaparte dynasty or a renewal of revolution in France which might lead again to aggressive war.[2]

The third result of the Allied efforts in 1814 and 1815 was the achievement of a large measure of international cooperation, together with the provision for certain machinery to be used by the Allies to carry on their collaboration in the future. Many names have been applied to the system of international cooperation prevailing after 1815, but whether one calls it a system of congresses, a Concert of Powers, a Directory of Europe, a system of diplomacy by conference, a Confederation of Europe, the beginning of an all-Euro-

---

[2] Hans W. Schmalz, *Versuche einer gesamteuropäischen Organisation 1815–1820, mit besonderer Berücksichtigung der Troppauer Interventionspolitik*, 10–16; Charles K. Webster, *The Foreign Policy of Castlereagh, 1815–1822: Britain and the European Alliance*, 51–55.

pean organization, or something else—and all these terms [3] have a
certain justification—the main point remains the same. During this
period the great powers of Europe felt themselves bound together
by an overriding common interest in the maintenance of peace and
order. So close was this harmony of conservative aims that they not
only were willing to commit themselves jointly to the tasks of maintaining the entire territorial system established by the Vienna Final
Act of June 9, 1815, and of keeping watch over France, but they
were also ready to join in consultation and conference on other diplomatic problems which might arise. Article VI of the Quadruple
Alliance Treaty of November 1815 specifically provided for regular
conferences of the four powers. The conferences were to be called
both to supervise the execution of the second peace treaty with
France—the Treaty of Paris of November 20, 1815—and to deal
with general questions and policies of common interest and benefit
as a means of cementing a union salutary for Europe and the world.[4]
This clause was the basis for the series of post-Vienna conferences
and congresses held from 1818 (Aachen [Aix-La-Chapelle]) to 1822
(Verona). The same principle of great-power unity and cooperation
was implied in other transactions as well, especially in the Vienna
Final Act, which bound all the signatory powers, great and small,
to the maintenance of the entire interlocking territorial system of
Europe, thus tying them together in a community of interest.[5]

The outstanding symbol of this newly felt European unity, though
it was meaningless as an operative instrument, was the Holy Alliance, concluded on September 26, 1815. As is now well known, the
idea of a Holy Alliance did not at first possess or deserve the sinister
connotation it later came to bear: that of a reactionary league of

---

[3] The only terms to which I would make mild objection are "the Confederation of Europe" (Phillips) and "an all-European organization" (Schmalz and
others). These phrases suggest too much structure to the very intangible forms
which this unity of the great powers assumed (though the authors themselves
do not make this error). Moreover, the terms tend to blur the distinction between the real "Confederation of Europe" and "all-European organization"
which Alexander I of Russia had in mind, and the much more limited ideas of
diplomacy by conference and great-power unity of interest and attitude which
more realistic diplomats like Castlereagh and Metternich sought to achieve.

[4] Webster, *Foreign Policy of Castlereagh*, 55.

[5] *Ibid.*, 51–54; Schmalz, *Gesamteuropäische Organisation*, 10–16; Rieben,
Metternichs Europapolitik, 56–59.

sovereigns against their peoples. As originally proposed by Tsar
Alexander I of Russia, it was one of the most advanced and liberal
ideas of the period. In fervently idealistic language it called for a
union of kings and peoples in the effort to govern Europe according
to principles of peace, Christianity, and brotherhood. Moreover, it
was intended by Alexander only as a part of a general scheme in
which sovereigns would find security in a joint European guarantee
of their territories and thrones, after which they would guarantee
freedom and happiness to their subjects by granting them liberal
institutions, particularly moderate constitutions like the *Charte*
which Louis XVIII of France, largely at the instigation of Alexander,
had granted to the French people upon his restoration in 1814. Alexander's proposal was, however, so cleverly revised by Klemens
Lothar Prince Metternich, foreign minister and leading statesman of
Austria, that it took on a completely different direction and tone.
Metternich expunged from it all traces of liberal ideas, all hints of
changes in existing institutions, and changed the alliance from a
fraternal bond between kings and peoples for their mutual benefit
and the promotion of Christian ideals into a paternal alliance of
sovereigns to strengthen and guide their exercise of authority over
their subjects. In this form it was signed by the three Eastern great
powers—Austria, Prussia, and Russia—with all the other monarchs
of Europe later acceding except three: the Ottoman Sultan, because
he was not invited; Pope Pius VII, because he felt no need of instruction on Christian principles of government; and the Prince-
Regent (later George IV) of England, because as a constitutional
monarch he could not make treaties without ministerial consent.
Realists like Metternich, British Foreign Minister Viscount Castlereagh, and Metternich's secretary and publicist, Friedrich von
Gentz, were secretly contemptuous of the alliance's mystical tone
and lack of concrete meaning; but the very fact that such a treaty
could be proposed and signed indicates the widespread sentiment
for peace and the feeling of European harmony and unity which
prevailed at the end of the Napoleonic wars.[6]

[6] Schmalz, *Gesamteuropäische Organisation*, 16–18; Schwarz, *Heilige Allianz*,
30–42, 48–61, 86–99; Phillips, *Confederation of Europe*, 7–9, 20–40, 148–156;
Schenk, *Aftermath of the Napoleonic Wars*, 29–43; Werner Näf, *Staat und
Staatsgedanke: Vorträge zur neueren Geschichte*, 9–15; Werner Näf, *Zur
Geschichte der Heiligen Allianz*.

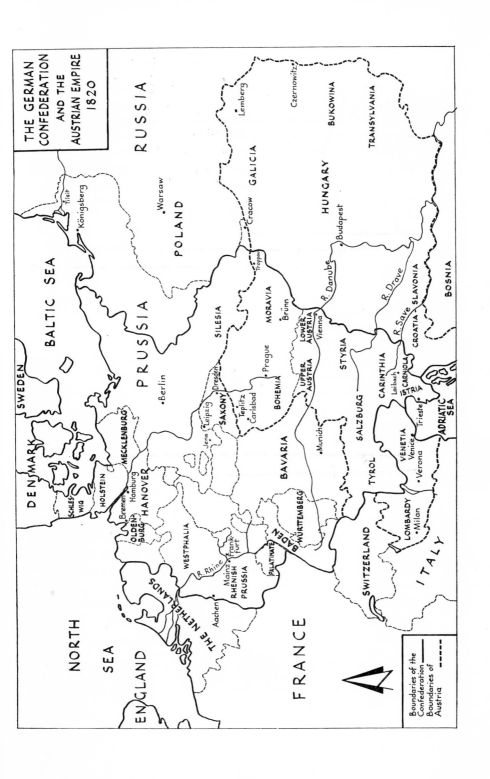

THE GERMAN
CONFEDERATION
AND THE
AUSTRIAN EMPIRE
1820

NORTH SEA

BALTIC SEA

SWEDEN

DENMARK

RUSSIA

ENGLAND

THE NETHERLANDS

•Tilsit
•Königsberg

POLAND

•Warsaw

PRUSSIA

•Berlin

SCHLES-WIG
HOLSTEIN
MECKLENBURG
Hamburg
Bremen
OLDEN-BURG
HANOVER

WESTPHALIA

R. Rhine

Aachen

RHENISH
PRUSSIA
Mainz
Frank-furt
PALATINATE
BADEN
WÜRTEMBERG

FRANCE

SWITZERLAND

Jena
Leipzig
Dresden
SAXONY
Teplitz
Carlsbad
BOHEMIA
•Prague

SILESIA

MORAVIA
Brünn•

BAVARIA

•Munich

Troppau

LOWER AUSTRIA
Vienna•
UPPER AUSTRIA

STYRIA

SALZBURG

TYROL

CARINTHIA
Laibach
CARNIOLA
ISTRIA
Trieste•

VENETIA
•Verona
Venice•

LOMBARDY
•Milan

ITALY

ADRIATIC SEA

GALICIA
•Cracow
Lemberg•

•Czernowitz

BUKOWINA

TRANSYLVANIA

HUNGARY

R. Danube

Budapest•

R. Drave

R. Save

CROATIA
SLAVONIA

BOSNIA

Boundaries of the
Confederation
Boundaries of
Austria

The fourth major result of the Congress of Vienna, and the one most important to Metternich, to his monarch, Emperor Francis I, and to the Austrian Empire, was the establishment of Austrian hegemony in Central Europe from the Baltic Sea to the Adriatic and the Mediterranean. Metternich's guiding principle throughout the War of Liberation and the succeeding negotiations, from 1813 to 1815, had been that of making Central Europe, especially Germany, strong and independent enough to resist the pressure of the two powerful flanks of Europe, France and Russia.[7] Metternich, to be sure, was not alone in this goal. He enjoyed, above all, the powerful support of Castlereagh, who was also interested in a strong center for Europe as a part of the traditional British system of maintaining the balance of power on the Continent, and who regarded Central Europe as Austria's natural sphere of influence. Nevertheless, Metternich's masterly diplomacy must receive the chief credit for Austria's remarkable success in achieving this goal. Not only did Metternich gain a substantial rounding-off and increase of the Habsburg domains, chiefly through the exchange of the long-lost Austrian Netherlands for the rich Italian province of Venetia (Lombardy, an Austrian province since 1714, also returned to Austrian rule), but much more important, he secured a political organization for Germany and territorial and dynastic arrangements in Italy which enabled Austria to enjoy a secure and generally unchallenged hegemony in both areas. In Germany, in spite of opposition both from the centripetal forces of liberalism and nationalism and the centrifugal forces of extreme particularism, he pushed through the formation of a German Confederation, a loosely-knit league of thirty-nine sovereign principalities under the presidency of Austria, organized largely for defensive purposes. The organization of the Confederation, though only roughly sketched in by the Federal Act of the Congress of Vienna, served to prevent the two dangers Metternich most feared: a unification of Germany under liberal auspices, on the one hand, and, on the other, the complete independence of the various states, which would encourage some, like Bavaria and

---

[7] This is the main point made by Emil Lauber in his *Metternichs Kampf um die europäische Mitte: Struktur seiner Politik von 1809 bis 1815,* although, as Srbik rightly points out (*Metternich,* III, 28), Lauber goes much too far in trying to make Metternich a Pan-German hero. For Srbik's view on the ticklish question of Metternich's attitude toward Prussia from 1809 to 1812, see *ibid.,* I, 135-140.

Baden, to gravitate toward France and would leave Germany as a whole too disorganized to resist Russian encroachments.

In addition, Prussia, Austria's historic rival in Germany, emerged from the war and the peace settlement with such severe internal problems to solve (especially that of uniting the Rhenish and East Elbean halves of the kingdom, separated by geographical location, by economic structure, by culture, and by religion) and with such heavy international commitments to meet (chiefly that of defending the left bank of the Rhine against France) that Austria was fairly safe from any Prussian challenge to her hegemony in Germany. Metternich, in fact, counted upon Prussia's becoming a good conservative partner and ally, once she overcame the liberal and nationalist sentiments inherited from her war of liberation. In Italy, to be sure, Metternich's achievements remained incomplete; his plan for a defensive league of princes, an Italian League (*Lega Italica*), similar to the German Confederation, could not be consummated, largely because the Italian princes were jealous of their sovereignty.[8] But Austrian dominance in Italy, based as it was on territorial and dynastic factors, was so complete that this was no great loss. In addition to possessing Lombardy-Venetia, Austria had dynastic ties with the Grand Duchy of Tuscany (Archduke Ferdinand III was Francis I's brother), the Duchy of Modena (Archduke Francis IV was Francis' cousin), and the Duchies of Parma and Piacenza (Archduchess Marie Louise, wife of Napoleon, was Francis' daughter). In the largest Italian state, the Kingdom of the Two Sicilies, Austria kept an army of occupation until 1818, and further bound the restored Bourbon King Ferdinand I by a secret treaty to introduce no liberal institutions into his kingdom. The Papal States, under the rule of Pope Pius VII and his foreign minister, Cardinal Consalvi, were far too weak internally to give Austria any trouble. The only state not under direct Austrian influence was the Kingdom of Sardinia-Piedmont, ruled by King Victor Emmanuel I. So long, however, as France was quiescent, Sardinia could cause Austria no serious difficulty. In addition, all the Italian princes, like the Ger-

[8] Two thorough studies of the Italian League and the international disputes, principally between Austria and Sardinia-Piedmont, which arose over it, are Antonio Maria Bettanini, "Un disegno di Confederazione italiana nella politica internazionale della restaurazione," *Studi di storia dei trattati e politica internazionale*, 3–50, and Karl Grossmann, "Metternichs Plan eines italienischen Bundes," *Historische Blätter*, No. 4 (1931), 37–76.

man ones, were bound together with Austria, by treaty obligations and by common interest, in the general task of maintaining their thrones and territories by upholding the Vienna settlement.[9]

On the whole, the diplomats of Vienna labored well, Metternich not the least among them. They achieved a peace settlement commendable not only for its moderation, especially toward France, but also because it satisfied the real existing political forces of that time—the great powers and the forces of monarchy and order—and enabled them to cooperate in maintaining the new system. Liberalism and nationalism, to be sure received scant attention at Vienna. Yet these were more ideas of the future than forces of the present. It is doubtful that the masses in 1815 were as much interested in constitutions and liberal reforms as in a return to peace and order.[10]

This is not to say, certainly, that the great powers no longer had particular interests to pursue after 1815, but rather merely that their interests, however divergent in details, converged on the one point of maintaining the Vienna system. Great Britain's post-Vienna policy was a simple one. The British wished, first of all, to cooperate in the Concert of Europe without, however, seeing it expanded to include guarantees other than the existing ones and without becoming involved in further entangling commitments. Second, they wanted to preserve the Continental balance of power, staying on guard against both a revival of French power and too great an extension of Russian influence into the center of Europe; last of all, the British desired to maintain the maritime supremacy upon which England's insular

[9] Srbik, *Metternich*, I, 182–229, 556–565. Especially interesting is Srbik's judgment (pp. 195–197) that Metternich's German policy was carefully thought out, clever, and backed by strong forces, but was not really statesmanlike, and that the time and conditions were ripe for Austrian leadership in a real federated Germany. See also Artz, *Reaction and Revolution*, 136–138, 142–146.

[10] As Schmalz rightly points out (*Gesamteuropäische Organisation*, 49), the policy of the great powers at Vienna, far from being reactionary, was not even conservative in the narrow sense. Their task was not one simply of preserving (*Erhaltung*) or clinging to (*Beharren*) the old order but rather of giving a renewed order to Europe (*Neuordnung* and *Wiederherstellung*). In contrast to this favorable appraisal, a typical doctrinaire liberal denunciation of the Vienna system is that of Antonin Debidour, in which, after denouncing the way in which the aspirations of nations and peoples were trampled upon, the author concludes, "The organization imposed upon Europe in 1815 appears to me a regime contrary to nature."—*Histoire diplomatique de l'Europe depuis l'ouverture du Congrès de Vienne jusqu'à la clôture du Congrès de Berlin, 1814–1878*, I, vii–xi.

security depended (though this took little effort after 1815) and to promote and retain markets for English goods and manufactures in Europe and the New World.[11] Especially because of the second of these aims—the maintenance of a Continental balance of power— Great Britain warmly supported Austria in her Central European policy, hoping to exclude Russian influence from the Austrian sphere.[12]

France, meanwhile, aspired to regain her lost place and prestige among the family of nations, an ambition already clearly evident in the tactics of the wily French diplomat Charles Maurice Talleyrand at the Congress of Vienna. Talleyrand's successes had been negated, however, by the return of Napoleon from Elba and the consequent fall and ignominious flight of Louis XVIII from France. After Waterloo, Louis was again restored, but the Bourbon prestige was more tarnished than ever, and France was punished with a harder peace, including a sizable indemnity and a partial occupation of her territory by Allied troops. Therefore the French goals for the next three years were perforce the modest ones of keeping the Bourbons in power despite internal intrigue and unrest and working to pay off the indemnity and get rid of the army of occupation as soon as possible.[13]

The Russian aims are more difficult to characterize, largely because of the enigmatic character of Tsar Alexander I. Most scholars agree that Alexander was sincere, if not very clear or consistent, in the liberal, philanthropic, and mystical ideas he displayed in the period during and after the Congress of Vienna.[14] What is not clear,

[11] Webster, *Foreign Policy of Castlereagh*, 47–52; Phillips, *Confederation of Europe*, 67–69.

[12] Phillips, *Confederation of Europe*, 87–90; Rieben, *Metternichs Europapolitik*, 61–62.

[13] Rieben, *Metternichs Europapolitik*, 60; Schwarz, *Heilige Allianz*, 18–21.

[14] Various estimates on Alexander's motives and policy in this period can be found in Webster, *Foreign Policy of Castlereagh*, 89–92; Schmalz, *Gesamteuropäische Organisation*, 28–35; Cresson, *Holy Alliance*, 1–35; Schwarz, *Heilige Allianz*, 6–8, 48–56, 117–119, *et passim*; Phillips, *Confederation of Europe*, 47–64, 114–116, 196–200; Constantin de Grünwald, *Alexandre Ier, le Tsar mystique*, 244–273; Karl Stählin, *Geschichte Russlands von den Anfängen bis zur Gegenwart*, III, 246–278; and Theodor Schiemann, *Geschichte Russlands unter Kaiser Nikolaus I*, Vol. I, 320. The only opinion of which I am aware that credits Alexander with no sincerity or idealism is that of Pirenne, *Sainte-Alliance*, II, 389–390, *et passim*.

however, is how he intended to implement his aim of substituting Christian principles of brotherhood and peace in European politics for the old selfish reasons of state. Equally vague was the role which the general European alliance (of which the Holy Alliance was for Alexander only a part) should play in this policy. What did seem clear to other heads of state, particularly to Castlereagh and Metternich, was that Alexander's schemes, and especially the intrigues of his agents, meant an extension of Russian influence all over Europe and a source of possible trouble for other powers. In Germany, Russian agents encouraged the princes of Bavaria, Baden, and Württemberg to grant constitutions; in France, Russian Ambassador Count Charles André Pozzo di Borgo exerted a powerful influence over the ministry of Armand Emmanuel du Plessis, the Duke of Richelieu, who was himself for ten years governor of Odessa under Alexander; in Spain, Ambassador Count Dmitri Tatistchev consorted with the camarilla surrounding the reactionary Bourbon King Ferdinand VII. The vagueness and lack of clear principles in Alexander's program encouraged each of his agents to pursue a policy of his own.[15]

As for Metternich, his aim—and that of Francis I—was simple: to preserve the internal quiet and external position of power gained for Austria in 1815 after long wars, great sacrifice, and enormous effort. This internal peace and international repose seemed not merely desirable but absolutely necessary to the continued existence of the Austrian Empire. For neither in internal nor in foreign affairs did Austria enjoy a natural security, composed as she was of many nationalities loosely bound together under the Habsburg Crown and surrounded by powerful nations, all potential or actual rivals. Austria's only safety thus lay in skillful diplomacy and in favorable international arrangements and guarantees—which Metternich was an unexcelled master at securing. In Central Europe the Austrian Prime Minister intended to preserve and strengthen the German Confederation in a conservative direction, to check liberal and national movements, and generally to bolster the hegemony of Austria. In Europe as a whole, his aim was to use the alliance system and the unity of the great powers to check individual national ambitions, keep the smaller nations in line, and suppress political innovations,

[15] Webster, *Foreign Policy of Castlereagh*, 92–96.

so that nothing would disturb the repose of Europe.[16] In this policy Metternich viewed England as Austria's natural ally and closest confidant; Prussia as a potentially valuable partner if she could be weaned away from the influence of Russia and from the constitutional ideas of the Prussian liberals; and France and Russia as troublemakers—France as the seat of revolution, Russia as the sponsor of dangerous liberal intrigues.[17]

This hold-the-line policy of Metternich's was much in evidence at the next general conference of the great powers, held at Aachen from the end of September to mid-November 1818.[18] The results of this Congress need only be briefly indicated here. The two problems for which the Congress was convened were quickly settled when the Allies agreed to remove their army of occupation from France at French request, while France, with the aid of the English banker Alexander Baring, made provision immediately to pay off the remainder of her indemnity. The Allies solved a third question, that of admitting France back into the circle of powers, not, as the Duke of Richelieu desired, by dissolving the Quadruple Alliance and forming a new alliance including France, but by secretly renewing the Quadruple Alliance, at the same time admitting France to the current deliberations as well as to all future conferences held under Article VI of the November 1815 treaty. The powers, in short, admitted France into the Concert of Powers while still maintaining

---

[16] Schmalz, *Gesamteuropäische Organisation*, 22–27; Srbik, *Metternich*, I, 556–573; Friedrich Carl Wittichen, "Gentz und Metternich," in Friedrich von Gentz, *Briefe von und an Friedrich von Gentz*, III, xxviii–xxxviii. Already in 1816, as so often later, one finds Metternich calling for a union of all "right-thinking" men everywhere against all innovators and agitators in order to preserve society from impending dissolution. Metternich (Trevise, April 23, 1816) to Cardinal Consalvi, in Hercule Cardinal Consalvi, *Correspondance du Cardinal Hercule Consalvi avec le Prince Clement de Metternich 1815–1823*, 124–126.

[17] Metternich's fear of Russia led him so far in 1816 and 1817 as to propose a secret four-power precautionary treaty against Russia. The project broke down on Castlereagh's refusal to credit Metternich's cries of alarm about an impending Russo-French-Spanish alliance. The British Foreign Minister believed that such a step as Metternich proposed not only would split the Quadruple Alliance, but also would drive Russia and France into taking the very step which Metternich feared.—Srbik, *Metternich*, I, 569–572; Webster, *Foreign Policy of Castlereagh*, 102–108.

[18] The best account of the Congress is in Webster, *Foreign Policy of Castlereagh*, 121–172.

their precautionary treaty against her. The only serious dispute at the Congress arose over the attempt by Alexander and his influential and mildly liberal secretary of state, Count John Capodistrias, to make the Allies the general guarantors of all territories and thrones in Europe against attack or revolution. This plan, which would have meant an enormous and incalculable extension of alliance commitments, was defeated chiefly by the determined opposition of Castlereagh. A similar proposal by Prussia, calling simply for a general territorial guarantee backed up by a standing European army to guard against France, met the same fate.[19]

Metternich did not play the leading role in this Congress, though he was well enough satisfied with its character and results.[20] Seeing possibilities both good and bad for Austria in Alexander's plan for a general guarantee of territories and governments, he had assumed an equivocal attitude toward it and was content to leave the chief opposition to Castlereagh.[21] His main concern at the Congress—as before and after it—was with other business: the task of solidifying the existing system in Germany against foreign influence, Russian intrigue, and liberal ideas. At the Federal Diet at Frankfurt before the Congress convened he had exerted himself to push through a plan of military organization for the Confederation in time both to anticipate the proposed evacuation of France and to forestall any discussion of the question of other German affairs at the Congress.[22] For similar reasons he strongly opposed Capodistrias' idea of inviting lesser powers to the Congress, fearing Russian intrigues with Württemberg, Baden, and other German middle- and small-sized states.[23] Finally, he took the opportunity at Aachen to warn the Prussians of the terrible dangers of revolution and dissolution which would threaten Prussia if the King fulfilled his promise of May 22,

[19] *Ibid.*, 142–166. See also Phillips, *Confederation of Europe,* 159–191; Schwarz, *Heilige Allianz,* 108–111, 122–144; and Schmalz, *Gesamteuropäische Organisation,* 37–45.

[20] Metternich (Aachen, October 5 and November 21, 1818) to his wife, in Clemens Lothar Wenzel Fürst von Metternich—Winneburg, *Aus Metternichs nachgelassenen Papieren,* III, 125, 129–130.

[21] Metternich's memoir on the Russian guarantee plan, n.d., *ibid.,* 159–160; Charles Dupuis, "La Sainte-Alliance et le Directoire européen de 1815–1818," *Revue d'histoire diplomatique,* XLVIII (1934), 469.

[22] Metternich (Frankfurt, September 4, 1818, and Aachen, October 7, 1818) to Francis I, in Metternich, *Nachgelassene Papiere,* III, 150–151, 156–157.

[23] Metternich (Franzensbrünn, August 18, 1818) to Francis, *ibid.,* 141–143.

1815, to grant his people a unified national constitution. The absolute limit for Prussia, said Metternich, should be the convocation of separate provincial estates; "everything else besides this," he argued, "is pure revolution." [24]

This same policy of securing Germany against external influence and internal political innovations governed Metternich's course in the famous Carlsbad Conference of 1819 and the Vienna Conference of 1819–1820. The problem with which the Carlsbad Conference was summoned to deal concerned the alarming spread of revolutionary doctrine in the German press and universities. Subversive activity seemed especially dangerous in the *Turnverein,* an organization founded by Professor Friedrich Jahn primarily for purposes of physical education but involved also in cultural and social pursuits, and in the *Burschenschaften,* nationalistic student organizations, whose center at this time was the liberal University of Jena and whose leading spirit was Professor Karl Follen. All the prevalent charges of revolutionary doctrine and conspiracy lodged against the universities and the *Burschenschaften* gained apparent confirmation when on March 23, 1819, the reactionary Russian agent and publicist August von Kotzebue was murdered by Karl Sand, a theological student at Jena and a follower of Follen.[25] Princes and governments all over Germany, especially in Prussia, lived in terror of imminent revolution. At Vienna, Gentz, deeply shaken and frightened, did everything he could to arouse Metternich to a sense of the grave danger. He must, in fact, be counted more than Metternich as the father of the repressive decrees of Carlsbad.[26]

For Metternich, who was journeying in Italy when the tragedy happened, the Kotzebue case and the previous activities of the

[24] Metternich (Aachen, November 14, 1818) to Prince Wilhelm Wittgenstein, *ibid.,* 171–172; supplement to this letter, 172–178. Since Wittgenstein, whose political principles were much like Metternich's, was at this time rapidly replacing the aged Chancellor Prince Hardenberg in influence, Metternich chose him as the vehicle for his suggestions.

[25] Stern, *Geschichte Europas,* I, 444–455, 554–556; A. F. Pollard, "The Germanic Confederation (1815–1840)," in *The Restoration,* Vol. X of *The Cambridge Modern History,* 363–365.

[26] Stern, *Geschichte Europas,* I, 556–562; Gentz (Vienna, April 1, 14, 23, and 25, 1819) to Metternich, in Metternich, *Nachgelassene Papiere,* III, 220–224, 231–232, 234, 237–242; Golo Mann, *Secretary of Europe: The Life of Friedrich Gentz, Enemy of Napoleon,* 267–268; Paul R. Sweet, *Friedrich von Gentz: Defender of the Old Order,* 220–227.

Burschenschaften were more occasion than cause of the policy he pursued. Though he hated and feared the long-range effects of liberal teaching in the universities, he regarded radical students and professors as the most unsuitable and impractical conspirators possible, and looked upon the Kotzebue incident and the attendant anxiety in Germany as an evil which he could turn to his own good and that of society.[27] Specifically, the antirevolutionary hysteria current in Germany could be exploited not so much to exorcise the largely nonexistent danger of immediate revolution as to settle the much more basic and serious question of liberal national constitutions in Germany. The constitutional issue was the more delicate and touchy because it involved the still-incomplete organization of the German Confederation and the undefined import of Article XIII of the Federal Act of June 1815. Article XIII called for constitutions based on the provincial estates (*landesständische Verfassungen*) for all the German principalities. Three states, Bavaria, Baden, and Saxe-Weimar, had already fulfilled the provision of the article by granting fairly liberal constitutions. Still worse, Prussia threatened to follow their examples. In May 1819, Chancellor Prince Karl August von Hardenberg had, in fact, recommended to King Frederick William III a constitution which, while conservative, was nonetheless both national and representative.[28]

Metternich objected to all such constitutions not merely because they were representative, and hence incompatible with absolutism, but also because they were national, and thus incompatible with the structure of the Austrian Empire. A national constitution, Metternich believed, would be the death of Austria. His recipe for ruling the Habsburg domains—the opposite of Emperor Joseph II's centralism—was provincialism, i.e., carrying on the administration in each separate part of the kingdom according to the old prescriptive forms, avoiding any attempt to unite the Empire into one

[27] Metternich (Rome, April 9 and 23, 1819, and Perugia, June 17, 1819) to Gentz, in Metternich, *Nachgelassene Papiere*, III, 227, 235, 250–251; Metternich (Naples, April 30, 1819) to Prince Paul Esterhazy, ambassador to England, *Weisungen, Grossbritannien*, Fasc. 210, No. 1. (As explained in the Preface, archival materials will be cited chiefly according to the name and number of the fascicle containing them. Any numbers, letters, or other designations given after the fascicle number [e.g., "Secret," "Reserved," and the like] refer to the particular letter or other document being referred to.)

[28] Stern, *Geschichte Europas*, I, 570–572.

whole.[29] But if it was in the best interest of Austria not to have a unified constitution, other German states should not set a bad example by having one, either—especially not Prussia.

Therefore Metternich moved shrewdly to deal with this problem in connection with the problem of revolutionary agitation in Germany, placing first importance on securing the docile cooperation of Prussia. With her safely in tow, he knew that Austria could lead the rest of Germany without difficulty.[30] In interviews with Frederick William and Hardenberg at Teplitz from July 29 to August 1, 1819, Metternich secured the agreement from Prussia which he desired by artfully playing on Prussia's fear of isolation. If his proposals were rejected, Metternich made clear, Austria would withdraw from the Confederation, leaving Germany to her own devices. Not only did the chastened Hardenberg and Frederick William promise to grant only a provincial constitution at some indefinite future date, but they further agreed to all Metternich's proposals for regulation of the universities and the press in Germany, which Metternich had already advanced to Prussian Prince Wittgenstein at the Congress of Aachen.[31]

With this secret agreement in his possession, Metternich repaired confidently to Carlsbad, where at his invitation delegates of the leading German states met (not the Diet at Frankfurt, as would have been in accordance with regular procedure) to discuss the danger of revolution in Germany. Here, in an intimate conference lasting from August 6 to September 1, Metternich, with Gentz active at his side, encountered no difficulty in putting over his proposals. Many delegates, in fact, were ready to go further in repressive decrees than Metternich wanted them to. The conferees passed resolutions calling for censorship of all newspapers, pamphlets, and publications of less than twenty pages in size,[32] the dissolution of

---

[29] See Metternich's letter and attached proposal to Francis I, Vienna, October 27, 1817, in Metternich, *Nachgelassene Papiere*, III, 62–75, especially pp. 66–69.

[30] Metternich (Naples, May 21, 1819, and Carlsbad, July 26, 1819) to Esterhazy, Weisungen, Grossbritannien, Fasc. 210.

[31] Stern, *Geschichte Europas*, I, 568–573; Metternich (Teplitz, July 30 and August 1, 1819) to Francis I, in Metternich, *Nachgelassene Papiere*, III, 258–268; Francis I (Schönbrunn, August 7, 1819) to Metternich, *ibid.*, 269–270; supplement to Metternich's letter to Wittgenstein, Aachen, November 14, 1818, *ibid.*, 178–181.

[32] The distinction maintained by Metternich between newspapers and "real

the *Burschenschaften* and *Turnanstalten*, the supervision of all universities by state inspectors to guard against subversive teaching,
and the establishment of a Central Investigation Committee at
Mainz to investigate plots and conspiracies. These resolutions became Federal decrees when they were adopted without dissent by
the Federal Diet at Frankfurt on September 20, 1819.[33]

Metternich considered Carlsbad one of his finest victories. Yet the
task of organizing and controlling Germany was not complete. At
Carlsbad, Metternich had deliberately deferred the question of defining Article XIII of the Federal Act to a later ministerial conference at Vienna, whose purpose it was not only to impose a check
on future German constitutions but also to fill out the skeleton of
the Confederation's organic act. The Carlsbad decrees had already
done something to limit the sovereignty of the confederate states; [34]
the conference at Vienna was to continue the process.

By November 25, 1819, the day the conference opened, the fear
of revolution in Germany had died down to some extent, and the
familiar concern of the middle-sized and small states for their
sovereign rights had revived. Hence, though he enjoyed general
success at the conference, Metternich had to be content with something less on certain points than he had hoped to achieve. The
Vienna Final Act, finished on May 15, 1820, and made a fundamental law of the Confederation by the General Assembly at Frankfurt on June 8, regulated the sphere of activity of the Diet, settled

---

works" should not be taken as an indication of his willingness to exempt
scientific research or substantial literature from censorship. As he wrote to
Gentz from Perugia, June 17, 1819 (Metternich, *Nachgelassene Papiere*, III,
255), "I regret indeed not being able to set up the principle of censorship for
all writings without exception." Unfortunately, some states, he noted, would
object too strenuously if this was done.

[33] Metternich (Carlsbad, September 1, 1819) to Count Buol, Austrian envoy
at Frankfurt, *ibid.*, 272–286 (with supplement); Metternich (Königswart,
September 3, 1819) to Esterhazy, *ibid.*, 286–289; Stern, *Geschichte Europas*,
I, 573–580, 582; Pollard, "Germanic Confederation," *Cambridge Modern
History*, X, 365–367.

[34] Although the primary responsibility for executing the Carlsbad decrees fell
upon the individual states, no state's laws were to be more lax (though they
could be stricter) than the Federal decrees, and any state that felt itself injured
or threatened by the lack of vigilance of another could bring complaint and
demand Federal execution against the offending member. In addition, with the
establishment of the Central Investigation Committee, the investigation of
revolutionary activity became a Federal function.

the procedure for enacting Federal laws, set up an Execution Ordinance for carrying them out, and provided for the settlement of judicial disputes between the states, all on the loosest confederate basis, with full respect shown to the sovereignty of the various states. The Confederation's competence in foreign affairs and the structure of its military establishment were also defined. Finally, on the crucial question of Article XIII, the Final Act strongly recommended provincial constitutions based wholly on the principle of monarchical, not popular, sovereignty, but did not entirely exclude national constitutions, either for the present or the future. Metternich congratulated himself—prematurely, as it turned out—that the Confederation had now received its definitive organization and that the Carlsbad decrees would really go into effect. Although his expectations on this point were not entirely fulfilled, the close partnership with Prussia achieved at Teplitz and Carlsbad and strengthened at Vienna proved durable,[35] and was actually more important to Metternich than the final organization of the Confederation.

During the Vienna Conference Metternich again had to exert himself to keep the Russians from interfering in German affairs. The possibility of Russian interference, always present because the Confederation had been organized under international agreement at the Congress of Vienna and because the powers maintained diplomatic representatives at the seat of the Confederation at Frankfurt, became more than theoretical when King William I of Württemberg, fearful of Austrian and Prussian domination of the Confederation, openly challenged the competence of the Vienna Conference to discuss and settle German affairs. Worse still, he appealed to his brother-in-law, Tsar Alexander, for help in preserving the sovereignty of the lesser states. Here, Metternich feared, was an ideal opening for Capodistrias' intrigues. By long argument and strenuous

---

[35] Stern, *Geschichte Europas*, I, 615–628; text of the Vienna Final Act, June 8, 1820, in *British and Foreign Papers*, VII (1819–1820), 399–414. See also Metternich's letter (Vienna, March 19, 1820) to Baron Ludwig Lebzeltern, ambassador to Russia, Weisungen, Russland, Fasc. 44, No. 1. At the conclusion of the Vienna Conference Metternich boasted to Emperor Francis that he had made Austria's word law in all of Germany (Metternich [Vienna, May 14, 1820] to Francis, in Metternich, *Nachgelassene Papiere*, III, 378). For evidence of continuing Austro-Prussian harmony, see Frederick William III (Berlin, September 29, 1824) to Metternich, and Metternich (n.p., n.d.) to Frederick William, *ibid.*, IV, 126–127.

efforts, however, Metternich convinced Alexander that the decrees
of both Carlsbad and Vienna not only were proper and benevolent
but also that they were no concern of non-German powers. At the
same time, he delivered a sharp rebuke to the Württemberg delegate, Count Heinrich Wintzingerode, for blocking the united will
of the German governments for a stronger and more effective confederation. The Württemberg protest thus went for nothing.[36] The
other European powers gave Metternich no trouble over his German policy. The British, in fact, supported it warmly. Castlereagh
favored Austrian control of the Confederation and approved of the
Carlsbad decrees as enthusiastically as Metternich applauded the
Six Acts passed by Parliament in 1819 to repress agitation in England. The Duke of Wellington, too, let it be known that he was
entirely in favor of the Vienna resolutions, particularly since they
strengthened Central Europe defensively against both France and
Russia.[37]

By early 1820 Metternich had thus succeeded in organizing Germany to his own satisfaction and in setting up Federal legislation
to repress revolutionary agitation and political innovations. At the
same time, certain developments on the European scene gave Metternich added reason for optimism about the future. An especially
hopeful sign was the apparent growing conservatism of Tsar Alexander. The Austrian ambassador, Count Ludwig Lebzeltern, reported that the Tsar was gradually but surely turning away from
his old liberal ideas under the influence of revolutionary disturbances in Germany, party strife in France, disappointment with the
progress of his experiment at liberal rule in Poland, and the persuasive arguments of Metternich and his ambassador.[38] The evi-

[36] Stern, *Geschichte Europas*, I, 626–627; Metternich (Vienna, January 1
and 23, 1820) to Lebzeltern, Weisungen, Russland, Fasc. 44, Nos. 1 and 1; two
letters of Metternich (Vienna, March 31, 1820) to Wintzingerode, in Metternich, *Nachgelassene Papiere*, III, 367–372.

[37] Webster, *Foreign Policy of Castlereagh*, 190–198; Metternich (Vienna,
November 7, 1819) to Austrian *Chargé d'Affaires* Neumann at London, Wei-
sungen, Grossbritannien, Fasc. 210; Neumann (London, February 17, 1920)
to Metternich, Berichte, Grossbritannien, Fasc. 211, No. 138A; Wellington
(London, January 5, 1820) to Austrian Ambassador Baron Vincent at Paris,
Berichte, Frankreich, Fasc. 340.

[38] Lebzeltern (St. Petersburg, June 4, 1820) to Metternich, Berichte, Russland, Fasc. 29, No. 38A; Metternich (Vienna, November 1, 1819) to Neumann,
and Metternich (Naples, May 26, 1819) to Prince Esterhazy, Weisungen,

dences of Alexander's change of heart were not yet clear enough to prompt Metternich to discard his suspicions of Russia, and in no way allayed his passionate aversion to Capodistrias, Pozzo di Borgo, Tatistchev, and other Russian agents, but they did give Metternich grounds for hoping that he could turn Alexander and Russia into faithful allies, just as he had done with Frederick William and Prussia.[39]

Developments in France in the spring of 1820, after more than a year of trends abhorrent to Metternich, also finally took a turn for the better. In the previous year, under the moderate centrist ministry headed by Élie Decazes (later Duke), who succeeded the Duke of Richelieu in December 1818, France had, in Metternich's opinion, gone from bad to worse. The victories of the Left in the elections of 1818 and 1819, the laws sponsored by the ministry granting considerable freedom of the press in 1819, the fierce struggles in the Chamber of Deputies between Left and Right, the Doctrinaires and the Ultra-Royalists, and above all the attempt of the ministry to rule by compromising between the contending parties had aroused Metternich's intense aversion and distrust.[40]

Metternich employed two of his favorite devices in his attempt to meet the danger of anarchy and revolution toward which he insisted the current ministry was leading France. Through private correspondence with Decazes, he tried to convince the supple French premier that unless France altered her press and election laws in a conservative direction and otherwise imitated the policies of the Carlsbad decrees, the monarchy of Louis XVIII was doomed.[41]

Grossbritannien, Fasc. 210; Gentz (Vienna, February 14, 1820) to Prince Alexander Soutzo, in Friedrich von Gentz, *Dépêches inédites du chevalier de Gentz aux hospodars de Valachie pour servir à l'histoire de la politique européenne (1813 à 1828)*, published by Count Anton Prokesch von Osten, II, 11–13.

[39] Metternich (Vienna, March 3 and 4, 1820) to Lebzeltern, Weisungen, Russland, Fasc. 44.

[40] Metternich (Vienna, March 19, 1820) to Lebzeltern, *ibid.*, No. 3; Metternich (Vienna, January 26, 1920) to Vincent, Weisungen, Frankreich, Fasc. 343, No. 1. See also Lady Blennerhassett, "The Doctrinaires," *Cambridge Modern History*, X, 57–62.

[41] Guillaume de Bertier de Sauvigny, "Metternich et Decazes, d'après leur correspondance inédite (1816–1820)," *Études d'histoire moderne et contemporaine*, V (1953), 84–85, 97–98, 101–102. Metternich actually originated the correspondence with a view to coordinating French secret-police activities and information with those of Austria, his final goal being a general European anti-

At the same time, in June 1819, Metternich proposed the establishment of a ministers' conference at London or Vienna to discuss the affairs of France, "serving, so to speak, as a rallying point and a center of moral support for the Quadruple Alliance." The conference, he argued, would be just as beneficial for Russia as for France; it would help "not only to settle the ideas of Emperor Alexander, but also to keep his mind occupied," thereby bringing all the powers, particularly Russia, "to direct . . . all their moral efforts toward a common goal—the only one they must and can have in view, that of the maintenance of repose in Europe." [42]

This proposal, like some others from Metternich, broke down on the polite refusal of Castlereagh to accept the Chancellor's method of dealing with the alleged dangers.[43] Another assassination like that of Kotzebue, however, opened the way to better trends in France. On February 13, 1820, Charles Ferdinand d'Artois, the Duke of Berry, heir-presumptive to the French throne, was murdered by Louis-Pierre Louvel outside the Paris Opera House. Though deploring the deed, Metternich nevertheless sought to produce the best consequences from it. He sent a special emissary, Count Wallmoden, to bear the Emperor's condolences to the King and at the same time to urge the ministry to take repressive measures against the press and to change the law of elections.[44] Before Wallmoden could reach France, however, the basic purpose of his mission had been achieved. He did not have to attempt to change the ministry's mind, for France had already changed ministries. Blamed by the entire Right for the death of the Duke of Berry, Decazes resigned, accepting as consolation a ducal title and the

---

revolutionary police system under his direction (pp. 61–65). Alarmed by the liberal trend of Decazes' government in 1819, however, Metternich turned the correspondence toward more immediate political goals.

[42] Metternich (Rome, June 8, 1819) to Esterhazy, Weisungen, Grossbritannien, Fasc. 210.

[43] Webster, *Foreign Policy of Castlereagh*, 206–207. Metternich's similar attempt to secure four-power intervention in French internal politics in 1818 had also failed.—Bertier, "Metternich et Decazes," 70–71, 76–78.

[44] Metternich (Vienna, February 24, 1820) to Lebzeltern, Weisungen, Russland, Fasc. 44, No. 1 and Reserved to No. 1; Metternich (Vienna, February 26, 1820) to Vincent, Weisungen, Frankreich, Fasc. 343, No. 1; Bertier, "Metternich et Decazes," 111–114.

post of ambassador to England. The Duke of Richelieu, who now formed his second ministry, was still, in Metternich's opinion, too much under the influence of Russia, but he was certainly a great improvement over Decazes. Moreover, the new ministry immediately reimposed press censorship and set itself the task of changing the law of February 1817 on elections. After severe struggles in the Chamber of Deputies, it managed to put through a new law on June 12, 1820, which, though far from ideal from Metternich's point of view, did shift the preponderant voice in France's very narrow electorate away from the urban upper bourgeoisie toward the landed aristocracy and gentry, a change which reflected itself in the Royalist victories in the elections of 1820 and 1821.[45]

Thus, so far as Metternich was concerned, conditions in France in the first half of 1820, though by no means satisfactory, were at least better than they had been for some time. A trip through Italy in 1819 with Emperor Francis also encouraged Metternich, convincing him that Austrian hegemony in the peninsula was still secure. He found the Court of Naples entirely loyal to the alliance and to Austria. Furthermore, though secret societies, notably the Carbonari, were active elsewhere in Italy, the Kingdom of Naples seemed to him commendably free "from all participation in the movement of the sects," and though Russian agents were trying to stir up trouble and weaken Austrian influence throughout Italy, Metternich judged that the other Italian princes were still loyal to Austria. The Duchy of Parma, he noted, "must at this moment be considered as an Austrian province." There were, true, some dangerous sentiments abroad in Italy, "some revolutionary dispositions which are common to a great mass of the population." Nevertheless, he was inclined to doubt that any revolution would break out. The lack of effective leadership for revolt, internal divisions among the sects, and the natural laziness and timidity of the Italians rendered them relatively harmless. Even the climate, Metternich believed, was in

[45] Vincent (Paris, March 10, 1820) to Metternich, Berichte, Frankreich, Fasc. 340; Metternich (Vienna, March 2, 1820) to Vincent, Weisungen, Frankreich, Fasc. 343; Metternich (Vienna, April 27, 1820) to Esterhazy, Weisungen, Grossbritannien, Fasc. 213, No. 2. See also Blennerhassett, "The Doctrinaires," *Cambridge Modern History*, X, 62–69; Nora E. Hudson, *Ultra-Royalism and the French Restoration*, 95–99; and Alfred Nettement, *Histoire de la Restauration*, V, 261–439.

his favor, for no Italian would have the energy to revolt during the long six months of summer.[46]

With Italy safe, Germany secure, England an intimate ally, and Russia and France at least improved in disposition, Metternich's system seemed more solid in the first half of 1820 than it ever had been before. Yet this was only the sunshine before the storm, for the revolutions which came in that year were to shake the system to its foundations.

[46] Two letters from Metternich (Florence, July 9, 1819) to Esterhazy, Weisungen, Grossbritannien, Fasc. 210. In them Metternich presented this analysis of the Italian situation to the British with characteristic modesty and caution: "Lord Castlereagh must know me well enough to nourish no doubts on the *certainty* of the facts which my communication contains. . . . I believe little, but I take pains to know very much; I am not even acquainted with the sentiment of fear, but I willingly follow the calculations of prudence." Unfortunately for Metternich, the next year's events were such as to nourish doubts on a great scale concerning the certainty of his information. This same dispatch also contained a complete disclaimer by Metternich of the notion of forming an Italian League in Italy. The idea that Austria was trying to form such a defensive league, he wrote to Castlereagh, "must be attributed solely to agitators and revolutionaries." True, Metternich was not negotiating with Piedmont to try to form the League at this time, as had been alleged; but he certainly always maintained the formation of the League as one of his important goals, one to which he repeatedly returned. The disclaimer is another instance of disingenuous dealing by Metternich with even his most intimate ally.

CHAPTER II

THE OUTBREAK OF REVOLUTIONS

The scene of the first revolution in 1820 was Spain, suffering since 1814 under the misrule of that most incompetent and reactionary Bourbon, Ferdinand VII. The immediate cause of the revolt was not so much the repressive domestic policies of the King and his camarilla as Ferdinand's insistence on attempting the quixotic project of reconquering his revolutionized Spanish American colonies. To this end he had gathered an expeditionary army and made some attempts to collect a seaworthy navy at the port of Cádiz. Disgruntled at their miserable pay and living conditions, disgusted at the graft and corruption which attended the enterprise, and unwilling to sacrifice themselves in an evidently hopeless expedition, the soldiers and officers of the army proved fertile soil for the growth of revolutionary doctrine and conspiracies. No one should have been surprised when revolution broke out. On January 1, 1820, Colonel Rafael del Riego y Nuñez, head of one troop of disaffected soldiers, raised the standard of revolt in Cabezas near Cádiz, proclaiming the radical 1812 Constitution, a product of the great rising in Spain against Napoleon from 1808 to 1814. The next day another force under Colonel Antonio Quiroga seized the town of San Fernando and then the Isle of León in the harbor of Cádiz, attempting to capture the important port city as well.

At first the revolution seemed to misfire. Quiroga failed to capture Cádiz and was himself besieged, while an expedition by Riego into Andalucía to raise the countryside in revolt ended in failure and the dissolution of his forces. When risings broke out in the north of Spain, in the provinces of Galicia and Aragon in late February and early March, however, the situation for the first time became really serious for the government. The revolt now spread very rapidly, reaching Madrid at the beginning of March and bringing mob agita-

tion to the streets of the capital. Ferdinand and his camarilla reacted in characteristic fashion. Having neglected to crush the revolt
in its beginnings, they now waited too long to make concessions and
finally capitulated completely. On March 6 the King promised that
he would summon the old Cortes. When this concession failed to
satisfy the crowds, he promised the next day to restore the Constitution of 1812, a radical instrument based largely on the French Constitution of 1791, which upheld popular sovereignty and put monarchical power largely at the mercy of a single electoral chamber.
On March 9, under mob pressure, Ferdinand took the first of many
oaths to the new constitution. A provisional junta then took over the
reins of government until the new Cortes should be assembled,
completing the astonishingly easy victory the revolutionaries had
gained.[1]

Until the revolution reached Madrid in March, Metternich showed
little concern with the risings in Spain, discounting their significance
and predicting that the legitimate government would easily suppress
them.[2] The capitulation of the King during the period March 6–9,
however, which Austrian ambassador Count Brunetti blamed wholly
on the cowardice and inaction of Ferdinand and "the imbeciles who
surround him" (the camarilla), caused a strong reaction in Vienna.
Gentz, while discounting any great material danger from the revolution, owing to the remoteness of Spain, feared that it would have a
very bad moral effect on the whole continent.[3] Metternich took sub-
stantially the same view, although he apparently had more fear of
an immediate revolutionary chain reaction than Gentz did. So far
as security against revolution was concerned, he considered both
France and England as doubtful and Germany and Italy as in grave
danger. Only the inherent tranquillity of Austria and the great
distance removing Russia from Spain rendered them immune to
contagion.[4]

[1] Stern, *Geschichte Europas,* II, 25–32; Artz, *Reaction and Revolution,* 152–
154; Rafael Altamira, "Spain (1815–1845)," *Cambridge Modern History,* X,
205–217.

[2] Metternich (Vienna, February 24, 1820) to Lebzeltern, Weisungen, Russland, Fasc. 44, No. 2.

[3] Brunetti (Madrid, March 8, 1820) to Vincent, Berichte, Frankreich, Fasc.
340; Gentz (Vienna, March 30, 1820) to Soutzo, in Gentz, *Dépêches inédites,*
II, 19–20.

[4] Metternich (Vienna, April 7, 1820) to Esterhazy, Weisungen, Grossbritannien, Fasc. 213, No. 1; Metternich (Vienna, April 25, 1820) to Lebzeltern,

But as some weeks went by without further international repercussions from the revolt in Spain, Metternich became convinced that
the danger of an extension of revolution was diminishing. If the revolt failed to spread beyond Spain, he felt, the revolutionary party
in Europe would find their victory in Spain turned into defeat in
Europe as a whole.[5] For a time Metternich's hopes were realized.
France, Germany, and Italy remained calm, while the English government greeted the revolution with quiet but firm disapproval.[6] So
long as the revolution showed no signs of becoming contagious, Metternich would have been glad to let it run its course.

This policy of masterly inactivity, however, was disturbed by Alexander, who, greatly perturbed by this successful military revolt,
wanted to try a cure which, from Metternich's standpoint, would
have been worse than the disease. Even before hearing of the success of the insurrection at Madrid, Alexander had proposed that the
Allies consult on what should be done to aid Ferdinand should the
Spanish King require their help. His *démarche* found a sympathetic
audience in Berlin, where Chancellor Hardenberg suggested setting
up an ambassadorial conference to discuss the question at Paris.[7] In
April, Russia renewed her proposal in a circular to her ministers at
Vienna, London, and Berlin, proposing that the Quadruple Alliance
powers at least exchange views on the internal condition of Spain
and France, and suggesting—very diffidently—a congress as a means
of activating the alliance to meet the danger.[8]

Castlereagh gave a blunt answer to the Russian proposal in his
State Paper of May 5, insisting that any foreign intervention in Spain
was useless and rejecting in still plainer terms than he had used at

---

Weisungen, Russland, Fasc. 44; Metternich (Vienna, April 1, 7, and 17, 1820)
to Vincent, Weisungen, Frankreich, Fasc. 343, Nos. 2, 1, and 1. Though showing more concern than Gentz, Metternich was far less frightened by the revolt
than Ambassador Vincent at Paris, who believed that the British had instigated
it and that a similar movement was about to take place in the French army.
Vincent (Paris, March 23 and April 6, 1820) to Metternich, Berichte,
Frankreich, Fasc. 340.

[5] Metternich (Vienna, May 6, 1820) to Esterhazy, Weisungen, Grossbritannien, Fasc. 213, No. 1.

[6] Esterhazy (London, April 7, 21, and 28, 1820) to Metternich, Berichte,
Grossbritannien, Fasc. 211, Nos. 145A, 146A, and 147A.

[7] Webster, *Foreign Policy of Castlereagh*, 229–231, 235.

[8] Text of the Russian circular, St. Petersburg, April 30, 1820, in *British and
Foreign State Papers*, VII, 943–947.

Aachen any idea of a generalized system of intervention for the alliance.[9] Metternich welcomed the British reply, for though he was not averse to lecturing France, Russia, and other states on the great morals to be drawn from the Spanish revolution, i.e., the danger of liberalism and the necessity for governments to forgo innovations, he was no more eager than Castlereagh to see the alliance set in motion on such a remote question as Spain.[10] Therefore he found a host of arguments to bolster the English position on intervention. Regrettable as was the revolution, Metternich argued, now that the trouble had begun, no foreign interference could possibly accomplish any favorable result. History showed, he insisted, that "foreign action has never either arrested or controlled the effects of a revolution." The cure must come from inside:

In such a situation [as in Spain] the remedies can only be found in the lands themselves which suffer from the errors and the faults committed by their own governments. Every *material* remedy which a foreigner directs against an internal evil of that kind serves only to augment the evil by giving a very special force to extreme parties.[11]

These general truths, he maintained, were particularly applicable to Spain, for as the Duke of Wellington had pointed out, no people were more resentful of foreign interference than the Spaniards.[12] The Quadruple Alliance, moreover, bound as it was to explicit stipulations of existing treaties, could not be applied beyond them.[13]

Thus at this time Metternich opposed intervention in principle as strongly as Castlereagh did. Privately, moreover, he expressed strong contempt for the Russian *démarche* and was suspicious of its motives. Russia, he said, having done nothing but stir up trouble and

[9] This dispatch is fully discussed by Webster, *Foreign Policy of Castlereagh*, 235–242. The text is in *Cambridge History of British Foreign Policy, 1783–1911*, II, 622–633.

[10] Metternich (Königswart, June 15, 1820) to Vincent, Weisungen, Frankreich, Fasc. 343, No. 1; Metternich (Vienna, May 24, 1820) to Lebzeltern, Weisungen, Russland, Fasc. 44, No. 1.

[11] Metternich (Königswart, June 15, 1820) to Vincent, Weisungen, Frankreich, Fasc. 343, No. 1.

[12] Metternich (Vienna, May 24, 1820) to Lebzeltern, Weisungen, Russland, Fasc. 44, No. 1.

[13] Metternich (Königswart, June 15, 1820) to Vincent, Weisungen, Frankreich, Fasc. 343, No. 1.

revolution for five years, now suddenly wanted to stamp it out.[14] But in dealing with Russia he thought it unwise to rebuff the Tsar as openly as Castlereagh had done, particularly since the Russian proposal had evidenced a fear of revolution and an attachment to the alliance which ought to be encouraged and guided into the proper channels. Metternich therefore instructed Lebzeltern to answer the Russian proposal by praising Alexander's fidelity to the alliance and his hatred of revolution, rejecting the Tsar's idea only on the grounds of the insuperable practical difficulties in the path of any joint action—the opposition of Great Britain, the fact that Ferdinand VII had accepted the revolution, and, above all, the fact that any Allied declaration condemning the revolution, however true, would only embarrass the moderates and endanger the King in Spain. The best the powers could do, Metternich suggested, would be to express their solicitude for Ferdinand's personal safety and to see that they repressed all agitation at home.[15] In addition, Metternich made two counterproposals which he hoped would allay any Russian disappointment at the Austrian attitude.[16] First, to substitute for the congress of sovereigns that the Tsar wanted, Francis I invited Alexander to a personal meeting near Pest in Hungary.[17] Second, Metternich, reversing a position he had previously adopted, took up the question with Russia of what should be done by the powers to protect the legitimate succession in France in case Louis XVIII were to die suddenly. Earlier in the year, when Russia had proposed a joint declaration by the powers on this question, Metternich had dodged the issue because it was embarrassing to England to have

---

[14] Metternich suspected that Capodistrias, taking advantage of Alexander's misguided zeal for the alliance, had tricked him into making an impossible proposal, knowing that it would be rejected and hoping that Alexander would detach himself from the alliance in disappointment. This was Metternich's favorite explanation of Capodistrias' tactics and it is not an implausible one. Metternich (Vienna, June 3, 1820) to Vincent, Weisungen, Frankreich, Fasc. 343, No. 1.

[15] Metternich (Vienna, May 24, and Prague, June 5, 1820) to Lebzeltern, Weisungen, Russland, Fasc. 44.

[16] As it turned out, according to Lebzeltern, Alexander received the Austrian rejection of his proposal with outward good grace. Lebzeltern (St. Petersburg, June 9, 1820) to Metternich, Berichte, Russland, Fasc. 29, Nos. 39A and 39C.

[17] Metternich (Prague, June 5, 1820) to Lebzeltern, Weisungen, Russland, Fasc. 44, No. 3.

such hypothetical matters brought up.[18] Now, however, without approaching England or notifying her, Metternich proposed a secret three-power agreement with Russia and Prussia engaging each power upon the death of Louis immediately to recognize the legitimate successor and to deny recognition to any pretender.[19] The three powers sent joint instructions to this effect to their ambassadors at Paris in September 1820. The action, insignificant in itself, takes on importance as a part of Metternich's campaign to win over Alexander and as the first step toward the erection of a bloc of Eastern powers independent of Great Britain within the Quadruple Alliance.[20]

Metternich's policy of leaving the Spanish revolution alone to burn itself out thus seemed to work well at first. The revolution failed to disturb the general European repose, while it gave Metternich an opportunity to bring Alexander under more direct Austrian influence. The next blow to Metternich's system, however, could not be similarly evaded. It came with the outbreak of a military revolt in the Kingdom of Naples somewhat like that in Spain.[21]

The revolt began on July 2 at the town of Nola, southeast of Naples, where a cavalry regime under two sub-lieutenants, Michele Morelli and Giuseppe Silvati, defected, and, joining a motley crowd composed of Carbonari and members of the militia led by a renegade priest, Luigi Minichini, set out on a march to arouse the countryside and demand a constitution. The revolt spread quickly throughout the surrounding area. Troops sent to stamp out the mutiny defected to the insurgent ranks, as much out of reluctance to fire on their compatriots as through sympathy with the rebel aims. By the night of July 5, according to the Austrian *chargé d'affaires*, Count

[18] Metternich (Vienna, February 23, 1820) to Lebzeltern, *ibid.*, No. 2; Metternich (Vienna, February 6, 1820) to Esterhazy, Weisungen, Grossbritannien, Fasc. 213, No. 1.

[19] Metternich (Prague, June 5, 1820) to Lebzeltern, Weisungen, Russland, Fasc. 44, No. 6.

[20] Schwarz, *Heilige Allianz*, 184–185.

[21] My account of the actual details of the revolution is drawn mainly from George T. Romani, *The Neapolitan Revolution of 1820–1821*, 37–66; Pietro Colletta, *Storia del Reame di Napoli*, II, 291–304; Cesare Spellanzon, *Storia del Risorgimento e dell'Unità d'Italia*, I, 799–804; and Antonio Monti, *Il Risorgimento*, I (1814–1860),39–42. On the background and causes of the revolution, see Romani, *Neapolitan Revolution*, 7–36, and Spellanzon, *Storia del Risorgimento*, I, 793–799. Some reference has also been made to Annibale Alberti, "La rivoluzione Napoletana, il suo Parlamento e la reazione europea 1820–1821," in *Atti del Parlamento delle Due Sicilie, 1820–1821*, IV, vii–cccxci.

de Menz, the number of insurgents had grown to fourteen thousand, against only four thousand remaining loyal troops.[22] General Michele Carascosa, sent to deal with the rebels, came to sympathize with their cause and recommended that the King voluntarily grant the nation a constitution. Not until July 6, when the insurrection had spread to the city of Naples and the threat of riots in the streets arose, did the aged Ferdinand I yield to the popular demand and promise a constitution. The mere promise of some unspecified sort of charter, however, was not enough to quiet agitation. On July 7, therefore, the King's son and heir-apparent, Francis Duke of Calabria, named Vicar-General by his father the day before, proclaimed the Spanish Constitution for his father's realms.[23] In bloodless, almost ridiculously easy fashion the revolution had triumphed.

The unexpectedness of the revolt and the ease of its victory contributed to making the revolution a great shock to Metternich and his associates. Plainly they had not seen the revolution coming. As has been noted, Metternich and Francis I had found the Kingdom of Naples in excellent condition during their tour of inspection in 1819. Even after the Spanish revolution in March 1820 had stirred up Carbonari activity, Austrian Ambassador Prince Jablonowski had reported that there was no particular danger. The people, he said, were calm; as for the government, "Its course is firm and wise; the people enjoy more real happiness than at any other epoch, and do not fail to recognize the beneficent intentions of the King." [24] Metternich accepted this appraisal of the situation, believing, in addition, that the general stupor of the Italians and the willingness of their governments to avoid innovations would help to preserve tranquillity in the peninsula. In June, to be sure, widespread arrests of Carbonari and small-scale risings in Salerno and Calabria had indi-

[22] Ambassador Prince Jablonowski (Naples, July 4, 1820) to Metternich, and De Menz (Naples, July 7, 1820) to Metternich, Berichte, Neapel, Fasc. 48, Nos. 25B and 26A (with Postscripts 1 and 2). Count Orloff puts the total number of insurgents, military and civilian, at sixty thousand on July 5.—Comte Grégoire Orloff, *Mémoires historiques, politiques et littéraires sur le royaume de Naples*, III, 378.

[23] The move to make his son Vicar-General was clearly a device of Ferdinand's to help him escape responsibility for further concessions to the revolution and further dealings with revolutionaries. It did not save him, nonetheless, from having to take numerous oaths to the new constitution.

[24] Jablonowski (Naples, April 27, 1820) to Metternich, Berichte, Neapel, Fasc. 48, No. 13C.

cated trouble in Naples, but the agitation seemed to be quickly suppressed; both Jablonowski and the British envoy Sir William A'Court reported conditions as quiet on the eve of the revolution.[25]

Hence the outbreak of the revolution was a surprise. The course it took after July 7 was equally unexpected. According to Metternich, the revolt should have been the prelude for a reign of Jacobin terror:

The blood will flow in streams. A nation half-barbaric, in absolute ignorance, of boundless superstition, hot-blooded as Africans, a nation that can neither read nor write, whose last word is the dagger, such a nation offers fine material for constitutional principles![26]

Yet the expected anarchy failed to develop. A provisional junta quietly took over power from the King's old ministry, while the capital of Naples and the kingdom in general (except for parts of Sicily) received the revolution with almost lighthearted calm. Even when General Guglielmo Pepe, who had taken charge of the revolutionary forces and was now commander-in-chief of the army, paraded the revolutionary troops into the capital city, the anticipated outbreaks of violence failed to materialize. Ferdinand and his sons took the oaths to the Spanish Constitution required of them with ceremony and with a great show of sincerity by the King, who gained great popularity with his subjects by his magnanimous renunciation of absolute power. Both the provisional junta and the new ministry, moreover, were composed of Muratists (i.e., moderate constitutional liberals who had served under Joachim Murat, Napoleonic King of Naples from 1808 to 1814). Not a Carbonaro was among them. What had happened, in other words, was that the revolution, inspired and begun by the more radical Carbonari, had been taken over by moderate aristocratic and upper bourgeois constitutionalists.[27]

---

[25] Metternich (Vienna, May 24, 1820) to Lebzeltern, Weisungen, Russland, Fasc. 44, No. 1; Jablonowski (Naples, June 6, 13, 20, and 27, 1820) to Metternich, Berichte, Neapel, Fasc. 48, Nos. 19A, 20, 23, and 24; A'Court (Naples, June 22, 1820) to Castlereagh, Varia, Grossbritannien, Fasc. 18.

[26] Letter from Weinzierl (Austria), July 17, 1820, in Metternich, *Nachgelassene Papiere*, III, 340.

[27] De Menz (Naples, July 9, 12, and 14, 1820) to Metternich, Berichte, Neapel, Fasc. 48, Nos. 27, 30, and 31 with supplements; Romani, *Neapolitan Revolution*, 64–85; Spellanzon, *Storia del Risorgimento*, I, 804–808.

There were, undoubtedly, strong factors pushing the new government toward radicalism and instability. The Carbonaro movement expanded rapidly and gained strength in the army and the militia. The radical and impractical Spanish constitution, with its single legislative chamber and lack of any real monarchical authority, was clearly an unfit instrument for moderate rule. The heavy financial burdens on the state, already serious and mounting before the revolution, were now worsened by the increase in the army and militia necessitated by the probability of foreign intervention. Worst of all, an outbreak of revolt in Palermo just ten days after the successful revolution at Naples soon developed into a really radical revolution, or more accurately, a civil war within Sicily, of the nature Metternich had predicted for the entire kingdom.[28]

Though the new regime thus faced grave problems, the Muratists showed the ability to retain control, at least for the time. The elections for the first National Parliament, which convened on October 1, took a surprisingly moderate turn.[29] Although it labored under the

---

[28] An indication of the financial difficulties of the prerevolutionary regime is the fact that in May 1820 Finance Minister Luigi de Medicis had had to secure a million-ducat loan from Paris to cover his mounting deficits. Jablonowski (Naples, May 21, 1820) to Metternich, Berichte, Neapel, Fasc. 48. On the problems of the constitutional government, see De Menz (Naples, July 21 and 25, August 1, 4, 7, 9, 22, and 26, September 12 and 21, 1820) to Metternich, *ibid.*; A'Court (Naples, July 25 and August 24, 1820) to Castlereagh, Varia, Grossbritannien, Fasc. 18; Romani, *Neapolitan Revolution,* 88–103, 132–137; Spellanzon, *Storia del Risorgimento,* 808–812. The Sicilian revolt began when the inhabitants of Palermo arose in behalf of Sicilian independence (such as the island had enjoyed from 1811 to 1814 under British protection) and succeeded in defeating and imprisoning the Neapolitan army contingent at Palermo. Most of the rest of the island, however, including Messina and Syracuse, refused to follow Palermo's lead, and when the rebels at Palermo tried to force the rest of the island to support the revolution, the revolt turned into civil war. The whole movement at Palermo was extremely radical and led by some of the lowest elements in society, including many freed criminals. Before it was over, it had produced riots, pillaging, forced loans and confiscations from the rich, government by committees of artisans and workers, and a general state of anarchy. In addition to the sources cited above, see Spellanzon, *Storia del Risorgimento,* I, 812–823. A detailed account of the Sicilian revolt (though one-sidedly favorable to the cause of Sicilian independence) is that of Giuseppe Bianco, *La rivoluzione Siciliana del 1820 con documenti e carteggi inediti.* See pages 1–19 and 311–312 for his account of the basic causes and character of the revolt.

[29] Only seventeen of the seventy-two deputies were Carbonari.—Romani, *Neapolitan Revolution,* 119–120. Even the High Tory A'Court, who was

financial strain of arming to meet the expected foreign danger, the government was able to meet its foreign obligations, to collect taxes (collection had been virtually suspended just before and after the revolution), and to stop the fall in value of public rents. The regime easily suppressed small dissident groups in further attempts at revolution, while two weeks of fighting by Neapolitan troops led by General Florestano Pepe, Guglielmo's brother, served to break the resistance at Palermo and to end the revolt and anarchy in Sicily.[30]

The moderate constitutionalists did not take firm steps to meet the two fundamental problems confronting the government—those of controlling the Carbonari and revising the constitution in a conservative direction—until it was too late.[31] This fatal delay was due to a feeling of weakness or to insufficient determination, however, not to ignorance of the problem or its solution. The ministry, along with moderates in general, wanted to execute both of these steps without knowing precisely how to do so, and would even have welcomed foreign intervention if it was designed to help carry them out.

The whole attitude of the ministry toward foreign powers was in fact, anything but hostile or radical. In sharp contrast to the Carbonari, who wanted to spread constitutionalism by secret activity elsewhere in Italy, the "moderate" ministry, represented by the foreign minister, the Duke of Campochiaro, did everything it could to convince other nations, especially Austria, that it would in no way disturb them in their repose. Many of the activities of Campochiaro and the government indicate this conciliatory purpose: protecting the diplomatic corps from insult or injury during the revolution; promptly meeting the government's obligations on the Austrian debt;

---

strongly opposed to the revolution, was agreeably surprised at the outcome of the elections. A'Court (n.p., n.d.) to Castlereagh, Varia, Grossbritannien, Fasc. 18, No. 76.

[30] Under Carbonari pressure, the convention that Pepe concluded with the Palermo insurgents was repudiated by the National Parliament. De Menz (Naples, September 21 and October 13, 18, and 24, 1820) to Metternich, Berichte, Neapel, Fasc. 48; Romani, *Neapolitan Revolution*, 136–137.

[31] Romani (*Neapolitan Revolution*, 88–93, 95–98, 171–172, *et passim*) regards the failure of the Muratists to meet these fundamental problems as the basic internal cause of the failure of the revolution. This contention is undoubtedly correct, but it must be remembered that the worst handicap for the Muratists was the constant threat of foreign intervention, which served to keep Carbonari agitation and radical patriotism at a high pitch and to prevent a sane approach to the constitutional problem.

suppressing a Neapolitan newspaper which had attacked Austria; announcing a policy of strict noninterference with Benevento and Pontecorvo, Papal enclaves within Naples; and finally, attempting repeatedly, despite the evident hopelessness of the project, to get on good terms with Austria, hinting broadly that Austrian or allied intervention in Naples to help the government suppress the sects and turn the revolution in a conservative direction would be only too welcome.[32]

Ferdinand I and Duke Francis of Calabria, meanwhile, each played an important but quite different role during the constitutional regime. The King conducted himself throughout in accordance with his most prominent traits of character—laziness, cowardice, cunning. Having turned over all duties of governing to his son as Vicar-General, Ferdinand proceeded to play a dual role, posing as the loyal and magnanimous constitutional monarch before his people but assuming the part of the terrified prisoner of the revolutionaries for the benefit of the foreign powers. Publicly he rendered his oaths to the Spanish Constitution with an excess of religious zeal, while privately he kept in touch with the Allied powers to plead for help in freeing him from his imprisonment in constitutional bonds. He publicly rebuked and disowned the Neapolitan ambassadors, Prince Castelcicala, at Paris, and Prince Alvaro Ruffo, at Vienna, for refusing to take the oath to the new constitution, at the same time maintaining a secret correspondence with them, pouring out to them a lurid account of his sufferings and fears in Naples. To the French *chargé*, Chevalier de Fontenay, who was suspected of liberal tendencies, the King declared himself to be satisfied with his new min-

[32] De Menz (Naples, August 31, September 29, and October 18, 1820) to Metternich, Berichte, Neapel, Fasc. 48; De Menz (Naples, September 23, 1820) to Metternich, Kongressakten, Troppau, Fasc. 38; and Campochiaro's circular note (Naples, July 13, 1820) to the Neapolitan envoys, Berichte, Frankreich, Fasc. 341. The clearest hint given to Austria that the Neapolitan ministry would welcome intervention to modify the constitution came in the mission of Prince Cimitile (to be discussed later). With other powers the ministers apparently spoke more plainly. For instance, Minister of War General Carascosa presented a plan to Count Stackelberg, the Russian minister, calling for the allies to exert pressure on Ferdinand to get him to open the National Parliament personally and to demand sweeping changes in the constitution. Carascosa, on his part, promised that the ministry and the army would support the King's demands, suppressing the Carbonari entirely if necessary. See A'Court's secret letter (Naples, September 20, 1820) to Castlereagh, Varia, Grossbritannien, Fasc. 18.

isters and hopeful of the future; to A'Court, whose antirevolutionary sympathies were well known, he displayed the most abject terror for his life, advising A'Court that he was throwing himself on the mercy of the Allied courts.[33]

His son, Duke of Calabria, on the other hand, identified himself with the moderate constitutionalist party. No friend of the Spanish Constitution and anxious to see the revolution turned into conservative channels, he nevertheless took his oath to the constitution seriously and refused to betray it. Though he proved weak and indecisive at crucial moments, the Vicar-General followed a course more honorable, if less adroit, than that of his father.[34]

The most important question for the revolutionary regime was, of course, the attitude that foreign powers took toward it. Here the views of the various Allied agents in Naples, from whom Metternich secured most of his information, were of potential importance in determining the policies of their governments. While the several envoys interpreted the revolution differently on various points, they agreed generally that the best solution to the Neapolitan problem lay in some program of conservative revision of the constitution like that contemplated by the Vicar-General and the Muratist ministry. Although A'Court's general reactions to the revolution were highly unfavorable and his reports emphasized the disorders in Naples, the growth of Carbonarism, and the existence of danger to the royal family, even he conceded that the revolution had wide popular support, remarking, "I do not hesitate to say that the great mass of the nation is decidedly in favor of a constitution." While he approved of Austrian or European intervention in Naples, even if it meant the ruin of the country, he believed that it was unwise to attempt a return to the old order and that the best outcome of all would be joint action by a strong prince and a wise Parliament to repress the Carbonari and modify the constitution.[35]

[33] Esterhazy (London, November 3 and 10, 1820) to Metternich, Berichte, Grossbritannien, Fasc. 212; Vincent (Paris, September 22, 1820) to Metternich, Berichte, Frankreich, Fasc. 342; A'Court (Naples, August 26, 1820) to Castlereagh, Varia, Grossbritannien, Fasc. 18; Romani, *Neapolitan Revolution,* 85, 105–107, 109 (note). It was at Ferdinand's insistence and A'Court's request that a British naval contingent was sent to the Bay of Naples to afford the royal family refuge in case of danger.

[34] See Chapter III for details.

[35] A'Court (Naples, August 24, 1820) to Castlereagh, Varia, Grossbritannien,

A more favorable view was that of the Austrian *chargé*, Count de Menz, whose professed aim was only to give an objective analysis of the revolution and the new regime. First of all, he maintained, the revolution was in a real sense a popular movement. "One must agree," he wrote Metternich, "that constitutional ideas do dominate and have taken root in the nation. The clergy, the nobility, the military, the bourgeoisie, and, above all, the judicial order are imbued with them." The revolt was a reaction not against monarchy or even against Ferdinand himself, but against the inept policy of his ministers since 1815 and especially against the burdensome taxes and "ministerial despotism" of Finance Minister Luigi de Medicis. The easy victory of the revolution was due to a vague and inchoate but widespread desire for some sort of change, some sort of constitutional protection against arbitrary rule, against which the party of those attached to the old order was too small in numbers and too insignificant in talents to hold the line.

These same facts, De Menz further pointed out, helped to account for the surprisingly peaceable course the revolution had followed since its victory (the plots, mutinies, and disorder which had occurred, the Austrian *chargé* declared, were no more than normal in the kingdom). The reason was that there had been virtually no unfavorable reaction to the revolution; except in Sicily, it had been accepted without question. The new government, moreover, showed no desire to persecute those who were ousted from power; indeed, pamphleteers who attacked the old ministers too viciously were cited for disciplinary action by the Committee of Public Safety. De Menz recognized grave problems ahead for the new regime, particularly in the matters of the Carbonari, finances, armaments, and Sicily. Nonetheless, he saw a chance for stability in the moderation of the present ministry, its ability to maintain a regular internal administration, and the willingness of the ministry and the Hereditary Prince to adopt major changes in the constitution, including an absolute royal veto and a hereditary Chamber of Peers.[36]

Fasc. 18; Castlereagh (Cray Farm, January 5, 1821) to Charles Stewart, ambassador to Austria, in *Memoirs and Correspondence of Viscount Castlereagh, second Marquess of Londonderry,* XII, 340–341.

[36] De Menz (Naples, October 18, 1820) to Metternich, Berichte, Neapel, Fasc. 48.

Thus De Menz held the opinion that the new regime was not inherently unstable and would establish itself if given a chance. The observations of the Prussian and Russian emissaries and observers at Naples go far in important respects to confirm this analysis.[37] The Bavarian envoy, Chevalier Gombernat, in fact, denied the official Austrian thesis on the revolution directly:

> Up to the present, nothing which has taken place in the kingdom since July 1 justifies the declamations of the *Austrian Observer* [*Österreichischer Beobachter*, Metternich's official journal]. Everything leads one to assume here that if foreign armies do not intervene the new institutions will establish themselves without resistance.

A foreign invasion, Gombernat conceded, could easily overthrow the present regime, but it would also bring with it the kind of confusion and anarchy from which Naples was now happily free.[38]

These appraisals fitted in ill, of course, with the official Austrian thesis on the revolution, for the simple reason that the Austrian attitude was not based on empirical evidence or testimony about the revolution, but on something else—an emotional horror of all revolution, combined with a realistic appraisal of the special dangers which this particular revolution meant for Austria. Among Austrian spokesmen horror and shock were the immediate and widespread reactions to the events in Naples. Gentz admitted frankly:

> In view of the general disposition of peoples, it is impossible to deny that we have arrived at one of those dark epochs where one is unable any longer to count on anything, and where a wise man must expect from day to day to see the very ground that he believed the most solid and the best supported crumble under his feet.[39]

In Paris, Ambassador Vincent believed the danger worse than in 1814: "Everything reduces itself to a very simple consideration and

[37] Friedrich Wilhelm Ramdohr, Prussian envoy at Naples (Naples, July 14, 1820), to Frederick William III, Korrespondenz, Neapel, Fasc. 50; Count Stackelberg (Naples, August 1, 1820) to Russian Secretary of State Count Nesselrode, *ibid.*; Jakob Bartholdy, Prussian *chargé d'affaires* at Florence (Naples, September 26, 1820) to Frederick William, *ibid.*

[38] Gombernat (Naples, September 26, 1820) to Count Rechberg, *ibid.*

[39] Gentz (Vienna, July 17, 1820) to Soutzo, in Gentz, *Dépêches inédites*, II, 70.

calculation indeed, that of the existence of every throne." [40] Metternich in Vienna, shared his fear. While angry enough at the cowardice and weakness of Ferdinand I and fearful of almost certain further repercussions and outbreaks in Italy, he was most of all in-
censed that the movement in Naples, which he declared "was reduced to the surprise attack of a few bandits and occult maneuvers
on the part of secret societies," should have placed the fate of the
Austrian Empire and other centuries-old institutions in the balance.[41]

In contrast, therefore, to the cautious appraisals of De Menz and
other observers, the picture Metternich painted of the revolution, a
picture drawn, he claimed, from incontestable facts, was simple and
clear-cut in the extreme. It was one of a benevolent and paternalistic
king imprisoned and terrorized by factious criminals; an enlightened,
able administration turned out in favor of a band of lawless sectarians; a populace formerly well-governed, peaceable, and contented
now holding life and goods at the mercy of a rebel faction and a
mutinous army; a revolutionary government set up solely "to proclaim anarchy as the law" and incapable of meeting a single one of
its problems; a revolution, in short, without a shadow of popular
support or justification, promising for the kingdom only the blackest
of futures.[42]

As for a solution to the problem, Metternich felt that a good course,
were it not so dangerous, might be to let the Neapolitans stew in
their own juice. "With them," he said, "*everything* was *good,* and

[40] Vincent (Paris, July 27, 1820) to Metternich, Berichte, Frankreich, Fasc.
341.

[41] Metternich (Weinzierl, July 17, 1820) to Esterhazy, Weisungen, Grossbritannien, Fasc. 213.

[42] *Ibid.;* Metternich (Vienna, July 26, 1820) to Count Rechberg, in Metternich, *Nachgelassene Papiere,* III, 382–383; "Recit succinct de la marche des
événemens de Naples depuis le 1 jusqu'au 14 juillet 1820," Korrespondenz,
Neapel, Fasc. 50. In contrast to Metternich's official view, however, his report
to Count Zichy, Austrian envoy at Berlin (Vienna, July 15, 1820, *Atti del
Parlamento,* V, Pt. 2, 8–9), conceding that the revolution had taken place
peaceably, attributed its success to the cowardice of King Ferdinand. Annibale
Alberti ("La rivoluzione Napoletana," *Atti del Parlamento,* IV, xix–xxiii) shows
how Metternich, true to his oversimplifying political philosophy, refused to pay
any attention to the distinction drawn between the radical Carbonari progenitors
of the revolution and its conservative Muratist heirs. Indeed, De Menz's objective and serene analyses of the Neapolitan scene earned him the displeasure of
Metternich, who much preferred the more colorful, if less accurate, reports of
A'Court.

now *everything* must *unconditionally* become bad." [43] The ideal solution, however, would come from within Naples itself in the form
of a counterrevolutionary *coup d'etat*. This was the recipe Metternich expounded to Prince Cimitile, sent by the Neapolitan government to confer with Metternich and, if possible, also with Alexander
at St. Petersburg before replacing Prince Castelcicala, the non-juring
envoy at Paris. A group of strong patriotic men of good will, said
Metternich, "ought to unite themselves into a band (*un faisceau*),"
and launch a full-scale counterrevolution in the name of the King.
The counterrevolutionaries should proceed to punish all the criminal
factious elements, try General Guglielmo Pepe and similar conspirators in military courts and execute them within twenty-four hours,
bring treason charges against the Carbonari, and annul all laws and
enactments made since July 6. From eighty to a hundred such men
would be sufficient, Metternich believed, to carry out this program.[44]

Thus Metternich's verdict on the revolution was as black and his
suggested remedy for it as drastic as they could be. The reasons, as
already indicated, were partly a matter of antirevolutionary principles, but chiefly they were reasons of Austrian interests of state.
While any revolution was in principle damnable enough, this one
could ruin Metternich's carefully-constructed system. Naples was
supposed to serve the same purpose in Italy as did Prussia in Germany: to act as Austria's partner in preventing innovations. A secret
Austro-Neapolitan treaty of June 12, 1815, bound Ferdinand I to
introduce no changes into his government incompatible with the

[43] Metternich (Vienna, August 10, 1820) to Gentz, in Gentz, *Briefe von und
an Gentz*, III, Pt. 2, 30–31.

[44] "Précis sommaire des entretiens du Prince de Metternich avec Mr le Prince
de Cimitelle [*sic*]," August 1820, Korrespondenz, Neapel, Fasc. 50. Cimitile,
whose mission was to secure diplomatic recognition of the new regime from the
Allied powers, tried to convince Metternich that if Austria would recognize the
constitutional government she could then intervene diplomatically in Naples,
using her enormous influence to repress agitation and to turn the revolution
into conservative channels. Cimitile gained the impression from Metternich
that if a counterrevolution was carried out at Naples, Austria might then
concede some sort of constitution there. Cimitile (Vienna, September 7, 1820)
to the Vicar-General, *Atti del Parlamento*, V, Pt. 1, 73–74. No trace of this
idea, however, can be found in Metternich's report. Annibale Alberti ("La
rivoluzione Napoletana," *ibid.*, IV, lxxxiii–lxxxvi) condemns the Cimitile mission
as ill-conceived and badly executed, a hopeless diplomatic gesture which did
Naples no good and afforded Metternich a welcome opportunity to size up the
weaknesses and insecurity of the revolutionary regime.

form used by Austria in governing Lombardy-Venetia.[45] De Medicis, with whom Metternich was in correspondence before the revolution, had been cooperating with Austrian secret police in suppressing the "ill-willed" factions in Italy.[46] Now the secret treaty was broken, the factions were in power at Naples, and a revolution had been ignited which could easily spread to Rome, Tuscany, Piedmont, and even Lombardy-Venetia itself.[47]

The consequences could be as disastrous in Germany as in Italy. If the Neapolitan revolution was allowed to continue, all the good results of Metternich's labors at Carlsbad and Vienna might be lost. How could Metternich expect the German governments to discipline professors like Follen and Jahn while at Naples revolutionaries like Pepe and Minichini were feted as heroes? Why should the relatively harmless *Burschenschaften* have to disappear if the Carbonari were permitted to thrive? How could Austria demand that the German governments limit themselves to purely monarchical provincial constitutions if she tolerated the very radical Spanish Constitution at Naples? Above all, how could Metternich keep other princes from submitting to revolution and other peoples from rising in revolt if the bad example set by Ferdinand and the Neapolitans went uncorrected? If nothing was done, even the Austrian domains, quiet and secure as they were, might not be immune from the spread of the revolutionary contagion.[48]

Therefore the revolution must be crushed. This was the alpha and

[45] Romani, *Neapolitan Revolution*, 4–6. The treaty further bound Ferdinand to subordinate all family and dynastic ties to the general interest, to contract no other alliance at variance with the treaty, to enter into no "defensive federation of Italy of whatever nature it might be," and to organize his army on an Austrian basis and under an Austrian commander. At Emperor Francis' instigation, Metternich tried to insert similar provisions in treaties with all the Italian states, but was thwarted by the resistance of Piedmont and the Papal States, supported by Russia.—Walter Maturi, "Il Congresso di Vienna e la restaurazione dei Borboni a Napoli," *Rivista storica italiana*, New Series, IV (1939), 58–62.

[46] Metternich (Vienna, January 18, 1820) to De Medicis, Korrespondenz, Neapel, Fasc. 50; Metternich (Vienna, August 8, 1820) to De Menz, *ibid.*

[47] Metternich (Weinzierl, July 17, 1820) to Esterhazy, Weisungen, Grossbritannien, Fasc. 213.

[48] This judgment on the dangers of the revolution to Austria was not merely Metternich's, but the general consensus in the Austrian government. See the memoir to Metternich by one of his opponents, Finance Minister Prince Stadion (Vienna, July 22, 1820), Kongressakten, Laibach, Fasc. 41.

omega of Metternich's policy on the revolution. The manner, the means, the time might be unclear, but the basic fact could never be in question. No finely-spun theories, no carefully-amassed evidence about the revolution, no prognostication about its future course within Naples entered into this decision. The question was simply one of Austrian state interests. Austria was in danger, wrote Metternich to Vincent, and "it is therefore up to us to direct ourselves according to our own calculations." [49] This remained Metternich's position from the beginning to the end of the Neapolitan revolution: Austrian interests must decide everything. As he wrote to Prince Stadion in March 1821, when the Austrian intervention was under way:

Any retreat in Italy in the present situation would mean making revolution for ourselves in the entire peninsula, and how could we retain our Italian provinces for ourselves if this happened?

Italy, he commented, would go to the devil and France and Germany with her, if Austrian actions were not decisive. [50]

Because Metternich could not, or dared not, strike immediately to crush the revolution, [51] he had first to make sure that it would be morally condemned everywhere in Europe. For if Austria could not act immediately, she needed moral support from the other powers, and if this moral support was to come from other powers who were not menaced as Austria was, they would have to share the same

[49] Metternich (Vienna, August 5, 1820) to Vincent, Weisungen, Frankreich, Fasc. 343.

[50] Metternich (Laibach, March 26, 1821) to Stadion, Staatskanzlei: Interiora: Korrespondenz, Fasc. 82. Stadion certainly was no opponent of the Austria-first policy; he claimed, in fact, to be its author. "In the very first conference on the affairs of Naples at Schönbrunn," he wrote Metternich, "I established the thesis, which you shared, that it was the purely Austrian interests which had to dictate to us our decisions in that unhappy complication." Stadion (Vienna, March 14 or 15, 1821) to Metternich, Kongressakten, Laibach, Fasc. 41.

[51] Metternich claimed more than once, some months after the revolution began, that, had sufficient force been available to him, he would have crushed it immediately. See Metternich (Troppau, November 10, 1820) to Vincent, Weisungen, Frankreich, Fasc. 343; Metternich (Troppau, December 31, 1820) to Count Rechberg, in Metternich, *Nachgelassene Papiere,* III, 395. These claims, however, must be heavily discounted. Metternich was never a man of bold action. It is almost impossible to conceive of him taking such a decisive step without first ascertaining the attitude of the Allies and the other German and Italian Courts on it.

horror of the revolution which Austria had. Hence the unreserved denunciation of the revolution which Metternich gave out to the world. The Austrian Foreign Minister, who just a few weeks before had been insisting that the Spanish revolution must be left alone, now had to convince other nations that the Neapolitan revolution must be crushed, and this not simply because it was bad for Austria (clearly too self-centered a reason) but because it represented an intolerable menace to Europe and the world.

He had little difficulty convincing the Italian and German Courts of the utterly malevolent character of the revolution, since most of the lesser princes were more frightened of it than he was. In a special proclamation to the German Courts, Emperor Francis assured his fellow princes that Austria was prepared to defend her own Italian territory, as well as that of any Italian sovereign who called for Austrian aid, and that she would in an emergency use force to suppress the revolution.[52] In Italy, not contenting himself solely with similar proclamations, Metternich sent a trusted envoy, Count Ficquelmont, then ambassador to Tuscany, as a special ambassador to Sardinia's King Victor Emmanuel I to prevent any possible misunderstanding with the one state in northern Italy large enough to cause Austria any concern.[53] The results of these actions were entirely reassuring. Gentz, back from a personal visit in Bavaria, reported that both King Max Joseph and Prime Minister Count Rechberg were wholly in accord with Metternich's views on the revolution and fearful only that Austria would not send enough troops to Italy to contain and suppress it.[54] Ficquelmont reported that Victor Emmanuel, in a state of terror over the revolution, pleaded for more Austrian reinforcements in Lombardy-Venetia and urged Austria to make no compromise with any kind of constitution in Naples. Sardinian Foreign Minister San Marzano also assured Ficquelmont that the army and populace in Sardinia were loyal to the existing regime.[55] Another important Italian prince, Archduke Ferdinand III

[52] Proclamation by Francis [Vienna, July 20, 1820], Weisungen, Russland, Fasc. 44.

[53] Metternich (Vienna, August 12, 1820) to Ficquelmont, Weisungen und Varia, Sardinien, Fasc. 56.

[54] Gentz (Salzburg, August 1, 1820) to Metternich, in Gentz, *Briefe von und an Gentz*, III, Pt. 2, 16–24.

[55] Ficquelmont (Turin, August 12 and 13, 1820) to Metternich. Weisungen und Varia, Sardinien, Fasc. 56. For evidence of the Sardinian government's

of Tuscany, wholeheartedly approved the Austrian stand. Only the Court of Rome, because of its insistence that the Pope must remain neutral, failed to endorse the Austrian circular or to respond to the offer of armed aid.[56]

Meanwhile, Austria automatically assumed a policy of nonrecognition of the new regime at Naples, rejecting three would-be envoys who came to represent it or to plead its case—Prince Cariati in July, Prince Cimitile in August, and the Duke of Gallo in early September.[57] But even before receiving the encouragement of his fellow sovereigns, the Austrian Emperor began reinforcing his army in Lombardy-Venetia with the aim of reaching a strength of eighty thousand men by October.[58]

Military reinforcements in Italy and moral support from the lesser German and Italian states, however, were not enough for Austria. The crucial question for Metternich was the attitude of the other great powers. If they supported him, all was well; if not, they could easily frustrate Austrian action. In soliciting their moral support and explaining the Austrian position, Metternich found it necessary to use slightly different arguments with each power. Tsar Alexander, whose attitude Metternich considered of prime importance, was known to be a bitter opponent of the French and Spanish revolutions. Metternich's approach with him, therefore, was to maintain that the Neapolitan revolt was just like those two revolutions, only worse. Since Alexander, however, favored joint Allied action against revolutions based on a general intervention principle, while Austria wished to act alone and unhampered, Metternich deliberately left

---

wholesale support of the Austrian position throughout the Neapolitan crisis, see Maria Avetta, "Al Congresso di Lubiano coi ministri di Re Vittorio Emanuele I," *Il Risorgimento italiano*, XVI (1923), 1–50, and XVII (1924), 212–250.

[56] Metternich (Vienna, August 8 and 12, 1820) to Esterhazy, Weisungen, Grossbritannien, Fasc. 213, Nos. 2 and 4.

[57] Cariati and Cimitile were received privately by Metternich, while Gallo was turned back at the border at Klagenfurt. Cimitile was also refused audience by the Russians. Campochiaro (Naples, July 23, 1820) to Metternich, Korrespondenz, Neapel, Fasc. 50; Metternich (Vienna, September 2, 1820) to Gallo, *ibid.;* Gallo (Klagenfurt, September 3, 1820) to Metternich, *ibid.;* Count Golowkin, Russian ambassador to Vienna (Vienna, September 8, 1820), to Cimitile, *ibid.;* copy of report, Metternich (Vienna, July 26, 1820) to Francis I, Weisungen, Russland, Fasc. 44.

[58] Metternich (Vienna, August 8 and 12, 1820) to Esterhazy, Weisungen, Grossbritannien, Fasc. 213, Nos. 2 and 4.

vague the question of what action Austria would take to suppress
the revolution. Metternich also thought it wise not to mention the
secret treaty with Naples. The Tsar did not approve of secret alli-
ances and special spheres of influence alongside the general alliance
of all of Europe.[59]

With Great Britain, on the other hand, Metternich could freely
discuss the secret treaty. For one thing, the British had found out
about it anyway; for another, England favored Austrian hegemony
in Italy and had no objection to special Austrian arrangements with
the Italian states. The British, however, could agree to Austrian intervention and give it moral support only on special grounds of necessity, not on the basis of general principles. For this reason Metternich found it expedient to explain to Castlereagh that the Neapolitan revolution was entirely different from the Spanish revolt or even
from the French revolution—that is, the Neapolitan revolution was,
per se, without regard to its further effects, so menacing that Austria
might for the sake of her existence be driven to steps she would not
dream of taking or sanctioning in Spain.[60]

From France, Metternich wished only two things: no interference
with Austria in Italy, and vigilance against revolution at home. He
therefore instructed Vincent to sound out Louis XVIII and Richelieu
on their reactions to the revolution and to try to make sure that
France did not revive the old Bourbon policy of rivalry with the
Habsburgs in Italy. The present crisis, argued Metternich, was too
dangerous for any power to be thinking of special interests. Louis
and his ministry ought rather to be busy making sure that they did
not share the fate of their fellow Bourbons in Spain and Naples.[61]
As for Prussia, Metternich still professed to see great danger of her
dissolution through revolution: "Prussia has advanced so far onto
the edge of the abyss that nothing in Europe is more problematical
than the duration of her existence." [62] The Prussian leaders, especially Frederick William III, Wittgenstein, and Foreign Minister

[59] Metternich (Vienna, July 28, 1820) to Lebzeltern, Weisungen, Russland,
Fasc. 44, Nos. 1 and 2.

[60] Metternich (Vienna, August 5 and 12, 1820) to Esterhazy, Weisungen,
Grossbritannien, Fasc. 213, No. 4.

[61] Metternich (Weinzierl, July 17, 1820) to Vincent, Weisungen, Frankreich,
Fasc. 343, Nos. 1 and 2.

[62] Metternich (Vienna, August 8, 1820) to Esterhazy, Weisungen, Grossbritannien, Fasc. 213.

Count Christian Bernstorff, were by this time themselves so frightened of revolution anyway that they could be expected, as at Carlsbad and Vienna, to follow Austrian leadership in docile fashion.

England's reaction to the revolution, even in advance of the Austrian explanations on it, was all that Metternich could wish. Castlereagh's first comment on it was the shocked exclamation, "What an event, and directed against a government without reproach!" According to Esterhazy, Castlereagh's opinion was shared by the whole Cabinet, including George Canning. Castlereagh indicated in a veiled way that Austria had a free hand to act as she desired in Naples, urging Metternich at the same time to keep a close eye on Sardinia and France. Wellington was even more frank. Speaking unofficially, he urged Austria to crush the revolution immediately, suggesting that she amass eighty thousand men in Lombardy-Venetia to handle the task, and that she justify her intervention on the basis of the violation of the secret Austro-Neapolitan treaty.[63]

Metternich had no objection to this advice,[64] since he wanted nothing better than to receive moral support and a free hand for Austria from the other powers. Unfortunately for Metternich, neither France nor Russia was so amenable as England. Neither of the two nations, to be sure, approved of the Neapolitan revolution. The French government, Vincent was convinced, had in no way instigated or approved the revolt. Richelieu expressed surprise at its outbreak and approved the Austrian policy of nonrecognition, urging, in fact, that the Austrian statements of principle ought to be followed by action.[65] And Russia, having condemned the Spanish revolution, could hardly approve its Neapolitan counterpart. The difficulty was rather that neither France nor Russia was disposed to give Austria carte blanche at Naples. Both wanted to make of the revolution a European matter in which all the Allies would have a voice on both the question of intervention and that of the future

[63] Castlereagh (London, July, 1820) to Sir Charles Stuart, ambassador at Paris, Varia, Grossbritannien, Fasc. 18; Esterhazy (London, July 20 and 30, 1820) to Metternich, Berichte, Grossbritannien, Fasc. 211; letters from London, July 21 and 30, 1820, Daria Khristoforovna Lieven, *The Private Letters of Princess Lieven to Prince Metternich 1820–1826*, pp. 53–54, 56.

[64] Metternich (Vienna, August 12, 1820) to Esterhazy, Weisungen, Grossbritannien, Fasc. 213, No. 4.

[65] Vincent (Paris, July 19 and 27, 1820) to Metternich, Berichte, Frankreich, Fasc. 341.

Neapolitan government. The two governments had similar reasons
for this stand, the first of which involved their prestige. France was
eager to play once again the role of a great power in Europe, one
which should be consulted on so vital a question as the suppression
of a revolution in Italy. At St. Petersburg, meanwhile, Alexander
was nursing a case of frustration. The growing diplomatic entente
between Austria, Prussia, and England, the increasing independence
of France, and the rebuff administered to the Russian attempts to
secure a general guarantee pact at Aachen or joint Allied intervention in Spain were all signs to the Tsar that the influence of Russia
was declining, that she was no longer playing the role in Europe
which befitted her power. This was important to Alexander, who
cared more about the figure he cut in European congresses than the
administration he gave to his own domains.[66]

In addition, the French and the Russian governments entertained
a certain suspicion of Austria and of Metternich. This feeling was
particularly strong in France, whose ministers suspected that Austrian intervention in Naples might lead Austria to extend still further
her influence and even her territory in Italy. The final ground for
French and Russian opposition, however, was the one most dangerous to Metternich and his plans. There existed a party in each
country, led by Capodistrias in Russia, and Foreign Minister Baron
Étienne-Denis Pasquier in France, which favored modifying the
Spanish Constitution in Naples to make it resemble the French
Charte instead of destroying it entirely.[67] This idea of employing
European intervention at Naples to bring about a moderate consti-
tution typified a positive nightmare for Metternich and Francis I.

---

[66] Lebzeltern (St. Petersburg, July 29, 1820) to Metternich, Berichte, Russland, Fasc. 29, Nos. 42A and 42D. Lord Stewart shrewdly remarked at the
Congress of Troppau: "It is unquestionably . . . the Emperor of Russia's passion to regulate these Congresses. He has a passion for the little war of the
Mémoires that are given in from each Cabinet, and the examination of them,
and the interest or rule he can excite in the other nations of Europe have a
far greater charm with him than governing his own." Stewart (Troppau,
December 21, 1820) to Castlereagh, in Webster, *Foreign Policy of Castlereagh.*
Appendix C, 534.

[67] Vincent (Paris, August 21, 1820) to Metternich, Berichte, Frankreich,
Fasc. 341; Lebzeltern (St. Petersburg, August 23, 1820) to Metternich, Berichte,
Russland, Fasc. 29, No. 45A; Webster, *Foreign Policy of Castlereagh,* 264–266;
Romani, *Neapolitan Revolution,* 108–111.

Metternich, therefore, faced much the same problems in dealing with France and Russia. The French opposition he never took too seriously. Annoying, incorrect, and even embarrassing though some of France's proposals were, Metternich found them no insurmountable obstacle to his plans, for he was convinced that neither the Richelieu ministry nor the Bourbon monarchy were secure enough in France to permit them to seriously oppose Austrian action in Italy.[68] Russia, on the other hand, presented an entirely different problem, for her attitude, as Metternich saw the situation, would decide everything. If Alexander was amenable, Austria could act in Naples, regardless of what France said or did; without his support, Austria could carry out no material action even if France and Great Britain approved of it; and were Russia to combine with France against Austria on the Naples affair, the Austrian hold on Italy would be shattered. Metternich thus had to construct his policy regarding Naples on two fundamental but divergent premises: first, Austria must act by herself and in her own interests to save her position in Italy; and second, she could not act without the moral support of Russia.[69] The difficulties involved in reconciling these two premises taxed Metternich's diplomatic skill to the utmost.

The Cabinet of France was the first to raise actual difficulties for Austria—with a proposal of a congress or reunion of Cabinets on the Neapolitan question. While Richelieu personally urged Metternich to agree to a congress as the best means of demonstrating Allied unity, a French Cabinet memoir made a similar plea to all the great powers, calling for joint action against the revolution and insisting that unilateral action by any power would only encourage popular agitation.[70]

Although the French here were turning one of Metternich's

[68] Metternich (Vienna, September 1, 1820) to Vincent, Weisungen, Frankreich, Fasc. 343, No. 7; Metternich (Vienna, August 8, 1820) to Esterhazy, Weisungen, Grossbritannien, Fasc. 213, No. 1.

[69] Metternich (Vienna, August 5, 1820) to Vincent, Weisungen, Frankreich, Fasc. 343, No. 1; Metternich (Vienna, August 8, 1820) to Esterhazy, Weisungen, Grossbritannien, Fasc. 213, No. 1.

[70] Richelieu (Paris, July 28 and August 10, 1820) to Metternich, Varia, Frankreich, Fasc. 93; "Mémoire du Cabinet des Tuileries sur les événemens à Naples," August 1820, Kongressakten, Troppau, Fasc. 38. Richelieu's letter of August 10 is printed in G. de Bertier de Sauvigny, *France and the European Alliance 1816–1821: The Private Correspondence between Metternich and Richelieu*, 99–101.

favorite arguments against him, he was not greatly embarrassed by it. A Cabinet conference was a good idea in theory, he replied to the French Cabinet, but impractical because England would not agree to it, and a conference without Great Britain would give the appearance of disunity within the alliance and therefore do more harm than good. Besides, a Cabinet conference was not necessary to convince the world of Allied unity. It was only necessary that the powers be one in principle—and this unity had already been achieved. If military measures against the revolution proved necessary, they would be on too small a scale to dignify with the name of "war" or to demand the attention of Europe.[71] Thus Metternich neatly parried the French proposal with fair-sounding words. Privately, however, he was intensely irritated with it,[72] blaming not so much France (the general French attitude on the revolution was a pleasant surprise) as the Russian Cabinet and Pozzo di Borgo, whom Metternich judged to be the instigators of the French proposal. The French *démarche*, Metternich felt, could easily be circumvented. However, if Russia insisted on a Cabinet conference, Austria might have to agree to it.[73]

Metternich's forecast about France's proposal proved accurate. The French Cabinet, though unconvinced by Metternich's arguments, gave way on its plan for a Cabinet conference, accepting instead Metternich's substitute: the formation of a center for information and moral action in Vienna to discuss the danger of revolution everywhere in Europe. This left certain points in the French attitude which were annoying to Metternich, but nothing which was dangerous.[74]

[71] Metternich (Vienna, August 5, 1820) to Vincent, Weisungen, Frankreich, Fasc. 343, No. 1; Metternich (Vienna, September 3, 1820) to Esterhazy, Weisungen, Grossbritannien, Fasc. 213.

[72] To Esterhazy, Metternich denounced the French proposal openly. The alliance, he insisted, had no right and no business intervening in what was essentially an Austrian concern. The interest of Austria was at stake, and "it is not in the form of conferences of the five Cabinets that it can be assured." Metternich (Vienna, August 8, 1820) to Esterhazy, Weisungen, Grossbritannien, Fasc. 213, No. 1.

[73] If a Cabinet conference could not be avoided, Metternich wrote Esterhazy, he hoped Castlereagh would help him make sure that it would be held at Vienna, or at least within the Austrian Empire, but, above all, not at Paris. Metternich (Vienna, August 12, 1820) to Esterhazy, *ibid.*

[74] Metternich (Vienna, August 22, 1820) to Esterhazy, *ibid.*, No. 1; Met-

Unfortunately for Metternich, even so mild and tentative an approach toward a conference as was his risked opposition from England. Indeed, in this quarter, signs unfavorable for Austria were in evidence. There was not only a growing tendency of the English government to withdraw from Continental affairs,[75] but also, much worse, indications that England would decline even to give Austria open moral support. Castlereagh insisted that Austria should act alone against the revolution in Naples and should not bring the alliance into the question at all. Moreover, he indicated that England would not publicly announce a policy of nonrecognition of the new regime at Naples or of refusal to receive the ambassador from it, because this would cause trouble with British public opinion, even though England intended quietly to follow this course.[76] Disturbed by these indications of English lack of zeal in the good cause, Metternich sent Castlereagh a series of questions to probe the British attitude on various contingencies possible in the Neapolitan question. The answers he received were in the main discouraging. Great Britain, Castlereagh reiterated, could take no public stand against recognizing the new regime at Naples, though she herself would avoid such recognition. Moreover, England did not consider herself bound by any treaties in the Neapolitan question, though morally she was on the same ground as her Allies. The Austrian circulars to the German and Italian Courts, Castlereagh indicated, were entirely satisfactory, but England could make no official comment on them. Moreover, should a Cabinet conference be called (a contingency Castlereagh preferred not to contemplate), England would probably decline to participate in it.[77]

ternich (Vienna, August 21, September 1 and 13, 1820) to Vincent, Weisungen, Frankreich, Fasc. 343, Nos. 1, 7, and 2; Vincent (Paris, August 21, 1820) to Metternich, Berichte, Frankreich, Fasc. 341, No. 41A; Metternich (Vienna, August 21, 1820) to Richelieu, in Bertier, *France and the European Alliance*, 103–107.

[75] One reason for the British attitude was the preoccupation of the ministry throughout August and September with domestic affairs, especially the sensational divorce proceedings against Queen Caroline.—Webster, *Foreign Policy of Castlereagh*, 217–225.

[76] Esterhazy (Windsor Cottage, August 11, 1820) to Metternich, Berichte, Grossbritannien, Fasc. 212.

[77] To these specific answers, themselves unsatisfactory, Castlereagh added other disquieting remarks. It was unfortunate, he said, that at Frankfurt, according to a report from Frederick Lamb, Austria should have created the

By the time Metternich received these answers, he was already committed to proposing an informal conference of ambassadors to satisfy Alexander.[78] An Austrian circular memoir of August 28 presented a five-point program for the Allies to consider: (1) joint recognition of a state of revolt in Naples; (2) a joint policy of non-recognition of the revolutionary regime; (3) common moral condemnation of the revolt; (4) the formation at Vienna of "a central point of information, explanations, and entente," to be composed of the Allied ambassadors or special envoys; and (5) full powers to be given to the ambassadors or envoys to act on this program. The proposal, in other words, called for an informal conference, strictly limited in competence and under Austrian auspices, and committed in advance to moral support of Austria. A general congress, the memoir argued, would only lose valuable time.[79] Metternich did his best to persuade Castlereagh that this was a sound program by appealing to the traditional British suspicion of France and Russia. Both powers, he said, were now displaying a tendency "to play a preponderant role on every occasion." Austria could control them in a conference if she had British support. Would not Britain agree to take part in it, even if Alexander insisted on having the conference of ambassadors at Troppau in Austrian Silesia, the site now set for the meeting of the two Emperors? He realized the limitations placed on British action by her constitutional system, Metternich conceded, but Castlereagh must also understand the Austrian problem, which was that of securing a common *démarche* "conformable to the views and, if need be, even to the fantasies of His Imperial Majesty of all

---

impression among the German delegates that she regarded Naples as one of her Italian provinces. Moreover, he hoped that Austria did not intend simply to destroy the revolutionary regime at Naples without taking some thought about what should replace it. There were many in England, he reminded Esterhazy, who disapproved of military revolt and the Carbonari but who would, nevertheless, be glad to see a moderate, sound constitution set up at Naples with the consent of the King. Esterhazy (London, August 28, 1820) to Metternich, Berichte, Grossbritannien, Fasc. 212.

[78] Metternich (Vienna, August 12 and 26, 1820) to Esterhazy, Weisungen, Grossbritannien, Fasc. 213, Nos. 1 and 1.

[79] "Propositions adressées par l'Autriche aux Cours de France, de Grande Bretagne, et de Russie," Vienna, August 28, 1820, Kongressakten, Troppau, Fasc. 38.

the Russias." The alternative to great-power unity in this crisis, he warned Castlereagh, was the dissolution of society.[80]

Metternich's arguments failed. Castlereagh continued to insist that the whole question should be treated as a special Italian affair for Austrian action rather than as a general European affair necessitating alliance action.[81] Nor would the Russians be put off with Metternich's schemes for a "center of information" or an ambassadorial conference at Vienna. They were determined to bring the alliance into full play, both on general principles and out of suspicion that Austria's predominant influence in Italy needed some restraint.[82] Capodistrias insisted on a general conference, arguing that any isolated or unilateral action by any power was wrong, that there was no good reason why England could not participate, and that even if she could not, her disability should not prevent other powers from taking joint action. The Russian memoir in answer to those of France and Austria contended that if the Allies had intervened in Spain as Russia had requested in April, there would now be no Neapolitan revolt, or at least the machinery would already be in existence to deal with it. In any case, the whole alliance—the same alliance that had crushed the revolution personified in Napoleon—must act in Naples. Nothing less than a full Cabinet conference would be equal to the task.[83]

Metternich tried his best to bridge the gap between the Russian demands and the British refusals. He sent Ambassador Lebzeltern, called home in August for consultations, back to Warsaw, where Alexander was presiding over the opening of his new Polish Diet, to try to obtain a moderation of the Russian demands.[84] Meanwhile,

[80] Metternich (Vienna, September 3, 1820) to Esterhazy, Weisungen, Grossbritannien, Fasc. 213.

[81] Esterhazy (London, September 16, 1820) to Metternich, Berichte, Grossbritannien, Fasc. 212, No. 164A. Castlereagh stated his position fully in his dispatch to Stewart, London, September 16, 1820, in Castlereagh, *Correspondence*, XII, 311–318.

[82] Lebzeltern (St. Petersburg, August 23, 1820) to Metternich, Berichte, Russland, Fasc. 29, No. 45A.

[83] Capodistrias (Warsaw, August 30, 1820) to Metternich, Kongressakten, Troppau, Fasc. 38; "Réponse aux communications de l'Autriche et de la France, en date du mois d'août 1820," n.p., n.d., *ibid.*

[84] Metternich (Vienna, July 29, 1820) to Lebzeltern, Weisungen, Russland, Fasc. 44; instructions, supplement to instructions, and secret instructions to Lebzeltern, Vienna, September 29, 1820, *ibid.*

he continued to plead for understanding and cooperation from England, and to try to calm her fears of moral commitments. All that Great Britain would have to do at a conference, Metternich insisted, was to acknowledge formally the general agreement on principles which in fact already existed. "We have never thought," he concluded, "to make of a police measure the action of a coalition." [85] To both sides, as well as to outsiders, the Austrian Foreign Minister strove to minimize the divergence of views as simply a dispute over forms [86] and to convince them that it was folly to allow such a trifling disagreement to disturb Allied unity when all the important questions—namely, the menacing nature of the revolt and the necessity of its prompt repression—were already settled. [87]

All this conciliatory activity, designed not so much to hold the alliance together as to prevent embarrassments for Austria, the chief one being the necessity of choosing between England and Russia, came to no result. Ultimately Metternich had to choose between one side and the other, and his choice could not long be in doubt. He chose Russia. England's position, after all, would not make much difference in the Neapolitan question. Her constitutional limitations prevented her from doing Austria much good; her general pro-Austrian position in regard to Italy and Germany prevented her from doing Austria much harm. Alexander, on the other hand, would be extremely valuable to have as a friend and disastrous as an enemy. As Metternich remarked to Esterhazy, "Of all evils, the greatest would be to see the Emperor Alexander abandon the moral tie which unites us and thus to set himself up again as the power

---

[85] Metternich (Vienna, September 21 and 29, 1820) to Esterhazy, Weisungen, Grossbritannien, Fasc. 213, Nos. 2 and 1.

[86] To Cardinal Consalvi, Metternich explained that the difference between the powers was comparable to that between different guests invited to a dinner, some of whom wanted to come in evening dress, some in business clothes. Metternich (Vienna, September 2, 1820) to Consalvi, in Consalvi, *Correspondance*, 271–275. To Francis I, Metternich, like Esterhazy, explained the British reservations as the products not of principle but simply of domestic political difficulties. Metternich (Vienna, October 2, 1820) to Francis, Weisungen, Grossbritannien, Fasc. 213; Esterhazy (London, September 16, 1820) to Metternich, Berichte, Grossbritannien, Fasc. 212, No. 164A.

[87] Metternich (Vienna, September 29, 1820), instructions to Lebzeltern, Weisungen, Russland, Fasc. 44; Metternich (Vienna, September 21 and 29, 1820) to Esterhazy, Weisungen, Grossbritannien, Fasc. 213, No. 3 and Reserved.

protecting the spirit of innovation." [88] Since Austria was compelled to choose between two evils, Metternich wrote Francis I:

Between the two, the European public will draw less sinister consequences from a strained attitude of the English government than from the free and voluntary defection of Emperor Alexander, a sovereign whom nothing strains in the execution of his plans.[89]

Despite his oft-repeated assertion that the exclusion of any power from the joint deliberations would be disastrous, it was on this basis of expediency that Metternich finally agreed with the Russians on having a Cabinet conference at Troppau in connection with the meeting of the Emperors. The decision inevitably led to strained relations and coolness between Austria and England. Metternich began privately to complain of the "chicanery" of British opposition, of Ambassador Lord Charles Vane Stewart's failure to grasp the issues, of British lack of understanding and sympathy. "It is only at Berlin that we have been understood," he asserted.[90] To Castlereagh's expression of astonishment that Austria should have accepted the Russian demand for a conference, Metternich replied, with hurt denial, that Austria had never agreed to the formal, plenary sort of congress Russia wanted. Great Britain, moreover, ought to understand the consequences of refusing Russia's demand entirely. It would mean the collapse of the alliance, forcing the isolation of Austria and her retreat within her own borders. Not only would the revolution triumph, but once Alexander was freed from moral ties "an alliance would be effected between France and Russia, and Germany, as well as Italy, would range herself under her [Russia's] banner." With this, European society would be doomed. While Austria could never possibly adopt the same policy as Russia on intervention, Metternich declared, Castlereagh should realize that Russia and France were "the elements that we have to use." [91]

[88] Metternich (Vienna, September 29, 1820) to Esterhazy, Weisungen, Grossbritannien, Fasc. 213 (Reserved).

[89] Report to Francis I, Vienna, October 2, 1820, *ibid.*

[90] Metternich (Vienna, September 21 and 29, 1820) to Esterhazy, *ibid.*, No. 3 and a reserved letter.

[91] Metternich (Vienna, October 3, 1820) to Esterhazy, *ibid.*, Nos. 1 and 2. With his remarkable powers of conforming to a changed situation, Metternich, who had strongly opposed a conference at the beginning, now contended, "I regard it, to the contrary [of Stewart's view], as one of the last anchors of safety." Metternich (Vienna, September 21, 1820) to Esterhazy, *ibid.*, No. 3.

This highly-colored picture of the dangers Austria faced failed to impress Castlereagh. Sharply repudiating once more the idea suggested by Metternich that the Allied proceeding against Naples was in any way connected with the existing alliance treaties, he declared that England now felt compelled not only to decline to participate actively in the conference but also to adopt a policy of strict neutrality on the whole question of Naples. Lord Stewart, at his own request, would be permitted to attend the congress at Troppau as an observer, but without powers to act. Castlereagh further hoped that the congress would be conducted as informally as possible. If there was a protocol, Stewart could only accept it *ad referendum* or sign it without obligation, and if there was a solemn declaration made to Europe, England would decline to join in.[92] Even that unity of moral attitude on which Metternich laid so much stress disappeared. In sharp criticism of Metternich's report of October 2 to Francis I, Castlereagh denied vigorously that England wanted the same things or held the same principles on this question as France or Russia, insisted strongly on the limited nature of the engagements binding England in existing treaties, and defended Great Britain's freedom of discussion and attitude on all issues outside the specific *casus foederis* of the Quadruple Alliance.[93]

Other annoyances arose to vex Metternich as the time for the congress drew near. For one thing, King Frederick William III of Prussia decided to attend the conference, not because he himself wanted to, but because Alexander insisted on it. This was annoying to Metternich because the presence of still another sovereign made the congress that much more formal and imposing, and, more importantly, because he had previously promised Castlereagh that he would keep Frederick William away.[94] France now became a source

[92] Esterhazy (Cray Farm, October 8, and London, October 15, 1820) to Metternich, Berichte, Grossbritannien, Fasc. 212, No. 167B; Stewart (Vienna, October 2, 1820) to Castlereagh, in Webster, *Foreign Policy of Castlereagh*, Appendix C, 524 (see also pp. 277–279).

[93] Esterhazy (London, October 25, 1820) to Metternich, Berichte, Grossbritannien, Fasc. 212, No. 169B with supplement.

[94] Metternich (Vienna, September 21, 1820) to Esterhazy, Weisungen, Grossbritannien, Fasc. 213, No. 4. Metternich had assured Castlereagh that Frederick William's attendance or absence was "a circumstance that I regard finally as placed in *our* will." Metternich (Vienna, September 3, 1820) to Esterhazy, *ibid.* See also Esterhazy (Windsor Cottage, August 11, 1820) to Metternich, Berichte, Grossbritannien, Fasc. 212. Frederick William's attend-

of irritation in a way Metternich had not anticipated. Instead of trying to make too much of the congress, using it to try to restrain Austrian action in Naples or to save a moderate constitution there, as she seemed initially disposed to do, France now seemed not to take the conference seriously enough and to be unwilling to participate fully in the very congress she herself had proposed in July. The discovery in August of a Bonapartist plot against the royal family and plans for a military *coup d'etat* had left the government and the King jittery over France's internal situation and afraid of taking a strong stand against the Neapolitan revolution for fear of arousing a reaction at home.[95] The bad example of England, moreover, proved contagious. If, as Ambassador Decazes reported from London, England intended to remain neutral, prudence dictated that France follow a similar course. In any case, Richelieu reasoned, with England's refusal to participate officially in the congress the show of unity among the powers was broken and the main point of the congress lost. Therefore, instead of making the Marquis de Caraman, who was the French ambassador at Vienna, the French plenipotentiary, as Metternich had suggested and Pasquier had previously agreed, the French government informed Metternich it would send both Caraman and its ambassador at St. Petersburg, Count de la Ferronnays, as observers without powers. As Pasquier admitted to Caraman, "We find ourselves in a certain way forced by the conduct of England to modify our original intentions."[96]

To Metternich this "retrograde course" of France smacked of bad faith and demonstrated a foolish lack of foresight by the ministry. Moreover, it further upset his plans for the conference. "The game

---

ance meant also that Hardenberg would come to Troppau with him. Metternich had discouraged this, too, hoping to have only the amenable Bernstorff present from Prussia. Metternich (Vienna, October 7, 1820) to Zichy, and Zichy (Berlin, October 16, 1820) to Metternich, in *Atti del Parlamento*, V, Pt. 2, 253, 280–282.

[95] Vincent (Paris, August 20 and September 2, 1820) to Metternich, Berichte, Frankreich, Fasc. 341 and 342, Nos. 41 (Postscript) and 44B.

[96] Metternich (Vienna, September 21, 1820) to Vincent, Weisungen, Frankreich, Fasc. 343, Nos. 1 and 2; Metternich (Vienna, September 21, 1820) to Esterhazy, Weisungen, Grossbritannien, Fasc. 213, No. 5; Vincent (Paris, September 11 and 22, 1820) to Metternich, Berichte, Frankreich, Fasc. 342, Nos. 45A and 45B; Pasquier (Paris, October 6, 1820) to Caraman, Varia, Frankreich, Fasc. 93.

at Troppau," he complained, "will be unequal." Now there would be a full congress of the Eastern powers, with all the sovereigns and foreign ministers present, while the two Western powers would have only observers. If any action should be required of England and France, their representatives would have to send back to London and Paris for authorizations—a process requiring from twenty-four to twenty-six and eighteen to twenty days, respectively. "What is one to do in the meantime?" fumed Metternich in exasperation. The new instructions to Caraman, he averred, were pitiful; the backsliding of France was evidence that French policy was still dictated by a ridiculous jealousy of Austria as a rival power.[97]

One more minor annoyance for Metternich in his diplomatic preparations for dealing with the Neapolitan revolution was the attitude of the Court of Rome. While the Pope and Cardinal Consalvi were wholly in accord with Austrian principles on the revolution,[98] a combination of practical considerations, caution, and religious principles prevented the Papal States from taking sides openly with Austria in the impending conflict. As Consalvi pointed out to Metternich, the Papal States, possessing a long and almost defenseless frontier bordering on Naples, as well as having two enclaves in Neapolitan territory, simply could not afford to invite Neapolitan attack. Moreover, it was impossible for the Pope to be the declared enemy of a wholly Catholic state, especially since on religious grounds there was no complaint to make about the revolution (the Spanish Constitution, as adopted also at Naples, made the Catholic faith the exclusive state religion).[99] The Austrian envoy at Rome, Count Apponyi, sensed an unspoken wish on the part of Consalvi that Austria would take no hostile measures against Naples, for in view of the nullity of Papal defenses Rome could be taken and sacked by the Neapolitans before Austria could do anything

---

[97] Metternich (Vienna, October 6, 1820) to Esterhazy, Weisungen, Grossbritannien, Fasc. 213; Metternich (Vienna, October 6, 1820) Weisungen, Frankreich, Fasc. 343, Nos. 1 and 2 (Secret).

[98] Consalvi (Rome, August 12, 1820) to Metternich, in Consalvi, *Correspondance,* 257–259.

[99] Consalvi (Rome, August 23, 1820) to Metternich, *ibid.,* 262–267. See also the comment by Charles van Duerm, in Consalvi, *Correspondance,* xcvi–xcvii. A very full study of the question of Papal neutrality is Joseph H. Brady, *Rome and the Neapolitan Revolution of 1820–1821: A Study in Papal Neutrality.*

about it.[100] Metternich considered this annoying policy of Papal neutrality the result not of principles but of a culpable fear.[101]

The neutrality of the Holy See, however, was a mere pinprick, and even the more serious matters of France's backsliding and the rift with England were only minor problems compared to the great test that Metternich now faced. Having yielded in substance to Russia's demand for a Cabinet conference, and having alienated England in the process, he would now have to see whether he could make the game worth the candle—whether he could obtain from Russia the kind of free, unconditional support that he desired.

[100] Apponyi (Rome, September 20, 1820) to Metternich, in Consalvi, *Correspondance*, 281.

[101] Metternich wrote to Esterhazy, "Those old cardinals there [the *Zelanti*, Consalvi's opponents] are worse fools than anything it is possible to conceive." Vienna, August 12, 1820, Weisungen, Grossbritannien, Fasc. 213.

CHAPTER III

THE CONGRESS OF TROPPAU

The Congress which opened October 23, 1820, at Troppau had, from Metternich's standpoint, a bothersome defect: lopsidedness. Alongside the imposing array of sovereigns, foreign ministers, and ambassadors from the Eastern powers was the meager representation of only three observers from the Western nations.[1] The Congress also had, however, an important asset: privacy. Troppau, a provincial city without the distractions of a capital, proved an excellent site for the intimate conversations and conferences in which most of the work was to be accomplished. In addition, here within the Austrian Empire Metternich was able to impose the measures of secrecy he thought desirable to prevent any publicity or leaks of information which might spoil the results of the conference in advance.[2]

Immediately upon arriving at Troppau on October 19, Metternich took up his main task—that of winning over Alexander and, by the

[1] The personnel of the Congress was as follows: for Austria—Francis I, Metternich, Lebzeltern, Count Zichy, and Gentz (who served as secretary for the Congress); for Prussia—Frederick William III, Hardenberg, Bernstorff, Wittgenstein, and Ambassador to Vienna General Krusemarck; for Russia—Alexander I, Capodistrias, Nesselrode, and Ambassador to Vienna Count Golowkin; for England—Stewart; and for France—Caraman and De la Ferronnays.

[2] Caraman (Troppau, October 22, 1820) to Pasquier, Kongressakten, Troppau, Fasc. 39. Metternich's precautions included the establishment of a special *Postloge* at Troppau (as was done later also at Laibach) for the purpose of intercepting and reading or deciphering all mail, including dispatches to the conferees. Verona, which had an established *Postloge*, needed no special precautions for the Congress in 1822.—Josef Karl Mayr, *Metternichs Geheimer Briefdienst. Postlogen und Postkurse,* 12, 14. The whole work gives an excellent account of *cabinet noir* activities under Metternich.

same token, neutralizing the influence exerted over the Tsar by Capodistrias. His first step in this direction was made in a three-hour interview with the Tsar on the twentieth, which left Metternich, already optimistic before, convinced that Alexander's conversion to the good cause was even more complete than he had hoped. The Tsar, Metternich reported exultantly, confessed all his errors of the past seven years, acknowledging that Metternich had been right and he wrong, and insisted that he had come to the Congress with no other fixed plans than to maintain the alliance and to support Austria. Even Capodistrias, in an interview the next day, displayed an astounding conformity with Metternich's plans and viewpoints. Nevertheless, the Austrian Foreign Minister still regarded Capodistrias with suspicion, an attitude which turned out to be well justified.[3]

This new evidence of Russian willingness to cooperate with Austria helped to push Metternich further along the course already launched—that of turning from England to Russia as his chief support and most intimate ally. As Gentz had pointed out before the Congress met, the three Eastern powers were in a position to ignore "the political pruderies" of England and France and act as they wished on the Neapolitan question:

Russia, Austria, and Prussia, fortunately still free in all their movements, and sufficiently powerful to enforce whatever they decree, would be able to adopt a system such as the needs and dangers of the moment require, *without* the concourse of England and France.

The only deterrent to their doing this, Gentz commented, was the desire not to split the alliance.[4]

But was this deterrent enough? After hard consideration of the question, Metternich came to the conclusion that it was not. The alliance, though not split, was already inwardly strained; it was hardly worthwhile to maintain the still-intact outward unity of the five powers at the cost of giving up the special advantages that Austria could gain in a special partnership with Russia and Prussia.

[3] Metternich (Trappau, October 24, 1820) to Esterhazy, Weisungen, Grossbritannien, Fasc. 213; No. 1; private letters of Metternich from Hollitsch, October 14, and Troppau, October 21, 1820, in Metternich, *Nachgelassene Papiere*, III, 349, 351–352.
[4] Gentz (Vienna, October 14, 1820) to Soutzo, in Gentz, *Dépêches inédites*, II, 84–85.

Therefore, after his interview with Alexander, Metternich decided to risk an open rift with the Western powers for the sake of obtaining the support which the Eastern allies could give to Austrian action in Italy. Although still willing to defer to England in matters of form,[5] he abandoned from the outset any hope for unity of action with England and France. Had Alexander not displayed such sound conservative views, Metternich would not, to be sure, have dispensed so readily with the support of Great Britain or have turned the Congress, as he did, into essentially an Austro-Russian affair.[6]

His motive in securing Alexander's support was, of course, still the same—to retain for Austria the initiative both in suppressing the Neapolitan revolution and in setting up the future Neapolitan government. In other words, Metternich was now bent on achieving in the Congress what he had tried and failed to gain in August and September by avoiding one. The revolution, he had long since decided, had to be crushed by Austrian arms, and an Austrian army of occupation had to be sent to Naples. The only problem was how to justify the intervention. Metternich could not simply, as the British Foreign Office advocated, claim the right to intervene on the basis of violation of the secret treaty and the special interests of Austria in Italy, for this would displease Alexander. Nor did he wish to accept intervention as a European commission given Austria by the alliance, as Russia and France had originally favored, for this would tie Austria's hands. Clearly some middle course had to be found. On the question of the future government of Naples, meanwhile, the only important concern was making sure that the revolution was destroyed without a trace, instead of arriving at some compromise in a moderate constitution, as the other powers (except Prussia) favored.

Metternich had developed his strategy on these two problems well before the Congress opened. To justify intervention he claimed

[5] In reference to Stewart, who wanted everything done "in the least solemn form," Metternich succeeded at the first conference session in rejecting Capodistrias' proposal for a formal Congress protocol in favor of a simple journal drawn up by Gentz. "Journal des Conférences de Troppau," No. 1, October 23, 1820, Kongressakten, Troppau, Fasc. 38.

[6] Metternich (Troppau, October 26, 1820) to Vincent, Weisungen, Frankreich, Fasc. 343, No. 6 (Secret); Metternich (Troppau, October 24, 1820) to Esterhazy, Weisungen, Grossbritannien, Fasc. 213, No. 1; Gentz (Troppau, October 20, 1820) to Soutzo, in Gentz, *Dépêches inédites*, II, 92–93.

a special Austrian right to act in Naples because of the violation of the secret treaty and the manner in which the revolution particularly menaced Austria, at the same time asserting that the general danger of revolution threatened Europe as a whole to such an extent that all the powers must unite in giving their approval and moral support to the Austrian action. To rule out any constitutional compromise at Naples, he proposed limiting the role and purpose of intervention solely to the destruction of the revolution and the liberation of the King. The whole point of Austria's intervention, he declared, was that Ferdinand was not free. Had the King yielded voluntarily to the rebels in granting a constitution, Austria would have no reason to intervene. The whole question of the future government at Naples and of a constitution lay strictly within the province of the King, who could be advised on the matter, but nothing more. Therefore any decision made by the Allies, or even any official discussion of the matter, constituted an unwarranted interference in the internal affairs of a sovereign state:

We regard as a matter placed outside our competence [the task] of deciding the future forms of the internal administration of the Kingdom of the Two Sicilies. That right belongs only to the legitimate sovereign. . . . To wish to impose any form of government whatsoever on the Kingdom, or to forbid any, would be, despite the difference of intentions, to take a course analogous to that of the factions who have imposed their own laws upon it.[7]

This approach, outlined by Metternich in his diplomatic correspondence prior to the Congress, was the one he chose for the opening Austrian memoir read in the first Congress session of October 23. After condemning the revolution, Metternich proceeded to set out Austria's guiding principles. The first principle was that the entire treaty system created since 1814 had to be maintained inviolate (this was intended to reassure those who suspected Austria of territorial ambitions in Italy). The second was that Austria had an "incontestable right of intervention," based not only on the intrinsic evil and menace of the revolution but also "on the overtures and the protestations of the legitimate sovereign." The third and

---

[7] Metternich (Vienna, August 12, 1820) to Vincent, Weisungen, Frankreich, Fasc. 343, No. 1; Metternich (Vienna, September 11 and 21, 1820) to Esterhazy, Weisungen, Grossbritannien, Fasc. 213, No. 1.

most important principle governed the method and purpose of intervention. There were two kinds of action to take against revolution, said Metternich, each distinct from the other. The first was negative moral action, consisting of nonrecognition and moral condemnation of the revolution, the policy already being followed by all five powers. The second kind, positive direct action, was for Austria alone to execute, with the moral support of the powers, her sole aim being, of course, to restore the King to full possession of his power:

The legitimate power is captive; it is a matter of breaking its chains. It is up to the King to decide what the real interest of his crown and his country demands at the conclusion of this first action. It is for him alone to pronounce it, for him alone to establish it. But to arrive at that legal end, it is necessary that the King be free in his thought and still more that he be supported in his action.

In order that the King might be thus "supported in his action," Metternich foresaw that he would request an army of occupation (or, to use Metternich's euphemism, "a foreign tutelary force") for his kingdom. Austria, of course, would furnish the soldiers, but the army ought to be established and maintained as the army had been in France from 1815 to 1818. Of the secret Austro-Neapolitan treaty of 1815, Metternich made only casual mention in the memoir. Emperor Francis did not, he emphasized, insist on any special rights or wish to act by virtue of secret clauses.[8]

Six days later, the Prussian answer to this memoir, delivered in the next conference on October 29, underlined the complete subservience of Prussia to the Austrian point of view. Expressing full confidence in the purity and disinterestedness of Austrian aims, Hardenberg stated only one positive preference—the desire for a joint solemn declaration by the powers condemning the revolution— and this with the express understanding that Prussia would, of course, accede to any wishes of the majority.[9] Although the full Russian answer was not ready for this conference, a brief provisional note read by Nesselrode concerning the Austrian memoir indicated serious difficulties to come. While conceding the necessity

[8] "Mémoire du Cabinet Autrichien," Troppau, October 23, 1820, Kongressakten, Troppau, Fasc. 38; Schmalz, *Gesamteuropäische Organisation,* 70–71.
[9] Prussian note, October 29, 1820, Kongressakten, Troppau, Fasc. 38; "Instructions pour le Ministre du Roi à la cour de Vienne," Berlin, October 8, 1820, *ibid.*

of opposing the revolution with moral force, and even with arms if need be, Nesselrode also called for action which would assure to the Allies the good will of "all the right-thinking men of Europe." The phrase was treacherously ambiguous, for it failed to specify whether "the right-thinking men of Europe" were sound absolutists, like Metternich, or moderate liberals, like Capodistrias.[10]

Thus Metternich had forebodings about the Russian memoir, and when it appeared on November 2 it more than justified his fears.[11] Written by Capodistrias, it embodied, among a host of other errors, the very two evils Metternich had tried to avoid: first, the establishment of a general principle of intervention in revolutionized lands based on the spirit of existing treaties: and second, the proposal to employ joint Allied intervention in Naples to set up some kind of moderate constitution. The Preamble of the long and tedious memoir consisted of an elaborate justification of the Allied right of intervention on the basis of the treaties and transactions of 1814, 1815, and 1818, designed principally to convince England and France that they could in good conscience subscribe to the principle of intervention. First of all, argued Capodistrias, there was a strong analogy between the situation in France in 1815 during the Hundred Days and that in Naples during the revolution. Second, the Neapolitan revolution and the Spanish Constitution posed a grave threat to all European thrones. Third, it was clear that neither the King nor the people in Naples had freely chosen the revolution or the Spanish Constitution. Had they been free to choose, Capodistrias maintained, they would have chosen either a constitution based on the ancient estates or one like the *Charte* of France. For these reasons and in view of existing treaties, both England and France, he argued, must agree to intervention—France especially, since she owed her present government to a similar Allied intervention in 1814 and 1815.

From this highly objectionable Preamble, Capodistrias proceeded

[10] Note read by Nesselrode, October 29, 1820, *ibid.* After this session the three Eastern powers began holding private meetings, excluding the French and English observers until the results of the secret deliberations could be communicated to the Western powers. "Journal des Conférences," No. 2, October 29, and No. 4, November 19, 1820, *ibid.;* Webster, *Foreign Policy of Castlereagh,* 291–292.

[11] The memoir bears the date of November 2, but was presented only after much private discussion in conferences on the sixth and seventh.

to a "System of Conduct" for the powers, which consisted of three principles. The first stated that revolutionized states "cease to belong to the European alliance." The second set forth Capodistrias' doctrine of intervention: All revolutionized countries that menaced others by their bad example or by sectarian activities automatically authorized the Allied powers to intervene "to protect the states thus corrupted against the progress of the evil and Europe against its contagion." The third principle declared that any intervention, because it was based on the existing treaty system, would *ipso facto* be designed solely to maintain the present territorial arrangements.

These three principles, Capodistrias asserted, served simply to support and reinforce the Austrian plan of intervention. The first principle, for instance, coincided with the policy of nonrecognition of the revolutionary government already adopted by the five powers. It was only necessary now, in the Tsar's opinion, for the Allies to state explicitly in a formal act or protocol that they considered revolutionary states to be excluded from the alliance.

This first Russian principle, however distasteful it might have been to England, was indeed compatible with Austria's plan of intervention. The second principle, especially as Capodistrias interpreted it, certainly was not. For by it Capodistrias intended not merely to make intervention at Naples a joint Allied project but also to make it subject to various prior conditions. Referring the Allies back to earlier Russian proposals regarding the analogous case of Spain, Capodistrias suggested that the Allies begin by making a joint proclamation to both the King and the people in Naples, seeking to persuade them to accept certain vital conditions of peace. These conditions were the disavowal of everything which had occurred since July 2, the liberation of the King and his people from the yoke of revolution, the proscription and suppression of the sects, and "the establishment of an order of things which would guarantee the realization of a wish authentically national." If these demands were accepted at Naples, then the Allies, England and France included, would join in negotiating with Ferdinand I on the future government of Naples. Only if the demands were rejected would the Allies use military force. Even then, before Austrian troops occupied the kingdom the Allies would have to proclaim their true motive, namely, their desire to assure peace and stability to Europe and "the peaceful enjoyment of that double liberty" (*i. e.*, national and political independence) to the inhabitants of Naples. Finally, concluded Capodistrias, if this second principle was properly applied, the third would take care of itself.[12]

Small wonder that this memoir caused Metternich some anxious moments; from the Austrian viewpoint almost everything in it was wrong. A private set of notes on the memoir, drawn up by Gentz and seen only by Metternich and Lebzeltern, denounced it from beginning to end. Capodistrias' assertion that the treaties of 1814 and 1815 formed the new public-law of Europe drew from Gentz the retort: "Here is the source which has caused all the embarrassments of our first deliberations, the primary falsehood ($\pi\rho\hat{\omega}\tau o\nu$ $\psi\epsilon\hat{v}\delta os$) of diplomatic romance." The treaties, he said, restored the old public-law, and did not establish a new one. The Russian attempt to derive the Allied obligation to intervene in Naples from the treaties, especially that of November 20, 1815, was diplomatically, materially, and logically false and absurd. To interpret the treaties in this manner, Gentz argued, "is to invalidate them, to falsify them, to kill them." But such an interpretation, Capodistrias had maintained, was necessary in order to bring England along with the other Allies. "Nonsense," replied Gentz, it would drive her away, for the one thing England would not endure was an extension of the commitments of existing treaties.

For Capodistrias' appeals to the general "Holy" alliance Gentz reserved a special contempt. The Russian memoir had maintained that the world now doubted the efficacy of the general alliance, and insisted that these doubts must be removed by alliance action. Of course the world doubted the "European" alliance's efficacy, answered Gentz, and it would continue to do so until this empty abstraction, this "purely nominal union," was replaced by a union that was real, useful, and suited to the times. Upon Capodistrias' praise of Metternich for upholding the unity of the alliance rather than seeking an isolated Austrian solution at Naples, Gentz commented bitingly:

By a wise policy or, to put it better, by his customary courtesy he [Metternich] has dissimulated as much as possible the dissolution of the

---

[12] "Réponse du Cabinet de Russie au Mémoire presenté par le Cabinet d'Autriche dans la conférence du 11/23, et aux communications faites par le Cabinet de Prusse dans la conférence du 17/29 octobre," Troppau, November 2, 1820, Kongressakten, Troppau, Fasc. 38.

Alliance, or, to speak more correctly, its nonexistence in relation to the problems which it is necessary today to answer; but he has not been the dupe of the incontinent and insipid phrases by which the present memoir has misrepresented every question.[13]

Anger, not contempt, was Gentz's reaction to the sentiments in the Russian memoir about public opinion. The Allies, Capodistrias had argued, must act to assure themselves of "the spontaneous co-operation of that part of Europe which desires only beneficent ameliorations." This, retorted Gentz, was precisely the sort of co-operation which Austria did not ask for and did not want; she wanted only moral support from the Allied sovereigns against a revolution which had been created by that very part of Europe, the factious elements, who were working for "beneficent ameliorations." The Russian talk of the "double liberty" and the "political and national independence" which the Neapolitan subjects should enjoy, said the Austrian publicist, represented the worst kind of attempt to separate the King from his people. Political and national independence consisted simply in the independence of the King. "We wish to deliver the royal authority," he said, "and, by this same action, the nation from the yoke under which it is enslaved by a criminal faction. That is the thing to which our mission restricts itself." Gentz scoffed at Capodistrias' contention that the Allies ought to base their intervention on something more sound than Ferdinand's appeals for help, since these appeals, if revealed, would ruin the King's reputation, have a bad effect on public opinion at Naples, and weaken the link between the Neapolitan Crown and the people it ruled. The basic point, said Gentz, was that Ferdinand's pleas formed a sound basis for Austrian intervention, whatever damage they might do to his cause at home. "The personal conduct of the King," he remarked, "is after all only a secondary consideration in the great process."

In the whole memoir Gentz found just one brief phrase to which he could give wholehearted assent. Where Capodistrias had written that the Allied intervention was motivated, among other things, "by the firm design to stop the revolutionary torrent," Gentz noted in the

[13] Copy of the Russian memoir with marginal notes by Gentz, n.d., *ibid.*, Fasc. 39.

margin, "Here is the sole motive on which it is necessary to establish our course." [14]

Gentz's critique clearly reveals how he and Metternich differed from Capodistrias. They were concerned with Austrian interests, not general principles; *Realpolitik,* not ideals; action to crush the revolution and restore absolutism, not vague ideas for mild liberal reform. Neither of them, however, could publicly express such total disapproval of the Russian memoir as Gentz had expressed in private, especially since at least part of the memoir reflected Alexander's thinking as well as Capodistrias', and it was vital not to alienate him. The necessary course, then, was to separate what was intolerable in the Russian proposal from what could be endured or even accepted and turned to Austrian purposes, and thereby conciliate Alexander while thwarting Capodistrias. A second, "polite" set of notes drawn up by Gentz, evidently designed for use in discussing the memoir with the Russian diplomats, indicate this strategy. Written in a tone of warm praise for the memoir's principles, it objected only to the inconvenience and practical difficulties caused by confusing the letter and the spirit of existing treaties and by linking the affair of Naples with that of Spain (though Austria had no objection to either of these steps in principle). The main criticism was reserved for Capodistrias' idea of a form of government adapted to the "national wish." Here Gentz argued:

The realization of an authentically national wish, a project which would appear to presuppose and demand popular assemblies—for in what other form would it enunciate the national wish authentically?—belongs entirely to modern public-law, and will never be admitted either by the Cabinets or by the publicists of the good old school, who, while recognizing the reality of a national wish, will never seek it in popular assemblies, but in the counsels of the sovereigns called by providence to be the sole organs and legitimate interpreters of the national wish. [15]

Although Gentz put the Austrian ideas down on paper, it fell to Metternich to try to make them prevail in the private conferences, an undertaking which proved to be no easy task. A three-hour conversation with Capodistrias on November 2 left Metternich depressed,

---

[14] *Ibid.*
[15] "Notes sur le Mémoire Russe par Mr. le Ch. de Gentz," *ibid.*, Fasc. 39.

not only at his failure to change Capodistrias' outlook on Naples, but also at his own inability to understand the Russian minister's ideas or to elicit from him any positive course of action. Metternich next issued a warning to Nesselrode. Austria, he said, would be compelled to act unilaterally in what was a matter of life or death for her if Russia did not give her support quickly and without unacceptable restrictions. Nesselrode, however, was as yet without great influence, and after further talks with him and Capodistrias yielded no results, Metternich made his appeal to Caesar, approaching Alexander directly as well as through Emperor Francis. Further delay, he hinted to the Tsar, might mean that Austria would have to look to her own devices and let the alliance go to pieces—an argument always effectual with Alexander.[16]

Along with the appeal for Russian support and the warning of unilateral Austrian action if it was withheld went an attack on the most objectionable features of the Russian proposal. To refute the broad Russian interpretation of existing treaties, Metternich argued that the Russian memoir, while interpreting the spirit of the treaties correctly, failed to distinguish between the spirit and the letter, between contractual and moral obligations, a discrepancy which might cause grave practical inconveniences.[17] To combat a more dangerous error, the Russian insistence on discussing the future government of Naples before settling the question of active intervention,[18] Metternich employed his argument on the necessity of limiting the aim of intervention. However noble in principle was the Russian proposal to set up a beneficent government at Naples, he said, Austria could agree

[16] Metternich (Troppau, November 5, 1820) to Esterhazy, Weisungen, Grossbritannien, Fasc. 213 (Secret); Stewart (Troppau, November 3, 1820) to Castlereagh, in Webster, *Foreign Policy of Castlereagh*, Appendix C, 524–527 (see also pp. 290–291).

[17] "Observations du Cabinet de Vienne sur l'interpretation des Traités," Troppau, November 5, 1820, Kongressakten, Troppau, Fasc. 38.

[18] Metternich suspected Capodistrias of planning to take the issue of intervention away from its true ground of "an attack against the repose of all of Europe" in order to put it on the basis of a violation of the Austro-Neapolitan treaty, simply so that Russia could then offer to mediate between Austria and Naples, thereby extending Russian influence all over Italy. Capodistrias' related suggestion—to invite Ferdinand and his council to confer with the Allies on the needs of Naples—Metternich termed "reprehensible and ridiculous." Metternich (Troppau, November 5, 1820) to Esterhazy, Weisungen, Grossbritannien, Fasc. 213 (Secret).

that the Allies had a right to intervene there only in order to destroy
the revolution and liberate the King; after this, the King's will must
be free:

> Thus Austria prejudices in no way the use which the royal power, once
> re-established, will consider that it ought to make of its incontestable
> faculty to take into consideration the real needs of its people. The Allies
> . . . can give advice . . . but they cannot infringe upon the rights of
> the legitimate authority.

However well meant, the Russian suggestion that the Allies attempt to persuade the King and his council to accept their conditions for revising the present system would, Metternich contended,
result in sanctioning the revolution and bringing about the triumph
of one faction or the other in Naples.[19]

Even more dangerous, Metternich declared, were the suggestions
about a new order of things designed to satisfy the "national wish."
In the first place, this "national wish" was a vague, risky abstraction
which should not be introduced in a grave practical matter like the
present crisis at Naples. In the second place, any action by the Allies
to produce this new order would constitute an inadmissible interference in the purely internal affairs of an independent state. Finally,
neither Austria nor Russia, he reminded Tsar Alexander, was itself
a constitutional state, and both were therefore ill-advised to counsel
others in that direction. The only sound course was to keep Allied
intervention within its proper bounds, i.e., "to protect all legitimate
power."[20]

The Austrian attack was shrewd and well directed. In supplementary explanations, Capodistrias found himself compelled to relin-
quish point after point that he had made. The Russian Cabinet, he
explained, concurred in the distinction between the letter and the
spirit of treaties. It had never intended to take the position that the
treaties made it obligatory for the powers to fight revolution, but
only possible and morally right to do so. Neither had it meant to imply that powers which declined to do so, like Great Britain, were out
of the alliance. To Metternich's request for a more explicit defini-

---

[19] "Apperçu sommaire au sujet de la réponse du Cabinet de Russie du 21
octobre/2 novembre," Troppau, November 5, 1820, Kongressakten, Troppau,
Fasc. 38. The original draft, in Metternich's hand, is in *ibid.*, Fasc. 39.

[20] *Ibid.*

tion of the "national wish," Capodistrias could give no clear answer, replying only that it implied a government freely accepted by the King and the whole people, and not one representing a mere faction. As for interfering in the domestic affairs of Naples, Austria was assured that Alexander had never intended to prescribe laws or domestic institutions to Ferdinand, but only to counsel with the Allies on what advice to offer if Ferdinand asked for it. Moreover, the Tsar had not considered the views given in the second part of the memoir as final.[21]

These were major concessions, but they still were not quite definite enough for Metternich. To settle the question of the basis for intervention, he proposed three points: first, that the Allies should aim in their moral and material action not only to set the King at liberty but also to assure to Naples and to Europe "some pledges *of repose and of stability*"; second, that to this end the King should consult the real needs of his land and people; and third, that whatever the King decided to adopt would be accepted "as satisfying to the interests of the kingdom and in consequence to the views of the sane part of the nation." [22] In the first and third points Metternich thus made slight verbal concessions to the Russian point of view without jeopardizing Austria's aims. This proposal satisfied the Tsar, who was in any case more interested in alliance unity than in Capodistrias' "national wish." In the general conference on the seventh the Russians presented a declaration accepting the Austrian formula, in which, the Russian note said, Alexander found the way to "a happy unanimity," "the elements proper to bring about a decision which can unite the votes of the Allied Courts." [23] Metternich accepted this declaration with delight as a decisive victory.[24]

---

[21] "Éclaircissemens supplementaires du Cabinet de Russie à son réponse au mémoire du Cabinet Autrichien et aux communications [sic] du Cabinet Prussien," Troppau, November 6, 1820, *ibid.*, Fasc. 38.

[22] "Propositions du Cabinet d'Autriche à la suite des éclaircissemens supplementaires du Cabinet de Russie, faites le 6 novembre 1820," Troppau, n.d., *ibid.*

[23] "Déclarations du Cabinet de Russie sur les propositions faites par le Cabinet d'Autriche le 6 novembre," Troppau, November 7, 1820, *ibid.*

[24] Metternich congratulated himself that Capodistrias' ideas of Russian mediation and the "national wish" were buried, never to rise again. Metternich (Troppau, November 11, 1820) to Esterhazy, Weisungen, Grossbritannien, Fasc. 213, No. 2. "The inclination of the Russian Emperor for me," he wrote, "is lasting. It is a return to the year 1813. Had he been in 1815 as he was

The Austrian Foreign Minister lost no time in exploiting and developing the results of this victory, one of which was an increased influence over the Tsar. Metternich had perceived that Alexander, no longer enamored of constitutions and liberal principles, was still as concerned as ever to make the alliance an instrument to be used against revolution by establishing a general intervention principle. In the conference of November 7, therefore, Metternich bestowed full approval upon this part of the Russian position. Emperor Francis, he said, had been especially impressed with the Russian arguments which "deduced the right and the moral obligation of the powers to intervene in the affairs of Naples from the transactions of 1814, 1815, and 1818, as likewise by the parallel established . . . between the events of 1815 and those of our day." Francis, Metternich added, also considered a general protocol on the manner of dealing with revolutionized countries a very useful proposal.[25] These ideas which Metternich now termed striking and useful were, of course, the very same as those he had opposed and denounced before the Congress convened and which Gentz had privately characterized a few days before as vague, confused, meaningless, dangerous, false, and absurd. But now that Capodistrias' liberal ideas had been defeated, Austria had little to lose and much to gain by an extended interpretation of treaties and a general protocol on intervention, both of which now would help tie Alexander to a thoroughly conservative, and Austrian, policy.

While he thus indicated to the Russians that Austria would support a general intervention principle, Metternich's main concern, now that he had got Russia to accept the Austrian basis for intervention, was also to persuade her to agree to the exact Austrian method for it. That matter, he told the Russians, was fortunately a relatively minor point; the Eastern powers were now agreed on the main points—the principle of intervention and the necessity both of armed military action against the revolution and an occupation of Naples afterward—which left only questions of procedure remaining to be settled. The Allies, he suggested, would probably want to precede their military action by a declaration of its causes and motives. Be-

in 1813, there would be no 1820." Letter from Troppau, November 10, 1820, in Metternich, *Nachgelassene Papiere*, III, 355.

[25] "Journal des Conférences," No. 3, Troppau, November 7, 1820, Kongressakten, Troppau, Fasc. 38.

cause this announcement of Allied intentions might cause grave dangers for the King, however, it would be wise before taking this step to invite Ferdinand to leave his kingdom to confer with the Allied monarchs. The invitation, to be an entirely personal one intended for the King alone, would have to be so worded that the revolutionaries could not use it to try to negotiate or to delay the proceedings of the Allies.[26]

Having the King with the Allies when intervention began, would, of course, enable the Allies to aid him to set up his new regime. Should the King be forced to remain in Naples, however, and should he and the government retire to Calabria when the Austrians invaded Naples, the Allies would have to rule temporarily in Ferdinand's stead, setting up a provisional Council at Naples, with the commander-in-chief of the Austrian army as president and General Count Ficquelmont as minister plenipotentiary representing the King. If the King later joined the Austrian army at Naples, the Council was to continue to act only in an advisory capacity. Even if the King was able to set up his government immediately at Naples, a conference of Allied envoys like that in Paris from 1815 to 1818 would be necessary to support and advise him.[27]

As these proposals showed, Metternich now wanted to concentrate on practical measures to suppress the revolution and give Austria control over the Neapolitan government afterward. The Russians, however, were still concerned with a general protocol on intervention. Hence the Russian answer to Metternich's proposal, entitled "Bases of a Transaction," combined this aspect of Russian theory with Austrian practice. The first three of its seven points advocated the usual Russian principles on intervention. The fourth point called for the Allies to attempt some unspecified "friendly moves" of conciliation with Naples; in the event that these failed to bring results, armed intervention would follow. The fifth and sixth points followed the Austrian suggestions on the army of occupation and the Allied conference of plenipotentiaries to advise Ferdinand. The seventh, finally, called for the Congress, first, to remain in session to

[26] "Pièce remise par le Cabinet Autrichien aux Cabinets de Russie et Prusse," November 13, 1820, Kongressakten, Troppau, Fasc. 39. Both the preliminary declaration and the invitation to Ferdinand were Russian ideas turned to suit Austrian purposes.
[27] *Ibid.*

await the results of the "friendly steps" to be taken with Naples, and second, to see what response England and France would give to the intervention protocol which was to be based on this document.[28]

Although Metternich had no serious objection to most of this memoir, the lack of clarity in two of the points disturbed him. On the seventh point he insisted that any communications made to England and France must not be allowed to hold up the course of action of the Eastern powers. His condition regarding the fourth point was even more important: If by "friendly steps" and "conciliatory moves" Russia meant simply a letter of invitation to Ferdinand, well and good. No other kind of "conciliation," however, could be considered, and even the invitation must conform to strict Austrian conditions. The King must be considered a captive. There must be no negotiating with the revolutionary government, the invitation must be a strictly personal one for the King alone, and the Allied goal must remain that of freeing Ferdinand and not that of mediating between him and his people. This understood, Metternich would endorse the invitation. He proposed as a site for the conference with Ferdinand the town of Laibach in Carniola—again, of course, in Austrian territory.[29]

While the Russians were thus working to secure agreement on a general protocol of intervention, Metternich was occupying himself with a far more important question, that of the future government at Naples. His ideas, completely changed now that it was his turn, and not Capodistrias', to propose what the new regime should be like, were set down in a document titled simply "Points." He began by laying down the fundamental principles which should govern the reorganization of Naples. First, he said, the revolution must be completely destroyed. After this, the reconstruction of the government could begin. But the vital thing was to create institutions of government at Naples that were stable, not simply ones that were good for Naples:

The reorganization of the Kingdom must offer the strongest possible guarantees of internal stability. The *good* must in this connection be

---

[28] "Bases d'un Transaction, remises par le Cab't. de Russie aux Cab't. d'Autriche et de Prusse le 14 novembre 1820," *ibid.*

[29] "Remarques du Cabinet Autrichien à la pièce intitulée Bases d'un Transaction," n.d., *ibid.*

sought and attained, but it must not and cannot proceed except from the
legal source of all good, from the legitimate sovereign authority.

This condition, Metternich held, was indispensable, for even a good
government was a terrible evil if it was the result of a revolution:

The good which proceeds from a false basis (and such a case can happen
in times of upheaval) is a very real evil for the entire society. It encour-
ages the factious, not in this respect, that they search for the good, but
rather because the deceitful appeal of that good delivers over to them
virtuous men and makes them their accomplices. Thus the organization
most favorable to the true well-being of the Kingdom of Naples, if it
was simply the immediate and direct consequence of the criminal enterprise of the factions who have leagued themselves together for the overthrow of their country, would have to be regarded as an immense evil
for Europe. There is not a single state which would not feel the result
of such a combination of things.[30]

Naples, Metternich conceded, might by itself amend the errors
and excesses of the revolution in the course of time; but this would
not eliminate the worst danger, namely, the terrible example which
Naples had given to other countries. If legitimate governments in
any way tolerated this example or accepted its results, they would
be signing their own death warrants.

Thus the basic question was not what was good for Naples, but
what was the best way to eradicate the revolution there for the good
of legitimate governments in Europe. The first step to this end was
the liberation of the King. Ferdinand's response to the Allied invitation would show whether or not he was free. If he proved to be, he
could overthrow the revolution himself; if not, the Allies would do
it for him.

The liberation of the King did not set him free to choose any kind
of government he wished, as Metternich had formerly contended.
Reversing his previous position, he now argued that the King had
instead to establish the *right* kind of government, which meant meeting certain definite specifications regarding both Naples and Europe:

The King, once free, will have to assure the future of his Kingdom. He
must to this effect,

   a) Consult the true needs of his country.

[30] "Points," Troppau, November 15, 1820, *ibid.*

These needs are composed, at Naples as everywhere else, of the strong and sustained action of the government and of guarantees which institutions suitable to the national character can offer, guarantees suitable at once to prevent the authority of government from going astray and the subjects from infringing on the authority.

b) Establish and regulate the form of his administration in a way which would not be in opposition to the internal tranquillity of neighboring states.[31]

These requirements, Metternich maintained, necessitated the absolute exclusion of any sort of representative government at Naples. Without going into the question of what value such a form of government might have in more advanced states, one could instantly see that it was totally unsuitable for Italy and especially for Naples. This was clear both from

the point of view of the national character, of the extreme and hot temper of the people and of the vivacity of their hatreds, . . . [and] in consideration of the total lack of culture in the lower classes of society; it is finally not less in opposition with the subdivision of the peninsula into numerous political bodies. The constitutional spirit in Italy is nothing else than that of fusion, and it could not be otherwise, since that spirit is spread only among the upper classes of society, while it is entirely unknown to the immense majority of the population, to whom it is indeed absolutely foreign, and upon whom it would have to be imposed.[32]

That Austria opposed any representative system, however limited, Metternich made clear in a definition of a representative government as any system

which admits an assembly more or less numerous, formed by elections more or less general, deliberating upon questions of state without distinction, and announcing its opinions by means of a parliament and formal addresses.[33]

Since any such system was absolutely incompatible not only with the Neapolitan character but also with Italian tranquillity and Euro-

[31] *Ibid.*
[32] *Ibid.*
[33] *Ibid.* It is worth noting that Metternich here does not include in his definition the right of popular assemblies to share in legislation. Even a system with purely advisory representative bodies was anathema to him, for he feared publicity, open discussion, and the influence of public opinion on questions of state as much as the division and sacrifice of monarchical power.

pean response, said Metternich, "the Emperor has decided not to permit the establishment of that system in any of the states of the peninsula." [34]

What, then, did Austria propose—the re-establishment of the old regime? Put in that form, said Metternich, the question did not deserve debate. Anyone could call the system to be re-established anything he liked—the old regime, the new order, or something intermediate. The one important condition was this:

Austria will admit as good, or at least as admissible, any regime resting on the following basis:

The supreme legislative, administrative, and executive power belongs to the King without restriction or division; except that he may designate certain bodies or individuals, as he may think proper, to concur in the exercise of this or that branch of that power, and may delegate to them by a formal act the functions with which they would be vested to that effect.

Any form of government which can be reconciled with that basis Austria will admit; she will not admit any which proceeds from a different basis.[35]

Metternich thus made two points perfectly clear: first, that Austria, and no one else, would decide what the future government at Naples and, indeed, those in all of Italy, would be like; and second, that the *sine qua non* for all governments was that they preserved unalloyed absolutism.

Even this sweeping arrogation of the very power of decision which Metternich had up to one week before insisted must be left wholly to the King did not represent by any means the sum of Austrian requirements at Naples. Next followed Austrian plans on how every major phase of the reconstruction of the government should be carried out. Austria, Metternich said, approved of the following steps to be executed by Ferdinand: first, the separation of the two kingdoms, Naples and Sicily, in terms of their local institutions; second, "the strongest possible organization of the government"; third, the creation of a Senate, appointed by the King and divided into Neapolitan and Sicilian sections, to advise the King; and, fourth, the establishment of "provincial congregations" to look after the well-

[34] *Ibid.*
[35] *Ibid.*

being of the provinces. To assure the permanence of this organization, he further proposed:

These diverse institutions ought to be confirmed in an act vested with
all the forms of a *pragmatic sanction,* sworn to as such by the King, his
successor, and the agnates of his house, as well as by the different bodies
of the state. That *pragmatic sanction* would be placed under the guarantee of the powers just as the constitutions of different states were of old.[36]

Thus Metternich intended that these corporate institutions of Naples—products of the Austrian will—should not be established
merely for the reign of the present king but should be imposed by
the guarantee of the powers also upon all his successors to eternity.
Metternich next laid down the exact course Ferdinand should follow
in setting up this new system upon his return. Obviously, "the King
will have to annul in their totality the institutions created by the
revolt." He would then have to establish a provisional government
and announce the summoning of a council of advisers (the *Consulta*), composed equally of Sicilians and Neapolitans, to counsel
him on the permanent institutions of the kingdom. In addition, he
should disband the army and abolish the law of conscription. The
new army was to be composed of Neapolitan volunteers and Swiss
and Albanian mercenaries, to be no larger than absolutely necessary
to give Naples internal security. A corps of gendarmes from three to
four thousand strong was also to be maintained for police duty.

Accompanying this prescription for the future constitution and
government of the kingdom were further measures to control the
new government—namely, provision for Italian and European supervision of the whole reorganization of the kingdom. As an initial
step, Metternich suggested, the Allies should inform the Italian governments of the principles on which the Neapolitan government was
to be rebuilt. This would serve not only to assure the other states
that their repose was not menaced but also to encourage them to
reorganize their own systems according to the Neapolitan pattern.
To promote this very desirable end, the Allies should call a congress
of Italian states. Meanwhile, to apportion the measure of control
over Naples which should be exercised by Ferdinand, the princes
of Italy, and the Allied sovereigns, respectively, Metternich proposed the following formula:

[36] *Ibid.*

Since it is extremely important that the Allied Courts should never depart from the most correct, and, by the same token, the only useful principles, everything relative to the reconstruction of the Kingdom of the Two Sicilies will have to be agreed upon and regulated in the following form:

1. The *initiative* on questions will have to belong exclusively to the King as the only appraiser and sole natural judge of the true interests and needs of his country.

2. The immediate *control* of the principles upon which His Sicilian Majesty will believe he ought to found the bases of the new organization of the kingdom will belong to the Princes of Italy, since they are most directly interested in avoiding having these bases contradict in any way the bases of their own existence.

3. Counsel and surveillance belong to the great courts in view of the attitude they have taken in the entire Neapolitan affair and the just and legitimate interest which they are called to bring to bear upon the reestablishment and maintenance of the general peace.[37]

So long as it helped him to get this sweeping Austrian program of reconstruction at Naples adopted, Metternich had no qualms about agreeing to the general Preliminary Protocol on intervention which the Russians wanted. Along with Capodistrias, Nesselrode, and Bernstorff, therefore, he signed the Protocol on November 19. Derived in form from the Russian "Bases of a Transaction," analyzed above, the document contained Capodistrias' phrases, but served Metternich's purposes.[38] Divided into three parts ("Preamble," "Principles," and "Application"), the Protocol, after a lofty statement of the Allies' aims and motives regarding Naples, restated Capodistrias' familiar three principles on intervention: the exclusion of revolutionary states from the alliance; the doctrine of nonrecognition of revolution; and the necessity of returning revolutionary states "to the fold of the alliance" if they menaced other countries "either by their proximity" or in some other way. This return of revolutionary states to the alliance was to be effected by peaceful means if possible, by force if necessary. The "Application" contained the Austrian proposals concerning armed intervention in Naples, the army of occupation, and the diplomatic conference to be established under Austrian presidency to advise King Ferdinand. The final point of

[37] *Ibid.*

[38] "The authorship of the intervention principle was Russian; once set up, however, it corresponded to the Austrian policy."—Schmalz, *Gesamteuropäische Organisation*, 80.

the Protocol called for its communication to France and England for their information and, it was hoped, their approval.[39]

In a supplement to this protocol, the signatory powers agreed to invite Ferdinand to a conference at Laibach and to send common instructions to their envoys at Naples explaining the invitation.[40] The supplement also provided that the courts at Rome, Turin, and Florence should be informed of the invitation to Ferdinand and that the French and British observers at the Congress should receive the documents not only for their information and approval, but also in order that France and England "might join them [the three Eastern powers] with friendly *démarches* in the same sense to His Sicilian Majesty." [41]

In agreeing to invite British support for this move, Metternich entertained no serious hope of securing it. He had gone into the Preliminary Protocol with the Russians with his eyes wide open,

[39] "Protocole Préliminaire," November 19, 1820, Kongressakten, Troppau, Fasc. 39.

[40] The supplement carefully stipulated that the purpose of the invitation was to set the King at liberty and "to offer to the [Neapolitan] nation in the august person of its legitimate monarch the only mediator who, after the deplorable consequences of the events of July 2, can reconcile the re-establishment of order in the Kingdom of the Two Sicilies with the tranquillity of the rest of Italy and of Europe." "Supplement au Protocole du 19 novembre 1820," *ibid.* Here again Metternich adroitly turned to his own advantage the lingering Russian ideas of avoiding armed intervention by some kind of mediation. By making the King the sole mediator between the needs of his country and the repose of Europe, he excluded any mediation between Austria and Naples or, still worse, between the King and the revolutionaries. He did the same thing with the Russian desire for "conciliation." His "Agenda pour donner Suite aux Dispositions du Protocole Preliminaire," (n.d., *ibid.*) called for, among other things, "deliberations on the measures to take to exhaust the means of conciliation and to legitimize the use of coercive force." He was careful, however, in his accompanying "Apperçu du Cabinet Autrichien sur les Agenda . . ." (n.d., *ibid.*) to define precisely what "conciliation" meant: "Not the conciliation of the revolt with the legitimate institutions, but [the conciliation] of the needs which the legitimate Sovereign will be able to recognize as being the most suitable to serve as a safeguard for the re-establishment of internal repose in his country now in revolt, with the general repose." The letter to Ferdinand, drawn up by Austria ("Projet de lettre de Cabinet au Roi des Deux Siciles," Troppau, November 20, 1820, *ibid.*) and the joint instructions to the envoys at Naples ("Instructions pour les Envoyés de Russie et de Prusse et le Chargé d'affaires d'Autriche à Naples," Troppau, November 22, 1820, *ibid.*) are without particular interest. The letter of the sovereigns to Ferdinand is printed in *British and Foreign State Papers*, VIII (1820–1821), 1147–1148.

[41] "Supplement au Protocole . . .," Kongressakten, Troppau, Fasc. 39.

fully aware that he was following a course which the constitutional powers could not follow, and only hoping that England would give passive assent to the Preliminary Protocol or at least keep quiet on it.[42] Dissatisfied with the hampering restrictions of Britain's constitutional system and insular position, and fearful of an impending fall of the Tory ministry,[43] he elected to cast his lot with Russia, whose absolutist system not only was more congenial to Austria than British constitutionalism, but whose interventionist principles also made her at the moment infinitely more useful to Austrian policy. Even though Metternich had received a good indication that England would neither assent to the Protocol nor keep quiet about it when Stewart vigorously protested to him against any renewal of a general intervention policy or guarantee pact, this protest did not deter him.[44]

Metternich proceeded in the hope that he might be able to slip the Preliminary Protocol past the Western envoys, none of whom had thus far played any important role in the Congress.[45] Having excluded them from the three-power conferences, he had given Stewart reason to believe that only the question of action against the revolution was being considered, not that of a general intervention principle. Hence he surprised the three observers completely in the conference of November 19 when he presented to them the completed and signed Preliminary Protocol which, along with its supplementary documents, established a general doctrine of intervention in revolutionized states and called upon England and France to sub-

[42] "What is clear to us is the duty of the states still free in their thought and action to counsel on these two goals [establishing general principles concerning the revolution and damming the revolutionary torrent]. It is to see what they are able to do and what their constitutional Allies cannot do." Metternich (Troppau, November 14, 1820) to Esterhazy, Weisungen, Grossbritannien, Fasc. 213.

[43] Webster, *Foreign Policy of Castlereagh*, 294. The Eastern powers were so fearful of what a Whig ministry might do that they secretly resolved in case of a change of ministries to make a joint demand for a declaration from England that she would not release Napoleon from St. Helena. Metternich (Troppau, November 11, 1820) to Esterhazy, Weisungen, Grossbritannien, Fasc. 213, No. 1.

[44] When shown a projected Act of Guarantee by Metternich, Stewart denounced it as unprecedented, rash, dangerous, and inevitably divisive of the alliance. Stewart (Troppau, November 15, 1820), to Metternich, Weisungen, Grossbritannien, Fasc. 213.

[45] Gentz (Troppau, November 21, 1820) to Soutzo, in Gentz, *Dépêches inédites*, II, 96–97.

scribe to it according to the spirit of existing treaties.[46] After reading the pieces, Metternich made a strenuous effort to justify his lack of candor. He advanced the arguments that secret sessions had been necessary since only the three Eastern Courts had their sovereigns present and could work effectively; that these private conversations were not really conferences in any formal sense; that the Eastern powers were now fulfilling their duty to the other Allies by informing them of the results of these conferences; and that the Preliminary Protocol should be no surprise to the Western powers, since it was only the logical outcome of the memoirs presented in the earlier conferences at which the French and English had been present.[47] His arguments convinced neither Caraman nor Stewart, both of whom protested vigorously. Stewart sent home bitter complaints about Metternich's deceit, and demanded and secured from Metternich the withdrawal of the signatures on the Protocol so that it could at least be presented to the Western powers as a project rather than a signed document.[48]

Somewhat dismayed by the force of Stewart's protest, Metternich prepared an elaborate defense of the Protocol for Castlereagh, hoping that England might still support its intent and purposes even if she had to reject its form. The Protocol, he protested, was not a treaty but only a statement of principles; needless to say, the Allies could not even conceivably contemplate any interference in the internal affairs of other independent states. Only the legal possession of power by the legitimate authority was in question, and this was and ought to be subject to international guarantee. "That [possession] of legal power," said Metternich, "is no less a property [than the possession of territory] . . .; that property is of right not less sacred than that of territory. . . . It therefore ought to be able to be placed under guarantee equally well." The only possible objection would be to the application of the principle, he argued, not to the principle itself; for the principle was simply a different version of the idea behind the November 1815 treaty against Napoleon.[49]

---

[46] Stewart (Troppau, November 20, 1820) to Castlereagh, in Webster, *Foreign Policy of Castlereagh,* Appendix C, 527–528 (see also pp. 294–296).

[47] "Journal des Conférences," No. 4, November 19, 1820, Kongressakten, Troppau, Fasc. 38.

[48] Stewart (Troppau, November 20, 1820) to Castlereagh, in Webster, *Foreign Policy of Castlereagh,* Appendix C, 530–531 (see also p. 296).

[49] Metternich (Troppau, November 24, 1820) to Esterhazy, Weisungen,

To clear himself of the onus of deceit and secretiveness in dealing with Stewart, Metternich confided that he personally would have been glad to admit Stewart to the conferences, but because the French envoys, especially De la Ferronnays, who was ambitious, a constitutionalist, and a friend of Capodistrias, would have caused trouble, all the observers had had to be excluded.[50] Moreover, Castlereagh should pay no attention to "the pitiful wording of the Preliminary Protocol." It was entirely Capodistrias' work, which Metternich had allowed to stand to appease his literary vanity.[51]

Arguments such as these were ill-designed to convince a statesman who had written the State Paper of May 5, 1820, and whose political principles included the sanctity of the Glorious Revolution. None of them, in fact, made the slightest impression upon Castlereagh, whose mind was already made up. Before news concerning the contents of the Preliminary Protocol arrived in England, the Russian ambassador to Great Britain, Prince Lieven, had suggested that if England could not support the Eastern powers, her best course was silence; Castlereagh had answered sharply that the English position must be made clear, not deceptive, even if the appearance of Allied unity were lost thereby.[52] When, therefore, he heard from Stewart about the Protocol and the manner of its presentation, he reacted with strong disapproval. Metternich's dispatches of November 24 did not improve his disposition in the least. After closer examination of the Protocol, Esterhazy reported, Castlereagh found it "odious."

Grossbritannien, Fasc. 213, No. 1. It is worth noting that while Metternich was making this apology to England, he was also engaged with Gentz in the preparation of a full-fledged treaty (the Act of Guarantee, discussed below) to present to Russia and Prussia, which embodied in still more drastic form all the features of the Protocol which England found objectionable.

[50] *Ibid.*, No. 4. Actually Metternich's hatred of De la Ferronnays, whom he called "a Jacobin without knowing it, an imbecile doctrinaire" (Metternich [Laibach, January 1821] to Count Floret, Staatskanzlei: Interiora, Korrespondenz, Fasc. 82), exceeded only to a certain extent his dislike of Caraman and Stewart.

[51] Metternich (Troppau, November 24, 1820) to Esterhazy, Weisungen, Grossbritannien, Fasc. 213, No. 1. In an accompanying reserved letter (*ibid.*, No. 2), Metternich frankly stated to Esterhazy the reasons of state which had dictated the Austrian course at Troppau. The revolutionaries, he said, "menace with total subversion the institutions upon which alone the power of Austria can be founded, in view of the essential difference which exists between the diverse parts which compose her."

[52] Esterhazy (London, November 29, 1820) to Metternich, Berichte, Grossbritannien, Fasc. 212, No. 174B.

The Foreign Office, which had formerly emphasized the impossibility of British participation in intervention and the uselessness of a general intervention principle, now turned to an outright condemnation of the principle and a determination, if necessary, to publicly protest against it.[53]

The net result was a long dispatch from Castlereagh to Stewart on December 16, in which the British Foreign Secretary restated even more sharply and emphatically than before the principles of his State Paper of May 5 and in which he subjected the Preliminary Protocol to a withering critique. Perhaps the most trenchant of Castlereagh's many comments was the statement that while the British government condemned military revolts and sectarian activity, it would never be pushed into the "not less fatal extreme of becoming (as the Protocole appears to contemplate) armed Guardians of all Thrones, without even regard to the Principles upon which the Powers of Government are administered." The dispatch, though not published, remained in reserve, Castlereagh intimated, in case the Protocol ever came to public attention.[54]

In the meantime, an earlier note sent by Castlereagh on December 4, more mild in tone than the later dispatch but no less firm in principle, was read by Stewart at Troppau on December 19. While conceding Austria's special position in Italy and affirming her continued friendship for the Eastern Allies, England announced that she was determined not to participate in any joint Allied move, and that she would not even bind herself to nonrecognition. This meant, of course, that England refused not only the Allied requests in the Preliminary Protocol but also Metternich's private plea that A'Court

---

[53] Esterhazy (London, December 4 and 10, 1820) to Metternich, *ibid.*, Nos. 175C, 176A, and 176B; Webster, *Foreign Policy of Castlereagh*, 298–303. Any possible impact of Metternich's dispatches was thwarted by Stewart, who, repaying Metternich tit for tat, had sent copies of them, shown to him by Metternich, on to London ahead of the originals. Thus when Esterhazy called to present them, Castlereagh was ready with a long, prepared commentary. Metternich's reaction was to denounce Stewart for his lack of principle, judgment, and powers of reasoning, and to blame Stewart's whole attitude on his preoccupation with domestic concerns instead of his ambassadorial duties and on his personal pique at having played such a poor role at the Congress. Metternich (Troppau, December 9, 1820) to Esterhazy, Weisungen, Grossbritannien, Fasc. 213.

[54] Castlereagh (London, December 16, 1820) to Stewart, Kongressakten, Troppau, Fasc. 38; Webster, *Foreign Policy of Castlereagh*, 303–305.

attach himself at least unofficially to the *démarche* of the other envoys at Naples. The English note further advised the powers not to consider interference in Spain and Portugal and referred them back to the English stand at Aachen should they be considering a general pact of guarantee.[55]

While expressing polite regret at the British stand, publicly Metternich continued to deny that there were any differences in principle between the five powers, still attributing England's divergence simply to the circumstances of English internal politics. Privately, however, he was bitter over the British attitude. There was a difference in principle, he admitted. The British considered the right of intervention so special as to admit of no general rule, while Austria believed that special cases could be foreseen, defined, and confronted in advance without violating the principle of the sovereignty of independent states. This was less important, however, Metternich maintained, than England's blindness not only to the danger confronting all thrones and institutions but also to the primary necessity of steering Russia out of her vagaries and onto a fixed course.[56]

The British stand had one result favorable to England: it eliminated the Preliminary Protocol from consideration as an operative instrument. On the idea of a pact of guarantee, however, the British position acted as a stimulant instead of as a barrier. For Metternich, who had so recently assured Castlereagh that he could never possibly adopt the Russian principles on intervention, was now, in view of Russian cooperation with Austria and English defection from her, ready to bind himself with Alexander to an Act of Guarantee more sweeping in principle than any the Russians themselves had yet proposed.[57] Gentz, who wrote the Austrian proposal, described it as

an *act of guarantee* for the maintenance of the legal order and of the fundamental institutions upon which it rests in every European state; an act which, if we are able to obtain it, will assure, as far as this is still

[55] "Journal des Conférences," No. 8, December 19, 1820, Kongressakten, Troppau, Fasc. 38; Castlereagh (London, December 4, 1820) to Stewart, *ibid.*; Metternich (Troppau, December 16, 1820) to Esterhazy, Weisungen, Grossbritannien, Fasc. 213.

[56] Metternich (Troppau, December 24, 1820) to Esterhazy, Weisungen, Grossbritannien, Fasc. 213, Nos. 1 and 2.

[57] Schmalz, *Gesamteuropäische Organisation*, 84–85.

in the power of the Great Powers, the *internal* peace of states, as the transactions of 1814, 1815, and 1818 have assured their possessions and the political peace of Europe.[58]

Gentz's proposal, after undergoing two revisions, was presented formally in an Austrian memoir of November 28. The memoir opened with three theses on the right of intervention:

1. Every revolution brought about by usurped power or in evidently illegal fashion, and by even stronger reason, every revolution conceived and executed by criminal means becomes by that fact alone, whatever otherwise may be its character, its course, and its effects, the object of a just and legitimate intervention by foreign powers.
2. Revolutions conceived and executed by the legitimate powers of the state justify foreign intervention only in cases where they expose the primary interests of their neighboring states or the whole of civilized society to evident peril by their character, their course, and their effects.
3. When a revolution unites these *two* characteristics—a manifestly illegal origin and a pernicious and hostile tendency for other states— the right of intervention attains its maximum force.[59]

These principles, the memoir continued, thus attributed to the powers a right of intervention which was "clear, positive, admitting neither exception nor restriction," and modified in its exercise only by considerations of prudence. Indeed, intervention was not merely a right "unlimited in its nature," but also "a severe and sacred duty" based upon divine precept. The role which the sovereigns of the great powers were called upon to play in suppressing revolution "is determined in advance by a law superior to all human authority." [60]

This was indeed lofty language and elevated principle, especially striking since it was voiced by the same man who had heaped such scathing contempt upon the "mystical nonsense" of the Holy Alliance and of Capodistrias' memoir. Once the act had stated its basic principles, however, its language became much more cautious and

[58] Gentz (Troppau, November 30, 1820) to Soutzo, in Gentz, *Dépêches inédites*, II, 97–98. The idea was also broached at the Congress by Caraman, who suggested that the Vienna Guarantees be extended to cover the internal, as well as the external, conditions of states, with legal changes to be recognized and illegal ones condemned. Note Verbale, Caraman (Troppau, November 1, 1820) to Metternich, Kongressakten, Troppau, Fasc. 39.

[59] "Mémoire du Cabinet d'Autriche," Troppau, November 28, 1820, *ibid.*

[60] *Ibid.*

qualified. Its main substance consisted of eight provisions of "Moral Guarantees," briefly summarized as follows:

1. The contracting powers and those who acceded to the act were to guarantee the "legitimate sovereignty" and "fundamental institutions" of each state in Europe.

2. The guarantor powers were not to intervene in any state's internal affairs so long as the legitimate authority was in control and regularly exercising the functions of government.

3. The right of intervention was not to apply to internal political changes brought about legally by the legitimate authority.

4. A new order of things carried out by a legitimate sovereign, or willingly agreed to by him, would be assumed under the guarantee, "at least if it is not in manifest contradiction with the fundamental principles of the social order."

5. Any other change illegally effectuated would be regarded as null and void.

6. The powers were never to recognize or have dealings with a revolutionary regime until the sovereign was restored to his full power and rights.

7. States that underwent illegal alterations in their government were to cease to enjoy the benefits of the guarantee until their situation was remedied.

8. Alterations brought about illegally, even if they were sanctioned *ex post facto* by the legitimate sovereign, would not be assumed under the guarantee "except when the Powers will have unanimously recognized [them] as compatible with the maintenance of public order and the general tranquillity of Europe." [61]

These moral guarantees, the memoir conceded, afforded no complete protection against all the evils of innovation. For one thing, they could not guarantee states against the changes made by imprudent or ill-advised sovereigns, though these were often as bad as revolution, simply because sovereigns were beyond human judgment. This fact, however, also presented a certain advantage. The powers would not have to inquire into the intrinsic faults or merits of a new system or institution (a matter often difficult to judge) but could sanction or condemn it solely on the much simpler basis of whether or not it was legally introduced. Moreover, since sov-

[61] *Ibid.*

ereigns could still introduce changes (though no one else could), not even the friends of reform would be able "to accuse the powers of wishing to arrest the progress of civilization, or to condemn society to a state of complete stagnation." [62] Although the moral guarantees would admittedly arouse only the contempt of the factious, they would, nevertheless, have the salutary effect of encouraging men of good will, particularly princes who might be intimidated by revolution, to resist agitation.

While this section concerning moral guarantees against revolution was itself none too clear, the second section, dealing with "Effective Guarantees," was even more vague. Indeed, the whole question of such guarantees, the memoir conceded, was too complicated and uncertain to admit of precise formulation without a great deal more discussion by the powers. Three main questions on the problem of what action to take against revolution, however, were indicated. To the first—concerning the active measures to be used against revolutions brought about by revolt—Austria suggested a cautious answer. While every such revolution unqualifiedly justified and demanded the intervention of the powers, the form and degree of action still depended on circumstances. For instance, if a monarch of a country in revolt appealed for aid or was plainly a captive of the revolutionaries, the powers would first consult on what steps, if any, were to be taken to remedy the situation. But if a revolt plainly menaced other lands, "whether by its proximity or any other cause," the powers would have to act, first with amicable, then with armed, intervention.

The second question concerned what should be done about revolutions which, even though they had been initiated or willingly sanctioned by the legitimate authority, menaced "the repose of other lands." This, said Metternich, offered a real problem:

If we would have to submit without any restriction to anything which an independent sovereign would wish to try by way of political experiments in his country, and would have to simply ignore the dangers that might result for his neighbors or for Europe as a whole, all our precautions against violent revolutions would not suffice to arrest the progress

---

[62] *Ibid.* In Gentz's original version and in the "Second Travail" this sentence then follows: "The only goal of our project is to restrict the right to make changes to those to whom this right ought exclusively to belong."

of the evil that we are fighting, nor to guarantee the social order against the most pernicious shocks.[63]

Nevertheless, he pointed out, the opinions of other Cabinets were still too unknown to permit a further examination of this question in the memoir. The third question, on what should be done to help a country included under the guarantee which was attacked by a foreign land in revolt, was suggested simply as a problem that needed thought.[64]

Thus the Austrian Act of Guarantee turned out after all to be much more a statement of principle than a call to action. The entire section on "effective guarantees" was very vague, no doubt by intent. In the final analysis, it said only that the powers should or should not intervene actively against a revolution, according to the circumstances involved. The whole part on "moral guarantees" also lacked clarity and content. What did it mean, for example, to say that a state that had undergone illegal political alterations would no longer enjoy the benefits of the guarantee? It seemed to say that any state that underwent revolt would no longer be guaranteed against revolt, which made it equally as meaningless as Capodistrias' principle that any state that by revolt withdrew from the European alliance should be excluded from the alliance. Metternich and Gentz themselves realized that such "guarantees" would deter no one from revolt who did not want to be deterred. Metternich's real purposes in proposing this act must be supposed to have been twofold: first, he wanted to get the other Eastern Allies to sign a formal treaty unqualifiedly condemning all revolution, in the hope that this would strengthen moral support throughout Europe and would encourage his Allies to agree to establishing a counterrevolutionary secret information center at Vienna, Metternich's constant goal; and second, he hoped to tie Russia even more firmly than before to a thoroughly conservative policy. To help effect this latter purpose and to enhance the memoir's appeal to Russia, he and Gentz borrowed and adapted ideas, principles, and even whole phrases in the act from earlier Russian documents. The act is significant, in fact, chiefly because it demonstrates how willing Metternich

---

[63] *Ibid.*
[64] *Ibid.* See also the original draft and the "Second Travail," *ibid.*

was at this fairly early date to abandon both his former principles and his former partner, Great Britain, to gain the support of Russia.

The attempt misfired, for the moment at least. Prussia, to be sure, welcomed the act and was ready to make it even stronger. Bernstorff suggested that all public servants and ministers ought to be required to take an oath against the subversive doctrine of popular sovereignty, and that the powers should announce that they would not recognize any new constitution which was based on popular sovereignty or any which failed to protect the royal right to legislate, the absolute royal veto, and the retention of all executive power in the monarch's hands.[65]

The Russian response, however, was negative. Capodistrias seized the opportunity to dissect the Austrian memoir as Metternich and Gentz had previously dissected his own, criticizing first the section on principles. Either the act was a new transaction not based on existing treaties, Capodistrias wrote, or it was based on the Vienna system. If it was something new, then it would have the following bad consequences: first, revolutionary countries would not recognize the new treaty or admit its force; second, constitutional states, like England, France, the Netherlands, and several of the German states, would refuse to sign it; and third, the whole Vienna system would be depreciated. If, on the other hand, the Act of Guarantee was based on the Vienna system—and this was the presupposition on which the powers had proceeded at Troppau—then no new act was necessary. All that was needed was simply a protocol like that Russia had proposed at Aachen, stating "definitively" the attitude of the powers on revolution and inviting other powers to sign it.[66] The Russian Foreign Minister also objected to certain features of the act itself, such as the distinction between "legal" and "illegal" revolutions, alleging finally that the whole piece was so unclear and negative that it would paralyze Allied action rather than strengthen it.[67]

Faced with such criticism, Metternich beat a hasty retreat. The memoir had been only a suggestion, anyway, he said; if it was

[65] Observations attached to the Austrian memoir, *ibid.*
[66] "Questions que présente le développement ultérieur de la première partie du Protocole du 7/19 Novembre, ou la partie intitulée: *principes,*" n.d., *ibid.*
[67] "Comments" attached to the Austrian memoir, *ibid.*

deemed unsatisfactory, he would withdraw it and welcome consideration of the kind of protocol the Russians wanted.[68] This ended
Metternich's attempts to formulate a general intervention principle
or act of guarantee with Russia at the Congress.

Toward the end of the Congress, Metternich also had to cope with
a final Russian proposal for mediation—a suggestion of Papal intercession in Naples. As the Russians conceived it, the Allies should
make a last attempt to avert the use of force, which would become
inevitable if Ferdinand was compelled to decline the invitation to
Laibach. The Pope, the Russians reasoned, might be able so to
enlighten the innocent masses in Naples on their real interests that
they would themselves overthrow the revolution and restore full
royal authority, making the use of force unnecessary. Metternich, of
course, would have nothing to do with such impractical optimism,
for he did not intend to permit anything to prevent an Austrian
occupation. However, he was not averse to having the Pope sanction the Austrian march into Naples and lecture the Neapolitans
into accepting it quietly. He therefore subtly changed the proposed
letter to Pope Pius and the accompanying instructions to the Allied
envoys at Rome to suit his ends. As altered, the Allied letter requested the Pope to mediate, not to secure "peace" between Naples
and the Allied powers, as the Russians had suggested, but to create
an "entente" between Ferdinand and the Allies against the revolutionaries, who would have to be beaten and punished in any case.
To make doubly sure that this *démarche* could not be misunder-
stood, Metternich sent Lebzeltern as special envoy to convey this
message to Rome and also to transmit a letter from Emperor Francis
calling on the Pope to anathematize the radical sects.[69]

Lebzeltern's mission was not entirely successful. Pope Pius had

[68] Note by Gentz on the Austrian memoir, *ibid.*; "Note Verbale," Metternich
[December 24, 1820] to Russian Cabinet, *ibid.*
[69] "Journal des Conférences," No. 6, December 11, 1820, Kongressakten,
Troppau, Fasc. 38; "Opinion du Cabinet de Russie sur les moyens de conciliation que les Cours Alliées pourraient employer envers Naples, si l'invitation
adressée au Roi n'etait point acceptée," December 6, 1820, *ibid.*; "Réponse du
Cabinet Autrichien . . .," December 10, 1820, *ibid.*; "Projet d'une dépêche à
adresser par les Cabinets d'Autriche, de Prusse et de Russie à leurs ministres
respectifs près du S. Siège," n.d., *ibid.*; "Projet de Protocole," December 8,
1820, *ibid.*, Fasc. 39; Francis I (Troppau, December 12, 1820) to Pope Pius
VII, *ibid.*; Gentz (Troppau, December 12, and Vienna, December 31, 1820) to
Soutzo, in Gentz, *Dépêches inédites*, II, 100–103.

already sent a letter to Ferdinand urging him to accept the Allied invitation and had indicated his own moral support for the Austrian campaign. Beyond this he would not go. Not only did the Papal Court, because of religious scruples and the danger of Neapolitan invasion, decline to undertake any further mediation or exhortation at Naples, but it also resisted other Austrian demands. It did not comply with the Austrian request for a Papal anathema against the sects—a request repeated the next April—until September 1821. The Court of Rome also refused to contribute any supplies to the Austrian troops that would cross its territory to move against Naples, and it resisted the Austrian demand for the occupation of Ancona, a strategic port and fortress on the Adriatic, until after the successful completion of the Austrian campaign against Naples in March 1821. A combination of principle, fear, and poverty thus made Rome the only Italian court to offer resistance to Austrian pressure.[70]

In the meantime, while Metternich had been thrashing out all the important questions at the Congress—the intervention at Naples, the plan of reconstruction there, a general intervention principle— with the Eastern powers alone, he had also taken care to keep a watchful eye on France. The main danger, that France would attempt to mediate in Naples, preventing an Austrian armed intervention and preserving a moderate constitution there,[71] seemed to have largely disappeared by the start of the Congress. The mission of Prince Cariati of Naples to Paris to secure such mediation failed; Cariati was received politely but only privately by Richelieu and Pasquier.[72] Not only were the French in no real position to risk intervention, but they considered it impossible to intervene unless

---

[70] Consalvi (Rome, December 5, 1820 and January 6, 1821) to Metternich, in Consalvi, *Correspondance*, 318–321, 337–348; Apponyi (Rome, January 4, March 27 and 31, 1821) to Metternich, *ibid.*, 335–336, 372–376 (note); Francis I (Laibach, April 12, 1821) to Pius VII, *ibid.*, 378–379; Introduction, *ibid.*, xcvii; Brady, *Rome and the Neapolitan Revolution*, 94–99. The Austrian demand for the occupation of Ancona was suddenly and surprisingly dropped in May 1821 after Rome had finally agreed to it.—Brady, *ibid.*, Appendix, 181–187.

[71] Metternich (Vienna, September 1, 1820) to Vincent, Weisungen, Frankreich, Fasc. 343, No. 7; Étienne-Denis Pasquier, *Histoire de mon temps. Mémoires du Chancelier Pasquier*, V, 13–15.

[72] Vincent (Paris, October 9, 15, 20, and 27, November 18 and 24, December 15, 1820) to Metternich, Berichte, Frankreich, Fasc. 342, Nos. 50, 53, 54A, 55B, 61A, 63, and 67A; Pasquier, *Mémoires*, V, 47–49.

the Neapolitan Parliament would first undertake to revise the Spanish Constitution sharply in a conservative direction.[73] France, therefore, took a neutral, retiring position on the Neapolitan question at the Congress. Her opening statement, read by De la Ferronnays, announced her withdrawal from active participation in intervention because of the dangers of war and the incompatibility of such intervention with her constitutional principles.[74]

France's neutral stand suited Metternich well enough, though he had hoped to be given more positive moral support for Austrian intervention. In his dispatches to Paris during the Congress, he concentrated on discouraging any thoughts of French mediation that might linger in the minds of Pasquier, Richelieu, or Pozzo di Borgo by identifying the Carbonari at Naples with the Jacobins in France and the Muratists with the Bonapartists. To favor either faction, he argued, would be suicidal for the French monarchy.[75] At the Congress, though excluding both French envoys from the secret conferences, he made the most of the rift between them, flattering Caraman with attention and seeking assurance from him that France would unofficially attach herself to the Allied course at Naples. Caraman, whose devotion to Metternich was obsequious, was only too willing to cooperate, assuring Metternich that only "his devil of a colleague" would make difficulties.[76]

Caraman was soon to learn how his confidence in Metternich and cooperation with him were to be repaid. Encouraged by the Preliminary Protocol to believe that Austria would welcome "amicable steps" with Naples before resorting to armed force, he proposed that

---

[73] Both Cariati and Chevalier Brancia, the constitutional regime's *chargé* at Paris, strongly supported the French counsel on revising the constitution. Brancia (Paris, October 25, November 7 and 14, 1820) to Campochiaro, in *Atti del Parlamento*, V, Pt. 1, 131, 147, 160–164; II, 518–521; Cariati (Paris, November 14, 1820) to Campochiaro, *ibid.*, V, Pt. 1, 164–166.

[74] Caraman (Troppau, October 22, 1820) to Pasquier, Kongressakten, Troppau, Fasc. 39; "Observations Préalables et Confidentielles," Troppau, October 26, 1820, *ibid.*

[75] Metternich also suggested to Pasquier and Richelieu that the Duke of Decazes was behind the whole intrigue for French mediation at Naples as a part of his bid to get back into power. Metternich (Troppau, October 26 and 31, November 10, 1820) to Vincent, Weisungen, Frankreich, Fasc. 343.

[76] Caraman's attitude, according to Metternich, was frank and correct. Metternich (Troppau, November 10, 1820) to Vincent, *ibid.*; Caraman, Troppau, October 30, 1820) to Metternich, Kongressakten, Troppau, Fasc. 39.

Louis XVIII, who was a relative of Ferdinand I and head of the house of Bourbon, might mediate between Naples and the powers and encourage Ferdinand to overthrow the revolution and make the necessary changes in the constitution. Although the idea had been in Pasquier's mind, Caraman was in no way authorized to present it. In any case, he communicated the proposal to Metternich in a private conversation, admitting that it was only his personal idea but asserting his confidence that his government would support it. Metternich could have told him immediately, of course, how repugnant such an idea would be to either Austria or Russia. Instead, he said he would take the matter under advisement, allowing the impressionable Caraman to believe that he was favorably impressed with it and would seriously consider it.[77] Caraman, in fact, intimated to his government that the proposal was as good as accepted. When the French envoy presented his idea in the full conference of December 7, Capodistrias rejected it indignantly. Metternich in turn shrugged off the proposal with the remark that these were only Caraman's personal views, and that Caraman was of course not acquainted with the "friendly step" already decided on by the Eastern powers, i. e., requesting the intercession of the Pope. When De la Ferronnays, in defense of his colleague, objected that France should have been informed about the Allied decision to seek Papal mediation before Caraman presented his proposal, Metternich replied that unfortunately the decision had so recently been made that this had not been possible.[78]

Caraman's embarrassment at this rebuff was not lessened by his having to read at this same conference the official French reply to the Eastern powers' memoirs of October 23 and 29 and November 2. The memoir reiterated France's neutrality, promising only moral support for the Allied intervention, which it hoped would be carried out peacefully and for liberal ends. To promote peace, Louis XVIII announced his intention of writing a letter to Ferdinand urging him

[77] Pasquier (*Mémoires*, V, 32–33) alleges that Metternich solicited the proposal from Caraman.

[78] *Ibid.*, 43–44; "Journal des Conférences," No. 5, December 7, 1820, Kongressakten, Troppau, Fasc. 38; proposal by Caraman, December 7, 1820, *ibid.* Metternich, of course, placed all the blame for Caraman's embarrassment upon Caraman himself for his "habitual levity." Metternich (Troppau, December 9, 1820) to Vincent, Weisungen, Frankreich, Fasc. 343.

to accept the Allied invitation to Laibach.[79] This same policy of preserving official neutrality but giving moral support to the Allies also characterized France's answer to the Preliminary Protocol. France was in sympathy with the Protocol's aims, the French note said, but could not sign or ratify it.[80]

After the questions of French mediation and Papal intercession were settled, only a few bits of business remained to be cleared up while the Congress waited for news from Naples. The council of Allied ministers to accompany and advise Ferdinand on his return to Naples was set up, with Metternich appointing Ambassador Vincent to head it.[81] The Preliminary Protocol having been abandoned, the Eastern powers met the need for giving the world some kind of formal statement on the results of the Congress by issuing a joint circular to their various missions on December 8. This Troppau Circular, while in the main simply a summary of the principles and actions agreed upon at the Congress, restated some of the very points to which Castlereagh had objected in the Preliminary Protocol. It flatly asserted, for example, that the Congress had resolved upon its action in the name of the general alliance; that England and France would surely agree that the principle behind the Allied action regarding Naples was "strictly conformable to treaties solemnly ratified by these two powers"; and that the principles followed by the three Eastern courts were not new, but were based upon the existing system and designed to strengthen it.[82] The ulti-

[79] Note from French Cabinet, read December 7, 1820, Kongressakten, Troppau, Fasc. 39; Vincent (Paris, December 5, 1820) to Metternich, Berichte, Frankreich, Fasc. 342, No. 66A; Louis XVIII (Paris, December 3, 1820) to Ferdinand I, *British and Foreign State Papers*, VIII (1820–1821), 1148–1149.

[80] "Communication aux Plénipotentiaires Français relativement du protocole préliminaire du 19 novembre . . .," read December 24, 1820, Kongressakten, Troppau, Fasc. 39.

[81] Metternich instructed Vincent, among other things, to "assure to the political voice of Austria the necessary weight in the council of Cabinets, composed of elements all too often heterogenous." Vincent should also be careful to have no contacts with the "the lower classes of people"—"your sphere of activity," Metternich admonished him, "will be the highest possible." Particular letters, Metternich (Troppau, November 10 and December 9, 1820) to Vincent, Weisungen, Frankreich, Fasc. 343.

[82] "Journal des Conférences," No. 5, December 7, 1820, Kongressakten, Troppau, Fasc. 38. The references to existing treaties were included in the circular at the insistence of Capodistrias, who wanted something even stronger on this point. Capodistrias (Troppau, December 12, 1820) to Metternich,

mate British reaction to these statements in the circular, as will be shown, was very sharp.

At the same time, the powers addressed a memoir to the courts of Italy explaining the resolutions of the Congress and conveying an invitation to them to attend the forthcoming congress at Laibach.[83] Although the invitation was couched in polite diplomatic phraseology, Metternich made it clear in his instructions to the Austrian *chargé* at Turin, Baron Binder, that the Italian Courts were being invited simply to accept the Allied proposals, not to consult with the Allies on them.[84]

Besides meeting the great questions of intervention in a satisfactory manner, Metternich had other incidental successes at the Congress. He succeeded in keeping the revolutions in both Spain and Portugal off the Congress agenda, despite the fact that appeals came to him from both countries and that he had taken a very compromising stand with Alexander in favor of a general principle of intervention against revolution everywhere. Spurred on by appeals for help from Ferdinand VII of Spain, Alexander had wanted to invite him along with his uncle, Ferdinand of Naples, to the coming congress at Laibach. Metternich was able to sidestep this highly inconvenient proposal, however, by the ever-useful device of praising it in principle but pointing out insuperable practical obstacles

------

ibid., Fasc. 39 (with accompanying enclosure). The circular is printed in Metternich, *Nachgelassene Papiere,* III, 391–394.

[83] Although most of this memoir consisted of the usual dogmas, there were in it one or two interesting points, chief of which was a warning to Italy against the subversive example of England. The French Revolution, the memoir said, was due in part to France's proximity to England, a country "imbued for almost a century with the errors of a false philosophy." All the Italian states were warned that making any concessions to popular demands, as England had done in the past, only weakened monarchies against revolution. "Among the monarchical states," the memoir continued, "those least exposed to the attacks of internal factions are without contradiction those who have altered nothing in the fundamental bases and the forms of their government. *Austria* offers a convincing example of this." It was not, moreover, by bad financial systems or heavy taxes that the seeds of discontent and revolution were sown, the memoir continued, but by the acts and omissions of governments—by introducing innovations and failing to suppress the sects. "Mémoire adressée simultanement aux Cours de Turin, de Rome, de Florence, de Modenè, de Parme, de Lucques," n.d., Kongressakten, Troppau, Fasc. 39.

[84] Metternich (Troppau, December 24, 1820) to Binder, Weisungen und Varia, Sardinien, Fasc. 56.

to such an invitation, especially the fact that while the Allies could back up their invitation with force at Naples, they could not in Spain.[85] A plea for intervention against the revolution in Portugal, presented by the Marquis de Marialva, prerevolutionary Portuguese ambassador at Paris, was more easily dismissed. Declining Marialva's request for permission to attend the congress, Metternich advised King John and his royalist supporters to appeal to Great Britain, giving the English no excuse to back out of their treaties with Portugal.[86] Having thus shunted Marialva's plea aside, Metternich had to deal in similar fashion with a certain amount of domestic opposition against his policy, headed by Austrian Finance Minister Prince Stadion, who was gravely disturbed at the bad effect armed intervention at Naples might have on Austria's shaky finances. Stadion wanted to see the whole matter made the subject of Cabinet deliberations before the Emperor,[87] but Metternich succeeded in keeping the reins of Austrian policy firmly in his own hands at Troppau.

All these minor successes put together paled in significance, however, when the good results of the Allied *démarche* at Naples became known. Ever since the outbreak of the revolution at Naples, Metternich, though happy that the revolutionists had chosen a radical constitution instead of a moderate one,[88] had been perturbed by the regrettable moderation displayed by the constitutionalists in control at Naples. His hope was that the radicals would take over the government and even that they would offer resistance to the Austrian intervention. "If it is necessary to fight, we will fight," he wrote Vincent, "and I desire it, for the rascals will receive a good lesson." [89] The ostentatious Austrian military movements in northern

---

[85] Ferdinand VII (Madrid, October 25, 1820) to Francis I, Kongressakten, Troppau, Fasc. 39; "Apperçu sur l'idée d'inviter le Roi d'Espagne à venir se réunir en congrès avec les Monarques," n.d. *ibid.*

[86] Metternich (Troppau, October 26, 1820) to Marialva and Vincent, Weisungen, Frankreich, Fasc. 343; Metternich (Troppau, October 26, 1820) to Baron Stürmer, ambassador at Lisbon, Interiora: Korrespondenz, Fasc. 81.

[87] Stadion (Vienna, November 3 and 17, 1820) to Metternich, Kongressakten, Troppau, Fasc. 39; Austrian Court Councillor Count Andreas Mercy (Troppau, November 12, 1820) to Metternich, *ibid.*

[88] Metternich (Vienna, August 17, 1820) to Bernstorff, in *Atti del Parlamento,* V, Pt. 2, 98.

[89] Particular letter from Troppau, November 10, 1820, Weisungen, Frankreich, Fasc. 343. Metternich later wrote to Stadion, "The revolution has in fact been

Italy, combined with the diplomatic pressure exerted on the new regime, served Metternich's ends effectively. For these measures forced a program of armaments on Naples and aroused the radicals against the constitutionalists, who, as noted, had been pursuing a peaceful foreign policy and even hoped to disband the Neapolitan army to save money. In September, well after the Austrian troop movements were fully under way, the Prussian envoy at Rome, the famous historian Barthold Niebuhr, commented, "The inconceivable inactivity of the Neapolitans in the face of the formidable armament which openly menaces them has finally ceased." [90]

The arming which took place at Naples was highly ineffective, however, for the Carbonari, infatuated with wild-eyed schemes of a nation at arms, gave little practical attention to munitions, supplies, or discipline. More important still, despite all that General Pepe and the Carbonari could say or do, the nation clearly had no stomach for a war in behalf of the Spanish Constitution. Mutinies and desertions increased in the army, particularly in those units sent to the northern frontier. De Menz confidently predicted that resistance to an Austrian invasion would be feeble or nonexistent, commenting further, "The nation appears disposed to receive the law from Troppau and the most sound part even desires this, for it is this alone which would be able to give a stable and solid basis to the kingdom." [91]

De Menz, as usual, was right. While the regime at Naples protested (largely *pro forma*) against the armed menace of Austria and

---

forced to take a character of deplorable mildness impossible to avoid in view of our armaments." Laibach, March 10, 1821, in Metternich, *Nachgelassene Papiere*, III, 455.

[90] Niebuhr (Rome, September 9, 1820) to Frederick William III, Korrespondenz, Neapel, Fasc. 50.

[91] De Menz (Naples, December 2, 1820) to Metternich, Berichte, Neapel, Fasc. 48, No. 64B. See also his letters of September 5 and 9, November 7, 17, 22, and 26, December 6, 1820, *ibid.*, Nos. 45E and 46A, and Fasc. 49, Nos. 59C, 61B, 61C, 62B, 63B, 63C, and 65B; reports based on A'Court's dispatches by Esterhazy (London, October 25 and November 3, 1820) to Metternich, Berichte, Grossbritannien, Fasc. 212, Nos. 169A and 171A; and Romani, *Neapolitan Revolution*, 102–104, 142. The Duke of Calabria characterized the Carbonari leaders of the resistance movement as hotheads and fools so irrational as to believe that "when the Austrian army shows itself, they will make it come over to their side by making Carbonaro signs at it." De Menz (Naples, December 7, 1820) to Metternich, Berichte, Neapel, Fasc. 49, No. 66A.

her refusal to recognize the new government, the Duke of Campochiaro continued to follow a policy designed to placate Austria and
the Allies [92] and to recommend that the National Parliament make
concessions to appease the powers.[93] The effort of the moderates to
control the Carbonari at home, however, was a feeble one; the constitutionalists pinned their main hopes on an intervention of the
right sort by the Allies convened at Troppau. The lack of news from
Troppau and the mounting evidence that the Allies had no intention
of compromising with the revolution at Naples served equally to
encourage the radicals and discourage the constitutionalists. A'Court
summed up the situation well:

The moderate constitutionalists (amongst whom we may class all the
nobility, the superior officers of the army and most of those who compose
the present administration) are cast down and alarmed in the same proportion [as the radicals were encouraged], for their hopes rest upon the
arrival of some firm and energetick [*sic*] declaration on the part of the
greater Powers, dictating those conditions which may, at the same time,
offer a sufficient guarantee to Europe, and secure to this country the
enjoyment of a constitution in which property may be admitted as the
basis of representation, and the Royal Prerogative be allowed that just
latitude which is denied to it by the Constitution of the Cortes—.
I have every reason to believe that the nation, generally speaking, is
prepared for and would agree to accept conditions of this nature, if proposed by the united voice of the Congress.[94]

The messages arriving from Troppau in early December contained, of course, no such beneficent declaration, but only a personal

---

[92] Campochiaro, for instance, accepted Consalvi's word that Austria would
not be invited to cross Papal territory to invade Naples, and on this basis
abandoned any idea of occupying part of the Papal States to meet an Austrian
attack. He also besought the Pope to mediate in behalf of Naples and persuade
Austria not to launch an invasion. De Menz (Naples, November 4, 1820) to
Campochiaro, and De Menz (Naples, November 12, 1820) to Metternich,
Berichte, Neapel, Fasc. 49, No. 60B; Campochiaro (Naples, November 3,
1820) to Chevalier de Fossombroni, foreign minister of Tuscany, Kongressakten,
Troppau, Fasc. 39. See also Campochiaro's report to the National Parliament,
October 4, 1820, in *Atti del Parlamento*, I, 209–210, and his letter to Consalvi,
Naples, November 3, 1820, *ibid.*, V, Pt. 1, 141–143.

[93] De Menz (Naples, November 26, 1820) to Metternich, Berichte, Neapel,
Fasc. 49, No. 63C.

[94] A'Court (Naples, November 24, 1820) to Castlereagh, Varia, Grossbritannien, Fasc. 18.

invitation to the King (delivered to Ferdinand on December 6 by the Allied ministers), together with the warning sent secretly to De Menz, that if the King was refused permission to come to Laibach, Austria would consider the royal family's safety as the responsibility of every Neapolitan.[95]

It was now discouragingly clear that both the Allied powers at Troppau and the radicals at Naples were intransigent in their attitude on the constitution, the former insisting on destroying it entirely, the latter on preserving it intact. Despite these ominous portents, the moderates, led by Campochiaro, the Duke of Calabria, and Finance Minister Giuseppe Zurlo, head of the ministry, made a last belated attempt to arrive at a moderate compromise constitution. Aided by A'Court and Count Stackelberg of Russia, the ministers played on the King's mounting fears that he would not be permitted to go to Laibach, thereby persuading him much against his will to send a message to Parliament promising that if he was permitted to go he would do all in his power to disperse the danger of war while still remaining true to his promises of constitutional freedom for his country. In eight specific points he guaranteed his subjects broad civil rights, along with an amnesty. At the same time he freed his hands to change the constitution in the manner already proposed by Campochiaro to the Parliament. The changes included establishing an absolute royal veto, a Chamber of Peers, and a ministry responsible to the King. Campochiaro, who had been holding out the hope of French mediation in behalf of this program,[96] accompanied the royal message with a special report urging Parliament to adopt it as the only way to avoid a disastrous war and to steer a middle course between democracy and despotism. Furthermore, in the hope of gaining provincial support for the move and of confronting the Carbonari with a *fait accompli*, the moderates went over the head of Parliament by sending the King's proclamation into the provinces in advance of Parliamentary approval.[97]

[95] De Menz (Naples, December 6, 1820) to Metternich, Berichte, Neapel, Fasc. 49, No. 65C; Metternich (Troppau, November 22, 1820) to De Menz, Korrespondenz, Neapel, Fasc. 50, Nos. 1–3.

[96] See the correspondence between Campochiaro and the Vicar-General, Naples, November 29 to December 4, 1820, in *Atti del Parlamento*, II, 341–345.

[97] De Menz (Naples, December 6 and 7, 1820) to Metternich, Berichte, Neapel, Fasc. 49, Nos. 65C and 66A; Ferdinand's message to Parliament, December 7, 1820, in *British and Foreign State Papers*, VIII (1820–1821),

The plan backfired completely. Although the King's message was well received in the provinces, the Carbonari, with their Grand Lodge at Naples, aroused the populace with the cry of treason against the Spanish Constitution and exerted such pressure on the Parliament to save the constitution that it rejected the King's message by a large majority, sending a reply to Ferdinand which denied him the right to infringe in any way upon the existing charter. Completely cowed and ready to do anything to escape from Naples, Ferdinand swore solemnly to uphold the Spanish Constitution in every particular, repeating the oath again and again in succeeding messages. On the basis of these promises and in the incredibly fatuous belief not only that Ferdinand would be true to them but also that the Allied powers would bow to the King's decision, Parliament by acclamation granted the King permission to leave his kingdom. The Neapolitan legislators even ignored the precaution, as suggested in the King's first message, of sending a Neapolitan delegation to accompany Ferdinand to Laibach. Meanwhile, in his reply to Emperor Francis, Ferdinand accepted the Allied invitation gladly, omitting any mention of the promises he had made to the Parliament and nation. Terrified and servile so long as he considered himself within reach of the revolutionaries, Ferdinand repudiated every promise immediately upon reaching friendly soil at Livorno, and began once more to act as an absolute monarch.[98]

In Naples, meanwhile, the internal situation deteriorated rapidly. The Zurlo ministry fell and was replaced by a radical one with the incompetent Duke of Gallo as foreign minister. Zurlo and Campochiaro were put on trial for treason; the rest of the moderates, who included practically all the men of sense and talent, were completely discouraged. With the radical faction in control, governmental dissolution was unmistakably approaching. At the same time, the

---

1151–1153; "Rapporto della commissione straordinaria del parlamento nazionale su l'intervento di S. M. al Congresso di Laybach," *Atti relativi all'intervento di S. M. il Re delle Due Sicilie nel Congresso di Leybach,* 3–12; Pasquier, *Mémoires,* V, 47–49.

[98] Messages exchanged between Parliament and Ferdinand, December 8–13, 1820, in *British and Foreign State Papers,* VIII (1820–1821), 1153–1161; De Menz (Naples, December 8, 9, 19, and 21, 1820) to Metternich, Berichte, Neapel, Fasc. 49, Nos. 66B and 66C with supplements, Postscript to 69, and 70B; Ferdinand I (Naples, December 12, 1820) to Francis I, *ibid.;* Ferdinand (Livorno, December 21, 1820) to Francis, Hofkorrespondenz, Neapel, Fasc. 32.

nation reacted apathetically to all plans for organizing resistance to foreign intervention.[99] No one, of course, witnessed these trends with greater satisfaction than Metternich. Though even the success of the Muratist attempt to revise the constitution would not have altered his policy on intervention in the slightest, it might have embarrassed him and given him some difficulty with Alexander. As it was, the revolution had taken the turn Metternich desired and had worked for.[100] The last serious obstacle in the path of Austrian intervention at Naples had now been cleared. Only the details needed to be settled at Laibach.

[99] De Menz (Naples, December 12 and 21, 1820) to Metternich, Berichte, Neapel, Fasc. 49, Nos. 66D and 70B; A'Court (Naples, January 1, 1821) to Castlereagh, Varia, Grossbritannien, Fasc. 19; Romani, *Neapolitan Revolution* 149–153.

[100] It is difficult, of course, to appraise how much danger the Muratists' move, if successful, woulld have meant for Metternich's policy. Webster (*Foreign Policy of Castlereagh,* 310–311) seems to feel that the danger would have been fairly great. I am inclined rather to consider the move as possibly a serious embarrassment for Metternich, but hardly a really formidable obstacle. For one thing, mediation in Naples by France would surely have been opposed, not only by Austria but also by England and Russia, out of suspicion of France. In addition, Metternich knew that he needed only Alexander's support to be able to act. By this time, however, Metternich's influence over Alexander was so great and the Tsar's horror of military revolt (intensified by the news reaching Troppau on November 14 of the mutiny of the Semyonovski Regiment in St. Petersburg) was so intense that even a successful modification of the constitution in Naples could hardly have prevented Metternich from drawing Russia with him in a crusade against revolution. (On the Semyonovski mutiny, see Stählin, *Geschichte Russlands,* III, 268–269; also Webster, *Foreign Policy of Castlereagh,* 294.) The Neapolitan envoy at St. Petersburg, the Duke of Serracapriola, repeatedly attempted to drive a wedge between Austria and Russia on the Neapolitan question by arousing Russian suspicions of Austrian motives in Italy, but without success. Serracapriola (St. Petersburg, September 23 and October 5, 1820) to Capodistrias, and Serracapriola (St. Petersburg, October 7 and December 2, 1820) to Nesselrode, in *Atti del Parlamento,* V, Pt. 1, 87–89, 114–120, 186–188. For the reaction of Metternich and Gentz to the Muratists' attempt to change the constitution, see Metternich (Troppau, December 24, 1820) to Esterhazy, Weisungen, Grossbritannien, Fasc. 213, No. 2, and Gentz (Vienna, December 31, 1820) to Soutzo, in Gentz, *Dépêches inédites,* 11, 110–111.

CHAPTER IV

THE CONGRESS OF LAIBACH

Essentially a continuation of the prorogued Congress of Troppau, the congress which opened at Laibach on January 11, 1821, resembled its predecessor in many ways. Much the same personnel was on hand, with some changes and additions,[1] and business was conducted in much the same way, with the chief work being done in private meetings and conferences. At Laibach, as at Troppau, Metternich took measures to ensure secrecy and prevent leaks of information, with the added precaution of keeping certain of those in attendance at the Congress under Austrian police observation.[2]

From the very beginning of the Congress Metternich held two trump cards: his influence over Alexander, and his control over Ferdinand. To make sure of the former's support, he had held long, intimate conversations with the Tsar over cups of tea at Troppau. There he had expounded to Alexander his political testament—a lengthy piece he called his "Profession of Faith," whose chief argument was that if there ever were occasions for reform, the present moment of distress was not one of them. At this time sane governments could only hold to sound principles, avoid innovations, maintain strong government, and suppress the agitation of the factious.[3]

[1] Besides Ferdinand I, the new delegates at the Congress were the Marquis of Molza, from Modena; the Marquis of San Marzano and Count d'Aglie, from Sardinia; Prince Corsini, from Tuscany; and Cardinal Spina, of the Papal States. Robert Gordon, British minister at Vienna, assisted Stewart; Hardenberg and Frederick William absented themselves from the Prussian delegation. "Journal des Conférences de Laybach," Kongressakten, Laibach, Fasc. 40.

[2] Folder titled "Beobachtungs–Resultate," *ibid.*, Fasc. 41; Friedrich von Gentz, *Aus dem Nachlass Varnhagens von Ense: Tagebücher von Friedrich von Gentz*, II, 382–393.

[3] Metternich (Troppau, December 15, 1820) to Alexander, in Metternich, *Nachgelassene Papiere*, III, 399–420.

These salutary doctrines had so impressed Alexander that Metternich was convinced that Capodistrias' malign influence over him was, for the moment at least, at an end.[4] As for Ferdinand, not only had he no other desire than to escape from his cares by throwing himself on the mercy of the Allied sovereigns and diverting himself with the pleasures of the hunt, but he was also completely under the influence of Prince Alvaro Ruffo, one of the most obsequiously loyal of Metternich's so-called "harem" of ambassadors at Vienna.[5] Metternich's only problem with the King was to overcome his distaste for work and his alternate spells of fear and bravado long enough to commit him firmly to the course of action that the Austrian desired.[6]

Metternich did not hesitate a moment to play these trump cards to full advantage at the Congress. In a private conference of January 13, he reached complete agreement with Alexander on all the major points of action to be taken concerning Naples.[7] In dealing with Ferdinand, meanwhile, he had only to try to conceal the Austrian hand in the Neapolitan glove. The most important papers

[4] "Capodistrias writhes like a devil in holy water," wrote Metternich on January 10; "he is, however, in holy water and can do nothing."—*Ibid.*, 424.

[5] "Beobachtungs–Resultate," entry for January 10, 1821, Kongressakten, Laibach, Fasc. 41. Assuring Metternich that he made it his "religion to undertake nothing without your approval," Ruffo had urged Metternich to make him the King's companion at Laibach, for, he argued, "if the King is in my hands, he is in yours." Ruffo (Vienna, December 12, 1820) to Metternich, in *Atti del Parlamento*, V, Pt. 2, 418–419.

[6] Gentz describes eloquently the contemptible figure that Ferdinand cut at the Congress. After mentioning the "sorry protestations" (still happily secret) with which the King had repudiated all his sacred vows, Gentz continued: "The King has arrived here without having with him a single man capable either of giving advice or of transacting business. He has never himself had the least taste for work; he has now so lost the habit of it that it is difficult to engage him to read a dispatch which consists of more than one page. . . . Like all weak men, he conceives nothing but extremes; he passes in turn from imprudence to the most fearful reserve, and from terror to temerity. Having subscribed on one evening to the most shameful capitulation, he believes the very next day that he can not only consider this as not having happened, but that he can also dictate the law as an absolute master to those to whom he engaged himself. This is the ally whom heaven has placed in our hands and whose interests we have to re-establish!" Gentz (Laibach, January 22, 1821) to Soutzo, in Gentz, *Dépêches inédites*, II, 121–123.

[7] "Points rédigés pour être lu à l'Emp. Alexander dans mon entrevue avec S. M. I. le 13 janv. 1821," Kongressakten, Laibach, Fasc. 41; "Résultats de ma Conférence avec S. M. I. de toutes les Russies le 13 janv. 1821," *ibid.*

which the King was to dispatch or proclaim were written for him by Metternich and his aides,[8] while all matters of policy were settled by the great powers—in effect, by Austria and Russia.

With this groundwork established, Metternich was able to make the Congress move smoothly through the motions of transacting business and reaching decisions in the first seven sessions, from January 11 to January 25. Ruffo, accepted as plenipotentiary for Naples, conveyed Ferdinand's expression of fervent gratitude to the Allied monarchs for their help, coupled with a request for their opinion on the situation in his country. Metternich, speaking for the Allies, pronounced their unconditional anathema on the revolution, asking Ferdinand, in turn, what he felt should now be done about it. Ruffo then presented Ferdinand's "proposal": a letter from him to his son, the Prince-Regent, accompanied by suitable instructions to the Allied envoys at Naples supporting it, announcing that it was necessary to completely overthrow the existing regime. In addition, the Duke of Gallo, then foreign minister of Naples, was to be summoned to the Congress solely to act as a messenger to bear to the revolutionary government the news of the King's firm decision to destroy the revolution.[9] The conferees readily agreed to these steps, all of which, of course, had already been planned long before by Metternich and agreed to by Alexander.[10]

Ferdinand thereupon sent to his son the two letters which Metternich had drawn up for him. The first, intended for publication at Naples, portrayed Ferdinand as powerless to keep his vows in the face of the unyielding insistence of the Allied sovereigns on doing away with the revolution entirely, and emphasized the necessity of giving the powers adequate guarantees of stability in Naples in the

[8] See, for instance, "Projet d'une lettre de S. M. le Roi de Naples au Prince Héréditaire" and a draft of the "Proclamation du Roi aux Napolitains," both with notes in Metternich's handwriting on the critical passages (*ibid.*). Metternich remarked that in dealing with Ferdinand and drawing up documents for him, he had to avoid "the delicate chord" of his oaths and vows to the Spanish Constitution and to his people, and to stress simply his paternal good will for his subjects. Metternich (Laibach, January 25, 1821) to Esterhazy, Weisungen, Grossbritannien, Fasc. 217, No. 1.

[9] "Table des Journeaux des Conférences tenués au Congrès de Laybach," and "Journal des Conférences de Laybach," Kongressakten, Laibach, Fasc. 40.

[10] "Résultats de ma Conférence avec S. M. I. de toutes les Russies le 13 janv. 1821," *ibid.*, Fasc. 41.

future.[11] All mention of an army of occupation, however, was expressly reserved for the second confidential letter, which the Prince-Regent could disclose or not as he saw fit. In it Ferdinand announced that the Allies, "in peaceful and amicable intent," had decided to dispatch to Naples an army of occupation.

The Allied envoys at Naples, meanwhile, were instructed to try to prevail upon the Prince-Regent to overthrow the revolutionary regime himself and so open the way for a peaceful occupation of the kingdom by Austrian forces. Metternich agreed to these instructions even though he had no enthusiasm for them or confidence in their practicability. He complied solely to appease Alexander, who had earlier favored direct secret negotiations with the Prince-Regent to avoid war, but had sacrificed this idea in deference to Austria's prior interests in Naples and in order to preserve the harmony of the powers.[12]

In its next two sessions, on January 26 and 28, the Congress devoted itself to securing the consent of the Italian representatives to the decisions it had taken. The only Italian diplomat who gave Metternich any trouble was Cardinal Spina,[13] who insisted on preserving Rome's complete neutrality in regard to Allied measures which, he pointed out, might provoke hostilities in the Holy See. The remonstrance of Capodistrias that the Pope could surely recognize and approve the benevolent purposes of the Allies without damaging his neutrality, and the rather surprising remark by Stewart that the British King and his government had found it possible to condemn and deplore the revolt while remaining neutral on inter-

---

[11] Ferdinand (Laibach, n.d.) to the Duke of Calabria, *ibid.*, Fasc. 40.

[12] Ferdinand (Laibach, n.d.) to the Duke of Calabria, *ibid.;* "Instructions pour les ministres et chargé d'affaires d'Autriche, de Prusse et de Russie à Naples," Laibach, January 31, 1821, *ibid.;* "Dépêche à Mr le Comte de Stackelberg," Laibach, January 31, 1821, *ibid.;* Russian note, January 16, 1821, *ibid.*, Fasc. 41. The French observers at Laibach also attached themselves to the Allied *démarche* at Naples. See their "Dépêche de Messieurs les Plénipotentiaires français à Mr de Fontenay chargé d'affaires de France à Naples," January 31, 1821, *ibid.*, Fasc. 40.

[13] Most of the Italian delegates made sure of advance approval of their statements from Metternich. San Marzano of Sardinia, for example, turned his declaration over to Metternich before reading it. "Declaration de Mr de St. Marsan [sic]," Laibach, January 27, 1821, *ibid.*, Fasc. 41.

vention made no change in Spina's position.[14] The announcement
of Papal neutrality, however, was only a trifling annoyance for the
Allies. On January 30, Metternich read the Allied decision to the
Duke of Gallo, who received the bad news meekly enough and
promised to do all in his power at Naples to "respond" to the views
of his sovereign and the Allies.[15]

Thus the first phase of the Congress ended; the way was finally
clear for sending Austrian troops to Naples. Metternich now invited
the Congress to consider his proposals governing the Austrian army
of occupation in Naples. According to his plan, the army, though
entirely Austrian in composition and under Austrian command,
should be regarded as an auxiliary of Ferdinand, in accordance with
the previous resolutions of Troppau and Laibach. If the Neapolitan
government submitted to the Austrian occupation peacefully, it
would not be required to pay an indemnity for the mobilization
previously carried out by Austria in her Italian provinces. This concession, the Austrian memoir pointed out, was further proof of
Emperor Francis' benevolence. If the Neapolitans offered any resistance to the Austrian occupation, however, Austria would then demand that Naples pay her for this earlier mobilization. In any case,
whether the occupation proceeded peacefully or not, once the Austrian army crossed the Po, all its expenses would be charged to
Naples. Emperor Francis and Ferdinand, with the other Eastern
powers participating, were to draw up a convention governing the
occupation, which provisionally would be set for three years. Another congress, to be held in Florence in 1822, was then to survey
the inner condition of Naples and determine whether the occupation
should be terminated, continued for the original period, or prolonged. Since Naples undoubtedly would be unable at first to meet
the costs of the campaign and the occupation, Austria volunteered

[14] "Journal des Conférences," January 26 and 28, 1821, *ibid.*, Fasc. 40. A
renewed appeal to the Pope for moral support for intervention had been one
of the steps agreed upon by Metternich and Alexander on January 13. See
"Résultats de ma Conférence . . .," *ibid.*, Fasc. 41.

[15] "Journal des Conférences," January 30, 1821, *ibid.*; "Allocution de M. le
Prince de Metternich au nom de la Conférence, à M. Le Duc de Gallo dans le
séance du 30 janvier 1821," *ibid.* Although Gallo made a sorry showing at the
conference, it may be said in his defense that he seems to have made a manful,
though unavailing, attempt at the Congress to secure an audience with Ferdinand and Ruffo to try to dissuade them from the course they were following.
"Beobachtungs–Resultate," January 31 and February 1, 1821, *ibid.*, Fasc. 41.

to be the guarantor of a loan to the kingdom, provided that the other powers join her in the guarantee and that the guarantee be purely precautionary, with Naples remaining the principal debtor.[16] Russia and Prussia, whose support was all Metternich needed or expected on this matter, readily accepted the Austrian proposals. Stewart declined to discuss them on grounds of British neutrality, and the French observers followed his example, though at the same time praising the generosity and disinterestedness of Emperor Francis.[17]

This matter settled, the Congress fell into a relative stagnation while awaiting the results of the Allied *démarche* at Naples. Metternich, meantime, occupied himself with drawing up Ferdinand's plans for reconstruction at Naples. He encountered here his first slight difficulty with Ferdinand and Ruffo, who wanted a pure-and-simple return to the old order at Naples.[18] At the same time, he had to fend off a last feeble attempt by Capodistrias to rescue some shadow of representative government there.[19] Nevertheless, Metternich was ready by February 20 to have Ruffo present to the Congress Metternich's plan for the future government at Naples. The plan was in all respects a typical Metternichean political program,

[16] "Point de vue sur l'armée d'occupation," Laibach, January 29, 1821, *ibid.*, Fasc. 40; "Journal des Conférences," February 2, 1821, *ibid*. It was Prince Stadion who insisted on the monetary provisions contained in the Austrian memoir, and who also advised Metternich that it would be advantageous for Austria to have the Neapolitan loan go through the House of Rothschild, with which Austria and Metternich had close connections. Stadion (Vienna, February 1, 1821) to Metternich, *ibid.*, Fasc. 41.

[17] "Journal des Conférences," February 2, 1821, *ibid.*, Fasc. 40. In the session of February 20 the Italian envoys expressed their opinions of the plan of occupation. Spina commented on it noncommittally, Molza praised it to the skies, and Corsini expressed gratitude particularly for the renewed assurance it contained that the costs of Austrian passage through foreign territories (including Tuscany) on the way to Naples would be indemnified.

[18] Nicomede Bianchi, *Storia documentata della diplomazia europea in Italia dall'anno 1814 all'anno 1861*, II, 56–57.

[19] *Ibid.*, 55. Capodistrias wanted to give the King's advisory council (the *Consulta*) a "consultative vote" on general questions of legislation and administration. Metternich vetoed the idea as smacking of a representative system, and convinced Alexander that it should be rejected. "Note éxplicative remise à S. M. I. de toutes les Russies, à Laybach, le 15 février 1821," Kongressakten, Laibach, Fasc. 41; "Opinion du Cabinet de Russie sur les bases d'une loi fondamentale pour le Royaume des Deux Siciles," Laibach, February 17, 1821. *ibid.*

providing for provincialism, separation of the functions—but not the powers—of the government, and the establishment of purely advisory bodies of the King's own making to counsel him. The specific proposals were those indicated at Troppau: separate administrations for the two kingdoms, each to have its own Council of State and advisory *Consulta*; provincial councils, likewise appointive; and local bodies of some unspecified type to take care of communal administration.[20]

With Ruffo's presentation of this plan, Ferdinand had, according to Metternich's scheme of things, now exercised his "initiative" in the reconstruction at Naples. He therefore next invited the Italian Courts to exercise their right of "control" over Ferdinand's plans. To no one's surprise, the delegates accepted the proposals, adding the quite unnecessary stipulation expressed by Prince Corsini that "the consultative body be organized in a monarchical form." [21] Finally, the Allied powers put to use their powers of surveillance and definite assent (no longer, as originally, surveillance and *counsel*). Austria did so by graciously expressing her "entire adhesion" to the King's plans. Prussia and Russia followed suit. The only faint remnant left of Capodistrias' ideas was the Russian expression of a desire that the system erected at Naples be strong enough to stand on its own feet without foreign help.[22] With this, the elaborate and farcical ritual of meaningless conferences was ended. The Congress closed on February 25 with the resolution to reconvene to consider the Italian question in September 1822.[23] The representatives of the Eastern powers, however, remained on at Laibach to await the outcome of the Neapolitan campaign.

The Congress of Laibach was thus a smooth and easy victory for Metternich, attended by practically none of the anxieties and difficulties of Troppau. Even from the French delegation he had re-

---

[20] "Journal des Conférences," February 20, 1821, *ibid.*, Fasc. 40.

[21] February 21, 1821, *ibid.*

[22] February 22, 1821, *ibid.*

[23] February 26, 1821, *ibid.* Although for purposes of public consumption Metternich was able to keep up the pretense that Ferdinand was acting of his own free will, he deceived no one at the conference and, one may suppose, few outside of it. In Paris, for example, Pasquier spoke of "imaginary conferences" at Laibach and a "fictitious correspondence" between Ferdinand and the Prince–Regent. Binder (Paris, February 10, 1821) to Metternich, Berichte, Frankreich, Fasc. 342.

ceived, in the main, unexpected cooperation. To be sure, De la Ferronnays had tried to cause trouble by proposing at the last minute that the question of governmental reorganization at Troppau be deferred until the King was back in his domains—a proposal which Metternich ascribed to Capodistrias' intrigues. This idea, however, was easily shunted aside,[24] and the French observers behaved well in all other respects, joining in with the Allied *démarche* at Naples and otherwise showing their sympathy for the Allied cause. In addition, Count Blacas, an unimpeachable Royalist, was appointed to serve on the Allied council attending Ferdinand on his return to Naples. The French government itself, to be sure, was not quite so cooperative. It not only regretted that its observers at the Congress had gone as far as they had, and wished that if the Eastern powers were determined to intervene at Naples, they would do it and get it over with without any more solemn proclamations to Europe,[25] but it also protested openly against the wording of the Allied declaration of February 6 opening the campaign against Naples. Denying the Allied implication that France had acceded "with restrictions" to the intervention principle agreed on at Troppau, the government at Paris insisted that on the question of general intervention its position was exactly the same as that of England. It had only agreed to give moral support to the Allied moves at Naples in the hope of preventing war.[26] The protest, however, had no effect upon the Allied course, and was partly responsible for Alexander's delivering a severe lecture to De la Ferronnays on the subject of France's unreliability.[27]

The sole dark cloud upon the horizon for Metternich at the Congress was the conduct of Great Britain. The neutrality her observers insisted upon maintaining at the Congress did not disturb him, for such action was only to be expected. Even when Stewart, who ar-

[24] Bianchi, *Storia della diplomazia*, II, 58.

[25] Pasquier also expressed regret that the Allies had not left some small loophole for mediation or negotiation at Naples. Binder (Paris, February 9 and 10, 1821) to Metternich, Berichte, Frankreich, Fasc. 342, No. 10 and two particular letters.

[26] Note Verbale, Paris, February 20, 1821, Kongressakten, Laibach, Fasc. 41. The note, arriving too late to be inserted in the conference journal, was sent separately to the Allied Courts. "Remarque relative à la Note Verbale," *ibid.*

[27] Metternich (Laibach, March 5, 1821) to Binder, Weisungen, Frankreich, Fasc. 346. The other reason for Alexander's displeasure was the vacillating French attitude on Spain.

rived late at the Congress and left early,[28] inconveniently demanded
that a British declaration disclaiming any commitment to any *procès-
verbal* reached at the Congress be inserted into the conference journal, and insisted that this same declaration be read to the Duke of
Gallo, along with the other documents, Metternich was annoyed
rather than really troubled.[29]

More important were the actions taken by the British outside the
Congress. Up till now, since England had made no public statement
of her position on the Alliance and the intervention question, Metternich could still claim that there was no difference in principle between the powers and could maintain that whatever rift existed was
purely the result of British misunderstandings, for which Stewart
was largely to blame.[30] Castlereagh, however, had hinted in his dispatch of December 16 that circumstances might at some time compel
England to take a public stand. Such compelling circumstances arose
when agents of the Eastern powers permitted the Troppau Circular,
with its broad implication that Britain and France supported the
action of their Allies on the basis of existing treaties, to leak out to
the public, and particularly when the liberal London *Morning
Chronicle* published the substance of the circular on January 15 and
attacked the Tory ministry for craven submission to the reactionary
designs of the Unholy Alliance. Forced to act in self-defense, Castlereagh sent a circular dispatch on January 19 to all British ministers,
repeating the familiar British doctrines in a very frank manner and
openly repudiating the doctrines implied in the circular.[31] Metternich keenly felt the blow of this dispatch, widely used by British
envoys in various capitals. Officially his reply to Castlereagh was
couched in a tone of aggrieved innocence, but privately he was

[28] See Gentz's diary, February 2, 1821: "Departure of Lord Stewart . . . (to
the great relief of everyone concerned)."—Gentz, *Tagebücher*, II, 386.

[29] "Journal des Conférences," January 25 and 30, 1821, Kongressakten,
Troppau, Fasc. 40; Webster, *Foreign Policy of Castlereagh*, 315–319.

[30] Metternich himself was, of course, under no illusion about what had
caused the rift: "I have sacrificed considerations which have had to appear to
me as secondary [i.e., Britain's objections to a general intervention principle]
to the foremost of all considerations, to the most complete possible *rapproche-
ment* of the course of the two Imperial courts." Metternich (Laibach, January
11, 1821) to Esterhazy, Weisungen, Grossbritannien, Fasc. 217, No. 2.

[31] Webster, *Foreign Policy of Castlereagh*, 320–324; Esterhazy (London,
January 18, 1821) to Metternich, Berichte, Grossbritannien, Fasc. 214, No.
179B, with supplement.

bitter in his recriminations, registering sharp complaints especially against the conduct and language of Stewart at Vienna and Lord Burghersh at Florence.[32] England, he said, had lost her head perhaps more than any of the Continental states in "the mania of the century."[33]

On the heels of this blow came further disturbing reports about Castlereagh's divergence from sound principles—comments of his to the effect that the old order should not be restored at Naples, and that a moderate constitution would be advisable; hopes that Ferdinand would not simply submit to the sovereigns at Laibach, but would consult the true needs of his people; advice to Austria and the Allied ministerial council not to interfere too much in the restored government at Naples; and regret that the French observers at the Congress had seen fit to support the Allied course.[34] Aggravating Metternich's displeasure still more were the debates in both Houses of Parliament following Castlereagh's dispatch of January 19. Metternich, following the debates closely through reports from English newspapers, found ample material to confirm his diagnosis that the mania of liberalism had infected not only the Whig opposition in England but even the Tory ministry. Although the government was sustained on the question of its policy by a good majority (194 to 125) in the House of Commons, no one there attempted to defend the principle enunciated by the Eastern powers, while in the House of Lords Metternich found the defense of the ministry given by Lord Liverpool far more shocking and distasteful even than the attacks of his Whig opponents.[35] Public opinion in England regarding Austria was so bad, Esterhazy admitted, that even her defend-

---

[32] Metternich (Laibach, February 11 and 24, March 5, 1821) to Esterhazy, Weisungen, Grossbritannien, Fasc. 217, Nos. 2 and 4, 2, and 4 and 6.

[33] Metternich (Laibach, March 5, 1821) to Esterhazy, *ibid.*, No. 6 (Secret).

[34] Esterhazy (London, January 10 and 30, February 13, March 1, 1821) to Metternich, Berichte, Grossbritannien, Fasc. 214, Nos. 178A, 180A, 181C, and 182A.

[35] The Austrian attitude is illustrated by a document, apparently drawn up by Gentz, recording lengthy comments on the debate in the House of Lords on Lord Lansdowne's motion, which called for England to intervene diplomatically to halt the Austrian march on Naples, or at least to protest against it. Dismissing Lansdowne's arguments as "nothing but commonplaces" and the liberal Lord Holland's as "fully detestable," Gentz concentrated his condemnation on the concessions made by the ministry thus: *"The principles upon which the motion rested were disputed by no minister.* The question of whether Austria was justified in intervening in the Neapolitan revolution *Lord Liverpool* termed

ers like Lord Aberdeen were forced into silence or driven to the other side.[36]

These signs of British disaffection, however, could not spoil the glories of the Austrian triumph in the Neapolitan campaign. On February 6, sixty thousand Austrian troops crossed the Po, accompanied by an Allied proclamation announcing their campaign as a crusade in behalf of "the sanctity of all existing rights," and blessed by Ferdinand with a proclamation calling on his people to welcome the foreign troops as liberators, not as enemies.[37] Metternich rejoiced that the campaign was actually under way and that the chances for "conciliation" were now over; the event, he said, made him again feel as he had in 1813.[38]

If it did, the resemblance to that earlier campaign stopped there. For the Austrian troops, as Metternich well knew, were going against no Napoleon and faced no danger of meeting effective resistance. All during the Congress of Laibach the incipient dissolution of the constitutional regime at Naples had proceeded apace, the growing disaffection in the provinces and among the troops and militia being matched only by the wild unreason of the radicals at Naples.[39] The Prince-Regent was confronted with a hard choice when King Ferdinand's letters and the Allied declaration, both proclaiming the necessity of destroying the revolution, were presented to him by the Allied envoys on February 9. Torn between filial duty and an awareness of the utter futility of resistance, on the one hand, and feelings of loyalty to the nation and to his constitutional oaths, on the other,

---

doubtful, problematic, and wished neither to affirm nor deny it. The principle of the Allied powers 'to recognize no forcible revolution' this same minister condemned as an *extreme* just as untenable and just as dangerous as the *opposite extreme* of conceiving every revolution as praise-worthy and desirable." Gentz's sad conclusion was that most of the English nation and a large proportion of her upper classes had fallen prey to revolutionary doctrines and had abandoned sound principles. "Britisches Parlament—Sitzung des Oberhauses," March 2, 1821, Kongressakten, Laibach, Fasc. 41.

[36] Esterhazy (London, March 20, 1821) to Metternich, Berichte, Grossbritannien, Fasc. 214, No. 183B.

[37] "Déclaration," Laibach, February 6, 1821, Kongressakten, Laibach, Fasc. 41; "Proclamation du Roi aux Napolitains," Laibach, February 23, 1821, *ibid.*

[38] Private letter, Laibach, February 6, 1821, in Metternich, *Nachgelassene Papiere,* III, 427. See also Metternich (Laibach, February 7, 1821) to Esterhazy, Weisungen, Grossbritannien, Fasc. 217, No. 1.

[39] De Menz (Naples, January 11, 16, 20, and 26, 1821) to Metternich, Berichte, Neapel, Fasc. 51, Nos. 4B, 5C, 6B, and 8C.

he laid the papers before Parliament, at the same time writing Ferdinand to plead with him to remember his oaths and to grant the nation some kind of a constitution, warning him of the anarchy which would follow the steps he was now taking.[40] Breathing defiance to the last, the National Parliament rejected the Laibach declaration, taking refuge in the fiction that Ferdinand was a prisoner of the Allies, and proclaimed a war of resistance.[41]

As could be expected, the resistance amounted to almost nothing, collapsing, in fact, before the Austrian troops even reached Neapolitan soil. In a foolhardy attempt to dissipate the spirit of defeatism in the Neapolitan forces, General Guglielmo Pepe on March 7 led his contingent, a badly-trained and poorly-equipped assortment of troops and militia, in an attack on the Austrian forces at Rieti, in the Papal States. The attack turned immediately into a terror-stricken rout in which Pepe's forces melted away. Since the other Neapolitan generals, especially Carascosa, had never really favored resistance, in less than a week after the Prince-Regent proclaimed a war of defense the fight was given up as hopeless.[42] On March 23, the Austrian army, whose march was a parade welcomed by the populace, entered Naples. The armistice convention ending the "hostilities" had already been signed on the twentieth.[43]

This complete and easy victory in Naples, however, was clouded and for a time gravely threatened by the eruption of another revolt on March 10 in Piedmont. Once again the blow to Austria in this event was the more severe because it was generally unexpected. To

[40] Journal of the conference of the Allied envoys, February 9 and 10, 1821, *ibid.*; two letters, Prince-Regent [Naples, February 1821] to Ferdinand, *Hofkorrespondenz, Neapel*, Fasc. 32.

[41] De Menz (Naples, February 11, 15, and 20, 1821) to Metternich, Berichte, Neapel, Fasc. 51, Nos. 12D, 13G, 14A, and 14C.

[42] Ficquelmont (Rieti, March 8, 1821) to Metternich, *ibid.*, No. 5; Proclamation of the Prince-Regent to the people of Naples, Naples, March 7, 1821, Varia, Neapel, Fasc. 53; Austrian Army Proclamation No. 4, Laibach, March 20, 1821, *ibid.* Learning later of a scheme led by General Carascosa to offer the surrender of all revolutionary forces immediately and unconditionally to Ferdinand in the hope of avoiding an Austrian occupation, Metternich thanked God that the rapid march of events had foiled this iniquitous plot. Metternich (Laibach, May 14, 1821) to Esterhazy, Weisungen, Grossbritannien, Fasc. 217.

[43] Ficquelmont (Teano, March 20, 1821) to Metternich, Berichte, Neapel, Fasc. 55, No. 10, with supplement. On the dissolution of the constitutional regime, see Romani, *Neapolitan Revolution*, 157–168; and Spellanzon, *Storia del Risorgimento*, I, 829–831.

be sure, there had been signs of trouble in Piedmont during the previous year, but the government had always seemed to be master of
the situation. It had apparently recovered in sound fashion from the
shock of the Neapolitan revolution and its repercussions. No Italian
Court was more ready than that of Turin to give Austria carte
blanche to deal with Naples as she saw fit, or more anxious to see
the revolution destroyed root and branch. The Austrian ambassador,
Prince Starhemberg, believed that the Sardinian army was as incorruptible and loyal as that of Austria and characterized the government's policy in dealing with agitators as "correct" and "firm." The
Austrian *chargé d'affaires*, Baron Binder, found Piedmont at the end
of 1820 enjoying a perfect calm.[44]

Tension in Piedmont was renewed by student agitation which
broke out at the University of Turin on January 12, 1821. It was
suppressed with considerable severity by the authorities,[45] and
Binder reported that the government also, alerted by this outbreak,
was taking the necessary security measures. As for the nationalist
propaganda spread by the Piedmontese members of the secret sect
of the Federati (*Federazione Italiana*), which called on Italians to
unite and evict the foreigners from Italy, Binder was openly scorn-
ful. "One can hardly persuade oneself," he commented, "that anyone
believes seriously that he can make a village rise by such means." [46]

The Austrian *chargé* soon proved to be a poor prophet. Unknown
to him, a revolutionary conspiracy was already far advanced in Piedmont. The sectarians, chief of whom was Santorre di Santarosa, had
long held secret meetings, using the French Legation at Turin,

[44] Starhemberg (Turin, January 1, May 6, July 19 and 23, August 9,
September 23, and October 4, 1820) to Metternich, *Berichte, Sardinien*, Fasc.
55, Nos. 1, 77, 111, 112, 128, 165, and 173; Binder (Turin, October 29,
November 18 and 24, December 16 and 18, 1820) to Metternich, *ibid.*, Nos.
7B, 10B, 12D, 18, and 19B.

[45] Binder (Turin, January 15, 1821) to Metternich, Berichte, Sardinien,
Fasc. 57, No. 4; Spellanzon, *Storia del Risorgimento*, I, 845–847. A full account
of the student rising is given by Pietro Egidi, "I moti studenteschi di Torino,"
in *La Rivoluzione Piemontese dell'anno 1821* (Vol. XI of *Biblioteca di Storia
Italiana recente (1800–1870)*, 103–165. Egidi's conclusion (pp. 164–165) is
that the rising and its repression helped to stir up agitation and bad feeling
against the government and to encourage the radicals, thus helping to prepare
the way for the March revolt, though the student movements were not connected with it.

[46] Binder (Turin, February 17, 1821) to Metternich, Berichte, Sardinien,
Fasc. 57. See also letters of January 19 and 24, 1821, *ibid.*

under the French envoy, the Duke of Dalberg, as a headquarters.[47] Since 1819 they had been conspiring for a constitution, the more radical of them hoping at the same time for war to throw the Austrians out of Italy. Having established contacts with the liberals in Lombardy led by Count Confalonieri, they looked to Charles Albert, the Prince of Carignan, scion of a cadet branch of the House of Savoy and heir-apparent to the Sardinian throne, as the potential leader of their movement. Charles Albert, French-educated, prone to express liberal and nationalist sentiments in highly imprudent fashion, known to be anti-Austrian, and given to associating with liberals, including Santarosa, had indeed given them reason to hope for his support.[48]

When, therefore, despite the evident coolness of the liberals in Lombardy to their plans and the warnings of moderates that military action now would be disastrous, the conspirators decided in early March 1821 to launch their movement, they took the Prince into their confidence and asked for his help. Their plan, an insanely bold one, called for raising the army in revolt, seizing control of Turin while Victor Emmanuel was away at his castle at Moncalieri, and then confronting the King with a demand for the concession of the Spanish Constitution and a declaration of war upon Austria; Victor Emmanuel, at the head of his troops, would then lead the nation into battle. Charles Albert should have refused, of course, any part of the plan, if not out of loyalty to the King, at least out of good sense. But his ambition was at war with his judgment, each in turn gaining the upper hand. From March 6 to 9 he vacillated between support for the plot, repudiation and betrayal of it, and conditional assent to it. By the ninth Santarosa and the other conspirators were disturbed enough at the Prince's changes of mind to try to postpone the execution of the plot.[49]

The wheels of revolt, however, could no longer be stopped. In the night of March 9-10, the garrison of the fortress of Alexandria rose, seizing the citadel, proclaiming the Spanish Constitution, and setting up a provisional governmental junta. While the government delayed in launching countermeasures, the revolt spread. On March

---

[47] Spellanzon, *Storia del Risorgimento*, I, 843.
[48] *Ibid.*, 842–843, 848–849; Stern, *Geschichte Europas*, II, 164.
[49] Spellanzon, *Storia del Risorgimento*, I, 848–849, 852–854; Stern, *Geschichte Europas*, II, 164–165.

12, revolutionary soldiers seized the citadel of Turin, demanding of the King the Spanish Constitution and war against Austria. This was too much for the aged Victor Emmanuel I. Abdicating his throne in favor of his brother Charles Felix, the Duke of Genevois, he left the country, assigning to Charles Albert, much against his will, the task of carrying on the government as Regent.[50]

This step of Victor Emmanuel's doomed the revolution to failure, for it was only in his name and with his cooperation that the rebels had really hoped to succeed. Charles Albert, losing whatever heart he might have had for the enterprise, was forced by the mob tumult in Turin to proclaim the Spanish Constitution on March 13 and to swear an oath to it on the fifteenth. Secretly, however, he was looking for a way to escape from the thankless role he now had to play. His opportunity came with the proclamation issued in Modena by Charles Felix, condemning the revolution, annulling all its acts, and summoning the Piedmontese army and nation to surrender under threat of Allied intervention. Private orders also came from Charles Felix to Charles Albert, commanding him to leave Turin and join the loyal Piedmontese troops gathered at Novara under General Count della Torre. On the night of March 21, Charles Albert did so, abdicating the Regency, urging the rebels also to submit, and leading his cavalry regiment with him to Novara. Once there, he received a further directive from Charles Felix ordering him to leave the country for Tuscany. Repudiated and despised by both sides, the Prince obeyed.[51]

The news of the Piedmont revolt reached Laibach on March 14, where it caused a great sensation.[52] The danger for Austria was pal-

---

[50] Binder (Turin, March 10 and 12, 1821) to Metternich, Berichte, Sardinien, Fasc. 57, Postscript to No. 22; proclamation of the junta at Alexandria, March 10, 1821, Weisungen und Varia, Sardinien, Fasc. 58; Spellanzon, *Storia del Risorgimento*, I, 854–857; Stern, *Geschichte Europas*, II, 165–167.

[51] Binder (Turin, March 16 and 17, 1821) to Metternich, Berichte, Sardinien, Fasc. 57, Nos. 23A, 23B and Postscript to 23; three letters, Charles Felix (Modena, March 21, 27, and 31, 1821) to Charles Albert, in Bianchi, *Storia della diplomazia*, II, 339–340; Spellanzon, *Storia del Risorgimento*, I, 857–860; Stern, *Geschichte Europas*, II, 167–171.

[52] Metternich insisted that he had long foreseen the revolt and had been warning the Sardinian government about it for three years. Metternich (Laibach, March 19, 1821) to Esterhazy, Weisungen, Grossbritannien, Fasc. 217. He also claims to have received the news calmly on the fourteenth as something

pable. Her Italian provinces were almost denuded of troops because of the Neapolitan campaign then in progress, heightening the danger of a companion revolt in Lombardy-Venetia, where signs of revolutionary plots were also beginning to leak out.[53] Moreover, the revolution in Piedmont, in contrast to that in Naples, had the avowed purpose of driving the Austrians out of Italy and creating an Italian nation.[54] Finally, the revolt revived the danger of French interference in Italy, since France had always taken a special interest in the affairs of Piedmont and the House of Savoy.[55]

The Eastern powers, still assembled at Laibach, reacted promptly and forcefully to this new threat. In a meeting of March 14, Alexander, Francis, and Metternich agreed on three points: first, pushing the operations in Naples to their conclusion as quickly as possible; second, reinforcing the Austrian army in northern Italy with troops drawn from other Austrian provinces, to a total of sixty thousand men; and third, sending ninety thousand Russian troops across the Austrian domains into Italy to aid Austria. Bernstorff, also present at

---

long expected, conferred with the two emperors, reached the decision by that noon on measures to be taken, and then sat down to a peaceful meal. Laibach, March 15, 1821, in Metternich, *Nachgelassene Papiere*, III, 433–434. This account is hard to believe, particularly when one compares it with Gentz's diary for March 14: "This unexpected blow struck me, like all of us, very hard. . . . The great decisions of this evening, principally the march of ninety thousand Russians, had lifted me up completely."—Gentz, *Tagebücher*, II, 396–397.

[53] Count Strassoldo, the Austrian governor of Lombardy, reported signs of trouble after both the outbreak of the Neapolitan revolution and the beginning of the Austrian campaign against Naples. Strassoldo (Milan, August 15, 1820) to Metternich, Weisungen und Varia, Sardinien, Fasc. 56, and February 24 and March 5, 1821, Staatskanzlei: Provinzen: Lombardei-Venezien, Fasc. 7. The fundamental weakness of the Austrian position in Lombardy, Strassoldo pointed out, was that her rule rested solely on armed force. There was, he said, "a total absence of a party . . . which would take a sufficiently strong concern in our favor to compromise itself in case of need against our enemies." Strassoldo (Milan, March 11, 1821) to Metternich, *ibid.*

[54] Binder, who had to flee for his life from Turin on March 20, insisted that the demand for the Spanish Constitution was only a pretext used by the revolutionaries to help whip up frenzy for a war on Austria. Binder (Geneva, March 23, 1821) to Metternich, Berichte, Sardinien, Fasc. 57.

[55] According to Binder, the French *chargé* at Turin, La Tour du Pin, had instigated the whole revolt. Binder (Turin, March 12, Geneva, March 23, and Milan, March 26, 1821) to Metternich, *ibid.*

this meeting, agreed with these decisions, though he was not em-
powered to promise any material aid from Prussia.[56]

These strong measures encountered violent opposition from an
unexpected quarter, the Austrian Finance Minister Prince Stadion.
Already disturbed that the Neapolitan campaign and other Austrian steps in foreign policy might upset his newly-rebuilt and still-
shaky structure of domestic financial solvency and public credit,[57]
Stadion reacted to the news of the Allied decisions with outraged
despair. On hearing of the Piedmontese revolt, he had advised withdrawing the Austrian army from Naples and concentrating all Austria's forces on the defense of her own possessions. This measure,
he argued, would erect a barrier against revolution and disorder and
would also avoid the shameful display of weakness evident in having Austria allow ninety thousand Russian troops to cross her territory to save Austrian provinces in Italy, a resort which could only
result in a permanent extension of Russian power and influence into
Central Europe.[58] The financial implications of the decisions were
even more distressing to the Finance Minister. Hearing rumors of
an impending order from the Emperor augmenting the Austrian
armed forces by one hundred thousand men, Stadion demanded of
Metternich to tell him "for the love of God" just how this was to be
paid for. A repetition of the miracle of the feeding of the five thousand, it stood to reason, would be required to do it. Apparently the
Emperor and Metternich looked upon the Finance Ministry as a
source of never-ending wealth. "With this manner of doing things,"
Stadion stated, "all responsibility on my part ceases." Having already
made many sacrifices of his reputation for the sake of the monarchy,
he refused to take on himself the responsibility for an impending
financial catastrophe.[59]

[56] "Précis de la Conférence tenué chez S. M. L'Empereur d'Autriche le 14
mars 1821," Kongressakten, Laibach, Fasc. 41; Metternich (Laibach, March
17, 1821) to Esterhazy, Weisungen, Grossbritannien, Fasc. 217. Alexander
apparently more than fulfilled his promise. The Austrian *chargé* at St. Petersburg, Count Bombelles, reported that almost the entire Russian Army was
ordered to be ready for mobilization, while one hundred thousand men were
immediately set in march. Bombelles (St. Petersburg, April 1, 1821) to Metternich, Berichte, Russland, Fasc. 31.

[57] Stadion (Vienna, February 26 and March 6, 1821) to Metternich, Kongressakten, Laibach, Fasc. 41.

[58] Stadion (Vienna, March 22, 1821) to Metternich, with supplements, *ibid.*

[59] Stadion (Vienna, April 8, 1821) to Metternich, *ibid.*

Metternich went his way undeterred by these cries of alarm, and events soon vindicated his policy. Although the revolt in Piedmont spread further to Genoa and to Savoy in later March, the abdication and flight of Charles Albert and, still worse, the news of the total defeat of the Neapolitans at Rieti by the Austrian army discouraged the revolutionaries and rendered their cause hopeless. Meanwhile, the Austrian forces in Lombardy under Count Bubna grew rapidly, promising soon to be ready to take the offensive. Realizing this, and hoping to win the forces of General Count della Torre to their side, the constitutional army attacked the loyalist forces near Novara on April 8. The appearance of advance Austrian reinforcements, however, turned the attack into a rout during which the constitutional army rapidly disintegrated. While the leaders of the revolution fled to France or Switzerland, first Alexandria, then Turin, and finally Genoa fell into the hands of the royal Piedmontese and Austrian forces. The Piedmontese revolution had collapsed almost as quickly as it started.[60]

After such successes as these, Metternich had no difficulty defending his policy against Stadion's charges. Not only, he said, had all of Stadion's fears of ulterior designs on the part of Alexander and the extension of Russian influence proved baseless, but even the Austrian finances would not suffer from the Piedmontese revolt. Indeed, the projected occupation of part of Piedmont by Austria might prove a financial blessing. "Our finances will make a profit, for the [Austrian] garrisons on the other side of the Ticino will be charged to the Sardinians even though they could well be counted as belonging to our forces in Lombardy, which ought to remain at our expense." [61]

The suppression of the Piedmontese revolt ended the period of acute danger in Italy, but it by no means eliminated all problems and concerns for Austria. One of these had to do with the new Sardinian king, Charles Felix. Although a divine-right absolutist of the purest persuasion, and thus highly satisfactory on this score of principle, he was much inclined to act as an absolute monarch, inde-

---

[60] Metternich (Laibach, March 24 and 28, 1821) to Binder, Weisungen, Frankreich, Fasc. 346; Metternich (Laibach, April 9, 1821) to Esterhazy, Weisungen, Grossbritannien, Fasc. 217, No. 2; Spellanzon, *Storia del Risorgimento*, I, 860–862; Stern, *Geschichte Europas*, II, 174–175.

[61] Metternich (Laibach, April 21, 1821) to Stadion, Interiora: Korrespondenz, Fasc. 82. Stadion was, as a matter of fact, pacified by the turn of the events. Stadion [Vienna, April 1821] to Metternich, Kongressakten, Laibach, Fasc. 41.

pendently of the alliance. While the Russian ambassador at Turin, Count Mocenigo, had been carrying on secret negotiations with the rebels to try to bring about their voluntary submission (a project Metternich approved simply because it gained time to send Austrian reinforcements in to Lombardy), Charles Felix from his post in Modena issued a proclamation solemnly forbidding any negotiation with rebels. This step, Metternich felt, like Charles Felix' action in banning Charles Albert from his presence, imperiled the common cause and discouraged the loyal army of Della Torre.[62]

For this and other reasons, Metternich and Francis urged Victor Emmanuel I to retract his abdication, arguing that he had been forced into it by the revolution and that, by resuming his throne, he would eliminate the remaining fruits of the revolt in Piedmont. Charles Felix himself was perfectly willing to give way to the old king.[63] When Victor Emmanuel solemnly confirmed his abdication, however, he left the Allies no choice but to deal with Charles Felix as lawful monarch.[64] Fortunately for Metternich, he had already secured a means to exercise a strong influence over the Sardinian policy in the future. In the crisis caused by the revolt, Charles Felix had requested an Austrian force to help him stamp it out, confirming this later with a request for an army of occupation to help him restore order and obedience in his domains. This step meant, of course,

[62] Metternich (Laibach, April 11, 1821) to Binder, Weisungen und Varia, Sardinien, Fasc. 58; Stern, *Geschichte Europas,* II, 173–174. Binder explained Charles Felix' position as follows: "Kings and those who exercise royal authority have only God above them, and he [the King] would rather renounce the exercise of the rights which his birth gave him than to treat with rebels." Binder (Modena, April 13, 1821) to Metternich, Berichte, Sardinien, Fasc. 57. Charles Felix, actually believed that the overthrow of the revolt was entirely due to his own firmness. Charles Felix (Modena, April 16, 1821) to Victor Emmanuel, in Bianchi, *Storia della diplomazia,* II, 340–341.

[63] Metternich (Laibach, April 7, 1821) to Binder, Weisungen und Varia, Sardinien, Fasc. 58; Francis I (Laibach, April 17, 1821) to Victor Emmanuel I, Geheime Korrespondenz, Fasc. IV; Binder (Modena, April 16, 1821) to Metternich, Berichte, Sardinien, Fasc. 57. Charles Felix, in fact, refused to assume the royal title, waiting not only until Victor Emmanuel should confirm his abdication but also until, as he put it, "my subjects show themselves worthy [of me] by a complete expiation of their crime, by a complete and blind submission to my unconditional authority." Charles Felix (Modena, March 21, 1821) to Della Torre, Weisungen und Varia, Sardinien, Fasc. 58.

[64] The abdication was confirmed at Nice on April 19. Binder (Modena, April 23, 1821) to Metternich, Berichte, Sardinien, Fasc. 57.

that willy-nilly the new King could not take a course independent of Austria's in Italy.[65]

In addition to having an occupation force in Piedmont, Metternich felt that the near-disaster of the Piedmontese revolution called for a general tightening of Austria's military hold on Italy. To this end he designated the army of General Frimont in Naples to watch over the Papal States and that of General Bubna in Lombardy to guard Tuscany and the rest of northern Italy, meanwhile encouraging all governments in Italy to strengthen their own authority and to call on Austria for military help against plots or revolution if they needed it.[66]

Meanwhile, the outbreak of still another revolution in another part of Europe threatened momentarily to disturb the course of the Allies in Italy. On March 7, Alexander Ypsilanti, an officer in the Russian army reserve, raised the standard of revolt against the Turkish overlords in the two Danubian principalities of Moldavia and Walachia, calling on all the Greeks and other Christian peoples of the Ottoman Empire to rise with him, and seeking at the same time the support of Tsar Alexander for the liberation of his co-religionists.[67] Once again, however, under Metternich's influence Alexander's loyalty to the alliance and the cause of peace withstood a severe test. The Tsar cashiered Ypsilanti, repudiated and condemned his project, and maintained a resolute hands-off attitude regarding the revolt, leaving it to be stamped out by the Turks themselves.[68] After the revolt spread to Morea, in Greece proper, Metternich redoubled his efforts to convince Alexander that the Greek revolt, whatever its par-

[65] Charles Felix (Modena, April 8, 1821) to Francis I and to Metternich, Geheime Korrespondenz, Fasc. IV; Count Thaon de Revel, envoy of Charles Felix (Laibach, April 14, 1821) to Metternich, *ibid.*

[66] In these military measures, Metternich probably went further than he himself would have cared to go, yet not so far as some of his advisers and subordinates suggested. He rejected suggestions from Vincent and Bubna, for instance, that Austrian troops be placed in the Papal States or Tuscany on the grounds that such actions would have a bad effect on public opinion. Metternich [Laibach, April 1821] to Count Bombelles at Tuscany and to Apponyi at Rome, *ibid.*; Metternich (Laibach, April 27, 1821) to Bubna, *ibid.*; Vincent (Florence, March 24, 1821) to Frimont, Varia, Neapel, Fasc. 54, Postscript to No. 7, with supplement; Metternich (Vienna, June 14, 1821) to Vincent, Weisungen, Frankreich, Fasc. 346, No. 2.

[67] Stern, *Geschichte Europas*, II, 181–182, 199–200.

[68] Metternich (Laibach, March 19, 1821) to Esterhazy, Weisungen, Grossbritannien, Fasc. 217.

ticular circumstances might be, was only a part of the universal effort of the factious of all lands to overthrow the existing order everywhere, to which the sovereigns must respond with complete unity in upholding the legitimate authority—in this case, that of the Turks. Above all, Metternich pleaded, Russia must not permit herself to be drawn into conflict with the Ottoman Empire over the question of Greece. "One village conquered on the soil of Europe," Metternich warned, "is the death-signal for the only system which can still be followed to stamp out the revolutionary hydra." The only safe course for Russia was one confined to upholding existing treaties and executed jointly with the other Allies.[69] Momentarily, at least, Metternich was again successful. The instructions sent from Laibach to all Russian missions bound Alexander to keep faith with all his treaties and to maintain peace with the Turks. Metternich, therefore, was confident that the Danubian and Greek revolts had not broken the firm Austro-Russian accord or tarnished the decisive victory already achieved over the forces of revolution.[70]

On this note of concord the Congress of Laibach finally came to a close. In the final session of May 12, the Eastern powers took one last precaution against revolution—a promise by Russia to maintain 123,000 men on her Austrian border until the next congress to help promote general tranquillity. In order to publicize the actions they had taken since the full Congress ended on February 25, they issued a joint declaration to the world, written mainly by Pozzo di Borgo. In addition, each Court sent separate but similar circular dispatches to all its missions, with special messages to their agents in Italy.[71]

The joint declaration and the circulars to all the missions contain little of interest beyond the usual doctrines on revolution and an elaborate defense of the Allied actions in regard to Piedmont.[72] The

[69] Memoir, Metternich (Laibach, May 7, 1821) to Alexander, "Sur les Affaires de la Grèce," Kongressakten, Laibach, Fasc. 41.

[70] "Copie d'une Circulaire aux Missions de Russie," Laibach, May 13, 1821, *ibid.*; Metternich (Laibach, May 9, 1821) to Esterhazy, Weisungen, Grossbritannien, Fasc. 217 (wherein Metternich affirms, "Our operations have broken the great [revolutionary] machine"). See Chapter VI for Metternich's further dealings with the Greek revolt and the Russo-Turk crisis growing out of it.

[71] "Journal de clôture des Conférences particulières de Laybach," May 12, 1821, Kongressakten, Laibach, Fasc. 40.

[72] "Déclaration" (Laibach, May 12, 1821), *ibid.*; "Dépêche Circulaire" [of Austria, Laibach, May 12, 1821], *ibid.* (also printed in Metternich, *Nachgelassene Papiere*, III, 482–483, 486–488). A copy of the "Déclaration" (in Kon-

circulars to the Italian missions are of more interest, for they reflect an attempt by Metternich to extend his plan for the reorganization of the government at Naples throughout the peninsula. The Austrian circular, first of all, indicated that this same sort of governmental "reform" which would be executed at Naples was also needed in Piedmont, and evidenced the intention to set up in Sardinia a ministerial conference of Allied envoys, like that at Naples, to advise the King on the reorganization of his government. Metternich also heartily recommended his plan and its underlying principles to all the other Italian governments for study and adoption, so that they might at the coming congress at Florence report their reforms to the Allies. Russia, to be sure, admitted in her circular that she had no right to request governmental reorganization from the Italian states. Nevertheless, in view of Austria's special position and interests, she supported Austria's right to call for such reorganization. Besides, the Russian note pointed out, the Italian states should recognize the great "advantage of opposing union to union and a common system to common attacks." The Prussian dispatch not only supported the Austrian call for a general reorganization but made it clear that the "reforms" it advocated simply involved strengthening royal authority, tightening police power, and repressing all agitation and political movement.[73]

"Reforms," however, even of the nature contemplated by the Prussians, were not what Metternich was most interested in achieving in Italy. It was still more important to him to establish the right of the Allied sovereigns (i.e., of the Eastern powers) to exercise a general supervision over all the governments in Italy. In a memoir drawn up at the Congress and designed, no doubt, for Alexander's perusal, Metternich made a strenuous attempt to establish such a right, using arguments of characteristically specious ingenuity. First, he said, the Allied monarchs possessed this right of supervision because they had rescued the Italian princes from revolution, and were therefore responsible for those whom they had rescued. The Italian princes,

---

gressakten, Laibach, Fasc. 41) bears the notation "Rédaction Mr. Pozzo di Borgo."

[73] "Circulaire aux Missions Autrichiennes en Italie," Laibach, May 12, 1821, Kongressakten, Laibach, Fasc. 40; "Circulaire aux Ministres [Russian] de l'Empereur en Italie," Laibach, May 12, 1821, *ibid.*; "Circulaire du Cabinet de Berlin aux Missions Prussiennes en Italie," Berlin, May 26, 1821, *ibid.*

Metternich contended, could not have stood by themselves against the onslaught of revolution; they owed their liberty and independence to the Allied sovereigns. "This being the case," he proceeded, "there is born from this combination certain reciprocal rights and duties for the liberating powers and the states which were liberated." What were these reciprocal rights and duties? The princes of Italy had the right and duty to strengthen their administrations; the powers had the right and duty to see that they did it.[74]

The Allied sovereigns possessed this right of supervision over the Italian princes on yet another ground—paradoxically, on the principle of the complete independence and sovereignty of each individual state. The argument by which Metternich deduces this remarkable conclusion deserves to be given in his very words:

They [the Allied monarchs] have proved, to the princes of Italy as well as to all of Europe, that the absolute independence of states is sacred to them. While respecting the independence of others, however, they have the right to demand that their own independence be equally respected; and this would not be the case if the Monarchs should be deprived by false and pernicious measures on the part of the governments of Italy of the possibility of seeing repose follow in place of movement.[75]

His argument may be summarized as follows: Every state is absolutely sovereign in its internal affairs. But this implies that every state must do nothing to interfere in the internal affairs of any other. However, any false or pernicious step taken by any state in its internal affairs may disturb the repose of another state, and this consequent disturbance of another state's repose constitutes an interference in that state's internal affairs. Therefore, every state—or rather, every sovereign of a great power——has the duty, in the name of the sacred right of independence of every state, to supervise the governments of smaller states and to prevent them from taking false and pernicious steps in their internal affairs.

This was no theoretical point with Metternich. What he wanted first of all was the same sort of control for Austria over Piedmont that he had arranged for Austria at Naples. As he pointed out, in Naples this principle of Allied supervision of the government was

---

[74] "Points à arrêter relativement à la conduite à suivre vis-à-vis les Princes d'Italie" [Laibach, early May 1821], Kongressakten, Laibach, Fasc. 41.
[75] *Ibid.*

already established; the next place for its immediate application should be Piedmont. There, said Metternich, "it is due alone to the efforts of the Powers that the King is able to reign; it is today up to the Powers to know the thoughts of the Sovereign, to judge them, to support them, and to control them." [76]

With the other states of Italy the supervision should be no less firm, though less direct. The Allies, always proceeding jointly, should send strong statements not only to Ferdinand and Charles Felix, calling upon them to observe the governmental bases decreed at Laibach, but also to Rome and Florence, demanding administrative reform and action against the sects. Wide latitude of action should be given to the commanders of the armies of occupation, and all the Italian Courts should be given a stern warning that the requirement to submit their programs of administrative reform to the next congress was no idle word. Without real action on their part, they could not expect future Allied aid.[77] Finally, as the best way of carrying out the desired program, Metternich contended, "it is necessary to form for that effect a point *of information, of entente,* and of joint *decision*"—a center for "true moral action." Here, in thin disguise, was Metternich's old plan of the Italian League cropping up again. The pattern is clear: first, the settlement of common forms of government on all the states, according to Metternich's formula of provincialism and separation of local and central governmental functions within the framework of absolute monarchy; then the establishment of a principle of Allied supervision of these governments, something like the organization of Germany under the aegis of the great powers at Vienna; then the founding of a central investigation committee for Italy like that in Germany (Metternich specified that the Italian information center—which could best be established at Milan, of course—should be patterned after the German center at Mainz); and finally, at some future date, the conclusion of an Italian League under Austrian presidency, which would stabilize Italy, prevent political movement, and assure Austrian hegemony forever.[78]

The arguments, for once, failed to convince Alexander. He had not so completely forgotten his erstwhile concern for the welfare of

[76] *Ibid.*
[77] *Ibid.*
[78] "Apperçu sur les affaires d'Italie et sur quelques remèdes à employer," Laibach, May 15, 1821, *ibid.* The memoir is in Metternich's hand.

the small states and his suspicion of Austrian designs as to agree to this scheme. The center of information and the Italian League remained projects only. This setback, however, could not spoil the real Austrian triumphs at Laibach. In Naples, in Piedmont, and even in the Balkan peninsula the Austrian policy had triumphed. By conferring upon his Foreign Minister upon his return from Laibach the title of House, Court, and State Chancellor (an honor borne by no other Austrian official since Kaunitz), Francis I paid tribute to Metternich's remarkable successes.[79] How durable these successes would be, only the future would reveal.

[79] Stern, *Geschichte Europas*, II, 180–181.

CHAPTER V

THE RESTORATION IN
NAPLES AND PIEDMONT

Knowing that the policy decreed at Laibach would be put to its severest test when the reconstructed government was set up at Naples, Metternich had, as we have seen, made the plan of reconstruction his own personal work and had with typical care and attention to detail hedged it about with every possible precaution. His professed aim was to avoid the twin dangers of representative government and arbitrary rule, and to achieve what he liked to call "temperate monarchy." [1] No connected account of the actions of the restored government at Naples need be given here,[2] but it is of interest to see how far Metternich's diplomacy achieved its acknowledged aims, and by what means.

[1] Metternich (Laibach, March 10, 1821) to Stadion, Interiora: Korrespondenz, Fasc. 82; Metternich (Laibach, March 5, 1821) to Esterhazy, Weisungen, Grossbritannien, Fasc. 217, No. 2. In the letter to Stadion, Metternich described the reconstruction project as one which had received "all my solicitude" from the very beginning, and commented: "The King has had sufficient difficulty submitting to our views. . . . I send you enclosed the protocol . . . which presents as a spontaneous proposition of the King what is [in reality] our idea." The letter in the archives, from which I have quoted, differs slightly in word order from the version printed in Metternich, *Nachgelassene Papiere*, III, 454–458.

[2] A good brief account is in Spellanzon, *Storia del Risorgimento*, II, 106–122. Two other important sources are Ruggero Moscati, *Il regno delle Due Sicilie e l'Austria: Documenti dal marzo 1821 al novembre 1830*, and Walter Maturi, *Il Principe di Canosa*. After finishing this chapter, I was finally able to find the fullest account of the Neapolitan restoration, Angelo Filipuzzi's "La restaurazione nel Regno delle Due Sicilie dopo il Congresso di Lubiana," *Annali Triestini di diritto economia e politica*, XI (1940), 161–206, 230–282. However, Filipuzzi's account proved to be based on the same sources as mine, and confirmed the views I had already formed.

From the outset Metternich's plans ran into serious obstacles. The first of these arose from the manner in which King Ferdinand chose to exercise his power of appointment. This was a power which, according to Metternich's theory, could not be infringed or restricted without destroying the institution of monarchy itself. Unfortunately for Metternich, Ferdinand made a very regrettable use of this imprescriptible right. The provisional government which he appointed to serve at Naples until his return was composed, as A'Court described it, entirely of ignorant, prejudiced Ultras. Hardly a man of them was under seventy years of age, and not one possessed the energy or intelligence to run a village.[3]

Already at Laibach Metternich could not have been unaware, of course, of the character and disposition of Ferdinand, but he had hoped that the ministerial council set up to advise the King—consisting of Vincent, Pozzo di Borgo, Blacas, and Kayserfeld (representing Prussia)—would have a salutary influence over him. In its very first session on March 14 in Florence, however, the council discovered that the King and Prince Alvaro Ruffo, who represented him, had gotten completely out of hand. Ferdinand was determined not to return to Naples until the rebellious kingdom had undergone a purge at the hands of his provisional regime. Ruffo not only backed him to the limit at the conference but sent off this same day a letter to Metternich protesting against the "interference" of the Allied ministers in this decision of the King's free will.[4]

At further conferences the Allied ministers pleaded with Ferdinand for moderation, for an amnesty, and above all for a speedy return to his own domains—all to no effect. The King had been reluctant enough to leave Laibach, and was panic-stricken at the news of the Piedmontese revolt; nothing could induce him to leave Florence.[5] By March 19, Vincent felt obliged to appeal to the two em-

---

[3] See the summaries of A'Court's reports from Naples in Esterhazy (London, March 21 and 22, 1821) to Metternich, Berichte, Grossbritannien, Fasc. 214. Ficquelmont's opinion on the provisional regime was much the same. Ficquelmont (Naples, March 29, 1821) to Metternich, Berichte, Neapel, Fasc. 51, No. 12A.

[4] "Journal des Conférences," No. 1, Florence, March 14, 1821, Kongressakten, Florenz, Rom, Neapel, Fasc. 42; Ruffo (Florence, March 14, 1821) to Metternich, Varia, Neapel, Fasc. 53.

[5] "Journal des Conférences," Nos. 3–7, Florence, March 15 to 23, 1821, Kongressakten, Florenz, Rom, Neapel, Fasc. 42; Ruffo [Laibach, early April 1821] to Metternich, Varia, Neapel, Fasc. 53.

perors to help him overcome Ferdinand's culpable timidity. By March 24 all three of the chief ambassadors—Vincent, Blacas, and Pozzo di Borgo—had threatened to leave unless Ferdinand would at least move to Rome, while Vincent complained bitterly to Metternich of Ruffo's ill will and bad influence.[6]

The conferees at Laibach did their best to overcome this crisis. Alexander and Francis, as Vincent had requested, dispatched admonitory letters to Ferdinand,[7] while Metternich rebuked Ruffo sharply for the King's stubbornness and cowardice.[8] Metternich also immediately dispatched Lebzeltern as a special envoy to Florence to prevail upon Ferdinand to return to Naples [9] (this was, of course, after the complete submission of the country to the Austrian army). Soon Lebzeltern himself was near despair at overcoming "the opinionated and invincible resistances" of the King.[10] Ferdinand replied to the Lebzeltern mission, in fact, by sending Ruffo as his own special envoy back to Laibach on the pretext that he did not understand precisely what it was the Allied sovereigns desired of him and needed more information directly from them. Ruffo, to the intense exasperation of the ministers at Florence, wrote back to his sovereign that he had gained the consent, if not the adhesion, of the Allies to Ferdinand's plans for delaying his re-entry into Naples, "and that," he said, "suffices us." [11] The King's determination not to go back seemed so strong that Metternich was obliged to make serious plans about

[6] Vincent (Florence, March 19 and 24, 1821) to Metternich, Varia, Neapel, Fasc. 54.

[7] "Journal des Conférences," No. 8, Florence, March 28, 1821, Kongressakten, Florenz, Rom, Neapel, Fasc. 42; Francis (Laibach, March 22, 1821) to Ferdinand, Hofkorrespondenz, Neapel, Fasc. 32.

[8] Telling Ruffo flatly that the only reason for the King's hesitation and obstruction was fear, and demanding to know how Ferdinand expected to be restored to his throne and to rule if he would not return to his kingdom, Metternich finally exploded in exasperation, "Good God, if I were King of Naples, what would you not see me do!" Metternich (Laibach, March 29, 1821) to Ruffo, Varia, Neapel, Fasc. 53.

[9] Metternich (Laibach, March 29, 1821) to Ficquelmont, Berichte und Weisungen, Neapel, Fasc. 52.

[10] Lebzeltern (Florence, April 5, 1821) to Metternich, Varia, Neapel, Fasc. 54.

[11] Report of letters of Ruffo (Laibach, April 10 and 11, 1821) to Ferdinand, in "Journal des Conférences," No. 18, Rome, April 19, 1821, Kongressakten, Florenz, Rom, Neapel, Fasc. 42.

what the Allies should do if they simply could never get him back
into his kingdom at all.[12]

Little by little, however, the King finally yielded. On April 7,
Lebzeltern, aided by all the pressure exerted by his colleagues at
Florence and superiors at Laibach, wrung from Ferdinand a promise that he would leave for Rome on April 14, and then go to Naples
on April 25. The first part of this promise was kept, but Lebzeltern's
skepticism that the latter half would be, soon proved justified.[13] For
Ferdinand now proved recalcitrant about leaving Rome, and it required renewed pleas, threats, and finally the actual withdrawal of
Vincent and Pozzo di Borgo from the ministerial conference to force
his hand.[14] On April 24, Ruffo and Baron Frilli, who had come from
Naples as a representative of the provisional government, reported
that the King would leave for his capital in ten or twelve days, if
his health permitted.[15] This condition made further delays possible,
until finally Ficquelmont, who had abandoned his hopeless dealings
with the provisional regime at Naples to replace Vincent at Ferdinand's side, succeeded in pinning the King down to a definite promise that he would return to Naples on May 15, which he did.[16]

Ferdinand's protracted absence from his domains for more than

[12] Metternich, considering that Allied inactivity in such a case would be
disastrous, planned to give Ferdinand the following alternative: Either he
would have to give unlimited powers to his government at Naples to rule the
country and invite the Allied special ambassadors to go there and serve as an
advisory conference to it, or he would have to form a ministerial council of his
own at Rome, again advised by the Allied conference of ambassadors, which
would make the decrees to be executed by the authorities in Naples. "In this
case," Metternich stipulated, "the general-in-chief of the army at Naples, and
in case of his absence, Count Ficquelmont, authorized to replace him, would
necessarily have to be permanent members of the Government at Naples."
Metternich (Laibach, April 12, 1821) to Vincent, Varia, Neapel, Fasc. 54.

[13] Lebzeltern (Florence, April 13, 1821) to Metternich, *ibid.*; "Journal des
Conférences," No. 13, Florence, April 7, 1821, Kongressakten, Florenz, Rom,
Neapel, Fasc. 42.

[14] Russian Cabinet (Laibach, April 11 and 22, 1821) to Pozzo di Borgo,
Varia, Neapel, Fasc. 54; Metternich (Laibach, April 21, 1821) to Vincent,
ibid.; Vincent (Rome, April 23, 1821) to Metternich, *ibid.*

[15] "Journal des Conférences," Nos. 19 and 20, Rome, April 23 and 24, 1821,
Kongressakten, Florenz, Rom, Neapel, Fasc. 42. The Neapolitan envoys excused
the delay with the ridiculous pretext that the King would have announced his
date of departure long before had not dispatches from Laibach led him to send
a courier there to seek further information from the Allied sovereigns.

[16] Ficquelmont (Rome, May 1, and Naples, May 15, 1821) to Metternich,
Berichte, Neapel, Fasc. 51, Nos. 20 and 24.

two months after the entry of the Austrian troops he was supposed
to follow, might, under some circumstances, have been of little significance. Indeed, the whole farcical episode of three great powers,
two emperors, and a whole host of ambassadors and plenipotentiaries having to force this petty Bourbon prince back onto his throne
would provide only comic relief for the historian were it not for
one fact: During Ferdinand's absence, intolerable misgovernment
reigned at Naples. The fault lay not only in the wretchedly incompetent men the King had appointed to run his provisional government, but also in the character of the King himself, whose decrees
reflected his alternate moods of fear and vengefulness. The measures
he ordered or sanctioned for Naples included declaring martial law,
providing for special military courts for the entire country, setting
up local committees of investigation to ferret out revolutionary sentiment and sedition everywhere, providing the death penalty for
bearing arms (this in a nation where brigandage had flourished for
centuries, and even peaceable citizens had to have means to defend
themselves), passing death sentences on apprehended revolutionaries without trial, and giving the police unlimited powers of search
and confiscation. The Allied ministers condemned these measures
vigorously, and pleaded for moderation, but without effect.[17] Ruffo
defended all the measures as necessary, reminding the envoys of a
truth that Metternich had often stated: only the King could decide
on the real needs of his country and people.[18] Further protests by
the conference against arbitrary arrests and despotic decrees were
similarly fruitless.[19] Ferdinand did not hesitate to continue to appeal
to Austria for aid—he requested from four to five thousand additional Austrian troops in mid-April to serve as an occupation force

---

[17] "Journal des Conférences," No. 17, Rome, April 19, 1821, Kongressakten,
Florenz, Rom, Neapel, Fasc. 42. The ambassadors called the King's measures,
among other things, "excessive," "too severe," "too sweeping," "a measure
worthy to alarm the security of everyone," "a gratuitous menace" attended by
"grave consequences," designed to spread alarm "against the domestic peace
even of peaceable subjects." "Such a tribunal [the military court]," they said,
"can be regarded as capable of every violence and every injustice." Pronouncing
upon the whole plan "the highest disapprobation on the part of the Allied
sovereigns," the envoys declared that it smacked of "a sanguinary vigor which
it is far from his [Ferdinand's] heart and principles to wish to exercise." *Ibid.*

[18] "Note Verbale," read by Ruffo at session No. 19, "Journal des Conférences," Rome, April 23, 1821, *ibid.*

[19] Session No. 21, April 26, 1821, *ibid.*

for Sicily and to repress renewed disturbances on the island [20]—but he showed no more signs of heeding the Allied remonstrances when they came from Metternich than when they originated in the ambassadors' conference.[21] The net result was that the ministerial council broke up on April 28, ostensibly because the date had then been set for the King's return to Naples, but actually because the envoys and their masters, especially those from Austria and Russia, had come to realize that they were wasting their time in talking to Ferdinand and Ruffo.[22]

Meanwhile, Ficquelmont had been dealing, or rather contending, with the provisional regime at Naples. His chief contact was with Marquis de Circello, eighty-three years of age, who at the outbreak of the revolution had counseled Ferdinand to give in momentarily to the revolutionaries and to grant a constitution only that he might repudiate the promise later and restore the old order. During the revolution Circello had kept in touch with Metternich and Ferdinand by maintaining a secret correspondence with Ruffo and had greeted the Allied decrees of Laibach with rapture. The King, who had followed Circello's advice and repudiated all his vows (albeit tardily and with Allied help) at Laibach, then rewarded Circello for his sound counsel, unimpeachable loyalty to the King's person, and obsequious flattery by making him head of his government.[23]

Unfortunately, however admirably suited to the post Ferdinand found Circello, Ficquelmont discovered him to be utterly without

---

[20] Session No. 16, April 18, 1821, *ibid.* The request was received by the ministers with the acid comment that the King had not been in his kingdom for so long that it was difficult to see how he could know what was needed there.

[21] Metternich (Laibach, April 28 and May 3, 1821) to Ruffo, Varia, Neapel, Fasc. 53. As if the misgovernment in Naples were not enough, Ferdinand and Ruffo began to entertain wild ideas in foreign policy as well. Ruffo, for instance, urged Metternich to meet the menace of the Piedmontese revolt by having two hundred thousand Russian soldiers sent to Piedmont and to the Prussian border, while Austrian troops should occupy all the rest of Italy. Ferdinand advised Vincent that he wished to break diplomatic relations with revolutionary Spain. Ruffo (Laibach [early April 1821]) to Metternich, Varia, Neapel, Fasc. 53; "Journal des Conférences," No. 9, Florence, March 28, 1821, Kongressakten, Florenz, Rom, Neapel, Fasc. 42.

[22] "Journal des Conférences," No. 24, Rome, April 28, 1821, Kongressakten, Florenz, Rom, Neapel, Fasc. 42.

[23] Ficquelmont (Naples, March 29, 1821) to Metternich, Berichte, Neapel, Fasc. 51, No. 12A; Circello (Naples, February 8, 1821) to Ferdinand, Kongressakten, Laibach, Fasc. 41; Romani, *Neapolitan Revolution*, 58–59.

talents or abilities for governing. Neither he nor his fellows could be moved to any firm, consistent course of action. Whatever law and order existed at Naples was due solely to the presence of Austrian troops. The only action which the provisional government was capable of was arbitrary and illegal.[24] Prince Antonio di Canosa, a reckless Neapolitan Don Quixote of reaction whose position as Minister of Police made him the most powerful man in the kingdom, conceived it as his and the government's duty not simply to punish those directly responsible for the revolution (as Metternich wanted),[25] but rather to destroy Jacobinism, Muratism, Carbonarism, and constitutionalism as the works of Satan, regardless of what laws might stand in his way. His program, designed to exorcise the demons from Naples through a white terror, enjoyed the wholehearted support of King Ferdinand.[26] Ficquelmont, who, ironically enough, had earlier advocated Canosa as the man of the hour needed at Naples,[27] quickly became disillusioned. Even before he began his main task of advising the King, he had concluded that the basic problem of Naples lay not in the revolution, but in the men who ran the kingdom and whose conduct had made revolution possible. As he wrote to Metternich: "There are great difficulties to conquer, my Prince; they are not in affairs, but in men; the reasons which have produced the revolution are the same which today make the remedy difficult." [28] The trouble, said Ficquelmont, was that there was so little talent among the men to whom the King gave power that effective administration was impossible. Ferdinand's "principles of exclusion" (he refused to use anyone who was tainted by the revolution or even with service under Murat) ruled out almost

[24] Ficquelmont (Naples, March 29, April 1, 5, and 24, 1821) to Metternich, Berichte, Neapel, Fasc. 51, Nos. 12A, 13, 14, and 18 with supplements.

[25] Metternich (Vienna, July 6, 1821) to Ruffo, in Moscati, *Il regno delle Due Sicilie*, I, 44–51.

[26] Canosa (Naples, April 17, 20, and 21, 1821) to Ferdinand I, and Ferdinand (Rome, April 20, 1821) to Canosa, in *ibid.*, I, 4-8, 10–16, 18; Maturi, *Canosa*, 154–161. Francis, Duke of Calabria, in what Maturi (p. 166) calls perhaps the only noble act of his life, attempted to shield his moderate colleagues in the revolution from Canosa's vengeance.

[27] Maturi, *Canosa*, 147, 150–151. Incidentally, although Metternich came to deplore Canosa's imprudent and violent methods, he always credited him with good principles and intentions (*ibid.*, 133, 337).

[28] Ficquelmont (Rome, April 30, 1821) to Metternich, Berichte, Neapel, Fasc. 51, No. 19A.

everyone who was competent. Furthermore, said Ficquelmont, "The King in no way inspires confidence in anyone; he is judged here in an irrevocable manner, and many individuals who would not be included in the exceptions [Ferdinand's exclusions] hold themselves aloof." [29]

It was not, then, with great confidence that Ficquelmont, on his return from Rome, took up the task of heading the ministerial conferences at Naples. Nevertheless, with the aid of his associates (Blacas, for France; Chevalier D'Oubril, for Russia; and Count Truchsess, for Prussia), he made a determined effort to change the course of things in the kingdom. The conference held forty-three official sessions (plus many unofficial and private ones) between May 1821 and April 1822, the majority of these coming in 1821. At most of the meetings Circello was also present. It would be fruitless to review these sessions; one can, however, indicate fairly well the nature and extent of the conference's activity. Among other things, the ambassadors delved into the following affairs: the proclamations and decrees to be made by the King in reorganizing the government, and particularly his delay in convoking a Council of State or setting up the *Consulta;* the problem of gaining better personnel for the government; the questions of amnesty and dealing with political prisoners; police personnel and procedure; the matter of arbitrary arrests and extraordinary tribunals; the committees of inquiry; judicial procedure, in particular that of the trial of ninety-nine insurgents in the camp of Monteforte; the organization of the gendarmerie; the method of disbanding the old army and organizing the new one; the manner of dealing with the sects; the disbanding of the militia; the questions of occupation forces and indemnity; and questions of finance, taxation, and tariff rates. To carry out its duties, the conference felt free to summon and interpellate the highest officers of the government, including Circello, Canosa, Minister of Grace and Justice Di Giorgio, War Minister General Fardella, and

[29] Ficquelmont (Naples, May 16, 1821) to Metternich, *ibid.* As a partial answer to the problem Ficquelmont suggested that they make some use of the Duke of Calabria in the administration; he believed that he had certain talents and energy which his father totally lacked. Metternich vetoed this proposal unequivocally out of suspicion of Francis' bad principles and ambition. The King, he said, was to be protected from his son's influence. See his secret letter to Ficquelmont, Vienna, July 21, 1821, Berichte und Weisungen, Neapel, Fasc. 52.

the Duke of Calabria. The conference demanded documents and detailed information for study and laid proclamations and projects of decrees before the King for his approval. In short, it intervened in every possible way with every possible pressure into virtually every conceivable internal affair of the Neapolitan government.[30]

The results could not be termed encouraging. Although the influence of the Allied ministers undoubtedly served to curb the worst excesses and stupidities of the reconstructed government and to prevent a repetition of Ferdinand's restoration of 1799, it did little to accomplish the aims decreed at Laibach. The sessions were one long series of complaints and denunciations from the very first session on. Besides the abuses already noted and protested against by the conference at Florence and Rome, the envoys found the King's promised amnesty too long delayed and then, when it was finally issued on May 30, 1821, so inadequate as to leave anyone who had taken any part in the revolution or the constitutional regime in danger of loss of life or property.[31] Extreme measures were continually proposed. The Duke of Canosa, for example, in addition to the arbitrary arrests, wanted unlimited police powers of search and confiscation to help restore order, while the Duke of Calabria, at Ferdinand's instance, proposed that Naples exile two thousand of its reputed revolutionaries on Austrian soil.[32] The King's conduct displayed alternate spells of rashness and inaction. On the one hand, he wished to summarily dismiss his entire army, stripping everyone of rank, uniform, and honors (the conference argued that this would create a whole new group of malcontents in the kingdom); on the other hand, he delayed an orderly disbanding of the army until the interminable investigations of the committees of inquiry would be finished.[33] The conferees had to protest as much against laxness and

[30] "Journals des Conférences," Nos. 1–43, May 14, 1821, to April 10, 1822, Kongressakten, Florenz, Rom, Neapel, Fasc. 42.

[31] *Ibid.*, Nos. 3, 9, 11, 31, Naples, May 18, June 27, July 11, December 31, 1821; Ficquelmont (Naples, June 6, 1821) to Metternich, Berichte, Neapel, Fasc. 51, No. 29A.

[32] "Journal des Conférences," Nos. 9, 10, 11, 13, Naples, June 27, July 4, 11, and 25, 1821, Kongressakten, Florenz, Rom, Neapel, Fasc. 42; Ficquelmont (Naples, June 28, 1821) to Metternich, Berichte, Neapel, Fasc. 51, No. 34A (in which Ficquelmont reports that the number of exiles was expected by some to exceed nine thousand).

[33] "Journal des Conférences," Nos. 5, 7, 8, 19, Naples, May 21 and 30, June 9, September 5, 1821, Kongressakten, Florenz, Rom, Neapel, Fasc. 42; Ficquel-

stupidity as against harshness and arbitrary action. The Carbonari, for example, were not suppressed, and the Duke of Canosa's attempts to make them ridiculous failed utterly to curb their resurgence of activity, while the Royalist sect of the Calderari was positively encouraged.[34] The new regime's censorship decree was bad, according to Ficquelmont, not because of its laudable principle of suppression but because of its incomprehensible wording and its stupid administration (characterized initially by burning the books of Voltaire, D'Alembert, and Rousseau).[35] The King simply would not be persuaded that he had to employ Muratists in his administration.[36] Canosa, whom the Allied ministers finally forced the King, much against his will, to dismiss in mid-July, committed such blunders as releasing numbers of revolutionary suspects on the day of the patron saint of the Carbonari, and arresting the general with whom Ficquelmont had arranged the occupation of Naples.[37] Perhaps most embarrassing of all was the trial of the ninety-nine insurgents accused of revolt at the camp of Monteforte. The case dragged on in confusion, delay, and general disorderliness far into 1822, long surviving the conference itself, which broke up convinced that the trial had succeeded only in gravely compromising the King, scandalizing Europe, and rendering the governments of Naples and the Eastern powers ridiculous.[38] The incompetence and blundering in

---

mont (Naples, June 28, September 10, 1821) to Metternich, Berichte, Neapel, Fasc. 51, Nos. 34A and 48B, and November 17, 1821, Berichte und Weisungen, Neapel, Fasc. 52, No. 57A.

[34] "Journal des Conférences," Nos. 9 and 11, Naples, June 27 and July 11, 1821, Kongressakten, Florenz, Rom, Neapel, Fasc. 42; Ficquelmont (Naples, June 13, 1821) to Metternich, Berichte, Neapel, Fasc. 51, No. 30A.

[35] Ficquelmont (Naples, June 6 and 13, 1821) to Metternich, Berichte, Neapel, Fasc. 51, Nos. 29D and 30A.

[36] Ficquelmont (Naples, June 13, 1821) to Metternich, *ibid.*, No. 30A.

[37] Ficquelmont (Naples, July 5 and 20, 1821) to Metternich, *ibid.*, Nos 36 and 39A.

[38] "Journal des Conférences," Nos. 26, 29, 31, 34, 37, 43, Naples, October 17, November 21, December 12, 1821, January 17, February 13, April 10, 1822, Kongressakten, Florenz, Rom, Neapel, Fasc. 42; Ficquelmont (Naples, December 3, 10, and 20, 1821) to Metternich, Berichte, und Weisungen, Neapel, Fasc. 52, Nos. 58A, with supplements, 59A, and 61; January 1 and 16, May 25, 1822, Berichte, Neapel, Fasc. 55. The worst embarrassment was the discovery in December 1821 that the King had on June 6, 1821, secretly confirmed his amnesty of August 8, 1820—which meant that all the accused ought to be set free. The Allied envoys tried to persuade Ferdinand to repudiate both the August 8 and the June 6 decrees, but he and the govern-

the government reflected itself in increasing unrest and turbulence in the country; disturbances grew, especially in Sicily, where a revolutionary plot had to be suppressed by Lieutenant General Count Wallmoden and the Austrian troops in January 1822.[39]

The constant pressure exerted on the government and the reiterated complaints of the ministerial conference inevitably caused tension and friction between the Neapolitan government and the Allied advisors. At first the Neapolitan authorities showed themselves outwardly docile enough. Ferdinand professed himself eager to fulfill all the desires of the Allies. The proclamation issued by him on May 26 was word for word a translation of that sent by Metternich from Laibach, and Ficquelmont himself drew up for the King the Preamble to be attached to his proposed decree disbanding the Neapolitan army.[40] Indeed, there was some difficulty at first persuading Ferdinand and Circello that they should take the trouble to make it appear that the decrees and resolutions they issued were the products of the King's will, rather than the work of the Allies.[41]

Getting words translated into action, however, was another matter. The most important parts of the Laibach plan remained unexecuted,

---

ment decided to proceed as if they did not exist, with the result that in January 1822 the Court of Cassation threw out the trial on account of irregularities, and the whole proceedings had to be begun anew. At the end of May 1822 no one knew exactly where the trial stood.

[39] Ficquelmont (Naples, July 15, August 17, and September 18, 1821) to Metternich, Berichte, Neapel, Fasc. 51, Nos. 38, 43C, and 50C; October 24, 1821, Berichte und Weisungen, Neapel, Fasc. 52; De Menz (Naples, January 28 and 30, 1822) to Metternich, Berichte, Neapel, Fasc. 55, Nos. 5 and 6A. Ferdinand, determined to make no concessions to the Sicilians, resisted Austrian and British urgings to grant them some shadow of the ancient Sicilian Parliament as a purely advisory body. The main cause of the revolt in Sicily, however, seems to have been economic distress.

[40] Ficquelmont (Rome, May 9, Naples, May 19 and 24, June 6, 1821) to Metternich, Berichte, Neapel, Fasc. 51, Nos. 23, unnumbered, 27A with supplements, and 29B.

[41] Rather than to summon an extraordinary council of advisers to "deliberate" the Laibach plan of reorganization, Ferdinand and Circello wanted simply to publish the plan immediately. Ficquelmont protested as follows: "It is essential to preserve the appearance that the mode of government to introduce would be the result of the discussions of the extraordinary council. . . . To publish the work of Laibach without the convocation of the extraordinary council would mean losing that advantage; it would mean indicating in all too plain a fashion that the King had imported it already made, and to deprive it thus of the advantage of appearing to be the result of Neapolitan wisdom." Ficquelmont (Naples, May 19, 1821) to Metternich, *ibid.*

while, vexed by Allied pressure, Ferdinand and his ministers began
to yearn to exercise some of that liberty of thought and action so
stressed at Troppau and Laibach.[42] Canosa loudly blamed the interference of the Allied envoys for his dismissal, a contention whose
truth Ficquelmont's vehement protests could not disguise.[43] Ferdinand balked at many of the conference's remonstrances. Circello
persisted in regarding the Council of State proposed at Laibach as
simply "a phantom," defending himself the principle of the independence of individual councilors. The Allied envoys accused the
Neapolitan ministers of leaking secrets of the ministerial conference
out to the public, and making it seem as if the King was not free to
do as he wished; tension between the ministry and the Allied conference grew daily.[44]

By mid-July of 1821, Ficquelmont was ready to give up the existing regime as hopeless. "A false system," "false measures," "weakness of character and intelligence," and even "immorality," according to him, were its characteristics. "We must, my Prince," he wrote
Metternich, "fight very much more here against the friends of the
King who serve him badly than against his enemies who are now
disarmed." Nothing better could be expected, he pointed out, of a
ministry composed of Circello, aged eighty-three and correspondingly feeble; Cardinal Fabrizio Ruffo, six years his junior but equally
senile, "who does nothing and says nothing"; Prince Scilla, "a man
devoid of ability"; the Duke of Gualtieri, alike "without assets of
mind or character"; and the remainder, subalterns inspired only by
selfish ambition.[45] The only remedy, Ficquelmont argued in a long,
formal memoir to Metternich in September, was to make a clean
sweep of all the incumbents and replace them with better men,
whether the King liked it or not:

[42] Already by mid-June Ferdinand was complaining about the interference
of the Austrians in everything. Ferdinand (Naples, June 13, 1821) to Ruffo,
in Moscati, *Il regno delle Due Sicilie,* I, 38–39.

[43] Ficquelmont (Naples, July 25, 1821) to Metternich, Berichte, Neapel,
Fasc. 51, No. 40A. It is interesting, however, to note that in a letter to
Ferdinand of August 21, 1821, Ruffo indicates that he and Metternich were
opposed to the ouster of Canosa.—Moscati, *Il regno delle Due Sicilie,* I, 66–67.

[44] Ficquelmont (Naples, August 4 and 16, 1821) to Metternich, *ibid.,* No.
43A; "Journal des Conférences," No. 12, with supplement, Naples, July 20,
1821, Kongressakten, Florenz, Rom, Neapel, Fasc. 42.

[45] Ficquelmont (Naples, July 15, 1821) to Metternich, Berichte, Neapel,
Fasc. 51, No. 38.

It will be difficult to make up the ministry in this manner; the King may have an invincible repugnance against it. . . . It is necessary, nevertheless, to profit from a moment where he finds himself supported by an army and by the consent of his allies. . . . I know how difficult it is to make the King admit men who do not have his confidence; this will, nevertheless, be the only means of saving Naples from a new catastrophe. Your Highness has the intimate conviction of the necessity of placing capable men at the head of affairs; it has, therefore, become my duty to name to you those whom I regard as such.[46]

Ficquelmont's list of candidates explains why he expected to encounter the King's opposition. Some of the men recommended were good royalists, like Marquis Tommasi and the Duke of Ascoli. To head the ministry as minister of finances, however, Ficquelmont suggested Chevalier de Medicis, whom Ferdinand feared and distrusted and whose financial policies had helped to bring on the revolution; and as minister of the interior he recommended no less a figure than Giuseppe Zurlo, head of the constitutional ministry from July to December 1820.[47]

Metternich had by this time come reluctantly to agree with Ficquelmont on the necessity of making sweeping changes. Always aware of the disappointing trend of affairs at Naples, he had for months relied on remonstrances to Ruffo and encouragement to the King, whom Metternich regarded (at least outwardly) as essentially good but weak, to carry out the plans agreed upon at Laibach and to exercise moderation.[48] To this and to certain other palliatives he looked for a remedy, refusing for a considerable time to admit

[46] Ficquelmont (Naples, September 18, 1821) to Metternich, *ibid.*, No. 50B, with supplements.

[47] *Ibid.* An accompanying "Mémoire sur la situation intérieure du Royaume de Naples" contains an elaborate refutation of the charges leveled by the Neapolitan ministry against the Allies, which were: (1) interference of the ministerial conference in the internal affairs of Naples; (2) unjustified charges by Metternich against the Neapolitan government; (3) the failure of the Austrian government to heed the pleas of Naples for a reduction in the costs of the army of occupation; and (4) the inordinate pressure exerted on Ferdinand to force him to oust certain of his ministers. The defense was essentially that everything the Allies were doing they did for the kingdom's own good.

[48] Metternich (Laibach, May 14, 1821) to Esterhazy, Weisungen, Grossbritannien, Fasc. 217, No. 1; Metternich (Vienna, July 5 and August 26, 1821) to Ruffo, Varia, Neapel, Fasc. 53; Metternich (Vienna, July 21, August 31, 1821) to Ficquelmont, Berichte und Weisungen, Neapel, Fasc. 52.

that the fault might lie with the King and his choice of advisers,[49] and never, of course, conceding that there could be anything wrong with the framework devised at Laibach.[50] By August, however, Metternich was convinced that the King needed a new adviser at his side, and at least by early December he had concluded, along with Ficquelmont, that the present ministry would have to go.[51]

The only question for Metternich was who should head the new ministry. Ficquelmont had suggested bringing back De Medicis; Metternich's choice, however, fell on Prince Alvaro Ruffo. It was not because Metternich thought the Neapolitan envoy particularly competent. To the contrary—already at the Congress of Laibach Metternich had made the sad discovery, as he put it, of *"the absolute nullity of Ruffo!"* [52] and Vincent's experience with Ruffo at Florence had been anything but encouraging. The Austrian envoy denounced his cowardice and inertia, asserting that Ruffo "only has one hour of life per day." [53] As late as December 1821, some months after Metternich had begun promoting Ruffo's candidacy for president of the Council of State, he admitted to Lebzeltern that he did not really like either candidate for the post. His preference for Ruffo, it would seem, was due to his being more amenable to Austrian influence

[49] See his reserved letter to Ficquelmont from Vienna, August 31, 1821, in which, urging upon Ferdinand the necessity of setting up the *Consultas* in the two kingdoms, he said: "The choices [of their members] belong to the King; I do not admit the possibility that he would ever be able to let them fall on men known to be factious or inept." Berichte und Weisungen, Neapel, Fasc. 52. One of the palliatives which Metternich hoped might improve the situation was to establish in Naples an official newspaper favorable to Austria, which Ficquelmont was to start and support. The dearth of talent in Naples, however, was such that Metternich had to appeal to Strassoldo to send writers down from Milan. Ficquelmont (Naples, June 13, 1821) to Metternich, Berichte, Neapel, Fasc. 51, No. 30C; Metternich (Vienna, July 6, 1821) to Strassoldo, Provinzen: Lombardei-Venezien, Fasc. 7.

[50] Of considerable interest is Metternich's letter (Vienna, December 3, 1821) to Lebzeltern in which Metternich strives at considerable length to prove that the bad situation in Naples was due to the contagion of the revolution, not to an inner decomposition in the government. If the latter were the case, he concedes, it would mean that the whole procedure at Laibach was wrong, Weisungen, Russland, Fasc. 45, No. 3.

[51] Metternich (Vienna, August 26, 1821) to Ruffo, Berichte und Weisungen, Neapel, Fasc. 52; Metternich (Vienna, December 5, 1821) to Vincent, Weisungen, Frankreich, Fasc. 346.

[52] Metternich (Laibach, February 8, 1821) to Count Zichy, ambassador at Berlin, Interiora, Korrespondenz, Fasc. 82.

[53] Vincent (Florence, March 24, 1821) to Metternich, Varia, Neapel, Fasc. 54.

than De Medicis, and his having unimpeachable absolutist principles, whereas De Medicis was suspected of tolerance toward
liberalism.[54]

In any case, though Ruffo much preferred the congenial life of
ambassador in Vienna to the hard task of wrestling with the insuperable problems of Naples, Metternich persuaded him that he was the
man the King needed to carry through the necessary measures of
governmental reorganization, army reform, and an amnesty.[55] Then,
with Francis' support and through the agency of Ruffo, Metternich
set out to convince Ferdinand that this was what he himself
wanted.[56] Ferdinand proved extremely hard to convince. Though
willing, and even insistent, that Ruffo should return to Naples as
his adviser, he not only did not want Ruffo as president of the Council of State, but neither he nor his present ministers wanted Metternich's proposed Council of State at all, preferring a simple ministerial council of independent ministers without a president.[57] Moreover, the King rightly suspected that accepting Ruffo would mean
divesting himself of his present ministers—with whom he got along
famously—and reappointing De Medicis.[58] Therefore, when Ruffo,
encouraged by Metternich, declined to follow the King's orders to
return to Naples until he first received a definite promise that he
would be named president of the Council, Ferdinand broke off the
correspondence in displeasure at Ruffo's insubordination.[59] Metter-

[54] Metternich (Vienna, December 3, 1821) to Lebzeltern, Weisungen,
Russland, Fasc. 45, No. 3. Ruffo's political outlook is illustrated by his comment
to Metternich that while the Carbonari were simply imbeciles, the real criminals
at Naples were the Muratists, all of whom deserved to be hung. Ruffo (Vienna,
December 20, 1820) to Metternich, in *Atti del Parlamento*, V, Pt. 2, 430.

[55] Metternich (Vienna, August 26, 1821) to Ruffo, Berichte und Weisungen,
Neapel, Fasc. 52; Moscati, *Il regno delle Due Sicilie*, I, xviii–xx.

[56] Metternich (Vienna, October 13, 1821) to Ferdinand, Hofkorrespondenz,
Neapel, Fasc. 32; Ruffo (Vienna, November 4, 1821) to Metternich, Varia,
Neapel, Fasc. 53.

[57] A thoroughgoing absolutist, Ferdinand viewed the distinction between the
head of state (himself) and the head of the government (the president of the
Council of State) as the entering wedge of liberalism and an attack upon his
monarchical rights.—Maturi, *Canosa*, 176.

[58] Count Truchsess (Naples, February 21, 1822) to Baron Krusemarck,
Varia, Neapel, Fasc. 57; De Menz (Naples, February 28, 1822) to Metternich,
Berichte, Neapel, Fasc. 55, No. 11B.

[59] From July 1821, when Ferdinand sent out his first summons to Ruffo, to
November, when the King's irritation reached the breaking point, Ruffo stead-
fastly resisted the flattery, pleas, and pressure of the King, even when Ferdinand

nich now felt that the time had come for him to use stronger measures with Ferdinand than mere recommendations. He summoned
Ficquelmont home for consultation, on the pretext of a leave of
absence to settle personal affairs, and gave the King clear indication
of Austria's serious displeasure at his failure to appoint Ruffo and
to execute the necessary administrative reforms.[60] After two more
months of delay and vacillation, Ferdinand finally capitulated, accepting both Ruffo and the fourteen-point governmental program
that Metternich drew up for him. As Metternich described the
King's decision to Esterhazy, this program was something "His Sicilian Majesty has spontaneously decided to adopt," subject only to
the approval of the Austrian Emperor.[61]

Meanwhile, Ficquelmont, who had shared with Metternich his
own ideas on what should be done at Naples,[62] was sent back with
Ruffo in May 1822 with instructions to support Metternich's fourteen-point program, which was purely administrative and contained

------

sent Count Ludolf on a special mission to Vienna to persuade him to return
and offered him Circello's present post of minister of foreign affairs. See the
Ferdinand-Ruffo correspondence published in Moscati, *Il regno delle Due
Sicilie*, I, 43–44, 53–115. Ruffo's genuine reluctance to return to Naples is
evident—as is his complete subservience to Metternich. The whole story of the
relations between Ferdinand, Ruffo, and Metternich, like other aspects of
Neapolitan history at this time, is reminiscent of *opéra bouffe*.

[60] Metternich (Vienna, December 20, 1821) to Ficquelmont, Berichte und
Weisungen, Neapel, Fasc. 52, No. 1.

[61] Metternich (Vienna, March 17, 1822) to Esterhazy, Weisungen, Grossbritannien, Fasc. 218, No. 3. Metternich explained the matter somewhat more
candidly to Lebzeltern. He had called Ficquelmont home, he wrote, to instruct
him on the program which had been agreed upon "and decreed [arrêté] here
between Prince Ruffo and me, and to charge him [Ficquelmont], together with
his colleagues, to follow, supervise, and facilitate the execution of the plan of
the King." Metternich (Vienna, March 31, 1822) to Lebzeltern, Weisungen,
Russland, Fasc. 54, No. 6.

[62] The last memoir Ficquelmont submitted to Metternich gives a good
picture of the sort of problems which the Austrian envoy, like his master,
believed the Neapolitan government should deal with. Its various sections are
headed: "Choice of employees," "Sects," "Police," "Police of the churches,"
"Clergy," "Direction of public opinion," and "Formation of the army." The
program, in short, was purely administrative. Conspicuous by their absence
were provisions designed to deal with finances, taxation, customs, agriculture,
trade, industry, education, brigandage, or any of the fundamental problems of
the Neapolitan nation. Ficquelmont (Vienna, March 28, 1822) to Metternich,
Varia, Neapel, Fasc. 57.

nothing new, as "the spontaneous decisions of the King." [63] Along with this, Ficquelmont was instructed also to take care that the Hereditary Prince did nothing to disturb the existing system, to refuse any Neapolitan request for a reduction in the Austrian army of occupation or its costs, and to make sure that Austria acquired most-favored-nation status in trade with Naples. [64]

Ruffo's return to Naples and his assumption of office did result in some improvement in the situation there. By June, after further delay and obstruction by the old ministers, he succeeded in getting new ministers appointed, among them De Medicis as finance minister. [65] He proceeded with the long-delayed reorganization of the army, throwing out the committees of inquiry, and put through other overdue administrative measures. [66] The Monteforte trials were finally brought to an end in September, and thereafter an amnesty and a new law against the sects were proclaimed which, though not ideal, were in Ficquelmont's opinion better than nothing. [67] Thus the most glaring abuses and scandals were eliminated and a sem-

[63] "Instructions pour M. le Comte de Ficquelmont," Vienna, April 19, 1822, Berichte und Weisungen, Neapel, Fasc. 58; Metternich (Vienna, April 19, 1822) to Ficquelmont, *ibid.*, No. 1. Metternich's parting letter to Ruffo (Vienna, April 19, 1822) reads like a foreign minister's instructions to one of his ambassadors. Varia, Neapel, Fasc. 57.

[64] The trade concessions which Metternich contemplated were in ill accord with the restrictive Neapolitan tariff system. If Ferdinand made any objections, however, Ficquelmont was instructed to point out "that this is the only means which he [the King] possesses to acquit himself of a sacred debt of gratitude toward Austria; . . . that we have surely acquired by the immense services rendered to the King the right to be treated like the favored nations, and that we cannot admit that this right should be contested to us in a moment when we have just made, and are still making daily, such great sacrifices for the restoration of the Kingdom of the Two Sicilies." Metternich (Vienna, April 19, 1822) to Ficquelmont, Berichte und Weisungen, Neapel, Fasc. 58, No. 1. Metternich neglected to mention that these "immense services" and "great sacrifices" magnanimously extended by Austria to Naples were costing the Neapolitan government annually three-fourths of its entire income and saddling its finances with an almost insupportable load of debt, while costing the Austrian treasuries not one florin, and, indeed, relieving Austria of the cost of supporting a considerable portion of its regular Army.

[65] Ficquelmont (Naples, May 15, 20, and 25, June 9, 1822) to Metternich, Berichte, Neapel, Fasc. 55, Nos. 26, 27A, 28A, and 30A.

[66] Ficquelmont (Naples, July 5, and August 16, 1822) to Metternich, *ibid.*, Nos. 34 and 41A.

[67] Ficquelmont (Naples, September 9 and 13, October 1, 1822) to Metternich, *ibid.*, Nos. 44B, 45A, and 48A.

blance of order and quiet restored to the government. None but the surface symptoms of Naples' ills, however, had been touched. The intense disaffection and turbulence in Sicily continued, growing worse with time; brigandage increased, even though Austrian troops were used to help stamp it out; and the appalling economic problems lying at the root of so much of the kingdom's trouble had not even been faced, much less solved.[68]

As for the much-heralded Laibach plan for reorganizing the government, it may be doubted that under the best circumstances it would have been the panacea Metternich claimed it to be. Ferdinand, whose capacity for passive resistance to all reform rivaled that of an Ottoman sultan, contrived in any case, encouraged and abetted by Ruffo, De Medicis, Tommasi, and the French envoy Count Blacas, so to delay, obstruct, amend, and emasculate the plan that when the separate *Consultas* for Naples and Sicily were finally established in 1824, they bore little or no resemblance to the original idea. But by this time Metternich had given up hope of administrative reorganization in Naples.[69]

That something more than administrative manipulations was needed at Naples in the long run was plain to more than one observer there. Ficquelmont's views were narrow and his vision was restricted almost entirely to political and administrative matters, but even he saw clearly, and so reported to Metternich, that the financial condition of Naples was desperate, and that the crushing burden of the Austrian occupation was making it infinitely worse. "If the charges we cause," he warned Metternich, "are so heavy that they exceed the resources of the country, all parties will unite in desiring our departure, and our presence, far from being protective, will become oppressive." [70] Moreover, he realized that the evils

[68] Ficquelmont (Naples, May 25, August 1 and 5, 1822) to Metternich, *ibid.*, Nos. 28D, 39C, and 40; Ficquelmont (Verona, November 15, 1822) to Metternich, Varia, Neapel, Fasc. 57; Spellanzon, *Storia del Risorgimento*, II, 123–124.

[69] Various letters and documents in Moscati, *Il regno delle Due Sicilie*, I, 121–125, 130–145, 231–250; II, 228–236, 240–247.

[70] Memoir titled "Considerations sur les moyens de porter remède à la situation dans laquelle se trouve le royaume de Naples," from Ficquelmont (Vienna, February 16, 1822) to Metternich, Varia, Neapel, Fasc. 57 (with supplements). According to Vincent, A'Court also believed that the occupation costs would have to be cut sharply. Vincent (Paris, April 2, 1822) to Metternich, Berichte, Frankreich, Fasc. 347, No. 10C.

existing at Naples went far deeper than political errors or the influence of revolutionary doctrines. In passing on to Metternich a report on the state of the kingdom submitted originally by Commissariat General Barattelli to Ferdinand, Ficquelmont commented: "This report merits attention because it shows by a series of facts that one must look for the unique cause of the evils which burden the Kingdom of Naples not in the *raison politique,* but instead in a general demoralization." [71]

The basic problem of Naples, said Ficquelmont in a report of the following year, was endemic: the progressive disintegration of the institutions upon which the state rested. The royalists were essentially a vengeful faction, and revolutionary ideas were gaining support both among doctrinaires and disgusted supporters of the monarchy. The reigning anarchy and poverty in Sicily, the great number of political prisoners and others accused of ordinary crime, the ignorance and corruption of the clergy, and the economic decline and intellectual insignificance of the nobility gave grounds for a gloomy prognosis of the kingdom's future. [72]

Similar, but even clearer, was the analysis of De Menz. Two main evils, he said, existed at Naples: first, "public demoralization," and second, "the paralyzing of the vital forces of the soil by the laws of navigation and customs." The first evil, he maintained, could not be cured by surveillance from above, but only by improvement from below: by better education for the people, by the reform and elevation of the corrupt clergy, and by attacking "the spirit of buffoonery" which pervaded everything and everyone. As for the second, under the present system trade and agriculture were stagnant, taxes harder to collect than ever, and the living of the average peasant or worker harder to procure, especially in Sicily. The government, he urged, should turn to encouraging agriculture and industry, rather than milking them to death to secure revenue; it should moderate the restrictive rights of landowners and get rid of the vexatious barriers against commerce. As for the Carbonari, De Menz contended that they were not then, and indeed never had been, the main evil and danger in Naples. Even during the revolution they had most of the

---

[71] Ficquelmont (Vienna, February 7, 1822) to Metternich, Varia, Neapel, Fasc. 57.

[72] Ficquelmont (Naples, July 1, 1823) to Metternich, in Moscati, *Il regno delle Due Sicilie,* II, 189–202.

time only been used by the party in power, and since then they had lost most of their adherents and influence. "It is not, then, the sect at all," he said, "which constitutes one of the essential evils of this kingdom, but the degradation of morals, which ought to occupy all the attention of the government." [73]

The problems with which Ruffo proposed to deal on his assumption of office were not these problems at all, of course. The program of Metternich called for administrative reform to bring about order and quiet in Naples. This being accomplished, Metternich was content—or not interested.[74]

The most important question of all in the reconstruction at Naples was that of the army of occupation and its effect upon Neapolitan finances. Here again Metternich's principles turned out to be singularly impotent in practice. For while he was in theory aware of the importance of a sound financial system in the success of the restored government at Naples and damned the revolutionary regime vehemently for its alleged ruinous wastefulness,[75] he was also compelled by pressures from home to make sure that Austria received full compensation for everything she did in Italy. If Neapolitan finances suffered in consequence, this could not be helped. Hence Ficquelmont's first instructions included a warning to prevent any measures

[73] De Menz (Naples, March 15, April 10 and 20, 1822) to Metternich, Berichte, Neapel, Fasc. 55, Nos. 14A, 19, and 21A.

[74] His loss of interest in Naples is indicated by the sharp shrinkage in the volume of correspondence on Naples, which during 1821 and the first half of 1822 was quite heavy, but which after Ruffo's accession to office, and especially after the Congress of Verona, returned to the normal low volume of correspondence on routine diplomatic matters.

[75] Metternich recognized, for instance, that "the blind fiscality" of De Medicis' system of taxation had helped to bring about the revolution. Metternich (Laibach, March 10, 1821) to Stadion, in *Nachgelassene Papiere*, III, 455. He instructed Ficquelmont to secure a report on all the expenses of the revolutionary regime, providing Europe thereby with a salutary lesson on the evils of revolution. Metternich (Laibach, May 20, 1821) to Ficquelmont, Berichte und Weisungen, Neapel, Fasc. 52, No. 6. Metternich's claim, however, that the revolution had cost Naples 40,000,000 ducats was enormously exaggerated. Lodovico Bianchini, the standard authority on Neapolitan finances, puts the moneys raised by extraordinary measures in 1820 at 447,283 ducats, required mainly on account of the Sicilian revolt and the armaments expenditures of October and November. In the general collapse of 1821, to be sure, the finances suffered, and a forced loan was attempted in February.—Lodovico Bianchini, *Storia delle finanze del regno di Napoli*, 453–454.

at Naples which might jeopardize Austria's indemnification in full for the campaign and the support of her army.[76]

One such danger to be averted was to let the loan that was to be extended to Naples fall into the wrong hands. The House of Barbaja at Florence, Metternich wrote Ficquelmont, had reportedly offered the kingdom 30,000,000 ducats as an outright loan at 6 per cent interest. In view of this dangerous offer, it was vital to act quickly to make sure that the House of Rothschild instead made the loan, "since," said Metternich, "we can count on his [Rothschild's] exactitude in turning directly over to our treasuries the funds which will be destined for us." [77] For this reason Charles Rothschild, representing the firm, accompanied the Austrian army to Naples, where he immediately proceeded to negotiate with the provisional regime. The first two offers he made were on such ruinous terms that the provisional government rejected them; a third, somewhat better— providing that Rothschild would sell 800,000 ducats of rents at 60 per cent, with 3 per cent commission—was accepted. A special clause was inserted in the loan agreement providing that the funds raised by Rothschild would be paid "to those who will be authorized to handle them"—a provision which guaranteed, Ficquelmont assured Metternich, that the great bulk of the money would go directly to Austria.[78]

This loan, according to Ficquelmont's reckoning, was supposed both to cover the war indemnity and to enable the Neapolitan government to get on its feet. Normal revenues, he calculated, would then enable it to bear the cost of the Austrian occupation. His calculation proved wildly optimistic. For one thing, the King's request

[76] Metternich (Laibach, March 1, 1821) to Ficquelmont, Berichte und Weisungen, Neapel, Fasc. 52.

[77] Metternich (Laibach, April 12, 1821) to Ficquelmont, *ibid.* A full account of the origins of the Neapolitan loan, as originally worked out at Laibach, is given in Egon Cäsar Conte Corti, *The Rise of the House of Rothschild*, 229–249, 255, 259–262, 269–270. It is important to note that, though Metternich favored and supported the Rothschilds for the loan, the financial arrangements themselves were largely the work of Prince Stadion.

[78] Ficquelmont (Naples, April 19 and 30, 1821) to Metternich, Berichte, Neapel, Fasc. 51, Nos. 17B, and 19B; "Propositions de Monsieur de Rothschild au gouvernement de Naples, au date de 19 avril 1821," *ibid.*, supplement to No. 17B. Rothschild's first two offers were for 51 and 54 per cent, respectively; even Neapolitan bankers, the provisional regime stated, had offered better terms. During the revolutionary period up to November, the rents had varied between 68 and 74 per cent.

for an Austrian occupation force in Sicily (six thousand men plus a small naval contingent) to quell risings centered at Messina led to further heavy expenses for the kingdom.[79] For another, the chaotic condition of the government, its inability at first to collect taxes regularly, and above all its failure to cut costs in the manner Ficquelmont expected (by a rapid and orderly disbanding of its own army) soon made it clear that the Neapolitan regime would have difficulty meeting its normal expenses, to say nothing of meeting the costs of the occupation.

These facts notwithstanding, Ficquelmont, on his return from Rome to Naples in May, proceeded to use the full powers granted him to negotiate the proposed convention governing the occupation and to secure from Naples full payment for the war and the occupation. Though he was, in view of the Neapolitan "resistance" met in the campaign, also instructed to reserve Austria's right to claim damages for her prewar mobilization in Lombardy-Venetia in addition,[80] it was almost immediately apparent that attempting to secure any more idemnification from Naples would be squeezing blood from the proverbial turnip. Indeed, even without this demand, Ficquelmont from the outset encountered stubborn Neapolitan resistance to accepting the crushing burdens to be placed upon her.[81] Only after repeated attempts by the Neapolitan government to gain a reduction of the sums demanded (including an appeal over Ficquelmont's head direct to Emperor Francis) had failed and Francis had flatly told Ferdinand that the matter was settled and that he

---

[79] The actual annual cost somewhat exceeded 250,000 ducats cash, plus payment in materials and services. Ficquelmont (Rome, May 2, and Naples, May 24, 1821) to Metternich, *ibid.*, Nos. 21 and 27B with supplements. A'Court protested against the Austrian occupation of Sicily, but Metternich brushed his protests aside with the comment that the mere fact that England had once (in 1811–1814) had special influence in Sicily did not mean that she still had rights of protection there. Metternich (Vienna, June 6, 1821) to Esterhazy, Weisungen, Grossbritannien, Fasc. 217.

[80] Metternich (Laibach, May 14, 1821) to Ficquelmont, Berichte und Weisungen, Neapel, Fasc. 52, Nos. 1 and 5.

[81] Ferdinand's attitude toward the occupation army was equivocal, if not self-contradictory. On the one hand, he complained bitterly of the scandalous extravagance of the occupation authorities; on the other, he was so terrified of the revolution that he feared the present occupation forces were far too few to combat it—if, indeed, the foreign soldiers were not lured away or corrupted by the sects. Ferdinand (Naples, May 26 and June 6, 1821) to Ruffo, in Moscati, *Il regno delle Due Sicilie*, I, 34–35, 38–39.

must give the order to his government to sign the agreement, was a convention, providing for a three-year occupation to be supported wholly by the Neapolitan government, concluded at Naples on October 18, 1821.[82] Ficquelmont, who resolutely attempted to put the best face on the matter, conceded, "There is no doubt that in the present state of affairs the charge which falls on the kingdom of Naples is very burdensome." Until November 1, 1821, he calculated, the occupation forces, numbering fifty-four thousand men, would cost Naples a yearly 11,574,428 ducats; for at least the next eight months the army would total forty-two thousand men, costing 9,002,333 ducats annually; and when the final reduction in strength had been made, the twenty-five thousand men on peacetime footing would cost, Ficquelmont hoped, only 5,376,428 ducats. Deducting the amount he hoped the Neapolitan government would save by greatly reducing the size of its own army, he believed the occupation eventually would add only about 2,000,000 ducats annually to the Neapolitan budget.[83]

Even had this calculation been reliable (it proved not to be), it meant cold comfort to Naples in 1821. For the cost of the war and occupation in the first nine months—April to December 1821—was staggering. According to Austrian figures, it ranged between 13,000,-000 and 14,000,000 ducats.[84] This compared to a governmental income for the entire year of 18,871,222.78 ducats, and an outgo, including only normal governmental expenditures and service of the first Rothschild loan, and exclusive of all war and occupation costs, of 18,723,676.50 ducats. In short, the cost of the Austrian campaign and occupation almost equaled the entire governmental income in

---

[82] Ficquelmont (Naples, August 8, 16, and 25, September 1, 1821) to Metternich, Berichte, Neapel, Fasc. 51, Nos. 41C, with supplement, 43F, 45A, with supplements, and 46A, with supplement; Ficquelmont (Naples, October 3 and 21, 1821) to Metternich, Berichte und Weisungen, Neapel, Fasc. 52, Nos. 52C, with supplement, and 55A, with supplements; Metternich (Vienna, July 21, 1821) to Ficquelmont, *ibid.*, No. 1; Francis (Vienna, October 18, 1821) to Ferdinand, *ibid.*

[83] Ficquelmont (Naples, October 21, 1821) to Metternich, Berichte und Weisungen, Neapel, Fasc. 52, No. 55A, with supplements.

[84] Ficquelmont (Vienna, February 16, 1822) to Metternich, Varia, Neapel, Fasc. 57. Also see "Uebersicht der baaren Geld-Leistungen der königlich Neapolitanischen Staats-Schatzes." *Ibid.*, Supplement No. 2. The figure includes the war indemnity, cash payments, and payments in goods for the occupation.

Naples for the last nine months of 1821, and the entire burden had to be borne by deficit financing.[85]

Under the circumstances the government could only resort to more loans. A second Rothschild loan in November 1821 sold another 840,000 ducats of rents at 65 to 66 per cent of their nominal value; still a third in September 1822 brought 1,100,000 ducats at 71.5 to 73 per cent.[86] Meanwhile, the Austrian government, despite Ficquelmont's warnings, did nothing to decrease its charges on Naples. The Austrian envoy pointed out in September 1822 that after the third Rothschild loan the Neapolitan debt stood at 4,000,-000 ducats of rents per year; that the Austrian army was still costing Naples nearly 12,000,000 ducats annually; and that even after De Medicis had raised taxes still higher and redoubled his efforts to increase the revenue, the annual income at Naples only slightly exceeded 19,000,000 ducats. In the face of all this, the Austrian army was still forty-two thousand strong and remained on a wartime footing, causing additional expense.[87] Stadion, apprised of the situation, sharply rebuked Metternich for not heeding Ficquelmont's advice of the year before about putting the army on a peacetime footing, reminding him that the Foreign Ministry had to take the initiative to make the War Ministry do it.[88] Yet even at the Congress of Verona, where both Ficquelmont and Ruffo approached Metternich with pleas for a reduction in the size of the army and for other economies, and cited statistics to show that the kingdom suffered an annual deficit of 1,550,000 ducats quite apart from the occupation and one of more than 13,000,000 if occupation costs were included, Metternich's initial response to their plea was anything but encouraging. Other than to put the army on a peacetime footing,

[85] *Ibid.*, Supplement No. 3.

[86] Ficquelmont (Naples, November 27, 1821, and September 1, 1822) to Metternich, Berichte und Weisungen, Neapel, Fasc. 52, No. 58, and Berichte, Neapel, Fasc. 55, No. 43A.

[87] Ficquelmont (Naples, September 1, 1822) to Metternich, *ibid.*, No. 43A. The Neapolitan debt, which was 800,000 ducats annually in 1815, and which had risen to 1,200,000 by 1820, did not increase during the revolution. Between 1821 and 1826 it went up to 5,190,000 ducats annually.—Spellanzon, *Storia del Risorgimento*, II, 117; Bianchini, *Storia delle finanze*, 460.

[88] Stadion (Vienna, September 22, 1822) to Metternich, Varia, Neapel, Fasc. 57. Since Ficquelmont was an able and experienced general as well as a diplomat, his advice on the military occupation should have borne additional weight.

he would promise no concessions, directing the Neapolitans to effect economies in their own administration.[89] Though concessions were finally made at Verona, including a reduction of the army to thirty-five thousand men beginning in April 1823, they were due, as Metternich himself tacitly admitted, to political necessity, especially the pressure of the other Allies upon Austria,[90] and not to any Austrian concern over Neapolitan finances.

None of these financial distresses suffered by his kingdom, to be sure, deterred Ferdinand from continued dependence upon Austrian bayonets. As Ficquelmont commented, the King would certainly insist on having an Austrian occupation force at his side as long as he lived.[91] To show his gratitude to the Allies for their support, he conferred the Grand Cross of St. Ferdinand upon all the Allied prime ministers at Laibach and all the envoys at Naples; the dukedom of Antrodoco, with an annual income of 220,000 ducats, upon General Frimont, commander of the occupation army; and, following the third loan, the Small Cross of St. Ferdinand upon Charles Rothschild.[92]

[89] Ruffo (Verona, December 3, 1822) to Metternich, Varia, Neapel, Fasc. 57; Ficquelmont (Verona, November 11, 1822) to Metternich, *ibid.*, with supplements titled "Mémoire du ministére napolitain sur les frais occasionés par l'armée d'occupation," and "Réponse au mémoire du ministére Napolitain."

[90] Metternich (Verona, December 14, 1822) to Ficquelmont, Berichte und Weisungen, Neapel, Fasc. 58. This minor concession did not bring the hoped-for reduction in costs, since the Austrian army, despite bitter protests particularly from De Medicis, remained on a wartime footing. Ficquelmont attempted to justify keeping the troops mobile by pointing to the dangers of the Spanish revolution and French intervention in Spain and alleging other general dangers in the European situation. Metternich himself admitted privately to Ficquelmont, however, that these arguments were irrelevant. The truth was that the Austrian Council of War under Count Bellegarde and the occupation army's commander, Frimont, had simply decided on their own authority to keep the army on a wartime basis—and Metternich could do nothing about it. Ficquelmont was instructed to try to conceal this fact from the Neapolitans. Ruffo (Venice, December 23, 1822) to De Medicis; De Medicis (Naples, January 4 and April 26, 1823) to Ruffo; and Metternich (Vienna, March 31, 1823) to Ficquelmont, all in Moscati, *Il regno delle Due Sicilie*, I, 188–191, 199–200; II, 186–188.

[91] Ficquelmont (Vienna, February 16, 1822) to Metternich, Varia, Neapel, Fasc. 57, with memoir titled "Considerations sur les moyens de porter remède à la situation dans laquelle se trouve le royaume de Naples."

[92] Ficquelmont (Naples, December 3, 1821, and September 10, 1822) to Metternich, Berichte und Weisungen, Neapel, Fasc. 52, No. 58B and Postscript; Berichte, Neapel, Fasc. 55, No. 44A. Metternich also owned the dukedom of

The remaining years of the occupation fall outside our purview but the story may be briefly summarized here. After the army was reduced in April 1823, the occupation, though originally scheduled to expire in October 1824, was extended to the end of May 1826 by a convention of May 1824. The long-overdue death of Ferdinand in January 1825, however, brought a change in the situation. The new king, Francis I, though fully repentant of his part in the revolution of 1820 and determined to make no changes in the governmental system, was not inclined to maintain the heavy burden on his country.[93] Therefore the convention of May 1824 was revised in May 1825 to extend the occupation to the end of March 1827, reducing the forces to only twelve thousand after March 1826. The occupation was thus finally terminated, six years after its beginning.[94]

The end of the occupation occurred despite the opposition of Metternich, who insisted to the end that the evacuation of Naples was dangerous and harmful in view of the revolutionary situation in Portugal, the menace of subversive English propaganda, and the presence in Naples of revolutionaries and secret sects.[95] The evacuation was due only to the persistent efforts of De Medicis, who had taken over as prime minister in 1823 after Ruffo had succeeded in escaping from Naples back to the refuge of an ambassadorial post in Vienna.[96] Even the departure of the occupation army did not end

Portella, with an income of 60,000 ducats a year, which Ferdinand had given him before the revolution.

[93] Francis I (Naples, February 2, 1825) to Prince Castelcicala, in Moscati, *Il regno delle Due Sicilie*, I, 254–258. As a precautionary measure, Metternich sent Count Apponyi on a special mission to the new King, to sound out his political principles and warn him of the intrigues of France. Apponyi reported that the new monarch seemed to be respectably absolutist, at least in regard to his own domains. Metternich (Vienna, January 25, 1825) to Apponyi, and Apponyi (Naples, February 16, 1825) to Metternich, *ibid.*, II, 258–265, 271–274.

[94] Convention of Milan, April 24, 1823, Österreichische Armee in Neapel, 1815–1827, Fasc. 41; Convention of Naples, August 31, 1824, *ibid.*; Convention of Milan, May 28, 1825, *ibid.*

[95] Metternich (Vienna, December 21, 1825) to Ficquelmont, *ibid.* (two letters); see also Moscati, *Il regno delle Due Sicilie*, I, 265–272, 295–296, 303–304.

[96] The entire question of the occupation army and its costs is closely connected with the bitter personal quarrel raging between Metternich and De Medicis throughout this period. For Metternich, the Neapolitan minister was a weak, false, intriguing ingrate, responsible not only for frustrating the Laibach reorganization scheme but also for spreading the vicious, calumniating rumor

the occupation question. The government of Naples now accused Austria of having overcharged Naples handsomely for the troops' support, and after an acrid quarrel, succeeded in procuring a partial restitution.[97] The total cost of the occupation is estimated by one authority to be 85,000,000 ducats [98]—about three-fourths of Naples' entire governmental revenue for the six-year period.

The Austrian experience with the restored government of Piedmont, meanwhile, was to some extent the story of Naples repeated, though on a much smaller and milder scale. As at Naples, Metternich's chief concern was that the government be strong and firm in "snuffing out the play of the faction" and restoring order.[99] For this task, he was fond of remarking, "one ought to have there a dictator rather than a king." [100] Charles Felix, to be sure, showed no want of rigor in dealing with rebels, but Metternich feared that his lack of a consistently firm policy might lead to laxity later on. A more immediate problem was the fact that, like his stepfather at Naples, Charles Felix was determined not to return to his domains until his subjects had undergone punitive discipline at the hands of his provisional regime. Both Metternich and Binder, complaining that his absence placed the main burden of preserving order on the Austrian troops and put the King's authority under question, strongly urged him to return home immediately. Not until his commissions of inquiry had finished their work, however, and nineteen of the most prominent revolutionaries who could still be apprehended were executed did Charles Felix enter his kingdom on Octo-

---

that Austria wanted to interfere in Neapolitan internal affairs. In addition, he suspected De Medicis of liberalism, constitutionalism, and Francophile tendencies. As for De Medicis, he considered Metternich slippery and superficial, and held him responsible for bleeding Naples white through the occupation.— Moscati, *Il regno delle Due Sicilie*, I, liv–lv, 272–289, 295–296, 302; II, 228–236, 290–292, 336–337. On Ruffo's transfer (which Metternich opposed and attempted to reverse by reviving the conference of ambassadors at Naples), see *ibid.*, I, lxii–lxv, 224–225; II, 202–210, 220–228.

[97] *Ibid.*, I, 305–306, 310–312; Bianchini, *Storia delle finanze*, 501.

[98] Bianchini, *Storia delle finanze*, 501. Of this sum, 74,000,000 was computed as the direct cost of maintenance, and 11,000,000 as the interest on the attendant debt.

[99] Metternich (Vienna, June 28, 1821) to Binder, Weisungen und Varia, Sardinien, Fasc. 58, No. 1.

[100] Metternich (Vienna, August 19, 1821) to Bubna, Geheime Korrespondenz, Fasc. IV, No. 2; Metternich (Vienna, August 24, 1821), Weisungen, Russland, Fasc. 45, No. 4.

ber 1 and his capital on October 15, at the same time proclaiming an amnesty and a law banning all secret societies.[101]

While the reaction at Piedmont was less severe than at Naples, and the confusion caused by the King's absence far less deleterious, the difficulty encountered by Austria in securing a convention governing the occupation was at least as great. Metternich knew that an Austrian occupation force in Piedmont could cause bad reactions, particularly in public opinion in both Piedmont and France. To head off any possible intrigues, he even considered the idea of using Russian troops—under the command of General Bubna, to be sure— for the task. The idea, at best a tentative one, broke down when the Russians disapproved it.[102] At Laibach, Metternich stressed above all the importance of getting the king to voluntarily request the Allied occupation. The trouble, however, was that Charles Felix, after requesting Austrian aid clearly enough in early April, began to regret his decision as soon as the revolution was over, and without repudiating it wished to keep the army of occupation as small, inexpensive, and easily disposed of as possible.[103] His ministers, meanwhile, persisted in regarding the occupation not as a magnanimous favor extended to the King by the Allies but as a grievous yoke fastened on Piedmont by Austria, which they as Piedmontese should try to evade and reduce as much as possible.[104]

Thus in the negotiations over the convention begun between Binder and Sardinian Plenipotentiary General della Torre, the difference of opinion, which ostensibly concerned the size of the occupation force and the extent to which Piedmont should support it,

[101] Metternich (Vienna, August 19, 1821) to Bubna, Geheime Korrespondenz, Fasc. IV, No. 2; Binder (Milan, June 23, and 28, July 25, September 25, 1821, and Turin, October 3, 13, and 16, 1821) to Metternich, Berichte, Sardinien, Fasc. 57; Metternich (Laibach, May 17, 1821) to Binder, Weisungen und Varia, Sardinien, Fasc. 58; Bubna (Milan, July 25, 1821), to Metternich, *ibid.*

[102] Metternich instructed Binder to conduct the negotiation with the King and to write the convention in such a fashion that "in principle it will be the King who explicitly asks *us* for the occupation." Metternich (Laibach, April 22, 1821) to Binder, Weisungen und Varia, Sardinien, Fasc. 58, with supplement. See also Russian Cabinet (Laibach, April 22, 1821) to Count Mocenigo, Geheime Korrespondenz, Fasc. IV; and Metternich (Laibach, May 10, 1821) to Esterhazy, Weisungen, Grossbritannien, Fasc. 217.

[103] Binder (Modena, April 25, 1821) to Metternich, Berichte, Sardinien, Fasc. 57.

[104] Binder (Milan, May 25, 1821) to Metternich, *ibid.*, Nos. A–C.

actually went much deeper.[105] Della Torre denied the necessity for the occupation, insisting that Piedmont was capable of taking care of itself and that the presence of Austrian troops, together with the heavy added expense they would entail, would damage, not support, the King's cause in Piedmont.[106] Other Sardinian agents, in particular Count Pralormo, formerly Sardinian emissary at Laibach and now minister at Paris, seized the opportunity to arouse suspicion of Austrian motives and actions at foreign courts. Pralormo went so far as to attack the Laibach circular of May 12 directly, arguing that the Austrian plans

tend plainly to prepare for the aggrandizement of Austria, to destroy the independence of the Crown of Sardinia, to discredit the Government of the King in the country, and finally, by the imposition of the most intolerable and most humiliating yoke, to re-animate *that national hatred* against Austria which was the chief driving force and motive of the revolution in the month of March.

Pralormo denounced further the intention of the Allies to set up a ministerial council at Turin to guide the King, and the evident desire of Metternich to promote "the establishment in all the Italian states of a uniform system of organization" to be sanctioned by the next congress.[107] Other Sardinian agents at other courts dwelt on the

[105] *Ibid.* The line of occupation (on which the Austrians were to occupy a series of fortresses in eastern Piedmont) was readily agreed upon. Bubna, however, wanted fifteen thousand men, Della Torre only twelve. Binder insisted on full Sardinian support as at Naples; Della Torre argued that Austria should at least supply accessories and equipment. See also Binder (Turin, June 23, 1821) to Metternich, *ibid.* Metternich, who had earlier confided to Binder that he considered ten thousand men ample, now instructed his envoy to grant Sardinia a reduction to twelve thousand men as an Austrian concession, if Bubna agreed to it and provided that they could at any time be reinforced simply by Austrian command and at Sardinian expense. Metternich (Laibach, April 22, Vienna, June 11, 1821) to Binder, Weisungen und Varia, Sardinien, Fasc. 58.

[106] Metternich (Vienna, June 23, 1821) to Lebzeltern, Weisungen, Russland, Fasc. 45, No. 3.

[107] Metternich (Vienna, June 28, 1821) to Binder, Weisungen und Varia, Sardinien, Fasc. 58, Nos. 1 and 2, with supplement titled "Rapport du Ministre de S. M. le Roi de Sardaigne à son Cabinet," n.d. Some of the Sardinian charges, to be sure, were false. Austria certainly intended to make no territorial aggrandizement in Italy. Others, however, were just as certainly true. Metternich unquestionably intended, if he could, to control the Sardinian government through a ministerial conference and to push through a common system of government for all Italian states, to be sanctioned by the next congress. It was this sort of opposition which kept him from realizing his aims.

same theme. Even Count Rossi, the envoy at Vienna, did his part to spread these ideas.[108]

Metternich protested vigorously against these calumnies and instructed his own agents to do everything in their power to combat the petty suspicions and intrigues generated by the Sardinians. Yet the stir they raised was sufficient not only to frustrate his ideas for setting up a ministerial council at Turin and reproducing the Neapolitan system of governmental organization throughout Italy, but also to make him consider withdrawing the Austrian occupation force from Piedmont and calling on his eastern Allies to raise one of their own to replace it, or even suspending the Laibach declaration with regard to Piedmont and leaving the kingdom to its own devices.[109] Fortunately for the Austrian cause, Binder, backed up by Metternich's protests, was able to secure support for it from the King at Modena. Foreign Minister Laval sent out a circular dispatch to his ministers rebuking and disavowing the anti-Austrian agitation, while at almost the same time, on July 24, Binder secured agreement to the Convention of Novara governing the occupation of eastern Piedmont. The Austrian force, twelve thousand strong, was to remain in the kingdom at least until the next year's congress, when the situation would be reviewed and further action determined.[110]

Thus the diplomatic difficulties were smoothed over and in time the government of Piedmont settled down to a normal, quiet course. When this happened, Vienna was satisfied. Binder commended the King for his just severity against the revolutionaries and his rigid absolutist principles,[111] while Metternich warmly praised his course of repression of agitation and the surveillance against revolution that he followed in late 1821 and 1822. Emperor Francis indicated his approval by bestowing upon Charles Felix the Order of the

[108] Metternich (Vienna, July 18, 1821) to Lebzeltern, Weisungen, Russland, Fasc. 45, No. 2.

[109] *Ibid.*; Metternich (Vienna, June 30, 1821) to Vincent, Weisungen, Frankreich, Fasc. 346, Nos. 1–3.

[110] Binder (Milan, July 12 and 25, 1821) to Metternich, Berichte, Sardinien, Fasc. 57, Nos, A, B, and A; circular dispatch by Laval, Modena, July 26, 1821, Weisungen und Varia, Sardinien, Fasc. 58.

[111] Binder (Milan, July 25, 1821) to Metternich, Berichte, Sardinien, Fasc. 57, No. A; (Turin, October 16, 1821), *ibid.*, Nos. 4A and 4B.

Golden Fleece and upon Della Torre the Grand Cross of St. Stephen.[112]

At least one Austrian observer, Baron Daiser, who had been appointed *chargé d'affaires* at Turin in 1821,[113] doubted, however, that Charles Felix was doing much about the basic ills of his kingdom. He traced the roots of Piedmont's recent troubles to the great changes of the previous quarter-century. Piedmont, once one of the most feudal and backward of European states, had been thoroughly transformed by the French Revolution and Napoleon. Victor Emmanuel's halfhearted and bumbling attempts to restore the old order, he said, had succeeded only in composing a government and army half of incompetent nobles and half of dissatisfied Bonapartists and liberals. This unstable mixture was partly responsible for the easy success of the revolution, for when it broke out there was no strong openly prodynasty party to oppose it. Even the loyalist forces of Della Torre would have readily been overthrown without foreign intervention, since the masses were at best neutral in the crisis. "Nearly the entire nation," Daiser contended, "was for practical purposes divided into only two parties, of which the one [the middle class] supported the Spanish Constitution, and the other [the upper class] that of France." [114]

What Charles Felix had done to cope with the situation, Daiser felt, showed praiseworthy monarchical principles but maladroit administration. During the six months of his absence from Turin, the government had done nothing more than to punish the guilty; "in the six weeks since he returned," continued Daiser, "nothing has been done but to re-establish scrupulously the old order of things— no indication whatsoever of amelioration can be discovered." Conditions, he felt, boded ill for the future tranquillity of the country. He warned Metternich prophetically:

Your Highness will deign to see by this exposé that the tranquillity which reigns in this country does not proceed from either the confidence or the

---

[112] Francis (Verona, December 14, 1822) to Della Torre, Weisungen und Varia, Sardinien, Fasc. 60; Francis (Vienna, January 30, 1823) to Charles Felix, *ibid.*; Metternich (Vienna, January 31, 1823) to Daiser, *ibid.*

[113] Metternich (Laibach, May 20, 1821) to Binder, *ibid.*, Fasc. 58.

[114] Daiser (Turin, November 26, 1821) to Metternich, Berichte, Sardinien, Fasc. 57, No. 10A.

loyalty which the government is able to inspire, but rather from foreign, and in part ephemeral, circumstances, and that the least glimmer of hope and a single spark thrown into the land will suffice to set it once again in flames.[115]

The only solution, Daiser argued, was for the Sardinian government to catch up with the times, to reorganize itself on a modern (though absolutist) basis, so as to render harmless "the almost universal desire for a representative system." The steps required were educational reform—particularly to train the nobility for state service—a new code of laws, a reform and reduction of the army, abandonment of the attempt to rule simply through the clergy and nobility, and measures to control the rising middle class and make it useful to the government. Charles Felix, Daiser said, was doing none of these things. Instead, "frightened by the very word 'innovation,'" he chose to remain with the old order, ignoring the state's new needs. The assembled sovereigns at Florence, Daiser suggested, ought to persuade him to change his course.[116]

Later measures taken by Charles Felix to carry out judicial reform and a military reorganization led Daiser to modify his judgment to some extent in 1822. He remained convinced, however, that the Austrian army and the threat of foreign intervention were the chief deterrents to further revolution and that if the government wished to sustain the existing system its main task—that of educating an ignorant and talentless nobility to be fit to rule—had hardly been touched.[117]

Daiser's reports made no apparent impact on Metternich. The Austrian Chancellor was not interested in problems such as these in Sardinia. His only concern, as before, was that the government remain watchful against revolution and take repressive measures against the the factious and the sects.[118]

[115] *Ibid.*

[116] *Ibid.* Daiser also condemned the King's closing of the universities in Piedmont all through 1822, the new severe direct taxes he levied, his purge of civil officials on suspicion of liberal opinions, and the new police system which created, Daiser said, "a system of espionage everywhere." Daiser (Turin, December 13 and 15, 1821) to Metternich, *ibid.*, Nos. 11C and 12, with supplements.

[117] Daiser (Turin, May 27 and October 29, 1822) to Metternich, *ibid.*, Fasc. 59, Nos. 26 and 45.

[118] Metternich (Vienna, June 6, 1823) Provinzen: Lombardei-Venezien, Fasc. 37.

Little need be said here on the vexed question of the future of Charles Albert, Prince of Carignan, and on the plan of Charles Felix, aided and encouraged by Francis IV, Duke of Modena, to set aside the Prince in the order of succession in favor of his infant son, Victor Emmanuel II.[119] The question belongs really to the Congress of Verona. It suffices to say that the problem of what to do with the Prince was a serious one for Metternich during 1821 and 1822, and that from the outset he was not clear on what was the best solution to it. At first he entertained the idea that Charles Albert might be drawn into the Austrian armed service, in order to keep him away from liberal influence. Discouraged by Bubna's disapproval of the idea and by the evidence of the Prince's complicity in the revolutionary plot at Sardinia, he quickly dropped this proposal.[120] Binder argued strongly for the proposal of Charles Felix to oust the Prince from the succession, and Metternich may at one time have favored it.[121] By early 1822, however, he was convinced that Austria would serve herself ill by interfering with the succession in the House of Savoy, not so much because it would violate the principle of legitimacy and be contrary to Article 86 of the Vienna treaty—given as the ostensible reasons—as because England, France, and Russia were all opposed to such a step. "It appears, then, to us," he wrote Bubna, "eminently dangerous to agitate a question so compromising." His suggestion at this juncture, in February 1822, was to postpone the question until the congress of Florence, where the Allied powers might join to see whether they could not persuade the Prince to renounce his rights voluntarily.[122]

Austrian relations with the other great powers over the Neapolitan and Sardinian questions during the restoration period, while not

[119] Stern, *Geschichte Europas*, II, 176; Spellanzon, *Storia di Risorgimento*, II, 179–180. Francis IV hoped thereby to become Regent for Victor Emmanuel II during his minority.

[120] Metternich (Laibach, May 14 and July 6, 1821) to Bubna, Geheime Korrespondenz, Fasc. IV.

[121] "Mémoire sur le Piemont," by Binder, n.p., n.d., Weisungen und Varia, Sardinien, Fasc. 58. For evidence of Metternich's thought on the matter, see Chapter VII.

[122] See Metternich's secret letter (Vienna, February 16, 1822) to Bubna, Geheime Korrespondenz, Fasc. IV. Also compare with Metternich (Vienna, December 6, 1821) to Zichy and Lebzeltern, in *Nachgelassene Papiere*, III, 495–497; and Daiser (Turin, July 6, 1822) to Metternich, Berichte, Sardinien, Fasc. 59, No. 37.

particularly important, merit brief comment. Metternich had no difficulty with Russia or Prussia, who gave him in general full diplomatic support on these problems. England, too, was quite willing to see Austrian influence predominant in Italy, and let Metternich go his way without disturbance.[123] France, however, did give Metternich some trouble. After the outbreak of the Piedmontese revolt, the French government had revived its ideas of intervening both at Naples and at Turin in the hope of mediating the conflict and introducing the French *Charte* in both countries. The plan was thwarted only by England's refusal to participate in the scheme.[124] At the ministerial conferences in Florence, Rome, and Naples, the Duke of Blacas, though an unimpeachable royalist, had tended to act apart from the other envoys and, still worse, had actively supported the Duke of Calabria instead of Ruffo as a candidate to head the new ministry at Naples. Meanwhile, the government at Paris had lent its ear to the complaints of Sardinian agents against Austria, making them worse by spreading its own "calumnies" against Austria, suggesting, for example, that Metternich was attempting in Naples to use the ministerial conference and his influence over Prince Ruffo to keep the King permanently dependent upon him and to subject the government to Austrian control.[125]

Metternich's private reaction to these monstrous insinuations was to deplore the "underhanded" activities of Pasquier and his agents and to warn Vincent and Ficquelmont to be on guard against the

---

[123] The only question which seriously disturbed the British was the arbitrary treatment of Sicily, and on this score Metternich could do nothing with Ferdinand.—Webster, *Foreign Policy of Castlereagh*, 336–337.

[124] *Ibid.*, 335–336; Vincent (Florence, March 29 and April 7, 1821) to Metternich, Varia, Neapel, Fasc. 54, Nos. 9 (Postscript 3) and 10C. It was at this same time that personal relations between Richelieu and Metternich, once warm and friendly, began to cool, with Metternich growing impatient with Richelieu's failure to really fight liberalism in France, and the French premier becoming weary of Metternich's importunate and patronizing advice. As Richelieu wrote to Caraman (Paris, April 28, 1821), "It seems to me that [at Vienna] they have the idea of exercising a regency over us and of tracing for us the course that we must follow in the internal conduct of our affairs."— Bertier, *France and the European Alliance*, 119–120. See also Metternich (Laibach, April 10, 1821) to Richelieu, *ibid.*, 115–119.

[125] Blacas (Naples, September 18, 1821) to Metternich, Varia, Neapel, Fasc. 54; Ficquelmont (Naples, September 18, 1821) to Metternich, Berichte, Neapel, Fasc. 51; Metternich's secret letters (Vienna, July 7 and December 20, 1821) to Ficquelmont, Berichte und Weisungen, Neapel, Fasc. 52, and (Vienna, January 4, 1822) to Vincent, Weisungen, Frankreich, Fasc. 350, No. 6.

intrigues of Blacas. Publicly he assured France repeatedly of "the loyalty and rectitude of our course," showering Blacas with flattery in the hope of enlisting him with Austria in the common cause of all thrones.[126] When the Richelieu ministry fell in December 1821, to be replaced by an Ultra government headed by Count Villèle, Metternich took pains to give the new foreign minister, Viscount Montmorency, a truer picture of Austrian foreign policy than his predecessor had conceived. Austrian leadership in Italy, he explained, was solely a matter of self-protection and represented the only possible dike against revolution there. Nothing could be further from the Austrian mind than any thought of selfish interests or aggrandizement, since Austria had long realized that the old ideas of balance of power and spheres of influence, with their inevitable attendant conflicts and jealousies, must be discarded. The simple truth was that every other nation had tried to exercise or claim special influence in other lands, but Austria never had and never could.[127]

Metternich succeeded without great difficulty in turning aside French hindrances and objections to his Italian policy, which were never very formidable in any case. That he succeeded in convincing anyone, however, that Austria had no desire to exercise a special influence in Italy or that the Neapolitan government was really independent is doubtful. In this regard, the comment to Ficquelmont of the new French envoy to Naples, the liberal Count Hercule de Serre, on his arrival at Naples in the summer of 1822, is significant:

You have the right to first counsel [in the government at Naples]; and above all today, since the existing ministry is your creation, you ought all the more to exercise it, since you are, so to speak, responsible for its conduct.[128]

[126] Metternich (Vienna, January 4, 1822) to Vincent, Weisungen, Frankreich, Fasc. 350, No. 5; Metternich (Vienna, December 20, 1821) to Blacas, Berichte und Weisungen, Neapel, Fasc. 52 (attached to a letter to Ficquelmont of the same date).

[127] Metternich (Vienna, March 6, 1822) to Vincent, Weisungen, Frankreich, Fasc. 350, No. 2. Along with this explanation of Austrian policy, Metternich also had two requests to make of Montmorency and the new ministry: first, some disciplinary action against the *Journal des Débats* for its "hostile conduct" against the Austrian policy in Italy; and second, the ouster of La Tour du Pin from his post at Turin for spreading false rumors about Austrian plans in Sardinia. Metternich (Vienna, March 6, 1822) to Vincent, *ibid.*, Reserved to No. 2; Metternich (Vienna, April 24, August 12, 1822) to Vincent, *ibid.*, Nos. 3 and 4 and 4 and 5.

[128] Ficquelmont (Naples, July 5, 1822) to Metternich, Berichte, Neapel, Fasc. 55, No. 34.

CHAPTER VI

METTERNICH AND THE

RUSSO-TURK CRISIS, 1821-1822

The revolt which Alexander Ypsilanti began in the Danubian principalities on March 7, 1821, was only incidentally connected with the general revolution which spread to Greece proper a month later. The movement led by Ypsilanti represented a military adventure without any deep roots, carried out over the heads of an indifferent and even hostile population, a venture which, even had it succeeded, would have accomplished little more than to transfer suzerainty in the principalities from the Sultan of Turkey to the Tsar of Russia. The Greek revolution, however, was quite different. It was a genuinely popular movement, incited by the most pervasive and terrible mass passions, rooted in the deep cleavage existing between Turk and Greek in respect to nationality, religion, and culture, and inspired by the memory of lost Greek glory, the history of Turk overlordship, and Greek degradation ever since the fall of Constantinople. For this reason, and because of the generally low level of civilization on which both peoples existed, the conflict assumed on both sides the character of a war of extermination from the outset.[1]

[1] This account of the background and course of the Greek revolution in 1821–1822 is drawn chiefly from Anton Graf Prokesch von Osten, *Geschichte des Abfalls der Griechen vom türkischen Reiche in Jahre 1821 und der Gründung des hellenischen Königreiches, aus diplomatischem Standpuncte*, I, 1–188; Stern, *Geschichte Europas*, II, 183–216, 226–247; Christopher Montague Woodhouse, *The Greek War of Independence, its Historical Setting*, 11–83; 89–93; W. Alison Phillips, *The War of Greek Independence, 1821 to 1833*, 30–112; George Finlay, *A History of Greece from its Conquest by the Romans to the Present Time, B.C. 146 to A.D. 1864*, Vol. VI: *The Greek Revolution, Part I, A.D. 1821–1827*, 96–307. Some reference has also been made to

The Ypsilanti revolt was quickly and easily crushed. Not only did Ypsilanti prove to be a vain and incompetent leader, but also his movement was supported almost solely by the Phanariot Greek overlords in the Danubian principalities, while the native Roumanian boyars and peasants greeted Ypsilanti and his army as anything but liberators. Even so, the Turk garrisons in Moldavia were weak and easily overthrown, with needless massacres perpetrated on them at Galatz and Yassy in the process. Had Ypsilanti acted with alacrity to seize both provinces and to hold the line of the Danube, he might have been able to offer the Turks real resistance. But while he wasted his time in making futile proclamations and posturing, the Turks, with Alexander's blessing, sent an army into the provinces. Defeated in a minor engagement with the Turks at Dragashan on June 19, Ypsilanti fled to Austria, crossing the border and being interned there on June 25. Other remnants of his erstwhile army fled across the Pruth into Russia, a last remnant making a gallant stand against the Turks at Skuleni on June 29.

Far more formidable was the Greek revolt beginning in Morea in early April.[2] As one historian puts it, the only connections between the two movements were the family of Ypsilanti (Alexander's younger brother, Demetrius, came to Greece in the summer of 1821 to lead the revolution) and the conspiratorial secret society of the *Hetaireia,* which, with headquarters at Odessa and adherents among many of the Russian agents and consuls, spread the doctrine of revolution among the Greeks everywhere it could.[3] The main reason for the Greek revolt was not material suffering, for generally the economic condition of the Greeks had improved considerably in the late

---

Alexandre Soutzo, *Histoire de la révolution grecque,* and F. C. H. L. Pouqueville, *Histoire de la régenération de la Grèce, comprenant le précis des événements depuis 1740 jusqu'en 1824,* Vols. III and IV. The best accounts on the Greek question and European diplomacy in this period are in Prokesch, *Abfall der Griechen;* Webster, *Foreign Policy of Castlereagh,* 349–400; and Harold W. V. Temperley, *The Foreign Policy of Canning, 1822–1827: England, the Neo-Holy Alliance, and the New World,* 319–337. Charles William Crawley, *The Question of Greek Independence: A Study of British Policy in the Near East, 1821–1833,* gives only a brief treatment of the subject up to the death of Canning (pp. 1–29 cover the years 1821–1823).

[2] The traditional date for the beginning of the revolution is April 6. Actual fighting, however, seems to have begun about April 9 and to have become general by mid-April.

[3] Woodhouse, *Greek War of Independence,* 43.

THE

BALKANS

1821

eighteenth and early nineteenth centuries. Nor was it chiefly a question of outright political oppression, for, though kept in the humiliating and inferior status of *raja,* the Christian peoples of the Ottoman Empire were within that status generally tolerated and even granted considerable local autonomy. Land hunger did play a part in causing the revolt, for the vast majority of land in Morea was held by the small minority of Moslems there. The main causes, however, were religious and nationalistic. The Greeks hated the Turkish government because it was alien, despised it because it was corrupt and inefficient, and no longer greatly feared it because it was believed to be in a state of decay.

The war against the Turks was from the start one of popular risings and savage peasant warfare. Within a few short months all of the Greek countryside from Thessaly to Morea had been swept clean of Moslems—up to twenty thousand of them, mostly Greek converts to Islam, having been killed or enslaved. The remaining Turkish troops and terrified settlers were bottled up in a number of remaining fortresses and towns, heavily besieged. Those who surrendered often fell prey to massacre, as happened at Navarino, Tripolitsa, and elsewhere. A Greek navy, hardly more than a collection of pirates made up by the merchant shippers based on several islands of the Aegean and Adriatic Seas, notably Hydra, arose to prey on Turkish shipping, disrupt Turk communications, harass the Sultan's attempts to send reinforcements and supplies to his troops, and terrorize the Turk navy with their fireboats. The Sultan, his best troops engaged in southern Albania in reducing the rebellious Ali Pasha of Janina, and himself harassed elsewhere by the revolt in the principalities and trouble in Arabia and on the Persian frontier, could for the moment do little to suppress the Greek revolution.

Because it did not greatly concern Metternich in Vienna, however, the story of this revolution—with its varying fortunes but invariable bestiality on both sides, its internecine struggles within Greece between primates, soldiers of fortune, and politicians over control of the revolution, alternating with the fierce guerrilla warfare against the Turk—need not concern us greatly here.[4] While in the general interest of peace and order Metternich damned the revolt and wished the Sultan well in suppressing it, he kept his eyes

---

[4] "As for the Greek revolution," Metternich wrote Stadion, "let it go." Laibach, March 26, 1821, in Metternich, *Nachgelassene Papiere,* III, 464.

always on Europe and had no interest in the Greek struggle for its own sake. "What will happen in the Orient," he commented, "defies calculation. Perhaps there is not much in it; beyond our eastern borders three to four hundred thousand persons hanged, strangled, and spitted do not count for much" [5]—a statement which as a historical observation had a certain justification.

What did occupy all of Metternich's concern and test his diplomatic skill was the danger that a Russo-Turk war would break out as a result of the Greek revolution. The antagonism between Russia and Turkey had roots almost as deep and far-reaching as that between the Greeks and Turks. Serious conflict between Russia and Turkey began with Peter the Great, who had first turned the vague role that Moscow enjoyed as a protector of the Balkan peoples into a definite policy aimed at driving the Turks out of Europe and, as Catherine the Great had pursued this policy, of seizing Constantinople in the bargain. Though she fell short of this long-range goal, Catherine made impressive gains, important among which were the concessions granted by the Sublime Porte in the treaty of Kutchuk Kainardji in 1774. Here for the first time the Sultan recognized the right of Russia to protect some of the Orthodox Greek Christians in the Ottoman Empire, creating a species of Russo-Turk condominium in the Danubian principalities where, though the provinces remained under Turkish suzerainty, the Turks were required to obtain Russian consent if they wished to send any troops into the principalities, and Russian approval of the hospodars (governors) they appointed to run the principalities' largely autonomous governments. The treaty also allowed Russia to make representations before the Sultan on behalf of the Orthodox clergy, and charged the Sultan with protecting the Christian cult in his lands.[6]

Alexander I, heir to these gains along with certain others made by Tsar Paul, seemed at first to wish to pursue the same policy that his predecessors had followed at the expense of Turkey. The threat of Napoleonic aggression, however, prevented him from fully utilizing the Peace of Tilsit to dismember the Ottoman Empire, while Napoleon's impending invasion of Russia compelled him to break off the Turkish war with the Treaty of Bucharest on May 28, 1812. Though this treaty represented a retreat from the Russian goals of

[5] Private letter from Laibach, May 6, 1821, *ibid.*, 438.
[6] Schiemann, *Russland unter Nikolaus I*, Vol. I, 252–258.

incorporating the Danubian principalities into Russia and gaining further ways of interfering in Turkish internal affairs, it reaffirmed previous Russian rights in regard to the principalities and the Orthodox clergy, and granted the Serbs a special status analogous to that of Moldavia and Walachia. The most important and controversial clause was the unclearly-worded Article 6, which called for the restoration of the prewar Russo-Turk boundaries, thereby requiring Russia to evacuate the border territories and fortresses in Asia which she had captured. The Turks claimed that this article required the exact restoration of the *status quo ante bellum,* while the Russians retained possession of certain fortresses and villages which they claimed had voluntarily incorporated themselves into Russia and were not covered by the treaty. In the past such disputed clauses had often proved for Russia a welcome means of renewing controversy and extending Russian influence.[7]

Metternich knew, of course, about this long-standing source of Russo-Turk difficulty. It did not disturb him nearly so much, however, as did the activities of Russian consuls and agents within the Ottoman Empire. These agents, he had long believed, not without reason, were deeply involved in the plots of the *Hetaireia* and were encouraged by Capodistrias in their work of stirring up revolution.[8] The Ypsilanti rising, therefore, served to vindicate Metternich's long-standing fears and suspicions. Both Alexander's and Capodistrias' initial reaction to it, however, could not have been more correct. Besides disavowing the entire project, rejecting the pleas of Ypsilanti and the Moldavian hospodar Michael Suzzo for help, and granting the Turks full freedom to stamp out the revolt, Alexander and his Prime Minister gave the Russian generals on the Turkish border, and the Russian agents in the principalities, orders to observe a strict neutrality. They also instructed Baron Stroganov, Rus-

---

[7] *Ibid.,* 264–283. Gentz, whose sympathies were with the Porte here as on many other occasions, advised the Sultan not to press the issue, even though the disputed areas were still in Russian possession, for fear of straining relations and increasing danger of war. Gentz (Vienna, June 2, 1820) to Soutzo, in Gentz, *Dépêches inédites,* II, 32–53. In early 1821 the negotiations on the issue were in a state of suspension. Austrian Internuncio to the Porte Count Lützow (Constantinople, January 25, 1821) to Metternich, Berichte und Weisungen, Türkei, Fasc. 11, No. 74D.

[8] Metternich (Vienna, January 4, 1820) to Neumann, Weisungen, Grossbritannien, Fasc. 213; Metternich (Vienna, May 16, 1820) to Esterhazy, *ibid.*

sian minister at Constantinople, to try to help the Turks bring an
end to the revolt, if possible, even before a Turk invasion of the
principalities would be necessary.[9]

Although his own personal sympathies were with the Greeks,
Stroganov at first followed his instructions to help the Turks suppress the Ypsilanti revolt well enough to convince the Austrian Internuncio, Count Lützow, of his sincerity. Northing he could do or
say, however, sufficed to allay the Turks' suspicions of Russian complicity in the conspiracy.[10] When the revolution spread to Morea, the
situation became far worse. The Sultan's subjects, their latent fanaticism kindled by news of the revolt and of Greek atrocities, perpetrated acts of outrage and terrorism against Christians everywhere
in the Ottoman Empire, subjects of European countries—and particularly Russia—not excepted. The ruthless but effective measures
of the Sultan to ferret out the conspiracy and to quell rebellious
sentiment in the rest of his domains, most spectacular of which was
his public hanging of the Patriarch of Constantinople, outraged
Russia and Europe generally.[11] The declaration of a holy war against
the rebels, the appeal to the Barbary States for aid against the Greek
warships, the threat to send Janissaries into the Danubian principalities, the affirmation that the Sultan had the right, if he chose to
use it, to exterminate all Greeks within his domains—all these things,
while understandable in the light of fundamental Ottoman principles and the circumstances of the revolt, were perfectly suited to
enrage the Russians. Economic measures exacerbated the conflict.
The police measures adopted by the Turks, with Russian consent, to
prevent Greeks from escaping or smuggling through Ottoman ports
raised havoc with Russian commerce, while an Ottoman decree
closing the Sea of Marmora to traffic in grain, ostensibly designed to
cut off supplies of food to the rebelling Greek islands, severely dam-

[9] Ypsilanti (Yassy, March 5, 1821) to Alexander, Orientalische Angelegenheit-
en, Türkei, 1810–1822, Fasc. 16; Soutzo (Yassy, March 5, 1821) to Alexander
and to Capodistrias, *ibid.*; Alexander (Laibach, March 25, 1821) to Ypsilanti,
ibid.; Capodistrias (Laibach, March 26, 1821) to Stroganov, *ibid.*; Metternich
(Laibach, March 13 and 26, 1821) to Lützow, Berichte und Weisungen,
Türkei, Fasc. 11. The Moldavian hospodar, Michael Suzzo, was not related to
the former Walachian hospodar, Alexander Suzzo (or Soutzo).

[10] Lützow (Constantinople, March 24 and 31, 1821) to Metternich, Berichte
und Weisungen, Türkei, Fasc. 11, Nos. 80I, 80K, 81C.

[11] Lützow (Constantinople, April 20 and May 10, 1821) to Metternich, *ibid.*,
Nos. 84C and 88F, with supplements.

aged the Russian grain export trade centered at Odessa.[12] Charges and countercharges, meanwhile, flew back and forth, Stroganov protesting vehemently but without avail against the Turk atrocities, the destruction of churches, and the inhumane measures taken to repress the revolt; the Turks denying every charge, accusing the Russians of having instigated the revolt, and charging Stroganov even now with trying to interfere with the Turkish attempts to repress it.[13]

The worst problem of all was that of the principalities. By late April, Ypsilanti, deprived of the Russian support he had counted on, was ready to abandon the revolt, while Michael Suzzo had fled to Russia. The Russians, regretting the unconditional permission they had granted to Turkey to stamp out the revolt with armed force, wished the Turks to allow Ypsilanti and his troops to escape into either Russia or Austria, to accept the submission of the boyars and other inhabitants, and to send only a minimum armed force into the country to restore order, at the same time naming new hospodars and restoring the established civilian government according to treaty stipulations. The Turks were determined to stamp out the revolt in their own way, which meant making a sanguinary example of all the revolutionary leaders they could apprehend and occupying the principalities with an armed force under a temporary military administration until the revolt in Morea was suppressed. To aid them in this effort, they demanded the extradition of Michael Suzzo and other fugitives from Russia. Both the Russian insistence on the evacuation of the principalities and the Turk demand for the extradition of the fugitives were based on clear treaty stipulations; yet neither side felt in the least willing or able to accede to what the other demanded.[14]

By early July matters were at a breaking point. The Grand Vizier appealed to Nesselrode with a long tirade against Stroganov and

[12] Lützow (Constantinople, April 10 and 25, May 25, 1821) to Metternich, *ibid.*, Nos. 82G, with supplement, unnumbered letter with supplements, and 91I.
[13] Lützow (Constantinople, May 18 and 25, 1821) to Metternich, *ibid.*, Nos. 89B, with supplements, and 91G, with supplements.
[14] Notes, Reis Efendi (Constantinople, April 25, 1821) to Stroganov, and the response by Stroganov, n.d., in Prokesch, *Abfall der Griechen*, III, 72–79. Many other documents cited hereinafter by me are also printed in this volume. Since I used them originally in the archives, however, they will be cited as archival materials.

his actions;[15] Stroganov in turn called upon his Cabinet to back up his unavailing protests to the Porte. The Cabinet's answer was all Stroganov could desire.[16] Under its instructions, he delivered to the Porte on July 18 an ultimatum of eight-days' duration. The note demanded not only that the Turks promptly evacuate the principalities but also that they make a distinction between the innocent and the guilty in repressing the revolt, that they guarantee the future protection of the Christian cult within the Ottoman Empire, and that they take steps to restore the churches destroyed in the recent outbreaks of violence, all on pain of having Russia withdraw her ambassador if the terms were not met. In addition to these four specific requirements, there were vague statements to the effect that the Ottoman Empire would have to change its system for ruling its Christian subjects, that Russia ought to participate in the pacification and amelioration of the Danubian principalities, and that Russia had the right under existing treaties to protect all Christians everywhere in the Ottoman Empire.[17]

The Turk answer to this ultimatum, delayed until the ultimatum had expired, was completely unconciliatory, rejecting all the Russian charges and insisting that the Turks had already fulfilled all the conditions the Russians had named.[18] Stroganov thereupon retired to Buyukdère, ready to depart as soon as the Turks would give him his passports. There was grave doubt that they would, for both Stroganov and Lützow feared that he might be imprisoned, in which case war would have become inevitable. Largely due to the intervention of Lützow and English Ambassador Lord Strangford, Strog-

---

[15] Translation of a note by the Grand Vizier (Constantinople, July 9, 1821) to Nesselrode, in Berichte, Russland, Fasc. 31 (copy also in Berichte und Weisungen, Türkei, Fasc. 11).

[16] Capodistrias even authorized Stroganov to change the wording of the Russian note to be presented to the Porte if he thought it necessary. Russian Cabinet (St. Petersburg, June 28, 1820) to Stroganov, Prokesch, *Abfall der Griechen*, III, 92–93.

[17] Lützow (Constantinople, July 26, 1821) to Metternich, Berichte und Weisungen, Türkei, Fasc. 11, No. 98E and Postscript (text of Stroganov's ultimatum).

[18] "Traduction de la Note officielle destinée à être transmise par la S. Porte à Mr. l'Envoye de Russie Baron de Stroganoff" [ca. end of July 1821], Weisungen, Russland, Fasc. 45; Grand Vizier (Constantinople, same date) to Nesselrode, *ibid.*

anov was able to leave on August 7. Relations between Russia and Turkey were now all but broken.[19]

Metternich, meanwhile, had been watching the situation with growing concern. He was convinced that the Greek revolution could and should be left to burn itself out or, better still, to be crushed by the Turks. The Russo-Turk crisis, however, had to be considered a matter of common interest for all European powers, since out of it might arise a war which would stimulate the factious everywhere to renewed revolutionary activity.[20] Austria, moreover, opposed any move to expel the Turks from Europe for one simple reason: "The interest of Europe," said Metternich, "pronounces against any major political change." [21]

As his early hope that the Turks would quickly crush the revolt faded [22] and as Russo-Turk tension grew, the Austrian Chancellor found himself in an increasingly difficult position. On the one hand, he had to stay on good terms with the Porte in order to influence the Turks toward moderation. On the other hand, his whole foreign policy bound him to Russia as his closest and most important ally. If he offended Russia by being too amenable to the Turks, he not only would risk losing an ally, but also he would lose the influence he needed to steer Russia away from war. Thus Metternich had to carry out a delicate balancing act, helping Turkey within the bounds of benevolent neutrality to deal with the revolution, but also generally supporting the representations of Stroganov at Constantinople and urging both sides, especially the Turks, to use moderation.[23] In

[19] Officially Stroganov's departure meant a suspension, not the rupture, of diplomatic relations. Lützow (Constantinople, July 25 and 30, 1821) to Metternich, Berichte und Weisungen, Türkei, Fasc. 11, Nos. 98E and 99A, with supplements (copies of correspondence between Stroganov and Lützow); Lützow (Constantinople, August 5 and 7, 1821) to Metternich, Berichte und Varia, Türkei, Fasc. 12, Nos. 100A and 101C.

[20] Metternich (Laibach, May 14, and Vienna, July 16, 1821) to Esterhazy, Weisungen, Grossbritannien, Fasc. 217.

[21] Metternich (Vienna, December 19, 1821) to Lützow, Berichte und Weisungen, Türkei, Fasc. 11.

[22] Metternich (Vienna, June 6 and 14, 1821) to Esterhazy, Weisungen, Grossbritannien, Fasc. 217, No. 2.

[23] Lützow was instructed to work with Stroganov and to try to convince the Porte that compliance with the Russian demands was a wise course fully compatible with the Sultan's dignity. Metternich (Laibach, April 29, and Vienna, July 17 and 31, 1821) to Lützow, Berichte und Weisungen, Türkei, Fasc. 11; Lützow (Constantinople, May 2 and July 2, 1821) to Metternich, *ibid.*, Nos. 84B–D, 96A.

dealing with Alexander, meanwhile, Metternich instructed Lebzeltern to follow the same tactics Metternich had used at Laibach: to praise the Tsar's principles and his loyalty to the cause of peace and the alliance, but at the same time to frighten him with the specter of universal revolution which would arise if Russia set out on a course isolated from her Allies.[24]

The July crisis in Russo-Turk relations which culminated in Stroganov's ultimatum further perturbed Metternich, though it did not fatally discourage him. The departure of Stroganov from Constantinople, he contended, was not an unmixed evil, for it at least meant that this controversial figure was no longer on the scene. Moreover, relations between the two powers were only strained, not broken.[25] Nevertheless, the situation clearly called for definite action. In addition to continuing to urge moderation at St. Petersburg and Constantinople, in the latter place in close conjunction with the envoys of England and France, Metternich now proposed an Allied conference of ambassadors at Vienna to act as a "foyer of deliberation" for all five Allied Courts on the Eastern question, to guide their envoys at Constantinople.[26]

This proposal broke down partly because Russia was unwilling to see her demands on the Porte so quickly shunted into the bog of five-power deliberations and partly because England was reluctant to become entangled in any joint deliberations or *démarches*.[27] Castlereagh, however, saw as clearly as Metternich the necessity of restraining Alexander from war, and was only too willing to cooperate informally with Metternich to this end. Thus the Russo-Turk crisis had the effect of largely closing the rift between Austria and England left by the Congresses of Troppau and Laibach.[28] English

[24] Metternich (Vienna, July 18, 1821) to Lebzeltern, Weisungen, Russland, Fasc. 45, No. 1.

[25] Metternich (Vienna, August 15, 1821) to Esterhazy, Weisungen, Grossbritannien, Fasc. 217, No. 1.

[26] Metternich (Vienna, August 24, 1821) to Esterhazy, *ibid.* (This was a circular dispatch to Austrian emissaries at the major courts.)

[27] Webster, *Foreign Policy of Castlereagh*, 364–365; Esterhazy (London, September 13, 1821) to Metternich, Berichte, Grossbritannien, Fasc. 215, No. 204A.

[28] Webster, *Foreign Policy of Castlereagh*, 360–366; Esterhazy (London, August 2 and 3, 1821) to Metternich, Berichte, Grossbritannien, Fasc. 215, Nos. 198A, 198B; Castlereagh (London, July 16, 1821) to Alexander, Varia, Grossbritannien, Fasc. 19.

cooperation was doubly welcome to Metternich because at Constantinople the Turks, regarding Austria with deep suspicion because of her association with Russia in the Holy Alliance (which the Turks persisted in viewing as an instrument for another anti-Moslem crusade), made a favorite of the English ambassador, the pro-Turk Lord Strangford. Strangford had endeared himself to the Turks by declining to participate in a joint Allied protest to the Porte against the Turkish measures of reprisal and repression in Constantinople, defending the Turks so warmly on this occasion as to cause bitter enmity between himself and Stroganov, and even some tension between himself and Lützow.[29] Hence Castlereagh's support, and thereby also that of Strangford, came to Metternich as a very welcome boon. He had been seeking it since the outbreak of the revolt.[30]

The Anglo-Austrian cooperation was not, to be sure, a perfect one. Metternich felt that the English were inclined to push Russia too hard and the Porte not hard enough.[31] He also disapproved sharply of a proposal by Strangford for a joint Allied proclamation to be made from Constantinople to the rebelling Greeks, calling on them to surrender within a given period under an Allied guarantee of an amnesty, unless they wanted to be abandoned to the mercy of the Sultan. Metternich saw that this step not only would be an unwelcome interference in Turkish internal affairs (the Sultan, in fact, immediately rejected it), but would also make the Allies guarantors of any armistice which would follow Greek surrender—a fact that made Nesselrode enthusiastic over the idea.[32] But on the main

[29] Lützow (Constantinople, May 2 and 25, 1821) to Metternich, Berichte und Weisungen, Türkei, Fasc. 11, Nos. 87C and 91K; Metternich (Baden, August 14, and Vienna, August 15, 1821) to Esterhazy, Weisungen, Grossbritannien, Fasc. 217.

[30] Metternich (Laibach, May 21, and Vienna, May 30, June 14, and August 14, 1821) to Esterhazy, Weisungen, Grossbritannien, Fasc. 217; Esterhazy (London, July 14, 1821) to Metternich, Berichte, Grossbritannien, Fasc. 215, No. 195A.

[31] Metternich (Baden, August 14, 1821) to Esterhazy, Weisungen, Grossbritannien, Fasc. 217 (a second, secret letter).

[32] Lützow (Constantinople, September 19 and October 10, 1821) to Metternich, Berichte und Varia, Türkei, Fasc. 12, No. 106A, with supplements and unnumbered; Lebzeltern (St. Petersburg, October 5, 1821) to Metternich, Berichte, Russland, Fasc. 31, No. 16A; Metternich (Vienna, October 5, 1821) to Lützow, Berichte und Weisungen, Türkei, Fasc. 11, No. 4; Metternich (Vienna, October 2 and 9, Frankfurt, November 9, 1821) to Esterhazy, Weisungen, Grossbritannien, Fasc. 217, Nos. 3 and 4.

points—that the Russo-Turk crisis must be a European, not a Russian affair, that both sides must separate past grievances from present issues, that the Porte must meet the just demands of Russia, without acceding to the vague implications which the Russian Cabinet attached to them, and that a Greek triumph in the revolution or a Russian intervention in their behalf would be disastrous for Europe—the two powers were happily agreed and could work together.[33] Castlereagh disavowed any thought of separate English action or mediation between Turkey and the Greeks, while at Constantinople Lützow cultivated Strangford and followed his lead and at St. Petersburg Lebzeltern and Sir Charles Bagot, the British ambassador, worked hand in hand.[34]

To solidify and direct even better this renewed Anglo-Austrian cooperation on the Eastern question, Castlereagh and King George IV invited Metternich to a personal conference at Hanover in October, to coincide with a visit of the King to his German subjects.[35] Metternich, who had been thinking of some such meeting himself, readily agreed, hoping not only to regulate the common approach to the Russo-Turk question but also to lead the separatist British back into the fold of the alliance.[36] The meetings, lasting from October 20 to 29, pleased Metternich immensely. He basked in the flattery King George showered upon him and thoroughly enjoyed the intimate talks with Castlereagh and the role of mentor to the crowned heads of Europe which his journey through Germany enabled him to play.[37] Besides this, he believed that he had been able to reach complete agreement with Castlereagh on the Eastern question. Now he felt sure that all of Europe, except for certain elements in Russia,

[33] Metternich (Vienna, August 24, 1821) to Lebzeltern, Weisungen, Russland, Fasc. 45, No. 2.

[34] Esterhazy (London, November 29 and December 9, 1821) to Metternich, Berichte, Grossbritannien, Fasc. 215, Nos. 206A, 298B; Metternich (Vienna, September 19, 1821) to Lützow, Berichte und Weisungen, Türkei, Fasc. 11; Metternich (Vienna, October 2, 1821) to Esterhazy, Weisungen, Grossbritannien, Fasc. 217, No. 1.

[35] Stewart (Vienna, September 21, 1821) to Gordon, Varia, Grossbritannien, Fasc. 19; Castlereagh (Aachen, October 1, 1821) to Metternich, *ibid.*

[36] Metternich (Vienna, October 9, 1821) to Esterhazy, Weisungen, Grossbritannien, Fasc. 217, No. 1; Metternich (Vienna, October 14, 1821) to Lebzeltern, Weisungen, Russland, Fasc. 45, No. 1. Since Webster gives a full account of the Hanover conferences (*Foreign Policy of Castlereagh*, 365–366, 372–382), my account will only summarize its results.

[37] Metternich, *Nachgelassene Papiere*, III, 450–452.

wanted peace in the Orient. News received at Hanover from Prince Lieven, Russian ambassador to England, who had just left St. Petersburg after conferring with Alexander, indicated that the Tsar also desired peace.[38]

Yet, as Metternich well knew, neither the Anglo-Austrian entente nor Alexander's good intentions could guarantee peace. The fanaticism and savagery of Turk and Greek, the stubborn pride and suspicion of the Porte, and the ambitious schemings of the war party in Russia were all factors in the situation, any one of which could prove too strong for the "spider webs" of Metternich's diplomacy to contain. Never was the Austrian Chancellor more conscious of the weakness of the purely moral weapons that he had at his disposal.[39]

The crucial factor, of course, was the struggle over policy within Russia. The information which Metternich received from Lebzeltern on the Russian internal situation, though not always clear and coherent, and which on the vital question of Capodistrias' views was perforce second- or third-hand,[40] plainly indicated some disturbing facts. First, the Greek cause was very popular in Russia, with many influential persons favoring a war to liberate the Greeks and expand Russian territory. Second, Capodistrias, while he had not actually instigated the revolt, was very sympathetic to it, and counted on the continued intransigence of the Porte and the prolongation of the Greek revolt to bring war between Russia and Turkey. In the third place, because Capodistrias and the war party knew that they would find it difficult or impossible to draw Alexander into war without the approval of the Allies, or at least their tacit consent, they were trying every device to obtain this consent at Allied Courts, attempting, for example, to draw a parallel between Austrian action in Naples and Piedmont and the projected Russian intervention in Greece.[41]

---

[38] Metternich (Hanover, October 24 and 29, 1821) to Francis, *ibid.*, 488–495; Metternich (Hanover, October 27, 1821) to Esterhazy, Weisungen, Grossbritannien, Fasc. 217; Metternich (Hanover, October 31, 1821) to Lebzeltern, Weisungen, Russland, Fasc. 45.

[39] The term "spider webs" is Metternich's own. Private letter from Vienna, July 23, 1821, in Metternich, *Nachgelassene Papiere*, III, 444.

[40] Lebzeltern was instructed to avoid Capodistrias as much as possible and to deal with Nesselrode only. Metternich (Vienna, December 3, 1821) to Lebzeltern, Weisungen, Russland, Fasc. 45, No. 9.

[41] Austrian *Chargé* Bombelles (St. Petersburg, June 29, 1821) to Metternich, Berichte, Russland, Fasc. 31; Lebzeltern (St. Petersburg, August 12 and 14, October 21, 1821) to Metternich, *ibid.*, Nos. 5C, 6, 17A; dispatch, Russian

What Capodistrias did or planned did not surprise Metternich. More disturbing to him were signs that Alexander was wavering in his peaceful intentions. Although the Tsar had displayed a strong desire for peace just before the dispatch of the Russian ultimatum,[42] the prolonged crisis and the failure of the Turks to meet the Russian terms were a great strain on his good intentions. He was also influenced in the wrong direction by a memoir which Johann Ancillon, director of the Political Division at the Prussian Foreign Ministry, had written and which Bernstorff, at the instance of Russian Ambassador Alopeus, had issued from Berlin. Its prediction of a breakup of Turkey's European domains and its recommendation for an independent Greece under European protection and guarantee encouraged dangerous ideas in Alexander.[43] He began openly to contemplate the possibility of war, to discuss its possible advantages, and to look for the least sign of encouragement from his Allies to undertake it. Plainly not disturbed by any fear of losses or defeat, he was deterred only by his concern for the European system.[44]

Metternich did everything possible to reinforce the deterrent factors. Although he did not agree with all the Russian charges against Turkey, he gave diplomatic support to the four points of the Russian ultimatum, especially to the most important: Turk evacuation of the principalities and restoration of their regular form of government. At the same time, he worked to restrict Russian demands to these four points, narrowly defined, and nothing more.[45] In addition, he flooded Nesselrode and Alexander with secret police reports purporting to show that the factious elements all over Europe were waiting only for the outbreak of a Russo-Turkish war to institute a general ris-

---

Cabinet (St. Petersburg, August 1821) to its missions, *ibid.;* Lebzeltern (St. Petersburg, January 9, 1822) to Metternich, *ibid.,* Fasc. 56, No. 24F.

[42] Lebzeltern (St. Petersburg, July 13, 15, and 16, 1821) to Metternich, *ibid.,* Fasc. 31, Nos. 1A–C.

[43] Lebzeltern (St. Petersburg, September 1, 1821) to Metternich, *ibid.,* Nos. 9A and 9B. The Ancillon memoir is printed in Prokesch, *Abfall der Griechen,* III, 336–346. See also Bernstorff (Berlin, July 27, 1821) to Alopeus, *ibid.,* 347–351.

[44] Lebzeltern (St. Petersburg, October 21 and December 1, 1821) to Metternich, Berichte, Russland, Fasc. 31, Nos. 17A and 21B.

[45] Metternich (Vienna, October 31, 1821) to Lebzeltern, Weisungen, Russland, Fasc. 45.

ing.[46] All these measures were, of course, no sure antidote for the war fever in Russia. Just as Capodistrias, in Metternich's opinion, was counting on time and the Porte's errors to bring on war, so had he to count on time, the faithfulness of Alexander, and his own ability to guide the Porte into the right course to help prevent it.[47]

The task of guiding the Porte into a wiser course, however, proved at this time to be beyond the combined diplomatic skills of Metternich, Strangford, and Lützow. Deplore as he might the Turk course as one of suspicion, obstinacy, and savagery, the Austrian Chancellor could not change it.[48] For a time in the late summer and early fall of 1821, it had seemed as if the Ottoman government would listen to Austria's counsels of prudence. On the crucial point of evacuation of the principalities, the Turks, after at first insisting that they would never leave until the last rebel there had been punished and the revolt in Morea suppressed—and not then so long as five hundred thousand Russians remained mobilized in Russia—began to show signs of giving way. The Reis Efendi, Hamid Bey, confidentially assured Strangford that the troops would be withdrawn soon if the Porte received a guarantee that Russian troops would not be sent in to replace them.[49] Strangford, eagerly pursuing this opening, succeeded in getting the Porte to convey through Metternich a feeler to Russia, proposing to evacuate the principalities in exchange for this desired guarantee.[50] Other signs of improvement in the Turk attitude appeared: a decree announcing clemency to a

[46] In one dispatch Metternich sent eighty double pages of such reports for Alexander's perusal. Metternich (Vienna, March 31, 1822) to Lebzeltern, Weisungen, Russland, Fasc. 45, No. 12, with supplements. Nesselrode at one time protested against Metternich's taking up so much of the Tsar's time with such trivia at a time of crisis, and also severely criticized Metternich's repeated attempts to overthrow Capodistrias by sending documents purporting to implicate him in the Greek revolt. Lebzeltern (St. Petersburg, September 10, 1821, and January 9, 1822) to Metternich, Berichte, Russland, Fasc. 31 and Fasc. 56.

[47] Metternich (Vienna, December 3, 1821) to Lebzeltern, Weisungen, Russland, Fasc. 45, No. 9.

[48] Metternich (Constantinople, July 3, 1821) to Lützow, Berichte und Weisungen, Türkei, Fasc. 11.

[49] Lützow (Constantinople, August 5 and 25, September 10, 1821) to Metternich, Berichte und Varia, Türkei, Fasc. 12, Nos. 100A, 104E, 105F.

[50] Strangford (Constantinople, August 26, 1821) to Charles Bagot, *ibid.*; Metternich (Vienna, October 6, 1821) to Lebzeltern, Weisungen, Russland, Fasc. 45, No. 1; Metternich (Vienna, October 5, 1821) to Lützow, Berichte und Weisungen, Türkei, Fasc. 11, No. 3.

number of Greek islands, along with steps taken by the Sultan to quiet anti-Russian agitation at Constantinople and to quell the intrigues of the Janissaries, who, fearing their impending reform, were among the strongest in opposing any concessions to the Greeks and the Russians.[51] Seeing all this as evidence that "the Porte has not been entirely deaf to the voice of reason," Metternich urged Lützow next to persuade the Porte quietly to drop its demand for the extradition of the Moldavian rebels fugitive in Russia, especially Michael Suzzo. The demand, said Metternich, was theoretically just but politically impossible for Russia to fulfill; Turkey would act the same as Russia was now acting if her co-religionists were fugitive in Turkish territory, and she had done so on previous occasions. The Ottoman government should be satisfied if the fugitives were removed from the border, where they could cause trouble.[52] This would leave only the questions of the restoration of the churches and the naming of the hospodars to deal with, and within the limits set by Turk principles and suspicions something might even be done to meet these problems.

This hopeful situation changed sharply for the worse, however, with the deposition of Hamid Bey because of his suspected leniency to the Greeks and his replacement as Reis Efendi by Sadik Efendi, characterized by Lützow as an incorruptible zealot and anti-Christian fanatic. The fall of Hamid Bey served, as Lützow soon discovered, to annul all the promises and concessions he had made to the foreign courts [53] and to renew the Turkish policy of delay and

---

[51] Lützow (Constantinople, August 18, September 17 and 23, 1821) to Metternich, Berichte und Varia, Türkei, Fasc. 12, Nos. 103A with supplements, Particular, and 107F; Strangford (Constantinople, August 6, 1821) to the Porte, *ibid.*

[52] Metternich (Vienna, September 1, 1821) to Lebzeltern, Weisungen, Russland, Fasc. 45; Metternich (Vienna, September 4 and 10, 1821) to Lützow, Berichte und Weisungen, Türkei, Fasc. 11. The Austrian argument on the extradition of the fugitives was complicated by the fact that Ypsilanti had been interned in Austria. Although Austria had intentionally opened this path of escape to him, Metternich told the Turks that he had managed to slip in because of the ruggedness of the Transylvanian frontier. A further embarrassment for Lützow was the fact that, lacking information, he had denied, a month after Ypsilanti was taken into custody, the whole story as a vicious rumor. Metternich (Vienna, July 17, 1821) to Lützow, *ibid.*; Lützow (Constantinople, July 25, 1821) to Metternich, *ibid.*, No. 98F.

[53] Lützow (Constantinople, November 10 and 20, 1821) to Metternich, Berichte und Varia, Türkei, Fasc. 12, Nos. 110H, 111C.

tergiversation with a vengeance. After four weeks of futile attempts to gain an interview with the new Reis Efendi, Lützow was finally granted one on November 22, only to find that the Turk attitude had hardened on every point. On the questions of evacuation and the naming of hospodars, the Turks returned to their intransigent position of July, at the same time reviving their demand for Russian extradition of the fugitives.[54]

Nor could any progress on the other issues be made, either. In Lützow's opinion the heated state of public opinion in Turkey, evidenced in November and December 1821 by renewed anti-European outbreaks in Constantinople and new atrocities in Smyrna and elsewhere, made concessions by the Sultan impossible.[55] Mohammedan fatalism at the same time apparently rendered the Ottoman government impervious to the threat of a disastrous war. When Metternich warned the Porte that if it resorted to arms or if peace was once broken, all the European peoples would side with the Greeks to help destroy the Ottoman Empire, the Turks replied that, however this might be, European sympathy for the Greeks would be powerless to save them, for before Russian troops could reach Constantinople, all the Christian peoples under Turk rule would have been massacred.[56] Metternich failed equally to rid the Porte of its erroneous notions about the Holy Alliance and absurd suspicions of Austrian intentions.[57] By the close of 1821, the negotiations in Constantinople were in a state of stagnation. While still convinced that

[54] Lützow (Constantinople, November 20 and 26, 1821) to Metternich, *ibid.*, Nos. 111C with supplements, 112F; Lützow (Constantinople, November 25, 1821) to Reis Efendi, Orientalische Angelegenheiten: Türkei, Fasc. 16; Reis Efendi (Constantinople, December 2, 1821) to Lützow, *ibid.* (translation).

[55] The Turk argument was that the Sultan had always protected the Christian cult and respected the distinction between the innocent and the guilty in the rebellion, and hence that on these points no possible complaint could be made. As for restoration of the churches, Lützow conceded that religious principles and public opinion forbade the Sultan from giving any direct aid for this purpose. At best he could only permit their reconstruction from funds privately collected for the purpose. Lützow (Constantinople, November 26, December 8 and 24, 1821) to Metternich, Berichte und Varia, Türkei, Fasc. 12, Nos. 112L, 114A, 114B, and 116F, with supplements.

[56] Metternich (Vienna, October 14, 1821) to Lützow, Berichte und Weisungen, Türkei, Fasc. 11; Lützow (Constantinople, December 8, 1821) to Metternich, Berichte und Varia, Türkei, Fasc. 12, No. 114C.

[57] Metternich (Vienna, November 17, 1821) to Lützow, Berichte und Weisungen, Türkei, Fasc. 11; Lützow (Constantinople, November 26, 1821) to Metternich, Berichte und Varia, Türkei, Fasc. 12, No. 112K.

neither the Sultan nor the Tsar actually wanted war, Metternich feared that the danger of it was greater than ever.[58]

To escape the treadmill upon which up to this time Austrian diplomatic efforts had floundered, Metternich tried a new diplomatic maneuver. This was to persuade the Russians to separate the objects now in dispute, viewing three of the issues (the restoration of the churches, the distinction between innocent and guilty, and the protection of the Christian cult) as settled in principle but deferred on arrangements for execution, while laying all the stress on the question of the evacuation of the principalities according to the Treaty of Bucharest. Should the Turks refuse to withdraw their troops and to name commissioners to rule the provinces (as an interim expedient for formally-nominated hospodars), all the powers should unite in declaring to the Porte that negotiation was ended.[59] Thus Metternich hoped to separate the vital from the subsidiary questions; to get the whole discussion away from vague ideas about amelioration of the lot of the Greeks and back on the safe ground of treaty rights; to persuade the Turks to accept the help of third powers in seeking reconciliation with Russia, and to get the Russians to renew diplomatic relations with Turkey solely on the basis of evacuation in the principalities; and to make all the subsidiary matters concerning the pacification and future treatment of the Greeks to be concerns of the Allies, not subjects for Russo-Turk negotiations.[60]

This ingenious maneuver in the long run fulfilled its purpose of avoiding war, but it came close to failure at the outset because of the suspicions of both sides in the dispute. Even Nesselrode, who did not want war, believed that the Allies were being far too squeamish in dealing with the Porte. The proper way to act, he insisted,

[58] Metternich (Vienna, December 23, 1821) to Lebzeltern, Weisungen, Russland, Fasc. 45, Nos. 1 and 8.

[59] *Ibid.*, No. 2. Apparently both Lützow and Strangford believed that the Porte would give in on the evacuation issue and would name commissioners if forced to, but could not make concessions on other issues. Strangford therefore requested the Foreign Office to express its opinion on the envoys' idea of extending an ultimatum to the Porte, demanding that it meet these two conditions or be abandoned to its fate. Strangford (Constantinople, November 9, 1821) to Castlereagh, attached to Metternich (Vienna, December 3, 1821) to Lebzeltern, *ibid.*, No. 12.

[60] Metternich (Vienna, December 23, 1821) to Lebzeltern, *ibid.*, No. 2; Metternich (Vienna, January 31, 1822) to Esterhazy, Weisungen, Grossbrittanien, Fasc. 218.

was for the powers jointly to prescribe the conditions of peace once
and for all, and together to break relations with the Sultan if these
were not promptly met. The ordinary procedure of exchanging notes
and memoirs, he said, only played into the hands of the Turks, enabling them to evade the issues and exploit the differences between
the powers. He further proposed that Austria assemble a corps of
observation on her Turkish frontier, as Russia had done for Austria at Laibach. As for Metternich's proposal to separate the objects
of negotiation, this appeared to him simply as an Austrian scheme
to get Russia to abandon most of her claims.[61]

Other signs of bad feeling cropped up in the Russian capital. Alexander, receiving from Metternich another veiled warning that Austria would have to look to her own interests if Russia weakened in
her attachment to the alliance, reacted with pained surprise to this
evidence of uncalled-for suspicion of his fidelity to his promises.[62]
Lebzeltern, tiring of Nesselrode's repeated complaints about the
weakness and colorlessness of Austrian policy at Constantinople, accused Nesselrode of having closed his mind on the negotiations and
charged Russia with having made up her mind for war. This was
not true, replied Nesselrode; but while Russia still wanted peace,
she could not wait forever for fulfillment of her just demands. She
was, therefore, he admitted, ready for any eventuality, and if results
were not reached with the Porte by March, the Emperor intended
to place himself at the head of his troops.[63]

At Constantinople, meanwhile, the situation was little better. Although Lützow's account of Nesselrode's threat of war to the Reis
Efendi, along with his report on certain steps Russia had taken to
meet Turk complaints regarding the rebel fugitives, apparently had
some good effect on the Turks,[64] the Porte still showed itself unwill-

[61] Lebzeltern (St. Petersburg, January 9 and 10, 1822) to Metternich,
Berichte, Russland, Fasc. 56, Nos. 24H, 25, 26.

[62] Lebzeltern (St. Petersburg, January 30, 1822) to Metternich, *ibid.*, No.
28B; Metternich (Vienna, February 18, 1822) to Esterhazy, Weisungen,
Grossbritannien, Fasc. 218, No. 1.

[63] Lebzeltern (St. Petersburg, February 6, 1822) to Metternich, Berichte,
Russland, Fasc. 56, No. 29A.

[64] Lützow (Constantinople, February 11, 1822) to Metternich, Berichte,
Türkei, Fasc. 13, No. 120F, and particular letter; Metternich (Vienna, January
28 and February 20, 1822) to Lützow, Weisungen, Türkei, Fasc. 14. The
moves included the removal of fugitives into the interior of Russia, steps against
the *Hetaireia* at Odessa, and the expulsion of Michael Suzzo to Austria.

ing to listen to reason. Strangford could elicit from it nothing but vague promises about future action, and Lützow encountered only evasion and delays.[65] When, after weeks of being put off, the Austrian envoy finally presented the plan for separation of the issues under negotiation, on which Metternich had laid great store,[66] it met with the worst possible reception. In a memoir of February 28 the Porte accused Austria of showing a pro-Russian bias and of ignoring the just claims and arguments of Turkey. The principalities, the Turkish note argued, were now in a state of perfect quiet, owing to the presence of Turkish troops; if these were removed, the revolt would flame up again and the provinces would become a haven for refugees from Morea and Rumelia. If Austria wished to insist on the fulfillment of treaties, she ought to put pressure on Russia to extradite the fugitives and deliver over the disputed Asiatic fortresses to Turkey. As for the Sultan's treaty obligations, he would fulfill them all, but this required time.[67]

Metternich now considered his argument with the Porte as exhausted and instructed Lützow, with whose conduct of the negotiations he was dissatisfied in any case, to intermit Austrian mediation and leave further dealings entirely up to Strangford. In reply to the Ottoman memoir, Metternich expressed deep indignation that the Turks should so completely have misinterpreted the Austrian labors for peace.[68] Metternich's efforts, it appeared, were resented by the one side and flatly rejected by the other. Never had the threat to

[65] Lützow (Constantinople, February 25, 1822) to Metternich, Berichte, Türkei, Fasc. 13.

[66] See Metternich's secret letter (Vienna, December 31, 1821) to Lebzeltern, Weisungen, Russland, Fasc. 45.

[67] Lützow (Constantinople, March 5, 1822) to Metternich, Berichte, Türkei, Fasc. 13, No. 122B, with supplement. Lützow believed that the Sultan was sincere in promising an early evacuation of the principalities, but that the promise was entirely contingent upon his being able to crush the Greek revolt first, which he expected his spring campaign of 1822 to do. Lützow (same date) to Metternich, *ibid.*, No. 122C.

[68] Metternich (Vienna, March 27, 1822) to Lützow, Weisungen, Türkei, Fasc. 14, Nos. 1 and 2, with supplement; Metternich (Vienna, March 17, 1822) to Esterhazy, Weisungen, Grossbritannien, Fasc. 218, No. 5. Besides the official Austrian protest, Lützow and Strangford presented a joint note of protest on March 10 and Strangford made clear his own displeasure with the Turk attitude—all, however, without apparent effect. Lützow (Constantinople, March 12 and April 10, 1822) to Metternich, Berichte, Türkei, Fasc. 13, supplement to particular letter, and No. 125I, with supplement.

peace seemed greater than at this point in late February and early March of 1822.[69]

This proved to be a period of darkness just before the dawn. However tempted he may have been by an Oriental war, Alexander never took his eyes completely off the European scene. The fall of Richelieu's ministry in France, even though the new ministry was a Royalist one, renewed his fears about the political stability of France and of Europe.[70] The Austrian policy of playing on these fears, holding Alexander to his professed principles, and depriving him of any moral ground for going to war, pursued with great skill by both Metternich and Lebzeltern, finally bore fruit. In a long interview with the Austrian ambassador on February 19, the Tsar, after registering strong complaints against Austria's failure to support him as he had supported her in Italy, announced that he would give one more proof of his devotion to the alliance. He would send General Tatistchev, former minister to Spain, as a special envoy to bear the Tsar's thoughts directly to Metternich and to consult with him on future policy. Lebzeltern perceived that the Emperor chose this move not only to avoid war but also to extricate himself from the difficulty created by the two divergent policies pursued at St. Petersburg—his own, and that of Capodistrias and Stroganov.[71] Metternich, agreeing with this interpretation, was as delighted over the news of the Tatistchev mission as Capodistrias was furious.[72] Alex-

[69] Lützow reported in March that both the Europeans and the Turks in Constantinople expected war soon. Lützow (Constantinople, March 12 and 24, 1822) to Metternich, Berichte, Türkei, Fasc. 13. Strangford's reports were also alarming. See Esterhazy (Brighton, April 7, 1822) to Metternich, Berichte, Grossbritannien, Fasc. 216, No. 219B. The extent to which Metternich's diplomatic resources were taxed by this crisis may be seen from his letter of January 29, 1822, to Esterhazy. In it Metternich conceded that he was convinced that the Allies would have to unite in proposing some concrete measures to the Porte to prevent future friction between Christians and Moslems within the Ottoman Empire. The question was, what measures? "I confess, indeed," he wrote, "that I do not know; but it appears to me demonstrated by a calculation of simple reason that it [sic] must exist, and that never will their use have been more necessary." Vienna, Weisungen, Grossbritannien, Fasc. 218, No. 1.

[70] Lebzeltern (St. Petersburg, February 6, 1822) to Metternich, Berichte, Russland, Fasc. 56, Nos. 29B and 29D.

[71] Lebzeltern (St. Petersburg, February 19, 1822) to Metternich, *ibid.*, No. 31A.

[72] Correctly interpreting Austria's policy as one of so diluting and restricting Russian demands that the Porte could easily fulfill them and Russia could not possibly go to war over them, Capodistrias avowed that Russia would do better

ander's decision on this mission did not mean that the trouble was over. Capodistrias and Stroganov were both still urging that Russia should occupy the principalities in order to compel the Turks to meet the Russian demands, and Alexander, Metternich suspected, was attracted to the idea, not realizing that war would be its certain consequence.[73] In addition, the Tsar, not yet entirely willing to abandon the Greeks to their fate, specifically charged Tatistchev with seeking Austrian support for the dangerous Russian proposals on the question of the pacification of the Greeks and the amelioration of their conditions under Turk rule. But the Austrian Chancellor, assured by Lebzeltern that Tatistchev's views on the Eastern question were not those of Capodistrias, believed he could persuade both the Tsar and his envoy to accept his position.[74]

Metternich's confidence in his powers of persuasion proved justified. Tatistchev, arriving in Vienna on March 5, insisted that the Emperor desired peace. Nevertheless, the Russian emissary immediately set out on his main task: to induce Austria to acknowledge the justice of Russian claims to a right of protection over Christian peoples within the Ottoman Empire, and to gain assurance of Austria's moral support for Russia in case war became necessary.[75] On the first point he ultimately gained no satisfaction at all, and on the second he secured only a meaningless verbal concession.

A detailed analysis of the various conferences (which lasted from March 8 to April 19)[76] and of all the notes exchanged would be

---

to have an enemy rather than a friend like Austria. *Ibid.*, No. 31D; Metternich (Vienna, March 6, 1822) to Esterhazy, Weisungen, Grossbritannien, Fasc. 218, **No. 2.**

[73] Lebzeltern (St. Petersburg, March 12, 1822) to Metternich, Berichte, Russland, Fasc. 56, No. 33B; Metternich (Vienna, March 17, 1822) to Esterhazy, Weisungen, Grossbritannien, Fasc. 218, No. 1.

[74] Metternich (Vienna, March 6, 1822) to Esterhazy, Weisungen, Grossbritannien, Fasc. 218, No. 2. Nesselrode requested Gentz, who was strongly pro-Turk, to advise Tatistchev during the latter's stay in Vienna. Supplement to above, Nesselrode (St. Petersburg, February 19, 1822) to Gentz, *ibid.*

[75] *Ibid.*

[76] Metternich and Tatistchev collaborated to exclude Count Golowkin, Russian ambassador at Vienna, from practically all the conferences. Metternich (Vienna, April 22, 1822) to Lebzeltern, in Metternich, *Nachgelassene Papiere*, III, 550–552. Metternich had in fact been trying to get Golowkin replaced since January, viewing him as a henchman of Capodistrias and a stupid nullity. Metternich (Vienna, January 28, 1822) to Lebzeltern, Weisungen, Russland, Fasc. 54, No. 7.

tedious; in general outline, however, the negotiations afford an excellent insight into Metternich's masterly diplomatic tactics. Tatistchev proposed in notes of March 8 and 14 that Austria support Russia in two main demands: first, that the Porte promptly evacuate the principalities and set up a civilian government under Greek caimacams; and second, that the Porte appoint plenipotentiaries to negotiate with the Russians over the changes necessary to pacify permanently the Christian provinces of the Ottoman Empire. The changes which Russia contemplated in these areas tended, without saying so outright, to reduce the Turk sovereignty to suzerainty and to put Greece in much the same position as the Danubian principalities, with a corresponding extension of Russian influence.[77]

Privately, Metternich ridiculed the idea of granting Greece partial autonomy under Russian protection as the kind of dangerous nonsense to be expected from Capodistrias.[78] In the conferences with Tatistchev, he and Gentz pooled their efforts to expose the weaknesses of the whole Russian proposal and to persuade the Russian envoy to distinguish sharply between the Russian demand for fulfillment of treaties—which Austria could support wholeheartedly—and the Russian desire for amelioration of the lot of the Greeks—which was, strictly speaking, an internal affair of Turkey in which Austria could not interfere except to offer advice and counsel. If Russia could not drop her efforts to ameliorate the lot of the Greeks, at least she could postpone these considerations until the vital question of evacuation and restoration of diplomatic relations had been settled.[79]

In a lengthy analysis of Russian dispatches, Metternich showed how often the Russian Cabinet had confused and amalgamated these two separate problems. A similar analysis of the Russo-Turk treaties then in force demonstrated how limited was the protectorate actually granted to Russia over Greek Christians, and how, outside of the Danubian principalities, it was the Sultan, not the Tsar, who was the protector of the Christian cult, a fact the Russians had repeat-

[77] Notes by Tatistchev (Vienna, March 8 and 14, 1822) to Metternich, in Metternich, *Nachgelassene Papiere*, III, 537–539.
[78] Metternich (Vienna, March 16, 1822) to Lebzeltern, Weisungen, Russland, Fasc. 54, No. 1.
[79] Record of conversation, Gentz with Tatistchev, March 8, 1822, Varia, Türkei, Fasc. 15.

edly ignored.[80] In his talks with Tatistchev, Metternich repeatedly emphasized the distinction between treaty questions and discretionary matters. In the latter, Austria could not intervene, no matter how noble and humanitarian the purpose. Refusing to even consider the question of what Austria would do if war came, the Austrian Chancellor rejected with equal vigor the idea of a Russian occupation of the principalities as a step both inadmissible and incomprehensible under the circumstances.[81] As for the Russian requests to be presented to the Turks, Metternich suggested, first, that Russia should ask Turkey to send only commissioners, not plenipotentiaries, to treat with Russia. Second, Metternich argued, Russia should not insist on action on those matters which the Sultan had already conceded in principle (such as the future protection of the Christian cult and the restoration of churches). It was, after all, impossible for the Sultan to fulfill his promises in a time of rebellion, and it was an affront to his dignity to be constantly pressed on them.[82]

Unable to get anywhere with his original aims, and secretly not too eager to pursue them, Tatistchev tried to cover his retreat by seeking from Metternich at least a declaration that, if the Sultan's stubbornness forced Russia to war, Austria would also break relations with the Porte. Metternich suffered some embarrassment over this request, since on March 14 Prussian Foreign Minister Bernstorff had been incautious enough to sign such a protocol with Russian Ambassador Alopeus, provided that the other Allies also approved it. Metternich had rebuked Bernstorff sharply for this ill-considered action and for going much too far in recognizing Russian claims in the Eastern question.[83] Nevertheless, he could hardly do less for Russia than the Prussians had done. Therefore he instructed Lebzel-

80 "Analyse des dépêches du Cabinet de Russie sur les affaires de Turquie depuis le 6 Juillet 1821 jusqu'au 12 Février 1822," and "Dispositions des Traités entre la Russie et la Porte, relativement aux Chrétiens /:grecs:/ habitans des Provinces Européennes de l'empire Ottoman," supplementing Metternich's letter (Vienna, April 24, 1822) to Esterhazy, Weisungen, Grossbritannien, Fasc. 218.

81 Résumé of conversations, Metternich with Tatistchev, March 8 and 12, 1822, *ibid.*, and April 5, 1822, Prokesch, *Abfall der Griechen*, III, 328–331.

82 "Observations sur la Note Verbale," by Metternich, March 12, 1822, Weisungen, Grossbritannien, Fasc. 218.

83 Metternich (Vienna, March 31, 1822) to Lebzeltern, Weisungen, Russland, Fasc. 54, No. 11 (with supplement, Metternich [Vienna, March 25, 1822] to Count Zichy).

tern to declare that if the case arose, Austria would join Russia, not only in breaking relations, but also in issuing a joint statement announcing this action to the Porte.[84] The declaration sounded good but committed Austria to nothing, since Metternich, knowing full well that England had no intention of breaking relations under any circumstances, had carefully added the provision that Austria would be able so to act only if all the other Allies did likewise.[85]

Tatistchev made one more attempt to gain a partial victory to take back to St. Petersburg. On April 12 he presented for Metternich's signature a protocol drawn up by himself and Ambassador Golowkin, setting out Russia's original demands without essential change. Metternich was to affirm that Austria recognized Russia's claims as just, but that since the points related to the pacification of the Greeks were not based on existing treaties they could not become part of an Allied *démarche*. Accordingly, Austria would leave to Alexander the decision as to whether or not war was necessary over any of these questions. If war came, however, Austria would break relations with the Porte and give moral support to the Russian cause.[86] Metternich refused to sign, of course, and Tatistchev gave up the project without a struggle.[87]

The official memoir of April 19 which Metternich finally communicated to Alexander with Tatistchev's and Golowkin's approval represented a complete victory for Metternich, yielding only innocuous concessions to the Russian position. Drawn up as a guide for future negotiations and policy, it maintained that the treaty question no longer presented any basic difficulty, since the Porte had admitted its obligations to evacuate the principalities and restore the regular government there, and since the execution of these obligations was only a matter of time. The real difficulty, said the memoir, lay in the general or discretionary questions. On these points, in order not to infringe upon Turkish sovereignty, future discussions or negotiations should be confined solely to legislative and administra-

---

[84] *Ibid.*, Postscript to No. 1.

[85] *Ibid.*; Metternich (Vienna, April 4, 1822) to Esterhazy, Weisungen, Grossbritannien, Fasc. 218, Nos. 2–4.

[86] "Projet de Protocole de signer," presented by Tatistchev (April 12, 1822) to Metternich, supplementing Metternich (Vienna, April 24, 1822) to Esterhazy, Weisungen, Grossbritannien, Fasc. 218.

[87] Metternich (Vienna, April 22, 1822) to Lebzeltern, in Metternich, *Nachgelassene Papiere*, III, 551.

tive measures designed to promote the protection of the Christian cult, the peaceful enjoyment of private property, and the regular administration of justice among the Sultan's Christian subjects. Having thus evaded the Russian proposal for a change of system in the Sultan's European domains, the memoir went on to define the goals of Allied policy, in order of their importance and urgency. The Allies should insist on Turkey's fulfilling her treaty obligations. They should furthermore urge the Porte to proclaim an amnesty to the Greeks, and offer their good offices to try to get the Greeks to submit to the Sultan. Finally, they should recommend (not demand) that the Porte send commissioners to discuss with the five courts (and not with Russia alone) the best way of pacifying the Ottoman domains in Europe (i.e., not changing the existing system in them).[88]

Thus Metternich steered clear of all the pitfalls in the Russian proposals. If Alexander accepted Metternich's reasoning and his program, not only would it be almost impossible for him to go to war, but also he would have to turn over the further negotiations on the Russo-Turk dispute to the Allies. Metternich also had a plan to deal with this eventuality. In another confidential letter to Tatistchev he suggested two possible ways to handle the proposed five-power negotiations with Turkey: either advancing the date of the forthcoming Congress in Italy to include the negotiations, or, failing this, setting up an ambassadorial conference at Vienna to deliberate and to decide on the measures to be recommended to the Porte regarding the Greeks.[89] The latter suggestion was what Metternich really wanted—an ambassadorial conference at Vienna would provide another means for delay and for Austrian control over the dangerous Greek question.[90]

[88] Memoir, Metternich (Vienna, April 19, 1822) to Alexander, in Metternich, *Nachgelassene Papiere*, III, 539–545.

[89] Metternich (Vienna, April 19, 1822) to Tatistchev, *ibid.*, 545–547. The other pieces which Metternich sent to St. Petersburg with Tatistchev—Metternich's letter (Vienna, April 19, 1822) to Nesselrode, *ibid.*, 547–549; his note to Tatistchev and Golowkin, supplement, Metternich (Vienna, April 24, 1822) to Esterhazy, Weisungen, Grossbritannien, Fasc. 218; and Francis' letter (same date) to Alexander, *ibid.*—add nothing of great significance. Metternich knew, to be sure, that the Russians were very eager to have the next Allied conference on Russian soil, but he was determined to have it nowhere else than at Vienna. Metternich (Vienna, April 22, 1822) to Lebzeltern, Weisungen, Russland, Fasc. 54, No. 3.

[90] Metternich (Vienna, April 24, 1822) to Esterhazy, Weisungen, Grossbritannien, Fasc. 218, No. 2.

The successful negotiations with Tatistchev represented a battle won, but not yet final victory in the campaign. Everything depended on the reception which the envoy and the proposals he brought would receive at St. Petersburg, for conceivably the active and malign influence of Capodistrias might yet upset matters.[91] By mid-May, however, the final decision was made. Alexander had accepted all of Metternich's proposals and was sending Tatistchev back promptly as a plenipotentiary to take up the question of the pacification of the Greeks with the ministerial conference at Vienna. Metternich's rejoicing, not to say gloating, over this victory was unrestrained. He considered it not only as a final and complete triumph over Capodistrias but also as a total destruction of the work of Peter the Great and his successors and as the greatest victory ever won by one cabinet over another.[92] To make the triumph still more complete, there came good news at last from Constantinople. The Sultan, now harassed still further by trouble with Persia which broke out in open hostilities in the summer of 1822,[93] finally, after more false starts and delays, consented on April 25 to begin the evacuation of the principalities by May 5.[94] The evacuation did not actually start till May 13 and proceeded then only with agonizing slowness, so that it was not until July 1822 that the Sultan nominated new hospodars and only in February 1823 that the Porte finally consented, with sufficient ill grace, to notify Russia of the evacuation and of the

[91] Metternich (Vienna, April 4 and 24, May 16, 1822) to Esterhazy, *ibid.*, Nos. 1, 1 and 6, and 4; Lebzeltern (St. Petersburg, April 8, 21, and 29, 1822) to Metternich, Berichte, Russland, Fasc. 56, Nos. 35A, 36, and 37B with Postscript.

[92] Lebzeltern (St. Petersburg, May 16 and 19, 1822) to Metternich, Berichte, Russland, Fasc. 56, Nos. 40A and 41A; private letter by Metternich, Vienna, May 31, 1822, and Metternich (Vienna, June 3, 1822) to Francis, in Metternich, *Nachgelassene Papiere*, III, 515–516, 554. Writing to Esterhazy, the Chancellor, after describing the affair as a humiliating defeat for Russia, commented: "It would be impossible for me not to recognize myself as being personally of merit in the success of the common cause." Thereupon followed Metternich's enlargement at length of the decisive role he had played in the affair by his own constancy, vision, profound understanding of men and affairs, invincible reasoning, and correct principles. Metternich (Vienna, June 2, 1822) to Esterhazy, Weisungen, Grossbritannien, Fasc. 218, No. 1.

[93] Lützow (Constantinople, January 25, 1822) to Metternich, Berichte, Türkei, Fasc. 13, No. 119G, with supplements; Metternich (Vienna, July 15, 1822) to Lebzeltern, Weisungen, Russland, Fasc. 54, No. 9 with supplement.

[94] Metternich (Vienna, April 4, 1822) to Esterhazy, Weisungen, Grossbritannien, Fasc. 218, No. 7, with supplement; Lützow (Constantinople, April 25, 1822) to Metternich, Berichte, Türkei, Fasc. 13, No. 126F, with supplement.

restoration of normal government in the principalities.[95] With the beginning of the evacuation, however, Metternich felt that the worst danger for Europe had subsided and congratulated Strangford on a masterly diplomatic victory.[96]

Averting war, important as this was, remained approximately the extent of the gains achieved by Metternich and Strangford during this period. The Oriental question in general remained far from solution. The conference at Vienna was slow to get into action, mainly because of the absence of the Prussian minister and the lack of full powers and instructions for Caraman and Gordon. Even when it finally got under way, it could accomplish little in the face of the absolute refusal of the Porte to send commissioners to treat with Russia or the Allied powers on anything.[97] Strangford, like his government, generally more sensitive to Turkish than to Russian arguments, wanted Russia to reopen diplomatic relations immediately upon the evacuation of the principalities, without seeking to get the Porte to name commissioners or to treat on the Greek question.[98] Metternich on the other hand, with the conference supporting him, insisted that the additional questions, now that they were in Allied hands, were also crucial if real tranquillity was to be assured in the East. His confidence, however, that united European representations could obtain what Strangford's pleas alone could not was misplaced.[99] Not only did the Turks remain intransigent on this point, but they renewed their measures affecting Russian grain commerce through the Straits, prompting Nesselrode to lodge a vigorous protest at the pre-Verona conference of Vienna against the whole manner in which

[95] Lützow (Constantinople, May 25, June 10 and 25, July 10 and 18, 1822) to Metternich, Berichte, Türkei, Fasc. 13, Nos. 128I, 129G, 130K, 131G, 132B, with supplement; Strangford (Constantinople, February 28, 1823) to Metternich, in Weisungen, Russland, Fasc. 60, with supplements.

[96] Metternich (Vienna, June 3, 1822) to Strangford, Varia, Türkei, Fasc. 16.

[97] Metternich (Vienna, July 9, 1822) to Esterhazy, Weisungen, Grossbritannien, Fasc. 218, No. 2, with supplement, "Précis de la conférence de ce jour," Vienna, June 28, 1822: Lützow (Constantinople, June 10, 1822) to Metternich, Berichte, Türkei, Fasc. 13, No. 129F.

[98] "Précis de la conférence de mercredi le 17 Juillet 1822," and Strangford (Constantinople, June 25, 1822) to Metternich, Weisungen, Russland, Fasc 54.

[99] Metternich (Vienna, July 31, 1822) to Strangford, in Metternich, *Nachgelassene Papiere*, III, 564–574; Metternich (Vienna, July 31, 1822) to Lützow, Weisungen, Türkei, Fasc. 14. A prolific correspondence between Metternich and Strangford from June to September 1822 is found in Varia, Türkei, Fasc. 15.

the Allies were dealing with Turkey.[100] The conference and the Congress of Verona, as will be seen, only put the problem aside. The same strains and tensions between Russia and Turkey so persisted that in mid-1823 Lebzeltern once again believed that war was a serious possibility. Metternich, discouraged at the sweeping successes of the Greeks, was by this time ready to listen to Strangford's plan for giving Greece a status akin to that of the Danubian principalities (the same plan of Capodistrias' which Metternich had foiled through the Tatistchev mission), but secretly he considered the whole Greek question as out of the control of diplomacy and in the lap of the gods.[101] In short, his victory over Capodistrias, which Metternich had confidently believed would bring a new era of life to the Ottoman Empire, had proved to be only one short chapter in the history of that Empire's decline. The Eastern question was already, as it would be for a century, a perennial problem in European diplomacy.

None of these developments were present to disturb Metternich in the summer of 1822. Instead, he had everything to be thankful for. The crisis of war was past, the conduct of England had been excellent throughout,[102] and even that of France had been reason-

[100] Lebzeltern (St. Petersburg, August 7, 1822) to Metternich, Berichte, Russland, Fasc. 57, No. 50C: "Projet de Note aux Plénipotentiaires des Cours d'Autriche, de France, d'Angleterre et de Prusse," by Nesselrode, Vienna, September 26, 1822, Varia, Türkei, Fasc. 15.

[101] Metternich (Venice, December 21, 1822, and Vienna, June 21, 1823) to Baron Ottenfels (Lützow's successor at Constantinople), in Metternich *Nachgelassene Papiere*, III, 586–587, and IV, 63–69; Lebzeltern (St. Petersburg, March 12 and June 13, 1823) to Metternich, Berichte, Russland, Fasc. 58, Nos. 19D and 33A; Metternich (Vienna, April 15, 1823) to Esterhazy, Weisungen, Grossbritannien, Fasc. 211, No. 5. How drastically Metternich had to revise and even abandon his policy under the impact of events and Canning's diplomacy in 1824 and 1825 can be seen in part in his letters to Esterhazy, Vienna, October 24, 1824, and to Lebzeltern, Vienna, January 15, 1825, in Metternich, *Nachgelassene Papiere*, IV, 133–138, 199–209.

[102] There was, to be sure, a mild difference between Austrian and English policy in the spring of 1822, with Metternich believing that Castlereagh followed too much a policy of "fire and flame" with Russia, and Castlereagh wishing that Metternich had never let the problem get away from the original four points. This, however, was only a question of tactics, not aims, and caused no difficulty between the powers.—Webster, *Foreign Policy of Castlereagh*, 394–397; Esterhazy (London, January 11 and 18, February 27, March 15, April 24 and 26, May 18, 1822) to Metternich, Berichte, Grossbritannien, Fasc. 216, Nos. 210A, 210B, 211A, 213A, 215A, 220A, 221, and 222B, with supplements; Castlereagh (London, April 27, 1822) to Prince Lieven, Varia, Grossbritannien, Fasc. 19; Castlereagh (London, April 29, 1822)

ably satisfactory,[103] while Germany and Italy had remained quiet throughout the period of danger. Still another revolution had failed to shake his European system. Only one now remained to be dealt with: that in Spain. To this revolution, much against his will and solely because Alexander desired it, Metternich now had to turn his attention.

---

to Charles Bagot, *ibid.*; Gordon (Vienna, May 16, 1822) to Strangford, *ibid.*; Metternich (Vienna, May 16, 1822) to Esterhazy, Weisungen, Grossbritannien, Fasc. 218, No. 1.

[103] Although Metternich at first complained that the attitude of the French envoys at St. Petersburg and Constantinople was colorless, he later noted an improvement in their cooperation with the other Allies. He was especially pleased that the French refused Pozzo di Borgo's request for a protocol like that of Berlin, promising the joint rupture of relations with the Porte. Metternich (Vienna, August 5, November 9, December 5, 1821) to Vincent, Weisungen, Frankreich, Fasc. 346; Metternich (Vienna, December 23, 1821) to Lebzeltern, Weisungen, Russland, Fasc. 45, No. 6; Vincent (Paris, February 14, March 18, 19, and 30, 1822) to Metternich, Berichte, Frankreich, Fasc. 347, Nos. 5A, 9A, 12, and 19B.

CHAPTER VII

THE CONGRESS OF VERONA

From the Balkan Peninsula, where the Greek revolt and the Russo-Turk crisis had held the stage for more than a year, the diplomatic attention of Europe shifted back in mid-1822 to the opposite end of the subcontinent, the Iberian Peninsula, and to the first of the post-Vienna revolutions which had arisen to plague European sovereigns—the revolution in Spain. By 1822 this revolt had come very close to fulfilling the pattern which, according to Metternichean doctrine, all revolutions should inevitably follow—that of chaos, unrest, and anarchy leading up to civil war and the dissolution of society. Attempts by the *Moderados* in the Cortes to curb some of the excesses of the revolution by amending the laws on freedom of the press, the activities of political clubs, and the right of petition, failed.[1] The country's finances ran into constant heavy deficits, with the administration of the state little short of chaotic. The provinces, especially in the north, were disaffected and heading toward civil war. Meanwhile, King Ferdinand VII repeatedly, although without great success, tried to secure French aid to promote a royalist rising which would deliver him from his captivity as a constitutional monarch.[2]

A movement to liberate Ferdinand actually took place in early July, culminating in a rising of the Royal Guard at Madrid against the revolutionary regime. The coup failed utterly, however, largely

[1] Brunetti (Madrid, January 28, 1822) to Metternich, Berichte, Spanien, Fasc. 189, Postscript to No. 274.
[2] Brunetti (Madrid, March 7, 18, 25, and 28, April 6, June 3 and 10, 1822) to Metternich, *ibid.*, Nos. 289, 291, Postscript to 292, 294, 309, Postscript to 309, and 311.

because of the King's cowardice, treachery, and indecision.[3] In the resultant reaction the moderates were swept out of the government, leaving the radical *Exaltados* in complete control and deepening partisan hatreds and confusion in Spain.[4] Meanwhile, Ultraroyalist insurgents had set up a provisional government at Urgel, in Catalonia, proclaiming a Regency in behalf of the "captive" Ferdinand VII. Led by clerics (notably the Archbishop of Tarragona) and aristocrats (especially the Marquis of Mataflorida), the Regency espoused doctrines of pure absolutism and an intimate union of Throne and Altar, and was soon sending appeals to Metternich, the European sovereigns, and the Pope for recognition, arms, and other aid in its fight against the constitutional regime.[5] Without large-scale foreign aid, however, the insurrection had no prospects of ultimate success, and could only hope to tie up the constitutional army and further ruin Spain's finances.[6]

A'Court, transferred from Naples to Madrid as English ambas-

---

[3] The rising, as planned with the support of the existing ministry, General Morillo of the constitutional army, and other important moderates, called for the Royal Guard to rise and lead the King out of Madrid into the provinces where, uniting with insurgents of the north, he would lead a movement for the overthrow of the existing system in favor of a very conservative constitution. Though Ferdinand had encouraged the plan, he refused at the crucial moment to accompany the Royal Guard out of Madrid, partly from fear and partly because he would be satisfied with nothing less than the restitution of his absolute power. Thus the coup misfired and the constitutional militia had time to converge on Madrid and to defeat and disperse the Royal Guard on July 7. Brunetti (Madrid, July 1, 4, 5, 8, 18, 1822) to Metternich, *ibid.*, Nos. 318–321, Postscript to 325; Vincent (Paris, July 17 and 25, 1822) to Metternich, Berichte, Frankreich, Fasc. 348, Nos. 23, 25A.

[4] Brunetti (Madrid, August 8 and September 23, 1822) to Metternich, Berichte, Spanien, Fasc. 189, Nos. 333 and Postscript to 345.

[5] Letters, Regency (Urgel, August 15, September 12, October 14, 1822) to Metternich, Kongressakten, Verona, Fasc. 43; Proclamation, Regency to the Congress of Verona, September 13, 1822, *ibid.*; Archbishop Veremundo de Valencia (Toulouse, October 20, 1822) to Cardinal Spina, *ibid.* Mataflorida had personally appealed to Metternich for help as early as November 1821. In order to distract Alexander from the Turkish crisis, Metternich had relayed his plea to the Tsar. Mataflorida (Toulouse, November 12, 1821) to Metternich, supplement to Metternich (Vienna, December 3, 1821) to Lebzeltern, Weisungen, Russland, Fasc. 45, No. 4.

[6] See "Analyse du mémoire lu aux Cortés extraordinaires par le Général Lopez Baños, Secrétaire d'État aux Département de la Guerre, dans le séance du 8. Octobre 1822," Kongressakten, Verona, Fasc. 43; Brunetti (Madrid, October 9, 1822) to Metternich, Berichte, Spanien, Fasc. 189, No. 348.

sador, on his arrival found all of Spain a picture of pettiness, confusion, incompetence, and impending governmental dissolution. Amid an atmosphere of widespread despair over existing conditions and hopelessness of any change for the better, A'Court found only one strong general emotion among the people—a fear of a return to the old order, not so much because of a horror of despotism in general as because of fear of Ferdinand VII in particular.[7]

The Austrian *chargé d'affaires,* Count Brunetti, drew a picture which was, if anything, still more dismal. Brunetti was completely dismayed at the Hobson's choice presented by the two contending factions in Spain—on the one hand, the wild-eyed *Exaltados,* who showed themselves incompetent to govern at Madrid; on the other, the reactionary Ultras at Urgel, who had no better program than that of restoring an alternately craven and ferocious king to full power. Though himself a strong absolutist, the Austrian *chargé* saw the only possible salvation for Spain in an intervention by the Allies which would legitimize certain results of the revolution while eliminating its excesses, and which would force Ferdinand VII to accept new institutions that would not only be suitable for the government of Spain, but would also serve to restrain Ferdinand's despotic will.[8]

Much more important to the powers than the internal course of events in Spain was the attitude maintained by France toward the revolution, since she bordered on Spain and was therefore directly affected by what happened there. During approximately the first two years of the revolution the French diplomatic attitude toward Spain had been correct, neutral, and circumspect. The French ministry's reply to Alexander's proposal for intervention against the revolution in April 1820 had been similar to that of England. In her memoir, France deplored the excesses of the revolt and expressed a hope that the fundamental bases of order would not be overturned, but she refused to condemn the revolution in principle or to consider armed or forceful intervention against it.[9]

[7] A'Court (Madrid, October 7, 1822) to George Canning, Varia, Grossbritannien, Fasc. 19.

[8] Brunetti (Madrid, July 12, October 9, 1822) to Metternich, Berichte, Spanien, Fasc. 189, Nos. 323, 348.

[9] Memoir of the French Cabinet, July 1820, Weisungen und Varia, Spanien, Fasc. 190.

The Congresses of Troppau and Laibach and the Austrian interventions at Naples and Piedmont had naturally aroused great agitation in Madrid. The Spaniards, aware that the antirevolutionary proclamations of the Congresses could be applied to Spain as well as to Italy, were apprehensive that France and the Allies might turn next to crushing the revolutions in the Iberian Peninsula. The Spanish ambassador to France, the Marquis of Santa Cruz, therefore persistently in January and February of 1821 demanded a statement of French intentions regarding Spain. At first Pasquier rejected the Spanish request for a written expression; to make any reply, he said, would be beneath the dignity of France. In April, however, he reaffirmed France's noninterventionist policy. This assurance banished the momentary sharpening of tension which had arisen between France and Spain.[10]

An important turn in French-Spanish relations came in December, with the fall of the Richelieu ministry, which had been under attack by the Ultras for its do-nothing foreign policy. In the new Villèle ministry, Viscount Montmorency, an ardent Royalist, replaced Pasquier as foreign minister. Inspired by the pleas for help which Ferdinand VII had sent out to the powers through the medium of Ferdinand I of Naples,[11] Montmorency, in April 1822, tentatively suggested the establishment of a ministerial conference at Paris to consult on ways and means of coming to the Spanish King's aid. Any sign of French initiative in regard to Spain was unwelcome in Vienna. Acting on Metternich's instructions, Ambassador Vincent used every means to discourage France from proposing such a conference or from adopting any other scheme of intervention or interference in Spanish affairs.[12]

Despite Austrian discouragement, the French ministry continued to take steps in the direction of intervention. It had already sent

[10] Adhémar, Comte d'Antioche, *Chateaubriand Ambassadeur à Londres (1822) d'après ses dépêches inédites,* 174–175, 177–178; Binder (Paris, February 24, 1821) to Metternich, Berichte, Frankreich, Fasc. 344, Postscript to No. 12.

[11] Ferdinand I (Naples, February 7, 1822) to Louis XVIII, in Moscati, *Il regno delle Due Sicilie,* I, 117–121. Similar letters were sent to the sovereigns of the other great powers.

[12] Vincent (Paris, April 2, 1822) to Metternich, Berichte, Frankreich, Fasc. 347, No. 10E. Vincent himself believed that such a conference might be a good means of restraining France and the Ultras (*ibid.*).

sizable forces to the Pyrenees, ostensibly to guard against the spread of yellow fever which had broken out in Spain. In June 1822 these forces were reinforced and organized as a *cordon sanitaire*. Meanwhile, eager to make Louis XVIII the mediator between Ferdinand and the Spanish people and thereby to substitute the *Charte* for the Constitution of the Cortes in Spain, at the end of June Montmorency instructed the French ambassador to Spain, Count de la Garde, to convey to Ferdinand the conditions France required of him before offering him any mediation or help in response to the pleas he had sent to Louis XVIII. If Ferdinand would agree freely to renounce a part of his absolute power and to proclaim a constitution for Spain as Louis had done for France in 1814, the French King would guarantee these concessions to Spain and would act as mediator between Ferdinand and the Spanish people. Not only would the powers assent to this step, Louis confidently predicted, but the people of Spain would accept it gratefully. The King of France refused, however, to consider intervention on any other terms and warned Ferdinand against relying on the help of Spanish insurgents or on foreign aid to carry out a *coup d'etat*.[13]

This advice arrived in Madrid too late to prevent the July rising of the Royal Guard. Even if it had come earlier, Ferdinand undoubtedly would have ignored it anyway.[14] After the royalist coup had blown up in his face, however, Ferdinand threw himself upon the mercies of France, promising complete obedience to De la Garde's advice. (His specific promises, to be sure, included only a pledge to summon the ancient Cortes after his restoration.) The ministry, headed by the cautious Villèle, justifiably entertained grave doubts about Ferdinand's change of heart. Sensing his unwillingness to meet the main French conditions for their support (that he grant a

[13] Binder (Paris, June 26, 1822) to Metternich, *ibid.*, Fasc. 348; Vincent (Paris, October 31, 1822) to Metternich, *ibid.*, No. 51; Louis (St. Cloud, June 28, 1822) to Ferdinand, with extract from secret instructions to De la Garde, Paris, June 29, 1822, Kongressakten, Verona, Fasc. 43.

[14] So far as Vincent could determine, the French ministry had not known or approved of the July royalist coup, though De la Garde and Russian Minister Count Bulgari had apparently encouraged it. Similarly, there was no official support given to the insurgents of the north and the Regency at Urgel, although the government did close its eyes to the activities of Spanish *émigrés* in France and the support given them by French Royalists. Vincent (Paris, July 9, 17, and 25, 1822) to Metternich, Berichte, Frankreich, Fasc. 348, Nos. 22A, 23, and 25A.

constitution, proclaim an amnesty, and ban all camarillas from the government), the ministers were reluctant to intervene in Spain. Nevertheless, Ultra pressure for French aid to the royalist insurgents and even for armed intervention continued to increase.[15]

Metternich, meanwhile, maintained the same attitude on the Spanish question that he had taken from the beginning of the revolution. His policy was very simple—to deplore everything and to do nothing. He blamed all the present and future evils of Spain on the folly and weakness which Ferdinand VII had displayed both before and after the revolution.[16] No prediction concerning the future of Spain was too dark for him to accept. An impending dissolution of the monarchy, a downfall of the Bourbon dynasty, and even the formation, with revolutionary Portugal, of an Iberian federated republic like the United States of America were developments which he considered only too likely.[17]

Still, Metternich had no answer to give on how to solve the grave problems of Spain, and he found insuperable difficulties for every solution that someone else proposed. When Ferdinand of Naples transmitted Ferdinand VII's plea for help to the Allies, Metternich remarked testily that it would have been better for both of them to keep quiet.[18] He delayed answering Montmorency's proposal for a ministerial conference at Paris on the Spanish question as long as possible, finally replying by throwing cold water upon the idea.[19] The best course to follow, he believed, was to support the "healthy part" of the Spanish nation. But he was always very vague about

[15] Ferdinand (Madrid, July 24, 1822) to Louis, Kongressakten, Verona, Fasc. 43; Brunetti (Madrid, July 28, August 1, and September 10, 1822) to Metternich, Berichte, Spanien, Fasc. 189, Postscript to No. 329, Postscript to 330, and Postscript to 342; Vincent (Paris, August 16, 1822) to Metternich, Berichte, Frankreich, Fasc. 348, No. 30D.

[16] Metternich (Vienna, August 24, 1821) to Lebzeltern, Weisungen, Russland, Fasc. 45, No. 9; Metternich (Vienna, July 21 and 23, 1822) to Francis, in Metternich, *Nachgelassene Papiere*, III, 563–564.

[17] Metternich (Vienna, December 3, 1821) to Lebzeltern, Weisungen, Russland, Fasc. 45, No. 5; Metternich (Vienna, February 27, 1822) to Lebzeltern, *ibid.*, Fasc. 54; Metternich (Vienna, February 18, 1822) to Esterhazy, Weisungen, Grossbritannien, Fasc. 218, No. 2.

[18] Metternich (Vienna, March 20, 1822) to Lebzeltern, Weisungen, Russland, Fasc. 54.

[19] Vincent (Paris, May 15, 1822) to Metternich, Berichte, Frankreich, Fasc. 348, No. 14D; Metternich (Vienna, July 5, 1822) to Vincent, Weisungen, Frankreich, Fasc. 350.

just who constituted this "healthy part": whether it was the royalist insurgents at Urgel, or the moderate supporters of the King, or even the Spanish masses who, according to Metternich, wanted nothing but the restoration of the old legal order as it had existed before 1807. Moreover, the "support" of which he spoke was moral support only, to be given secretly and unofficially by the Allies. Any open or material support rendered by France to the Spanish insurgents would be worse than dangerous for Spain and the French monarchy alike.[20]

As for the rising of the Royal Guard in Madrid and the insurgent movement in the north, Metternich denounced these as great blunders, not because they were counterrevolutionary, for a counterrevolution was the legitimate device of any monarch against revolt, but because Ferdinand had failed through cowardice to seize his opportunity to overthrow the revolution in July, because the plotters in Madrid had intended to modify the constitution rather than to overthrow it completely, and because the insurgents at Urgel had gone ahead without waiting for the support of the Allies—which, to be sure, would have been moral support only.[21] In the future, Metternich fervently hoped that Ferdinand would not try another venture like this. As for the French idea of mediating between Ferdinand and his people in order to establish the *Charte* in Spain, this was in Metternich's opinion unquestionably the worst and most damnable of all possible courses of action.[22]

[20] Metternich (Vienna, July 10, 1822) to Vincent, Weisungen, Frankreich, Fasc. 350.
[21] Metternich (Vienna, July 31, 1822) to Lebzeltern, Weisungen, Russland, Fasc. 54, No. 2.
[22] The horror with which Metternich viewed the French idea of mediation is shown by a document titled "Observations du Cabinet de Vienne sur les differentes pièces" (i.e., the exchange of letters between Louis XVIII and Ferdinand VII and the French instructions to De la Garde), n.d., Kongressakten, Verona, Fasc. 43. Metternich denounced the attempt at mediation as a scheme to promote harmony between legitimacy and revolution, order and anarchy, the throne and the scaffold. He condemned the concessions required of Ferdinand VII in no uncertain terms: "A king must never make the sacrifice of any part of his authority whatsoever. To propose this to him is to propose his degradation to him . . . to counsel to him a crime . . . The only sense of the word *Constitution* that is admissible in the monarchical system is that of an organization of public powers under the supreme, indivisible, and inalienable authority of the *monarch* . . . In every other sense, *Constitution* is the equivalent of *anarchy* and the supposed *division of powers* the death of

It is not hard to understand why Metternich had no better counsel to offer on Spain than this mass of inconsistent, confusing, and really quite unhelpful advice, and why he could agree to no action bolder than that of giving unofficial, secret, moral support to some unidentified "healthy part" of the Spanish nation. Nor is it difficult to see why he was particularly horror-struck at the thought of French mediation or intervention in Spain. His interest in the fate of the Spanish revolution, the Spanish King, and even Spain herself was almost nonexistent.[23] Yet his interest in political stability and the *status quo* in Central Europe required an unyielding opposition to all political movement, especially to a revival of French chauvinism and the spread of French constitutional ideas.[24] His policy, therefore, was designed neither to help Spain nor to counsel France, but to discourage any action in regard to Spain because it might rock the equilibrium of Europe.

Hence it was not Metternich—nor, for that matter, the French ministry—who brought up the Spanish question for European discussion. It was rather the restless zeal of Alexander which forced the subject into the spotlight. Frustrated in his proposal for action in Spain in the spring of 1820 and thwarted again at the Congresses of Troppau and Laibach, Alexander now found in the idea of intervention in Spain an outlet for his energies and a means of distracting attention from the inglorious outcome of his dispute with the Turks. Responding to Ferdinand VII's plea for help, he came up with a proposal for intervention in a form particularly repugnant to the other powers: the formation of a European army to suppress the

------

monarchical government." The document went on to condemn in similar vein the civil liberties that the French wished to establish in Spain.

[23] Some idea of how slight his interest was may be gained by comparing the very slender volume of Metternich's instructions regarding Spain in 1820 and 1821 (one slim convolute for 1820, 27 folio pages in 1821, all on routine matters) with the 175 pages of fairly weighty and important documents sent in 1823, when Austria was involved in the diplomacy connected with the French intervention. Weisungen und Varia, Spanien, Fascs. 190, 191.

[24] Metternich was particularly suspicious of the French ambassador to England, Viscount Chateaubriand, and his organ, the *Journal des Débats*, because of their ambition to restore French glory, and warned Montmorency against them. Metternich (Vienna, April 22, 1822) to Lebzeltern, Weisungen, Russland, Fasc. 54, No. 4; Metternich (Vienna, May 16, 1822) to Vincent, Weisungen, Frankreich, Fasc. 350, No. 3.

Spanish revolution and liberate Ferdinand.[25] Just how this army would function was not—as was characteristic of Alexander's projects—made fully clear. At first the Tsar thought of sending forty thousand men across Austria, Lombardy, Piedmont, and southern France into Spain. When Austria raised objections to this idea, he retreated somewhat from this position. The European army should be formed, the Tsar now suggested instead, so that it could stand by to intervene in France in case of trouble and revolution there, as might happen, for example, if Louis XVIII died, and then from France it could intervene also in Spain; or the army could stand by to protect France from revolution in case the French should take up the task of intervening in Spain.[26]

Metternich, it need hardly be said, was infuriated by these dangerous proposals, considering them at least in part as an insidious plot hatched by Capodistrias, Pozzo di Borgo, and Stroganov. These sinister intriguers, Metternich believed, were following their old tactics of persuading Alexander to propose impossible plans, knowing full well that the Allies would reject them, and hoping then to convince Alexander that he ought to abandon the alliance and follow a policy based on Russian national interests.[27] Precisely because Alexander might come to feel that the alliance was a snare and a delusion, therefore, and because Austria had so often restrained Russia in the past and was at that very time engaged in keeping her from war with Turkey, Metternich dared not oppose Alexander's plans too openly. He fell back instead on the time-honored device of praising the Tsar's principles and motives, but pointing out the grave practical difficulties confronting the proposal: the certain opposition of England to it, the blow that it would give to the national pride of France, the difficulty of intervening in any useful way with a people as proud and stubborn as the Spaniards, and the danger to Ferdinand's life involved in any foreign intervention.[28]

[25] Lebzeltern (St. Petersburg, April 29, 1822) to Metternich, Berichte, Russland, Fasc. 56, No. 37D.

[26] Lebzeltern (St. Petersburg, May 19 and 28, 1822) to Metternich, *ibid.*, Nos. 41B and 44B.

[27] Metternich (Vienna, May 7, 1822) to Lebzeltern, Weisungen, Russland, Fasc. 54, No. 4 (Secret). See also Metternich's private letter, Vienna, April 29, 1822, in Metternich, *Nachgelassene Papiere*, III, 510.

[28] Metternich (Vienna, May 16, 1822) to Esterhazy, Weisungen, Grossbritannien, Fasc. 218, No. 5; Metternich (Vienna, May 7, 1822) to Lebzeltern, Weisungen, Russland, Fasc. 54, Nos. 2 and 3.

These arguments, plus the opposition of England and France, served to quell the idea of a European army at least temporarily. At the same time, nevertheless, Alexander insisted that the Spanish question be made a major topic of discussion at the next congress. This demand could not be so easily dismissed, especially since France was willing to have the matter taken up. Montmorency ostensibly felt, just as Metternich actually did, that foreign intervention in Spain was undesirable. But, he pointed out, cases might arise wherein France would be compelled to intervene—for instance, the revolutionaries might endanger Ferdinand VII's life or might menace France with war. In anticipation of such exigencies, France would be glad to have assurance of Allied support for her action.[29]

Under these circumstances, Metternich, who would have himself liked nothing better than to leave the Spanish question strictly alone, felt it wise to give in to Alexander. In July he wrote the Russians that Spain now demanded the full attention of the assembled sovereigns. The matter, he said, could no longer be left "to the often blind laws of necessity"; the alliance must once more prove its existence by action.[30]

The acceptance of the Spanish question for the agenda of the coming Congress, threatening to strain the close ties he had but recently reknitted with England, created new problems for Metternich. Clearly England had to be included in any Congress that discussed the question of Spain. Yet Castlereagh was not only averse to the idea of another five-power Congress, but ever since April 1820 he had vigorously opposed even a joint *démarche* or consultation on the Spanish question. He had in fact firmly rejected the idea of merely offering Spain friendly counsel—a proposal which Pasquier had advanced in 1821.[31] Although he tried in every way not to hurt Alexander's feelings in turning down Russian proposals on what should be done to help Ferdinand VII, he considered the Tsar's European army idea as worse than a war in the Orient.[32]

[29] Lebzeltern (St. Petersburg, May 28, 1822) to Metternich, Berichte, Russland, Fasc. 56, Nos. 44B and 44C; Binder (Paris, June 5, 1822) to Metternich, Berichte, Frankreich, Fasc. 348.

[30] Metternich (Vienna, July 15, 1822) to Lebzeltern, Weisungen, Russland, Fasc. 54, No. 1.

[31] Antioche, *Chateaubriand*, 146–148.

[32] Esterhazy (London, May 31 and July 5, 1822) to Metternich, Berichte, Grossbritannien, Fasc. 216, Nos. 223B and 226B.

Within Spain itself the British followed such an independent policy and were so suspicious of the intentions of France there that during the July uprisings Lionel Hervey, British *chargé* at Madrid, refused to take part in a joint Allied representation to the Spanish government on behalf of the safety of the King.[33] There were, in addition, other disadvantages for England connected with the proposed Congress: the danger that the conference might bring to light the differences between England and Russia on the Eastern question; the fact that the Congress would discuss Italian questions which, on principle, England wanted nothing to do with; and the perennial preoccupation of English statesmen with their own internal policies.[34]

Knowing that the Spanish question was urgent, however, and that his presence would be needed at the Congress to help Austria restrain France and Russia, Castlereagh was willing to attend if Metternich would spare him all possible embarrassments.[35] Metternich was, of course, eager to have Castlereagh's help. In his invitation to Castlereagh he emphasized his reliance on the support which only England, as Austria's "most intimate ally", could give him, and the good she could do at the Congress in solidifying the alliance, frustrating the schemes of Pozzo di Borgo to push France into active intervention in Spain, and preventing any action on the Spanish question.[36] Metternich solved the problem of dealing with Italian affairs in a way that would not embarrass Castlereagh by dividing the Congress into two periods. General questions, including the Spanish and Eastern questions,[37] were to be discussed by the foreign ministers assembled at a pre-Congress conference in Vienna from September 1 to 15, before the sovereigns arrived. Another week of sessions with the sovereigns would then enable them to conclude

[33] Antioche, *Chateaubriand*, 318–324.

[34] Esterhazy (London, July 5, 1822) to Metternich, Berichte, Grossbritannien, Fasc. 216, No. 226B.

[35] *Ibid.*; Esterhazy (London, June 22, 1822) to Metternich, *ibid.*; Webster, *Foreign Policy of Castlereagh*, 476–481.

[36] Metternich (Vienna, June 6 and July 9, 1822) to Esterhazy, Weisungen, Grossbritannien, Fasc. 218, Nos. 2 and 3.

[37] Actually, as Metternich wrote confidentially to Lebzeltern, he did not want to see the Russo-Turk question brought into the conference at all, since his discussions at Vienna with Tatistchev and the other ambassadors were going smoothly. He had to mention it, however, in order to give Castlereagh an excuse for coming. Metternich (Vienna, July 15, 1822) to Lebzeltern, Weisungen, Russland, Fasc. 54, Nos. 3, with supplement, and 11.

these matters, whereupon Castlereagh could leave for home while the representatives of the other Courts repaired to Italy for the Italian section of the Congress.[38] On the basis of these arrangements Castlereagh agreed to attend the Vienna conference.

One more step was necessary to complete Metternich's preparations for the Congress: to move the site from Florence, in Tuscany, to Verona, in Venetia, to keep it more closely under Austrian control. The proposed change caused Nesselrode to protest—quite correctly—that Austria seemed determined to exercise a monopoly on the Congresses.[39] But Metternich's arguments on the superiority of the Venetian police to the Tuscan police and the necessity of excluding all strangers, curiosity-seekers, and foreign agents from the scene of the Congress readily convinced Alexander that Verona was the better site.[40] With the news of his agreement to the change of site came the still more heartening news that Capodistrias would definitely not attend—that, fallen from grace, he had asked and received indefinite leave from the imperial service.[41]

Metternich's preparations now seemed complete. Yet a totally unforeseeable event intervened to ruin them. On August 12, 1822, Castlereagh committed suicide. Not only was Metternich deprived of the support of the only British statesman with whom he could work closely, with the unpredictable and independent George

[38] Metternich (Vienna, July 10, 1822) to Vincent, Weisungen, Frankreich, Fasc. 350, No. 8 and Postscript to 8.

[39] Nesselrode objected most of all to seeing the Tsar playing the game of European Cabinets far from home while his own domains went neglected. Lebzeltern (St. Petersburg, July 1, 1822) to Metternich, Berichte, Russland, Fasc. 57, No. 46E. Lebzeltern was quite willing to cooperate with Nesselrode in trying to persuade Alexander to give up the trip to Italy and confine himself to the conference at Vienna, or even to stay home entirely. Not even the bad impression made on Alexander by the July fiasco in Spain, however, sufficed to make him give up the Congress. Lebzeltern (St. Petersburg, August 7, 1822) to Metternich, *ibid.*, Nos. 50F and Postscript to 50A.

[40] Lebzeltern (St. Petersburg, July 20, 1822) to Metternich, *ibid.*, Nos. 48A and 49C; Metternich (Vienna, June 20, 1822) to Lebzeltern, Weisungen, Russland, Fasc. 54, No. 2. Metternich instructed all his agents neither to issue nor to honor any passports for Verona or Lombardy-Venetia during the time of the Congress. Circular dispatch, Vienna, September 28, 1822, Kongressakten, Verona, Fasc. 45.

[41] Lebzeltern (St. Petersburg, July 20, 1822) to Metternich, Berichte, Russland, Fasc. 57, Nos. 48A and 49C.

Canning replacing him,[42] but, more immediately, Metternich's carefully-laid plans for the conference were disrupted. Although the Duke of Wellington, as Metternich had hoped, was appointed to replace Castlereagh as British plenipotentiary at the Congress, the Duke's illness, the change in the English administration, and the fragmentary state of the instructions left by Castlereagh for the British plenipotentiary combined to delay his departure from England till mid-September. En route he stopped over at Paris to confer with Villèle and to try to discourage French intervention in Spain. Hence he did not arrive in Vienna until September 29, well after the general conferences were scheduled to have been over.[43]

Metternich fumed at the delay. Not only did Wellington's absence prevent the Vienna conference from reaching decisions, thereby threatening grave inconvenience for the Congress at Verona, but still worse for Metternich, it made more difficult his task of controlling France and Russia in the interim.[44] Metternich was playing the crafty game of pitting each side against the other, telling Alexander that intervention in Spain was necessary, but that France was far too unreliable and subject to revolution herself to be trusted with the task, and at the same time warning Montmorency not to trust Alexander, for if Russian troops once marched into Spain, they would destroy the French constitution on their way back.[45] Such tactics, even if they served to delay rash action by either power, had their risks. Therefore Metternich, along with Stewart, in hopes of speeding matters up, requested the English government to send Wellington directly to Verona so that the Congress could commence there without further delay.[46] The slowness of communications,

[42] Already on September 21 the Austrian *chargé* in London, Neumann, had written to Metternich of the new era in Austro-British relations that had come with the accession of Canning. Berichte, Grossbritannien, Fasc. 216.

[43] Neumann (London, September 14, 1822) to Metternich, *ibid.*, Nos. 233C and 233E; Arthur Wellesley, First Duke of Wellington, *Despatches, Correspondence, and Memoranda of Field Marshal Arthur Duke of Wellington, K.G.*, I, 319.

[44] Metternich (Vienna, September 12 and 15, 1822) to Neumann, Weisungen, Grossbritannien, Fasc. 218, Nos. 1 and 2.

[45] Ferdinand Franz Tarnawski, "Der Kongress von Verona" (unpublished doctoral dissertation, University of Vienna, 1925), 79–80.

[46] Metternich (Vienna, September 15, 1822) to Neumann, Weisungen, Grossbritannien, Fasc. 218, Nos. 1 and 2; Stewart (Vienna, September 15,

however, and the Duke's determination not to proceed to Verona without definite orders, delayed his departure from Vienna until October 5 and postponed the opening of the Congress until mid-October.[47]

The period which should have concluded the resolution of all important business thus saw nothing really accomplished. It was, it is true, marked by certain important developments behind the scenes, especially at Paris. Montmorency had undertaken the task of representing France at Vienna with considerable reluctance, rightly fearing a political stab in the back from such rivals as Chateaubriand and Blacas during his absence.[48] When he left Paris, moreover, there were certain fundamental uncertainties in the French policy and differences of opinion between himself and Villèle which had not been resolved. Villèle, supported by Louis XVIII, wanted to use the Congress chiefly to distract Russia from a war with Turkey and to frustrate the Austrian designs for strengthening her hegemony in Italy. As for the Spanish question, he wanted the alliance kept out of it. The French envoys at Vienna and Verona were therefore instructed to avoid inciting the Congress to deliberate on the question of Spain and especially to avoid committing France to any action regarding Spain. The question of Spain was France's affair, in Villèle's opinion, to be handled in France's own way. Yet at the same time, the French envoys were also supposed somehow discreetly to sound out the other powers' views on Spain. If the matter came up, they were to indicate that France would accept a treaty with the Allies which, without committing France to anything, would assure her of Allied support in case she decided to intervene in Spain and particularly in case England then tried to oppose this action. As for the Regency at Urgel, Villèle's view was that its cause was hopeless and that any aid to it would be compromising and dangerous for France.[49]

1822) to Secretary for War and the Colonies Earl Bathurst, Varia, Grossbritannien, Fasc. 19.

[47] Wellington (Vienna, September 30 and October 4, 1822) to Canning, in Wellington, *Correspondence*, I, 319–322, 354.

[48] Vincent (Paris, August 24, 1822) to Metternich, Berichte, Frankreich, Fasc. 348, No. 32.

[49] Vincent (Paris, August 27 and October 21, 1822) to Metternich, *ibid.*, Nos. 33A, 48, and 48B; "Les Préludes du Congrès de Vérone," in Jean Baptiste Comte de Villèle, *Mémoires et Correspondance du Comte de Villèle*, III, 32–39;

Montmorency, less adroit than Villèle and more inclined to Ultra and European views, was uneasy about this policy from the outset and soon became convinced at Vienna that it constituted an impossible assignment for him. It was out of the question, he reported, to secure any kind of new formal treaty with the Allies, much less the blank check Villèle wanted; anything the Allies resolved would have to be based on the existing treaty system. Moreover, if France expected to secure any support from the Allies on the Spanish question, it was unavoidable that she, as the power most directly concerned, should open the discussion and state her views and aims on it. Montmorency also suggested that France would do best to set out the specific contingencies which might arise in regard to Spain and provide for these by means of a written agreement with the Allies. He also thought that France, while preserving her independence of action, should cloak her policy in the guise of the alliance. Finally, he favored breaking relations with Spain and openly supporting the Regency at Urgel.[50] All these ideas, so divergent from Villèle's, led Villèle to express sharp dissatisfaction with the way his foreign minister was conducting the diplomatic campaign, though he did not propose any practical alternative.[51]

Villèle (Paris, September 6, 17, October 4, 1822) to Montmorency, *ibid.*, 45–46, 55–57, 97–98.

[50] Montmorency (Vienna, October 1, and Innsbruck, October 9, 1822) to Villèle, in Villèle, *Mémoires*, III, 89–91, 104–112.

[51] Villèle (Paris, October 15 and 17, 1822) to Montmorency, *ibid.*, 120–126, 129–131. Tarnawski's contention ("Kongress von Verona," 198–200) that Villèle was always just as much in favor of war with Spain as was Montmorency, and only more nationalistic and independent in his relation to the alliance, has something to recommend it. The evidence appears to me to indicate, however, that Villèle was at this moment neither pro- nor antiwar, but simply, like the canny politician he was, unwilling to be committed to any step which might prove embarrassing later, and that he was only too ready to leave to Montmorency the onus of difficult and compromising negotiations. Certainly the task he gave Montmorency was an impossible one, and the solution he suggested to help him out of the difficulty (an attempt to get all the powers to make a joint *démarche* to Spain regarding her revolted colonies, offering Allied mediation and threatening recognition of the colonies' independence if Spain refused) was, as Montmorency pointed out, in view of the Eastern powers' known views on revolutions and recognition, utterly chimerical. Villèle (Paris, October 15, 1822) to Montmorency, in Villèle, *Mémoires*, III, 120–126; Montmorency (Innsbruck, October 9, and Verona, October 23, 1822) to Villèle, *ibid.*, 104–112, 142–144. For a recent statement of the view that Villèle genuinely wanted peace and neutrality with Spain, and that his policy was

Pressures in France, meanwhile, were steadily building up in favor of war. The army on the Pyrenees, its excuse for existence as a *cordon sanitaire* long since vanished, was in early October reinforced and openly transformed into a corps of observation.[52] The Ultras, led by Monsieur (the Count of Artois, Louis' brother, later Charles X), put constant pressure on Villèle to intervene in Spain. The ambassador at London, Viscount Chateaubriand, in response to his pleas, had been sent as an additional French representative to Verona. But instead of being, as Villèle had thought, more representative of the ministry and less eager for war than Montmorency, he soon showed himself to be the most ardent proponent of war on Spain, anticipating an easy conquest which would restore the tarnished prestige of France and the Bourbon dynasty.[53]

Wellington had tried to counteract all this war fever during his stay in Paris in September, and had left Paris convinced of Villèle's determination to maintain peace. The impression that Villèle gave of their meeting, however, was quite different from that of the Duke. According to Villèle, after listening to Wellington's arguments about the inconveniences and dangers which France would encounter in a war with Spain, he had replied with a full account of all the wrongs that France had suffered from revolutionary Spain, the various possible events in Spain which might force France to intervene, and the comfort which Allied moral (not material) support through a *traité eventuel* would be to her in such circumstances.[54] Clearly Villèle did not wish either to be forced by Russia or the Ultras into war, or to be constrained by England into maintaining peace. Wellington, however, believed that Villèle wanted

deliberately sabotaged by Montmorency in violation of Villèle's instructions, see Irby C. Nichols, Jr., "Great Britain and the Congress of Verona" (unpublished doctoral dissertation, University of Michigan, 1955), pp. 78–81, 90–91, 116–118, 143, 239–243, 254.

[52] Vincent (Paris, September 30 and October 7, 1822) to Metternich, Berichte, Frankreich, Fasc. 349, Nos. 41A and 42B.

[53] Vincent (Paris, September 30, 1822) to Metternich, *ibid.*, No. 41A; various letters of Chateaubriand to Villèle, London, April 2 to August 6, 1822, in Villèle, *Mémoires*, III, 22–32; Chateaubriand (Verona, October 31, 1822) to Villèle, *ibid.*, 168–170; Charles Stuart (Paris, October 21 and 28, 1822) to Canning, in Wellington, *Correspondence*, I, 407–408, 454–455.

[54] Villèle (Paris, September 22, 1822) to Montmorency, in Villèle, *Mémoires*, III, 59–64; Wellington (Paris, September 21, 1822) to Canning, in Wellington, *Correspondence*, I, 288–294.

peace just as he did and was therefore confident of a favorable outcome on the Spanish question at the Congress. His brief stay at Vienna only served to reinforce this optimistic outlook. For though he had the chance there to become personally introduced to the Tsar's grandiose ideas about action in Spain, Metternich and Bernstorff also convinced him in personal conversations that they were on his side in opposing all action regarding Spain, though they had to act with great discretion for fear of offending Alexander.[55]

By October 16 the delegations of the five powers were complete at Verona and the Congress could begin. It was an impressive assembly, worthy of this last European Congress of the post-Vienna era, with sovereigns, chief ministers, ambassadors and plenipotentiaries, councilors, generals, and elaborate retinues of attendants present.[56] As usual Metternich made his bid to control the policy at the Congress before the official sessions opened. In a confidential memoir delivered on October 15 to Russia and Prussia, he urged that the three Eastern powers, free in thought and action as the constitutional states could not be, should take the lead in carrying out moral action against the Spanish revolution, aiming to destroy

[55] Wellington (Vienna, October 4, 1822) to Canning, in Wellington, *Correspondence,* I, 343–348.

[56] The more important members of the delegations were as follows: Austria was represented by Emperor Francis, Metternich, Gentz, Count Wrbna, Count Bubna and Baron Wimpffen (generals of the armies of occupation in Italy), Esterhazy, Zichy, Lebzeltern, Ficquelmont, and Bombelles (envoy at Florence). The Russian delegates were Tsar Alexander, Nesselrode, Tatistchev, Prince Lieven, Pozzo di Borgo, Stroganov, and Count Stackelberg (envoy at Naples). Those from Prussia were King Frederick William, Prince William and Prince Charles, Chancellor Hardenberg, Bernstorff, Prince Wittgenstein, and Prince Hatzfeldt (envoy at Vienna). France was represented by Montmorency, Caraman, De la Ferronnays, and Chateaubriand. The English delegates were Wellington, Stewart, Strangford, and Frederick Lamb (envoy at the German Diet at Frankfurt). Most of the business of the Congress was transacted by Metternich, Nesselrode, Bernstorff, Montmorency, and Wellington, but the Italian Courts were also represented, some of them with sizable delegations. The Italian princes and their chief ministers present were: Ferdinand I and Prince Ruffo from Naples; Charles Felix and Count della Torre from Sardinia; Archduke Leopold and Prince Corsini from Tuscany; Archduchess Marie Louise and Count Neipperg from Parma; Cardinal Spina from Rome; and Archduke Francis IV and Count Guicciardi from Modena. One notes that England, the richest of all the nations, had one of the smallest and least pretentious delegations, while Naples, poor and debt-ridden, had one of the most elaborate. See the folder titled "Verzeichnisse des Gefolges der Monarchen auf dem Congresse zu Verona," Kongressakten, Verona, Fasc. 45.

it, not to modify it, and inducing all five courts, if possible, to break relations with Spain to that end. Any material action by France against Spain was, he argued, so dangerous for France herself that the other powers should discourage it and should restrict themselves to supporting France if she was attacked.[57] Metternich, while determined to preserve the intimate alliance of the Eastern autocracies at any cost, was plainly counting on moral action in Spain to satisfy Alexander. He had to keep his plans secret for the time, however, in order to retain the help of Wellington as long as necessary, since he had earlier given the Duke to believe that he was opposed to doing anything in regard to Spain, including breaking diplomatic relations with her. The question of what action should be taken against the revolution after a diplomatic rupture had been made with Spain Metternich intentionally left unanswered, though he may already have been contemplating recognizing the regency at Urgel.[58]

Along with restraining and appeasing Alexander, Metternich had as his second task the job of finding out what the French intentions were in order better to control them. This problem was solved for him when in the first five-power session of October 20 Montmorency proceeded incautiously to lay his cards on the table. In response to Metternich's request for information on the French position regarding Spain, Montmorency read to the powers an *aide-mémoire* assuring the Allies that France wanted peace and was maintaining a defensive posture with Spain, but stressing also the danger of a Spanish attack on France and the possibility that France might have to break relations with Spain, which might also unavoidably lead to war. Montmorency then posed three questions: First, if France was compelled to recall her minister at Madrid, would the other powers follow suit? Second, if war broke out, how and under what form would the Allies give France moral support? Third, what material support would they be prepared to give on the condition that France called for it and subject to the restrictions which France

[57] "Mémoire confidentiel sur les affaires d'Espagne et de Portugal," October 15, 1822 (original by Gentz), *ibid.*, Fasc. 43.

[58] Gordon, the most pro-Austrian of all the British diplomats, commented in a pre-Verona memorandum on Metternich's strong inclination to promote the counterrevolution in Spain, adding, "The late proclamations from Catalonia breathe Prince Metternich's sentiments, and are as if written by himself." Vienna, September 22, 1822, in Wellington, *Correspondence*, I, 298.

would impose in deference to French public opinion? By posing these questions—even giving them to the powers in writing—Montmorency had done just what Metternich wanted and Villèle wanted to avoid. Although the French Foreign Minister had tried to safeguard French interests by emphasizing French initiative in all action and by being intentionally vague about the possible causes for a French break in relations with Spain, he had opened the door to making France's dispute with Spain a matter for alliance discussion and control.[59]

Montmorency was not long in discovering what embarrassments he had created for himself. His talk of the possibility or probability of war with Spain had not only renewed Alexander's impatient zeal to see troops set in motion but had also revived his notion of forming a European army—this time of 150,000 men—to stand guard on the French frontier ready to come to France's aid. While Alexander assured Montmorency that Russia would give France any help just as she requested it, he also wanted France to be more clear on the reasons for the possible withdrawal of the French ambassador at Madrid and also to stipulate clearly what should be the *casus foederis* in the *traité eventuel* which the French wanted from the Allies. Wellington also wanted more information on the causes of French-Spanish tension, but he wanted it in order to work against French intervention and suggested that France might solicit England's good offices in settling her dispute with Spain.[60]

Metternich avoided committing himself openly. He continued to give Wellington the impression that, although he was considering Brunetti's suggestion of a joint Allied mediation in Spain, he and Bernstorff were still on England's side in promoting peace.[61] To

[59] "Précis des communications verbales faites par M. le Vicomte de Montmorency dans la réunion confidentielle de MM. les Ministres d'Autriche, de Grande Bretagne, de Prusse and de Russie, à Vérone le 20. Octobre 1822," Kongressakten, Verona, Fasc. 43; Montmorency (Verona, October 23 and 25, 1822) to Villèle, in Villèle, *Mémoires*, III, 139–145, 155.

[60] Report of conversation between Montmorency and Alexander, October 24, 1822, in Villèle, *Mémoires*, III, 147–152; Montmorency (Verona, October 28, 1822) to Villèle, *ibid.*, 158–166.

[61] Wellington (Verona, October 22 and 29, 1822) to Canning, in Wellington, *Correspondence*, I, 408–410, 457–460. Wellington insisted (*ibid.*, 484) that Metternich not only favored using British good offices for mediation between France and Spain, but that he had actually originated the idea. It is entirely possible that Metternich did do this (the suggestion about using British good

Stewart, however, Metternich came closer to revealing his real intentions. He congratulated himself that he had now led both Russia and France to commit themselves to what they each desired and opposed. Since Russia wanted a joint Allied military action but was afraid of unilateral action by France, while France wanted Allied moral support but would not tolerate a single foreign soldier on French soil, Metternich believed he could play each side off against the other, finally uniting all parties in taking moral action only against Spain.[62] Prussia, while siding as always with Austria, took a very passive, timid position on the whole question.[63]

Metternich's plan was complicated, however, by the fact that Alexander had evidently changed his mind. Apparently convinced before the Congress opened that France was completely unreliable and could not be trusted to intervene in Spain, Alexander now seemed determined to push France forward toward intervention. Metternich and Gentz used the ten-day cooling-off period between the first and second conferences to try without great success to discover what hidden motive lay behind the sudden change.[64] At the next confer-

---

offices is indicated as one of three alternatives in the Austrian memoir of October 31, discussed later in the text). To pretend support for England's policy at this time in order to use England to restrain France and Russia and to keep these two powers from joining in a common policy is completely consistent with Metternich's regular diplomatic methods. Once he gained his main point, however, i.e., making sure that Russia and France would not join in a common *démarche* or even an alliance, Metternich was certain to abandon any pretense of support for Wellington's idea of promoting peace between France and Spain (or, as Gentz called it, "his [Wellington's] whole highly unedifying system on the Spanish question").—Gentz, *Tagebücher,* III, 102. For thereafter Metternich's interest lay not in promoting peace or staying on good terms with England, but in appeasing Alexander with moral action against Spain. These were points which Stewart, who knew Metternich better than Wellington did, was acute enough to recognize. See his memorandum No. 2, November 2, 1822, in Wellington, *Correspondence,* I, 484–486.

[62] Stewart's memorandum No. 1, October 29, 1822, in Wellington, *Correspondence,* I, 475–477. Montmorency agreed with this view of Metternich's position. Montmorency (Verona, October 28, 1822) to Villèle, in Villèle, *Mémoires,* III, 158–166.

[63] "Positions des Cabinets au 28 Octobre, relativement à la question d'Espagne" (by Gentz), Kongressakten, Verona, Fasc. 43.

[64] The Austrians also failed in their attempt to moderate the terms and tone of Wellington's answer to Montmorency's proposals. *Ibid.* See also Gentz's memoir titled "Spanische Frage," n.d., *ibid.,* Fasc. 45. Gentz describes this period aptly as one of "persistent great confusion in the course of the Spanish question."—Gentz, *Tagebücher,* III, 101. Alexander undoubtedly revealed his

ence of the five chief ministers on October 30, all the latent conflicts of position between the powers came out into the open when the various responses to Montmorency's three questions were read. The Russian note expressed delight that France had finally recognized the fact that the Spanish revolution must be crushed—a fact which Russia had been proclaiming for more than two years. Answering all of Montmorency's questions with unqualified answers of support, it proposed that the Allies should act in concert immediately on breaking diplomatic relations with Spain, on defining the moral support to be given France, on stipulating the material support they would make available if armed intervention should become necessary, and "on the restrictions with which she [France] believes she must accompany the stipulations relative to this aid." [65] The Austrian and Prussian notes were far more hedging, promising France that they would break relations if she did, pledging their moral support in case of war, with reservations as to the best form in which to give it, and agreeing to give material support in case of necessity, though qualifying this promise with so many restrictions as to render it worthless.[66]

But if the Russian answer was an eager "Yes" and the Austrian and Prussian a cautious "Perhaps," that of England was a blunt "No." Ruling out any interference in Spain's internal affairs on principle, and denying any real possibility that Spain in her present weakness could menace or attack France, Wellington refused to even consider Montmorency's questions or the possibility of a diplomatic break until his government knew more about the grounds on which such a step might be based; if such a step was taken, England would try to

---

underlying design in a conversation with Wellington on November 27. He was hoping, he said, that French intervention in Spain would cause internal troubles in France, whereupon the Allies could intervene in France with their European army. When Wellington asked him whether he thought the government in France could endure a war with Spain, the Tsar answered, "No; but if it should not, we have the means of setting all to rights!" Memorandum, Verona, November 27, 1822, in Wellington, *Correspondence*, I, 614.

[65] "Réponse confidentielle du Cabinet de Russie au précis de communications verbales faites par Mr. le Vicomte de Montmorency, à la Conference du 20. Octobre," Kongressakten, Verona, Fasc. 43 (also printed in Wellington, *Correspondence*, I, 496–499).

[66] Austrian and Prussian memoirs, October 30, 1822, Kongressakten, Verona, Fasc. 43.

alleviate the resulting irritation in Spain and help preserve peace.[67] In the discussion which followed, Wellington disparaged so completely the French grounds for fear or complaint about Spain and denied so firmly the usefulness of any joint intervention or *démarche* that the Congress plainly threatened to break down as a result of his opposition.[68]

The next day, at Alexander's demand and in the hope of repairing the breach, Metternich called a full conference of all the plenipotentiaries to discuss the Spanish question (previous sessions had included only the chief ministers). Here he presented an Austrian memoir designed to unify the powers in some ill-defined kind of moral action regarding Spain. The Allies, it proposed, should make representations to Spain against the revolution and its terrible effects there, and should support the "healthy part" of the Spanish nation. Thus Metternich hinted that the Allies should break relations with Spain and recognize the Spanish insurgents, without saying so outright. He suggested three forms in which the Allies could make their representations to Spain: first, sending instructions, either joint or separate but similar, from each of the powers to their ambassadors in Madrid; second, letting four of the Allies make representations in behalf of France, the party injured by the revolution in Spain; or third, delegating one of the powers (unspecified, but Metternich had England in mind) to make the representations in behalf of the others.[69] This proposal received hardly any attention in this meeting, however. Montmorency and Wellington instead wrangled over what should or should not appear in the protocol which the Congress would prepare, while Nesselrode indicated that Alexander was determined that the powers ought to arrive at a definite treaty stipulating the *casus foederis* for war on Spain, as well as to decide the makeup of the European army and the line of march over which it should move.[70]

---

[67] "Memoir on the Observations of the French Minister respecting Spain," Verona, October 30, 1822, in Wellington, *Correspondence*, I, 499–502.

[68] Wellington's minute of the meeting, *ibid.*, 503–505.

[69] "Propositions du Cabinet Autrichien dans la Conférence du 31 Octobre 1822," original by Gentz, Kongressakten, Verona, Fasc. 43. See also Wellington, *Correspondence*, I, 506, minute of the meeting of November 1.

[70] Minute of the meeting of October 31, 1822, in Wellington, *Correspondence*, I, 505.

Wellington warned at the conclusion of this meeting that he would be compelled to make a solemn protest against the whole direction which the Spanish question was taking. At the next five-power ministers' conference of November 1 he made good his warning, delivering a sharp protest against the Austrian memoir of October 31 and insisting that England would not be a party to any attempt to interfere in the internal affairs of Spain or to do more than restore good relations between Spain and France. He also opposed holding any more sessions with the other plenipotentiaries present, causing the scheduled full conference of November 2 to be adjourned without meeting.[71]

Clearly the Congress could make no progress with Wellington; perhaps, Russia suggested, it should try to get on without him. The Russians proposed that the four Continental powers continue to meet, drawing up, in the sense of the Austrian memoir of October 31, separate but similar notes to their ambassadors in Spain (the procedure which the other three powers had agreed was the best of the alternatives suggested by Austria). These notes, when completed, could then be submitted to Wellington. If he approved them, or at least if he did not actively oppose them, well and good; if he was adamant, the other powers would send them anyway. This proposal was accepted, thus overcoming what Gentz called "the very critical position of things at present," and enabling the Congress to proceed.[72] The four cabinet ministers thrashed out among themselves the question of the *casus foederis,* along with the tenor of the notes to be sent to Spain. On the latter point, they decided that their notes should be such as would lead unfailingly to a break in relations with Spain.[73] Metternich, meanwhile, ingenious as always in devising expedients designed to keep matters under his control and to prevent unilateral action by anyone else, persuaded the pliable Montmo-

[71] Declaration by Wellington and minute of the meeting of November 1, 1822, *ibid.,* 503, 505–507; Montmorency (Verona, November 5, 1822) to Villèle, in Villèle, *Mémoires,* III, 177–179; "Spanische Frage," Kongressakten, Verona, Fasc. 45.

[72] Montmorency (Verona, November 5, 1822) to Villèle, in Villèle, *Mémoires,* III, 180; responses of Russia, Prussia, and France to the Austrian memoir of October 31, all dated November 3, 1822, Kongressakten, Verona, Fasc. 43; entry of November 2, 1822, in Gentz, *Tagebücher,* III, 104.

[73] "Spanische Frage," Kongressakten, Verona, Fasc. 45.

rency to agree to having a ministerial conference at Paris help decide the question of French intervention in Spain in cases where the *casus foederis* could not be defined in advance.[74] At the same time he continued to warn his Eastern Allies, especially Russia, about the unreliability of France, and the grave dangers of entrusting France with the task of intervention in view of internal French instability and England's separatist position. The Eastern Allies, he urged, should keep firmly in mind their three goals of preventing intervention, restoring order in Spain, and preserving the alliance.[75]

By November 14, Montmorency was ready to present to the Allies his draft of a protocol governing Allied support of France on the Spanish question. He stipulated as *casus foederis* (cases which would bring war and therefore call for immediate Allied support of France) any Spanish attack on France, any Spanish provoking of revolution in France, any attack by force or legal process against the King of Spain or his family, and any attempts to overthrow the Spanish dynasty. As *casus belli* (situations which would lead to a break in relations and hence probably to war) he included all lesser attacks or menaces to the royal family in Spain, insults to France or her ambassador, menaces to French subjects in Spain, and the like. These latter cases were to be submitted to the ministerial conference at Paris before France would decide whether to break relations.[76] In conferences on November 17, 18, and 19, the Allies reached agreement on the protocol, making only two changes worth noting—first, that the instances of *casus belli* were left unspecified, and second, on Russian insistence, that the right of demanding joint consultation in such instances was not confined to France but made reciprocal for all the Allies.[77] This meant that Russia, if she wished, could also take the initiative in proposing action against Spain.

These sessions of November 17–19 were arduous enough; the one of November 20 with Wellington was really explosive. As early as

[74] Note Verbale, Metternich (Verona, November 8, 1822) to Montmorency, Kongressakten, Verona, Fasc. 43.

[75] "Mémoire secret. Coup d'oeil sur la position de la question d'Espagne, le 15. Novembre 1822" (distributed only to Russia and Prussia, with a special edited copy for Montmorency), *ibid.*

[76] "Projet d. Protocole," November 14, 1822, *ibid.*

[77] "Spanische Frage," *ibid.*, Fasc. 45; "Précis de la conférence de Dimanche 17 novembre," and "Précis des conférences du 18. 19. et 20 novembre," *ibid.*, Fasc. 43; Verona Protocol, November 19, 1822, in Metternich, *Nachgelassene Papiere*, III, 575–576.

November 2 Stewart had seen what Metternich was doing, but Wellington, reluctant to abandon his optimistic predictions of a favorable outcome on the Spanish question in the Congress, refused to face the fact that Metternich had now abandoned his original policy of preventing all Allied action regarding Spain—on the basis of which policy Metternich had persuaded England to send a plenipotentiary to the Congress. Wellington still retained the hope that he could bring the Congress back to what he was sure was its original purpose: the promotion of peace between France and Spain.[78] The Verona protocol and the projected Allied dispatches to Spain, shown to him on the nineteenth, finally convinced him how unfounded his optimism had been.[79] In the next day's conference he attacked the dispatches and the protocol from every conceivable angle—as injudicious, unwarranted, irritating to Spain, unhelpful to France, unkind to England, and ruinous to the cause of peace. He concluded his solemn protest with the statement that England's action at Madrid would be confined to attempting to allay the furor and bad feeling these dispatches would cause. Wellington succeeded, however, only in getting the protocol changed to a simple *procès-verbal*, an empty concession. Moreover, even though Wellington still hoped that Villèle would prevent France from breaking relations with Spain, he learned that the Eastern Allies' dispatches would be sent whether or not the French Cabinet approved Montmorency's policy and sent the French dispatch jointly also. Ruefully Wellington recognized too late that he had been used. Metternich had first employed him, along with Montmorency, to discourage Alexander's ideas of a European army. Once this was done, Metternich had then immediately gone over to the Russian position in regard to a *traité eventuel*, the dispatches to Spain, and the deliberate promotion of a break in relations with Spain. Having brought about Capodistrias' fall, Wellington observed, Metternich was now pretty much the Russian as well as the Austrian prime minister, and therefore had to pursue a Russian policy.[80]

[78] Stewart's memoranda, Nos. 2–5, November 2, 3, 8, and 14, 1822, in Wellington, *Correspondence*, I, 484–489, 510–511, 534–535; Wellington (Verona, November 12, 1822) to Canning, *ibid.*, 531–533.

[79] Wellington (Verona, November 19, 1822) to Canning, *ibid.*, 555–557.

[80] Wellington (Verona, November 22, 1822) to Canning (with enclosures of the projected Russian and Austrian dispatches), *ibid.*, 562–572; "Précis des conférences du 18, 19, et 20 Novembre," Kongressakten, Verona, Fasc. 43;

After the conference of November 21, devoted to receiving Wellington's written declaration of protest, Metternich considered the Spanish question as settled.[81] True, Montmorency, in deference to his instructions, had refused to commit France to joint action, and left this same day for Paris to seek confirmation of what he had resolved with the Allies at Verona. But Metternich, having made sure that the Eastern Allies' dispatches would be sent, come what might, felt confident that France was now tied to the alliance on the question of Spain.[82] Exulting over his defeat of Pozzo di Borgo's intrigues and the skill with which he had managed Montmorency, he at last

---

"Cadre d'Instruction pour le Ministre de France à Madrid," and "Dépêche du Cabinet de Berlin, adressée au chargé d'affaires de S. M. le Roi de Prusse à Madrid," both undated, *ibid.* In contrast to the relative moderation with which Wellington characterized Metternich's course of action, the Austrian Chancellor privately heaped ridicule on Wellington and his conduct. The Duke's whole course of "moral opposition," according to Metternich, was based on only two points: first, that the Spanish revolution, unlike those in Italy, was not dangerous or contagious; and second, that in view of the accord established between himself and Villèle no effective action could be taken in regard to Spain in any case. All in all, one might comment, this is a highly truncated and misleading account of Wellington's position and arguments. In refutation, however, Metternich simply dismissed the first point as an "empty polemic," conveniently forgetting that he had himself used this very argument for two and one-half years, especially at Troppau and Laibach. The second point he rejected as a false supposition. He then went on to denounce Wellington's conduct as full of foolish mistakes—his own or George Canning's—and to deplore the impotence to which England had now reduced herself, closing with the prediction that "England is for once isolated and will remain so until she is forced by circumstances to return to the ranks of the Allies." Metternich (Verona, December 2, 1822) to Neumann, *Weisungen, Grossbritannien,* Fasc. 218. In a similar vein Gentz characterized the British notes and Wellington as "nothing but sorrowful monuments of a government fallen away from all good principles, and at the same time of the most pitiful diplomat which this government has perhaps ever employed in important business." "Spanische Frage," *Kongressakten,* Verona, Fasc. 45. Metternich's predictions that Britain would find her isolation painful and that she would eventually be forced to return to the alliance were premature, to say the least. The conclusion to which Canning had already come, and the policy which he followed with great success in the coming years, was that England should break with the Concert of Powers and turn to the Americas, which were far more valuable to her than Europe anyway. Canning (London, November 8, 1822) to Wellington, in Wellington, *Correspondence,* I, 511.

[81] Gentz, *Tagebücher,* III, 112.

[82] Procès-verbal, confidential conference of November 25, 1822, *Kongressakten,* Verona, Fasc. 43; "Spanische Frage," *ibid.,* Fasc. 45; Metternich (Verona, November 27, 1822) to Vincent, *ibid.,* Fasc. 43.

divulged to Vincent a clear policy on Spain. He wanted, it turned out, "to place a royalist Spain opposite a revolutionary Spain"—to encourage "the good Spaniards" by giving them moral support and by breaking relations with the bad Spaniards. But more important, he wanted to make the royalist insurgents the sole channel for any material intervention that France would make in Spain, and therefore a good means for Allied control of France's action. Did the Spanish royalists need gold, arms, means of war? France should furnish them at Spanish request, subject to conditions set by the Allies. Did the Spanish insurgents require troops? Again it was up to France to furnish them, under the same conditions and with the understanding that of course France could never be allowed to go to war with Spain herself. In other words, it was up to France to provide all the aid requested and required by the "good Spaniards" and, Metternich stipulated, "up to the Allies to limit it within precise bounds and to supervise its employment."[83]

If Metternich seriously hoped to make France the lackey of the alliance and the commissariat and recruiting ground for the Spanish royalists, he was reckoning without Villèle. The French Prime Minister had been watching with growing inquietude and aversion the course pursued by Montmorency. He disapproved highly of the way France had appeared to seek help from the Allies and to accept a European commission at their hands. He had also warned Montmorency sharply against trusting Metternich (Montmorency had gone so far as to allow Metternich to review and revise the proposed French dispatch to Madrid). Moreover, Wellington was still pouring words of peace into Villèle's ear, and while Villèle, like Metternich, was not above pretending more agreement with the Duke's position than he really felt, he also was astute enough to make good use of the danger of English intervention to help check France's trend toward war and preserve her independence of action vis-à-vis the Allies. Hence the warning which Villèle had early in the Congress given Montmorency that his policy might be repudiated became more and more a real possibility.[84] There were strong factors

[83] Secret letters, Metternich (Verona, November 27 and December 2, 1822) to Vincent, *ibid.*, Fasc. 43. Also in Weisungen, Frankreich, Fasc. 350.

[84] Villèle (Paris, November 12, 1822) to Montmorency, *ibid.*, Fasc. 43; Villèle (Paris, November 4, 6, 19, 20, and 24, 1822) to Montmorency, in Villèle, *Mémoires*, III, 174–177, 182–190, 220, 236–244; "Memorandum on the

working in Montmorency's favor, to be sure. He enjoyed the support
not only of Chateaubriand and the other envoys at Verona, but also
that of most of the Cabinet at Paris and of the Ultras, who had just
scored a sweeping victory in the November elections and were impatient with Villèle's wait-and-see policy.[85] Villèle, however, had the
King on his side and the argument that France's dignity and independence must be preserved in his favor.

In a conference of December 1, immediately after Montmorency's
return, the issue was thrashed out in the French Cabinet. With
strong support from Louis XVIII, Villèle secured acceptance of his
view that the whole situation in regard to Spain was now changed.
The complete dispersal of the insurgent army of the Faith and the
collapse of the Regency at Urgel, the danger of open British opposition to intervention, and the bad effect war would have on French
commerce and public opinion meant that France would have to
delay the dispatch drawn up at Verona for De la Garde in Madrid.
With Montmorency's reluctant support, Villèle instructed Chateaubriand at Verona to request that the Allies also hold back their dispatches to Madrid until France was ready to send hers.[86] Chateaubriand, who wanted France to act jointly with the Allies, had to report
that the Allies, though willing to grant France a few days' delay, could
not agree to let her set the time for sending the dispatches. This
might mean, Metternich had pointed out, that the Congress would
close without taking any decisive step regarding Spain, a consequence
which would be intolerable to Russia and would have a bad effect
on public opinion in Europe.[87] While the Allies thus remained firm

State of the Spanish Question," Verona, November 12, 1822, in Wellington,
Correspondence, I, 519–523.

[85] Chateaubriand (Verona, November 20 and 28, 1822) to Villèle, in Villèle,
Mémoires, III, 231–236, 247–252; Villèle (Paris, November 18, 1822) to
Montmorency, *ibid.*, 218; Vincent (Paris, November 4, 23, 25, 29, 1822) to
Metternich, Berichte, Frankreich, Fasc. 349, Nos. 52, 59A, 60.

[86] "Les Suites du Congrès de Vérone," in Villèle, *Mémoires*, III, 267–280;
Villèle (Paris, December 5, 1822) to Chateaubriand, in François Vicomte de
Chateaubriand, *Congrès de Vérone; Guerre d'Espagne; Negociations; Colonies
Espagnoles*, I, 164–167; Montmorency (Paris, December 5, 1822) to Met-
ternich, Kongressakten, Verona, Fasc. 43; Vincent (Paris, December 5, 1822,
to Metternich, *ibid.*

[87] Chateaubriand (Verona, December 12, 1822) to Villèle, in Chateaubriand,
Congrès de Vérone, I, 170–172; Metternich (Verona, December 14, 1822) to
Vincent and to Montmorency, Kongressakten, Verona, Fasc. 43; Nesselrode
(Verona [ca. December 14, 1822]) to Pozzo di Borgo, *ibid.*

in their decision to send out their notes regardless of what France did, Villèle held out successfully against the rest of his ministry for a policy of restraint with regard to Spain, insisting that France must not break relations with Spain until her troops were ready to march on Spanish soil. This decision, taken December 25, forced Montmorency to resign. After some insincere hesitation, Chateaubriand accepted the post of foreign minister.[88] The year 1822 and the Congress thus ended with the Eastern powers determined to break relations with Spain, France determined to delay her action, England dissociated from all the other powers, and the whole question of Spain, as Gentz said, "more *broken open* than *terminated.*" [89]

The remaining matters considered at the Congress, though not unimportant, were far less controversial. The first to be disposed of was the Russo-Turk question. The problem, brought before the pre-Verona conference at Vienna, threatened to explode over Russian grievances against the Turks and Strangford. The Turks, Russia claimed, had failed to carry out in good faith their promises to evacuate the principalities and to name hospodars and had renewed their harassment of Russian navigation through the Straits. In addition Strangford had failed to defend Russia in a conference of August 27 against Turk charges that Russia had instigated the Greek revolt. These complaints culminated in a strong note denouncing both the Turks and Strangford, circularized by Nesselrode to the other delegates on September 26.[90]

Strangford arrived at Vienna this same day expecting to receive

[88] "Les Suites du Congrès de Vérone," in Villèle, *Mémoires*, III, 274–279. According to Villèle, Chateaubriand was chosen chiefly to prevent a break with the Eastern powers. Doubtless Chateaubriand's strong backing among the Ultras was also a factor.

[89] Gentz (Innsbruck, December 26, 1822) to Prince Gregory Ghika, hospodar of Walachia, in Gentz, *Dépêches inédites*, II, 164.

[90] Unsigned Russian note, Vienna, n.d., accompanied by supplements of Russian correspondence to support the Russian complaints, Kongressakten, Verona, Fasc. 44; another copy of Nesselrode's note, September 26, 1822, Varia, Türkei, Fasc. 15; Wellington (Vienna, October 2, 1822) to Nesselrode, in Wellington, *Correspondence*, I, 337–339; Tarnawski, "Kongress von Verona," 82–85. The *précis* of the August 27 conference shows that Strangford actually did defend Russia as well as he could.—Prokesch, *Abfall der Griechen*, III, 406–427. For a detailed account of the handling of the Russian grievances at Vienna, see Irby C. Nichols, Jr., "The Eastern Question and the Vienna Conference, September 1822," *Journal of Central European Affairs*, XXI, No. 1 (April 1961), 53–66.

acclaim for his successful handling of the negotiations, only to meet recrimination from Nesselrode and cold dislike from Alexander instead. Wellington believed there was real danger in the commerce issue and urged his government to support the Russian request for a return to the former Ottoman practice of allowing ships to pass the Straits under false flags—a policy which Canning, Liverpool, and Strangford all opposed because of the damage it would bring to the British carrying trade.[91] Metternich, meanwhile, tried anxiously to soothe the Russians' wrath with promises of full diplomatic support for Russia in all her legitimate grievances.[92]

Fortunately, Alexander, thoroughly tired of the Turkish question, was easily appeased, and his moderation prevented any real crisis. The issue was postponed to Verona where, after several private conferences, the delegates of the original Vienna conference on the Eastern question— Metternich, Tatistchev, Caraman, Hatzfeldt, and Wellington (replacing Stewart)—met to discuss the issues. Their first conference on November 8 ran into difficulty because Wellington refused to support the Russian claims regarding commerce through the Straits as fully as the other powers were willing to do. The next day's session, in which Tatistchev restated the Russian grievances and demands at length and Metternich responded by praising Alexander's moderation and promising support for his demands in general terms, served to clear the air.[93] Final conferences were called on November 26 and 27 at Tatistchev's request, but they produced nothing more than statements of wholehearted approval of the Russian position read by Caraman and Hatzfeldt, and one of very qualified approval read by Wellington, followed by a statement by Tatistchev conveying the Tsar's thanks for the Allied support and returning the negotiations to the hands of Strangford at Constantinople. This, of course, was exactly what Metternich and

[91] Wellington (Vienna, October 2, 1822) to Nesselrode, in Wellington, *Correspondence*, I, 337–339; Wellington (September 30 and October 4, 1822) to Canning, *ibid.*, 319, 350–354; Canning (London, October 25, 1822) to Wellington (with enclosures), *ibid.*, 431–433; Strangford (Verona, October 29, 1822) to Wellington, *ibid.*, 469–470.

[92] Metternich (Vienna, September 30, 1822) to Nesselrode, *ibid.*, 332–333; "Note verbale rémise au Comte du Nesselrode le 22 septembre 1822," Kongressakten, Verona, Fasc. 44.

[93] Wellington (Verona, November 12, 1822) to Canning (with enclosures), in Wellington, *Correspondence*, I, 523–529; Tarnawski, "Kongress von Verona," 158–164.

Wellington had wanted in the first place.[94] The Greek cause, meanwhile, was entirely ignored at Verona. A would-be envoy of the provisional Greek government (one Metaxas) was confined at Ancona by the government of the Papal States, while his appeals to the Congress and the Pope went unheard.[95] Metternich, in short, got his way entirely on the Russo-Turk question by treating it as a cabinet, not a Congress, affair.[96]

Italian affairs were settled at Verona with equal ease, though the Austrian victory was less complete. As has been seen, Metternich had hoped to use this Congress to promote his system of Allied supervision over the governments of Italy and, if possible, to bring about the creation of a central investigation committee like that in Mainz as a step toward the Italian League. His scheme, however, had been divined by some of the Italian states, notably Sardinia, which had, along with the Papal States and Tuscany, secured the powerful support of Villèle and France in their determination to frustrate these plans. Villèle, in addition, gave full support to Sardinia's demand for an end to the Austrian occupation and intended also to try to force Austria to reduce her occupation forces and their costs in Naples.[97] With active French support for Sardinia looming in the background, Count della Torre of Sardinia convinced the three Eastern powers that Charles Felix had fully pacified and reorganized his domains, and the Count secured an agreement for the

[94] Procès-verbal, conference of November 26, 1822, with declarations, Kongressakten, Verona, Fasc. 44; procès-verbal, conference of November 27, 1822, *ibid.;* memoir by Gentz, "Türkisch-Griechische Frage," *ibid.,* Fasc. 45.

[95] Greek government (Argos, August 7, 1822) to Pope Pius VII, *ibid.,* Fasc. 45; Metaxas (Ancona, November 3, 1822) to the Pope, *ibid.;* Cardinal Spina (Verona, December 2, 1822) to Metternich, *ibid.;* "Türkisch-Griechische Frage," *ibid.*

[96] Gentz, (Verona, December 6, 1822) to Ghika, in Gentz, *Dépêches inédites,* II, 139–140. Metternich's victory was accompanied by his usual self-congratulation, included in it his boast that "Strangford came here entirely without ideas and was completely mastered by mine." Metternich (Verona, December 3, 1822) to Gentz, in Gentz, *Briefe von und an Gentz,* III, Pt. 2, 39.

[97] Villèle (Paris, September 17, 1822) to Montmorency, in Villèle, *Mémoires,* III, 57–58; Neumann (London, September 14, 1822) to Metternich, Berichte, Grossbritannien, Fasc. 216, No. 233D; résumé, interview of Sardinian Envoy Count d'Aglie with Castlereagh, London, August 7, 1822, in Wellington, *Correspondence,* I, 272–273. As early as June 1821, Consalvi had expressed the fear that Austria intended by means of its Laibach decrees to interfere in the internal affairs of the Papal States. Metternich (Vienna, July 18, 1821) to Lebzeltern, Weisungen, Russland, Fasc. 45, No. 3.

withdrawal of all Austrian troops in gradual stages during the year 1823.[98] It was so plain to everyone that Naples could no longer support the existing burden of the Austrian occupation that the Eastern powers also resolved on a reduction of these forces to thirty-five thousand men beginning in April 1823. Ferdinand I, however, more concerned with his personal security than with his country's finances, pleaded for an extension of the occupation beyond the scheduled termination date of 1824. Despite Russia's impatience with Ferdinand for failing to take hold and rule in his country, the powers indicated their willingness to extend the occupation if it became necessary.[99]

The high point of the Italian section of the conference was supposed to have been the presentation and review of each Italian government's past actions and future plans for strengthening itself against subversion and political innovation. In this connection Metternich had intended to use the Habsburg Duke of Modena, Francis IV, as a stalking-horse for his Italian plans.[100] In the face of the opposition of most Italian princes and of France to any further extension of Austrian hegemony in Italy, however, the sessions produced only a series of meaningless declarations. The Italian princes one after another praised the principles of the Allies and announced their "reforms," usually in very vague terms; their programs ranged from the mildly progressive one of Parma, read by Count Neipperg, to the utterly reactionary one of Francis IV of Modena, read by the Marquis of Molza. The powers then accepted these declarations as satisfactory.[101] Metternich also secured one more action

[98] Procès-verbal, conference of December 2, 1822 (with Della Torre's memoir, same date), Kongressakten, Verona, Fasc. 44; procès-verbal, conference of December 5, 1822, *ibid.*

[99] Procès-verbal, conference between the Eastern powers and Prince Ruffo, December 8, 1822, *ibid.*; procès-verbal, five-power conference, December 8, 1822, *ibid.*; procès-verbal, Eastern powers conference with Ruffo, December 9, 1822, *ibid.* That reducing the size of the occupation army did not at all mean reducing political surveillance over Naples is indicated by the presence among the Congress documents (*ibid.*, Fasc. 45) of long lists of generals, nobles, political figures, and even civil servants in Naples, with comments concerning their political principles and reliability. Whether these were drawn up by Austrian agents or Neapolitan agents, I cannot tell. Other documents bear on the Neapolitan political organization, the now moribund scheme of separate *Consultas*, etc.

[100] Tarnawski, "Kongress von Verona," 52.

[101] Procès-verbal, conference of December 11, 1822, Kongressakten, Verona,

from the Congress regarding Italy—a joint approach by the four Continental Allies to Switzerland, demanding that the Swiss cantons remove all Piedmontese revolutionary fugitives from their Italian borders.[102]

The problem of the future of Charles Albert, Prince of Carignan, raised at the Congress by Sardinia, was dealt with entirely behind the scenes. Charles Felix, supported by Francis IV, had instructed Della Torre and Count Pralormo to promote his plan to cut Charles Albert out of the succession. Metternich's earlier views on this scheme are open to some doubt.[103] Assuredly, however, by the opening of

---

Fasc. 44; procès-verbal, conference of December 13, 1822 (with the various declarations), *ibid.* Molza announced the following program of "ameliorations" carried out by Francis IV: (1) promoting religion and the clergy as supports of the throne; (2) elevating the nobility for the same purpose; (3) extending the exercise of monarchical authority; (4) strengthening the laws against *lèse-majesté*, and facilitating convictions and preventing judicial pardons for this crime; (5) improving education by limiting the number of schools and holding separate schools instead of a university "to avoid the inconveniences which arise when there are too many students convened at a university"; and (6) watching over the press and suppressing bad books.

[102] Procès-verbal, conference of December 14, 1822, *ibid.* Metternich had instigated Sardinia to make this demand of Switzerland already in May 1821. "The excessive condescension" shown by the Swiss to the refugees, he said, "could be regarded by the Allied powers as a moral violation of neutrality." At this time Metternich wanted not only the removal of the refugees from the border, but the extradition of some of them to face trial. Metternich (Laibach, May 14, 1821) to Binder, Weisungen und Varia, Sardinien, Fasc. 58. The pressure exerted by the Eastern powers, especially Austria, on the Swiss cantons in regard to the asylum granted to German and Italian political refugees is described in Paul Schweizer, *Geschichte der schweizerischen Neutralität*, 659–687. Ultimately Metternich succeeded in getting the cantons and the Diet to oust some refugees and to curb the activities of others.

[103] The judgment of Tarnawski ("Kongress von Verona," 172–173) that Metternich originally favored Charles Felix' plan but had to retreat because of the opposition of France, Russia, and Tuscany, seems to me correct, though not absolutely proved. Certainly Della Torre and Pralormo thought Metternich favored their plan, though recognizing that he had to act with delicacy because of the Habsburg connection with the Duke of Modena. See William Hill, the British envoy at Turin (Turin, October 17, 1822) to Canning, in Wellington, *Correspondence*, I, 428–431. All Metternich's arguments about legitimacy, Article 86 of the Vienna treaty, and even his fear of too great an aggrandizement of Francis IV and Modena (memoir titled "Confidentiel. Branche de Carignan" [n.d., n.p.], Kongressakten, Verona, Fasc. 45) seem to me *ex post facto* rationalizations of his gradual change in position. It may be worth noting that in 1814 Metternich had been willing to allow Sardinia-Piedmont to have Lombardy up to the line of the Mincio—if Francis of Modena

the Congress he had become convinced that the scheme was in any case politically impossible in view of the absolute and determined opposition of France and the very considerable aversion of Russia and Tuscany to it. His plan, therefore, as communicated secretly to Alexander and to Wellington, was to leave the Prince in possession of his rights, though he was gravely compromised in the Piedmont-ese-Lombard conspiracy, but to bind him by an oath to the Allies to make no change in the fundamental laws of the kingdom.[104] Despite Wellington's belief that such an extorted promise was unwise, and Count Pralormo's observation that the oath would be invalid the moment Charles Albert mounted the Sardinian throne, since in Sardinia the principle that "the will of the ruler is the only law" held good,[105] Metternich's solution was tacitly adopted.

Other minor topics were dealt with at the Congress. On November 24 Wellington introduced a long memoir dealing with the slave trade and suggesting various means to attack it. His proposals met with such lukewarm support from the Eastern powers and such a caustic attack from France (the chief power still responsible for the extent of the illegal traffic, according to the English) that the powers finally resolved only upon issuing a pious but worthless statement condemning the slave trade.[106] At the same time, Wellington announced that England was compelled by circumstances to give *de facto* recognition to certain Spanish American governments in order to be able to deal with them in regard to commerce, the suppression of piracy, and the protection of British subjects. A protest by France against this step as a unilateral action which hurt the solidarity of the alliance, and a protest by the other powers against it as an infringement of the legitimate rights of Ferdinand VII, failed to alter the English policy.[107]

---

had been named to succeed Victor Emmanuel I.—Griewank, *Wiener Kongress*, 187.

[104] Stuart (Paris, October 24, 1822) to Canning, in Wellington, *Correspondence*, I, 410–411; "Mémoire confidentiel sur Mons. le Prince de Carignan pour Sa Majesté l'Empereur Alexandre" [October 1822], Kongressakten, Verona, Fasc. 45.

[105] Wellington (Verona, November 29, 1822) to Canning, in Wellington, *Correspondence*, I, 610–611; "Mémoire du Cte. de Pralorme," Verona, end of November 1822, Kongressakten, Verona, Fasc. 45.

[106] Procès-verbal of the conferences of November 24 and 28, 1822, with the declarations relative thereto, Kongressakten, Verona, Fasc. 44.

[107] *Ibid.* Much more important to Metternich than these matters were his

The epilogue to the Congress of Verona—the intervention of France in Spain—constitutes a distinct and rather complicated story in itself. Leaving aside, however, the developments in French internal politics leading up to the intervention, the unsuccessful attempts by Canning to head off or to halt intervention through British mediation, and the story of the successful French military campaign in Spain from March to September of 1823, one may review it briefly here simply from the standpoint of Metternich's diplomacy. If the Congress of Verona was on the whole a victory for Metternich, its epilogue was mainly a defeat. In an unsuccessful attempt to prevent French intervention, control French policy, and keep France under the supervision of the alliance, Metternich was forced to retreat from position after position, failing with one expedient after another to accomplish these purposes.

The first blow to Metternich's policy came with France's decision to delay sending her dispatch to Madrid, thus separating her action from that of the Allies. Metternich believed for a while that somehow the end of the Congress would compel France to end her delay and act with the Allies in breaking relations with Spain.[108] But though the Allies waited as long as they could, it did no good;[109] the continued French delay in sending her note to Spain, culminating in Montmorency's resignation, disabused Metternich's mind of the illusion that the French would in the end make a joint *démarche* with the Allies. The French dispatch was finally sent out in January 1823, deliberately later than those of the Allies and conspicuously independent of them. With it, moreover, went secret instructions to De la Garde in which Metternich found evidence that Chateau-

---

attempts at the Congress to gain Alexander's support for strengthening the repressive laws of the German Confederation and, once again, for the establishment of a secret European antirevolutionary information center. See the "Mémoire secrèt pour Sa Majesté Impériale de toutes les Russies sur la position des choses dans la fedération Germanique," and "Mémoire secrèt pour Sa Majesté Impériale de toutes les Russies," Verona, n.d., *ibid.*, Fasc. 45. Also in Metternich, *Nachgelassene Papiere*, III, 589–596.

[108] Metternich (Verona, December 11, 1822) to Francis I, in Metternich, *Nachgelassene Papiere*, III, 577–578.

[109] Metternich (Venice, December 24, 1822) to Vincent, Weisungen, Frankreich, Fasc. 350; Metternich (Vienna, January 18, 1823) to Vincent, with supplement, *ibid.*, Fasc. 354.

briand was entertaining dangerous ambitions about retaining a moderate constitution in Spain.[110]

It now became all the more important for Metternich, who had been urging peace upon Chateaubriand, to try to prevent armed French intervention, especially since France's break in diplomatic relations with Spain—which was, as intended, the result of her dispatch to De la Garde—moved France that much closer to war. Metternich attempted all kinds of expedients to prevent French intervention, which he feared might lead to establishing the *Charte* in Spain and compromising with the revolution there. One stratagem was to suggest—an astounding suggestion after what had happened at Verona—that the French turn to the English for mediation of Spanish-French difficulties. It was one of Villèle's fundamental mistakes, Metternich insisted, to make a diplomatic rupture with Spain an inevitable prelude to war. Even now war was not necessary; indeed, Metternich claimed in early February 1823 that the French ministry did not really want it. The best way, then, for France to avoid a conflict, now that she had broken relations with Spain, was to delay taking any further steps and to ask England what she could do to help preserve the peace.[111]

The French paid absolutely no attention to this advice; the last thing Villèle or Chateaubriand intended to do was to call on England, whom they regarded as their worst rival in Spain, for mediation there. This expedient failing him, Metternich turned to another. If he could not prevent French armed intervention altogether, he would try to restrict it to giving aid to the Spanish royalists. Pro-

[110] Brunetti (Madrid, January 5, 10, 11, 1823) to Metternich, Berichte, Spanien, Fasc. 190, Nos. 372–376; Caraman (Vienna, March 1, 1823) to Chateaubriand, Varia, Frankreich, Fasc. 97A; Metternich (Vienna, March 20, 1823) to Esterhazy, Weisungen, Grossbritannien, Fasc. 221, No. 5.

[111] Record of interview, Verona, December 12, 1822, in Chateaubriand, *Congrès de Vérone*, I, 219–220, 226–228; Metternich (Vienna, January 30, 1823) to Vincent, Weisungen, Frankreich, Fasc. 354, No. 3 (also secret letter, same date); Metternich (Vienna, February 4, 1823) to Lebzeltern, Weisungen, Russland, Fasc. 60, No. 1 (Secret). Nothing shows better than this last letter Metternich's reluctance even at this date to see France launched into action on her own or England separated from the alliance, and the hopeless expedients and arguments with which he tried to prevent it. Clinging, despite everything that had happened at Verona, to his proclamation of the unity of the Allies in their principles, he insisted that all the powers, including England, desired a speedy end to the Spanish revolution and that even England must admit that Spain posed the same threat to Europe in 1823 that France had in 1789.

foundly distressed at hearing French spokesmen, even Louis XVIII, speak in favor of war against Spain, Metternich protested that material action by France in Spain was indeed possible, but a war by France against Spain—never! If a French army did enter Spanish soil (which by the end of February was all but certain), it must, according to Metternich, act solely as a reserve or auxiliary for the Spanish royalists. This, after all, had been the policy that Austria had followed in Italy. "The Austrian army never bore any other name than that of the auxiliary army of Naples." [112] Finally, when it was clear that France could not be restrained from military intervention on her own, Metternich tried to bring the action under Allied supervision by insisting that Allied commissioners ought to be attached to France's military headquarters in Spain. [113]

The French went their way undeterred by these protests. They had learned from Metternich at Troppau and Laibach how to act in one's own interests after receiving the moral support of the Allies. The tactics which Metternich now so strenuously deplored and condemned were simply his own turned against him. Distressing as was the prospect of independent French action in Spain, however, the worst danger was still that the French would establish a constitution there. [114] Indeed, Metternich believed that he had found evidence of Villèle's intrigues in this direction on the very eve of the opening of the French campaign. [115] To stave this off, Metternich warned the French that the Allies might withdraw their promise of aid if France did not carry out her intervention under alliance supervision. He instructed Vincent to demand from Chateaubriand more information on the French plans regarding Spain and more consultation by France with the Allied ministers at Paris, reminding the French Foreign Minister that he must not think that the Allies had promised France support at Verona without control over how that support would be used. At the same time, he urged his Eastern Allies to

[112] Metternich (Vienna, February 19, 1823) to Lebzeltern, Weisungen, Russland, Fasc. 60, No. 1; Metternich (Vienna, March 1, 1823) to Vincent, Weisungen, Frankreich, Fasc. 354.

[113] Metternich (Vienna, March 6, 1823) to Lebzeltern, Weisungen, Russland, Fasc. 60, No. 3, with supplement.

[114] Metternich (Vienna, February 6, 1823) to Vincent, Weisungen, Frankreich, Fasc. 354; Metternich (Vienna, March 20, 1823) to Esterhazy, Weisungen, Grossbritannien, Fasc. 221, No. 2.

[115] Metternich (Vienna, February 24 and March 23, 1823) to Vincent, Weisungen, Frankreich, Fasc. 354, Nos. 3 and 3 (Secret).

make joint representations with him at Paris in demanding a four-power ministers' conference there in order to bring French action in Spain back where the Congress of Verona had implicitly placed it: under the control of the alliance.[116]

Chateaubriand knew, of course, that Austria and Prussia had no intention in any case of giving France any material support. Besides, France had already secured all the help she needed in Alexander's promise to come to her aid if the English openly opposed the French intervention. Hence the Austrian warning about withdrawing alliance support was an empty threat. By the time the French campaign opened on April 7, under the command of the King's nephew, the Duke of Angoulême, Metternich had perforce reconciled himself to it, consoling himself with the thought that action of this kind was better than leaving an army on the Pyrenees indefinitely, where it would be exposed to revolutionary plots. In fact, he said, he had always known that war was inevitable.[117] Moreover, he was by this time somewhat happier with Chateaubriand, largely because the Duke of Angoulême's initial proclamation to the Spanish people gave no evidence of any French plans to establish a constitution in Spain.[118]

This did not mean, however, that Metternich was now finally willing to let the French proceed on their own. Instead, in what was surely the strangest and most desperate of all his diplomatic expedients during the whole period of 1820–1823, he launched an attempt to gain for Austria control over the French intervention by making Austria's puppet, Ferdinand I of Naples, the regent of Spain. The original idea came from Ferdinand I. As the uncle of Ferdinand VII and the nearest agnate of the Spanish branch of the Bourbons who was not in the hands of the Spanish revolutionaries, he claimed

[116] Metternich (Vienna, February 24 and 28, 1823) to Vincent, *ibid.*, Nos. 2 and 1 and 2; Metternich (Vienna, February 19, 1823) to Lebzeltern, Weisungen, Russland, Fasc. 60, No. 1.

[117] Metternich (Vienna, February 28, 1823) to Esterhazy, Weisungen, Grossbritannien, Fasc. 221, No. 2; Metternich (Vienna, April 7, 1823) to Lebzeltern, Weisungen, Russland, Fasc. 60, Nos. 2 and 4. In another letter to Lebzeltern on the same date, Metternich admitted that the French and British policies had brought about the failure of his own policy, which was to allow the Spanish revolution to collapse by itself under Allied moral pressure. *Ibid.*, No. 8.

[118] Metternich (Vienna, April 19, 1823) to Vincent, Weisungen, Frankreich, Fasc. 354, No. 4.

imprescriptible rights to head any regency which the French might set up during their intervention. Metternich took over Ferdinand's idea, assuring the Neapolitan representatives of his support but urging them to leave the matter to him and to do nothing premature.[119] Although delicately broached, Metternich's plan met instant and formidable opposition from many quarters. Chateaubriand, describing the whole affair as "this puppet show, of which M. de Metternich was the Seraphin," opposed it firmly but quietly, not wishing to offend Austria too openly.[120] Nesselrode, however, rejected it vigorously because of Ferdinand's terrible post-restoration record at Naples and the bad effect the proposal would have on Spanish public opinion.[121] Alexander could see no reason why a king who could not rule his own country should be made regent of another; even Prussia reacted coolly to the proposition. Finally, Ambassador Vincent himself at Paris expressed the opinion that Ferdinand I should stop pressing his claims to the regency.[122]

Despite this opposition, when Chateaubriand announced his intention of setting up a provisional government at Madrid, with the Duke of Angoulême as regent for Ferdinand VII, whom the fleeing revolutionaries had taken to Cádiz, Metternich reversed his earlier promises that he would extend diplomatic recognition and representation to such a provisional government. He now insisted that no regency could be named or recognized that did not have Ferdinand I as its titular head. Besides basing his main argument on the

[119] Metternich (Vienna, February 24, 1823) to Vincent, *ibid.*, No. 2 (Secret); Metternich (Vienna, February 19, 1823) to Lebzeltern, Weisungen, Russland, Fasc. 60, No. 1. A good account of Austro-Neapolitan cooperation in the regency project is given by Moscati, *Il regno delle Due Sicilie*, I, xxxii–xli. The correspondence between Prince Castelcicala, Neapolitan envoy at Paris, and Prince Ruffo (*ibid.*, 197–199, 202–216, *et passim*) demonstrates that Ruffo acted consistently as the tool of Metternich.

[120] Chateaubriand, *Congrès de Vérone*, I, 380; Metternich (Vienna, March 23, 1823) to Vincent, Weisungen, Frankreich, Fasc. 354, No. 2; Vincent (Paris, April 7, 1823) to Metternich, Berichte, Frankreich, Fasc. 351, No. 91E, with supplement.

[121] Lebzeltern (St. Petersburg, March 12, 1823) to Metternich, Berichte, Russland, Fasc. 58, No. 19C. In answer to Nesselrode's objections, Lebzeltern admitted that had this measure been suggested at Verona, Metternich would have been the first to oppose it. Now, however, it gave the alliance a good means of controlling the regency and spoiling the ambitious plans of France. *Ibid.*

[122] Vincent (Paris, May 23, 1823) to Metternich, Berichte, Frankreich, Fasc. 352, No. 98F.

legitimacy of Ferdinand's claims to the regency as based on the rules
of dynastic succession, he also tried to convince Chateaubriand that
granting Ferdinand's claim would give great moral prestige to the
Allied cause, would prove the selflessness of France, and would—in
some undefined way—be a shrewd blow at England.[123] These arguments deceived Chateaubriand not a moment as to Metternich's
real intentions. Concealing his inward contempt for the scheme, he
pointed out patiently that France did not question Ferdinand's rights
of succession, but simply denied his right and capability to run the
show in Spain without having paid the bills.[124] Prussia gave no support to the Austrian proposal, while Nesselrode, Alexander, and
Pozzo di Borgo actively opposed it.[125] Nevertheless, even after the
proposal had been decisively rejected in a ministerial conference
with Chateaubriand at Paris on June 7, Metternich continued to
delay giving recognition to the provisional regime at Madrid, embarrassing and hampering the Austrian ambassador, Count Brunetti, in
his relations with the Madrid government. Not until mid-July, five
months after he had begun the attempt to make Ferdinand I regent,
did Metternich finally abandon the project quietly and recognize
the provisional regime.[126]

[123] Metternich (Vienna, April 4 and 19, 1823) to Vincent, Weisungen,
Frankreich, Fasc. 354, No. 3; Metternich (Vienna, May 28, 1823) to Vincent,
ibid., Nos. 1-4, with supplements (printed in part in Metternich, *Nachgelassene
Papiere*, IV, 45–57). In his secret dispatch to Vincent on May 28, 1823,
Metternich expressed confidence that Louis XVIII would find an acknowledg-
ment of Ferdinand's rights unavoidable though distasteful. Weisungen,
Frankreich, Fasc. 354, No. 4.

[124] Chateaubriand (Paris, May 27, 1823) to De la Ferronnays, in Chateaubriand, *Congrès de Vérone*, II, 28–30; Chateaubriand (Paris, May 29, June 2
and 8, 1823) to Caraman, Varia, Frankreich, Fasc. 97A.

[125] Lebzeltern (St. Petersburg, June 23, 1823) to Metternich, Berichte,
Russland, Fasc. 58, Nos. 3 and B; Vincent (Paris, June 2 and 8, 1823) to
Metternich, Berichte, Frankreich, Fasc. 352, No. 103.

[126] Metternich (Vienna, June 28, 1823) to Lebzeltern, Weisungen, Russland,
Fasc. 60, No. 1; Metternich (Vienna, June 24, 1823) to Brunetti, Weisungen
und Varia, Spanien, Fasc. 191, No. 1, with supplements; Chateaubriand (Paris,
June 26, 1823) to Talaru (French envoy at Madrid), in Chateaubriand,
Congrès de Vérone, II, 68–69; Brunetti (Madrid, June 28, July 4 and 24, 1823)
to Metternich, Berichte, Spanien, Fasc. 190, Nos. 1, 2, and 5. Ironically
enough, the abortive regency project served not only to estrange France and
Naples but also to begin the estrangement between Austria and Naples.
Ferdinand I considered that his own just cause had been abandoned by
Austria.—Moscati, *Il regno delle Due Sicilie*, I, xli.

After this fiasco, Metternich relaxed his efforts to control the course of the French intervention, partly because it was apparent that he would not succeed in his efforts, and partly because the ideas of Chateaubriand on the restored government in Spain were actually not too different from Metternich's own.[127] He did, however, take the precaution of making a secret *démarche* to Ferdinand VII with the other Eastern powers, urging him to make no promises or commitments whatsoever to anyone prior to his release from captivity. The purpose of this move, of course, was to try to forestall any possibility of Ferdinand's promising any constitutional concessions to Spain under French influence.[128] Ferdinand obeyed these instructions in principle, if not to the letter, by making many promises to the revolutionaries before his release and then repudiating them all immediately upon being liberated on October 1.[129]

The defeat suffered by Metternich in the French intervention—his failure to prevent intervention or to control the action of France, as well as his inability to keep England from breaking with the alliance—did not, to be sure, shake his confidence that his policy had been perfectly correct throughout. It was rather France, he said, that had made two great mistakes. The first was that her government had believed for a long time "that *material action* against the Spanish revolution could be avoided," whereas Metternich had always known that it could not be. The second mistake was that, having finally been forced by circumstances into intervention, France had acted alone instead of with the alliance.[130] As for England, Metternich consoled himself with the thought that that nation, "corrupted to the bone by the spirit of revolution," was headed toward eventual

---

[127] Vincent (Paris, June 25, 1823) to Metternich, Berichte, Frankreich, Fasc. 352, No. 107D.

[128] Brunetti (Madrid, September 15, 1823) to Metternich, Berichte, Spanien, Fasc. 190, No. 26.

[129] See Ferdinand's declarations to the Spanish people at Cádiz, September 30, 1823, and Port St. Mary, October 1, 1823, in *British and Foreign State Papers*, X (1822–1823), 998–1000, and XI (1823–1824), 860–862.

[130] Metternich (Witzomierzitz, Moravia, September 24, 1823) to Brunetti, Weisungen und Varia, Spanien, Fasc. 191, No. 1. The truth is, of course, that this alleged "mistake" of supposing that material action against the Spanish revolution could and should be avoided was the very foundation of Metternich's policy on Spain from the outbreak of the revolution to the very eve of French intervention three years later.

dissolution and that Canning, like Villèle in France, was destined soon to fall.[131]

Some of Metternich's worst fears in regard to the French intervention in Spain were, it is true, not realized. No constitution was granted to Spain after the restoration—the incorrigibly reactionary character of Ferdinand VII and his supporters saw to that. Nor did France gain a new sphere of influence, for Ferdinand proved to be as ungrateful to his liberators as he was vengeful toward his domestic enemies, and the French soon gave him up as hopeless. France's national ambition and desire for glory, however, had been reawakened, and, as Metternich was fond of saying, an ambitious France even under Ultraroyalist rule was a revolutionary France. Moreover, England, with Canning more firmly in control than before at the Foreign Office, now stood wholly outside the alliance, ready to make trouble for Metternich in the New World, in Greece, and elsewhere. What did remain in Metternich's possession was the achievement on which he had laid the greatest importance since 1820—the close alliance of the conservative Eastern powers, together with their bevy of Central European satellites.

Nevertheless, with the French overthrow of the Spanish revolution, an important turning point for Metternich's diplomacy had been reached and passed. No longer would Austria be able to use the fear of universal revolution to push through her policies everywhere in Europe. Count de Serre, French envoy to Naples, described the change and its significance well when he wrote to Chateaubriand:

The fear of revolutions is the common sentiment which, for the past eight years, has held the great powers united and Europe in peace. A peril, once it is past, is quickly forgotten, and this fear will be greatly enfeebled once the Peninsula will have been restored and pacified. Then the politics of the interests, of the ambitions of one power versus the other, the old politics, if you wish, will resume all its rights.[132]

[131] Metternich (Vienna, March 6, April 24, June 5, 1823) to Lebzeltern, Weisungen, Russland, Fasc. 60, Nos. 1 and 3. This was one of the occasions on which the "astounding foresight" which Srbik attributes to Metternich did not serve him well. Villèle remained in power until 1828 and Canning until his death in 1827.—Heinrich Ritter von Srbik, "Der Ideengehalt des Metternichschen Systems," *Historische Zeitschrift,* CXXXI (1925), 261.

[132] Naples, August 9, 1823, in Chateaubriand, *Congrès de Vérone,* II, 114.

CHAPTER VIII

METTERNICH–
EUROPEAN STATESMAN
OR AUSTRIAN DIPLOMAT?

FACTS

It is not too difficult to judge Metternich's diplomacy during 1820–1823 simply from the standpoint of his success or failure in achieving his objectives. The period was in general one of striking victories for Metternich. At Troppau and Laibach he achieved his goals of destroying the Italian revolutions and restoring undisputed Austrian hegemony in the peninsula without having to make any concessions to liberalism and constitutionalism or having to tolerate any interference with the Austrian action by the other powers. He was even able to secure wholehearted cooperation and support from two of them—Russia and Prussia—and the moral support of a third —France. He more than compensated for his one loss—the rift with England—by converting Alexander from liberalism to thorough-going conservatism and thereby transforming Russia from a potentially dangerous rival to a congenial friend and powerful ally.

The difficulties that Metternich encountered with the restored governments of Naples and Piedmont were, to be sure, embarrassing and annoying to him, but they were no serious setback for his policy. For in the end Metternich secured what was really important to him: the restoration of absolutism and the suppression of political change and agitation in Italy. Moreover, he saw to it that Austrian control over the Italian states emerged even from this difficulty strengthened rather than weakened—an important success for him.

Another striking achievement was the Austrian Chancellor's success in preventing an outbreak of war in the Russo-Turk crisis of 1821–1822. To be sure, Metternich's diplomacy was not the only or even the chief factor involved in preventing war. Castlereagh must be credited with helping to restrain Russia, while the efforts of Strangford did the most to wring tardy concessions from the Turks. The main reason why war was avoided, moreover, was undoubtedly the willingness of Alexander to be restrained by his Allies from following a course dictated by Russian national interests.[1] Nevertheless, Metternich showed great skill in playing on Alexander's European sentiments, counteracting the influence of Capodistrias and the war party in Russia, and keeping open the diplomatic alternatives to a war which might have been ruinous to his standstill European system.

Even the Congress of Verona, as long as it lasted, represented at least in good part a victory for Metternich. Although he was forced to abandon his original stand of wishing to leave the Spanish revolution entirely alone, he did succeed in restraining Alexander from open military intervention and in inducing Montmorency to align France with the Eastern powers. The price he paid—the renewed alienation of England—was a high one, but probably inevitable in any case. His inability once again to implement his plan for an Italian League and secret Italian and European antirevolutionary organizations was a significant failure, but he did manage to keep the existing system for Central Europe intact. Only the aftermath of Verona—France's success in carrying out the intervention in Spain independently of the alliance, and England's open break away from the Continental autocracies—brought real defeats for Metternich.

---

[1] This is one of many instances in Alexander's policy which make it, in my opinion, quite impossible to accept J. H. Pirenne's thesis that Alexander, under the guise of idealistic proposals, was actually following a "pitilessly realistic" power policy.—*Sainte-Alliance*, II, 389–390, *et passim.* Had Alexander wished to pursue such a policy, nothing could have dissuaded him from going to war with the Turks in 1821. He had the best possible pretext—persistent Turkish violation of the Treaty of Bucharest; the best possible objectives—extension of Russian territory and influence into the Balkans; and every prospect of an easy military victory. The worst that could have happened with regard to the other powers is that Britain would have declared her neutrality. The possibility of an anti-Russian coalition like that of 1854 was nil. See Castlereagh (London, April 29, 1822) to Bagot and to Strangford, *Varia, Grossbritannien*, Fasc. 19. In my opinion, Schiemann is entirely correct in maintaining that from the Russian viewpoint Alexander made two great mistakes: first, he subjected himself to the European Areopagus of his own making, denying Russian interests thereby; and second, without giving up the hope of eventually driving the Turks out of Europe, he wanted the alliance and "Europe" to share the responsibility for it.—*Russland unter Nikolaus I*, I, 320. It was these two tendencies in Alexander that Metternich successfully exploited.

One may argue that Metternich's victories were quite temporary, and that they would have been impossible without vital conditions which were in his favor. Both objections are true enough as far as they go. Certainly Metternich's success in maintaining an outward show of European unity up to the Congress of Verona could not cancel the fact that after this Congress the Concert of Europe was broken and the old policy of conflicting alignments and national interests was once more openly followed.[2] His success in averting a Russo-Turk war in 1821–1822 did not keep the Greek revolution from making such strides that Metternich increasingly lost control of the situation, being driven after 1825 into a defensive, entirely passive position.[3] Nor was he able to prevent England from going her own way in Latin America, or France and Belgium from dealing heavy blows to the whole Vienna system in the revolutions of 1830 and 1831.[4] It is also clear that conditions unusually favorable to Metternich's diplomacy existed in Europe following the fall of Napoleon —the widespread desire among governments and people for peace and order above all else, the prevailing harmony of conservative interests and dispositions among the great powers, and the great fear of revolution which made especially the lesser princes amenable to Metternich's repressive policies. Furthermore, Metternich never had to face the kind of opposition that many diplomats have encountered. No other great power, for instance, ever threatened to oppose him to the point of a war or even a break in relations with Austria during this period.

Yet to concede all this is not to disparage Metternich's achievements. Even the best diplomatic victories have a way of being temporary. It does not detract from Bismarck's successes to point out that they collapsed very rapidly after 1890. Some of Metternich's achievements, moreover, were by no means ephemeral, one instance being the close union of the Eastern powers which persisted until the debacle of 1848, although after 1825, with the accession of Nicholas I, Russia tended to become more and more the dominant partner. Metternich's system for Central Europe—his most important and most desired achievement—also survived until 1848, though in

---

[2] Charles Dupuis, *Le principe d'équilibre et le concert Européen de la paix de Westphalie à l'acte d'Algésiras,* 190–192.

[3] Rieben, *Metternichs Europapolitik,* 80–84, 93.

[4] *Ibid.,* 98–117.

commercial matters Prussia and her customs union had already become a dangerously divisive force within the German Confederation.[5] In any case, a quarter-century or more is not a bad record for
the endurance of a system in European affairs.

It may be supposed, furthermore, that diplomatic victories are
never won without having at least some important conditions favoring them. Certainly not *all* the relevant factors were favorable to
Metternich. He had to cope with the serious handicap of Austria's
internal instability and military and financial weakness, which compelled him to compromise or retreat whenever he met serious opposition and forced him on the defensive whenever his means of persuasion and moral influence proved unavailing. Arrayed against him,
moreover, were the very forces, not yet at full flood, which would
bring his system crashing to the ground in 1848—liberalism, nationalism, and revolution.

It cannot be denied, then, that Metternich displayed diplomatic
talents of a high order, amounting almost to genius. In this respect,
no one in the nineteenth century matched him except Bismarck.
More open to dispute are the questions of what ends Metternich
sought to achieve with his diplomacy, and how worthwhile these
ends were. Few even of Metternich's detractors would deny his
diplomatic skill, while his defenders, notably his eminent biographer, Heinrich Ritter von Srbik, insist that something better and
deeper is required to account for Metternich's achievements than
mere diplomatic skill and maneuvering.[6]

Before attempting to add my bit to the acrid and not wholly edi-
fying controversy over Metternich, I wish to stress two points by
way of precaution. First, my own interpretation covers only Metternich's foreign policy during 1820–1823, and is thus at most a limited
contribution to a general interpretation of Metternich's policy. This
condition applies to all the rest of this chapter, even where it is not
explicitly stated. Second, the evaluation of Metternich's policy given
here is intended to be simply descriptive and historical, not moral.
Even where I use words unavoidably charged with moral connota-

[5] *Ibid.*, 49–55.
[6] Srbik, *Metternich*, I, 317–320; Srbik, "Ideengehalt des Systems," *Historische
Zeitschrift*, CXXXI (1925), 240–241; Arnold O. Meyer, "Der Streit um
Metternich," *ibid.*, CLVII (1938), 76.

tions (e.g., "repressive," "standstill") in characterizing Metternich's policy, the intent is to give an accurate description, not a moral judgment.

Plainly, it would be presumptuous as well as futile for me to attempt in a brief space a point-by-point analysis and critique of Srbik's interpretation of Metternich. Srbik's main thesis, however, has become familiar and widely accepted, and has influenced to a greater or lesser extent such historians as Hugo Hantsch, Werner Näf, Constantin de Grunwald, Hans Rieben, and, most recently, Henry A. Kissinger.[7] According to this interpretation, Metternich was a man of many faults and shortcomings, indeed, but withal a political figure far removed from the blind reactionary pictured by nineteenth-century historians. Despite grave mistakes, he was, all in all, a constructive European statesman. His program for Austria and Europe was based on a system of coherent principles, not a patchwork of day-to-day diplomatic maneuvers; his policy was highly conservative, but definitely not reactionary.[8]

The objection to this construction of Metternich, in my opinion, is that, though persuasive and convincing at first appearance, it does not, when applied to the period under consideration, seem to fit the evidence at hand. My own impression, in dealing with Metternich from 1820 to 1823, is that, instead of finding the long-range principles and plans of a constructive European statesman, one is continually confronted in the documents with the short-range maneuvers and expedients of a repressive Austrian diplomat. Three basic questions regarding Metternich's policy and attitudes in this period may explain and defend this conclusion. First, was his policy constructive? Second, was it "European"? Third, was it genuinely conservative? The answer to each question, properly understood and qualified, must, I believe, be in the negative.

As to the first, Metternich's policy in this period was not constructive for the simple reason that he was not trying to construct anything. His aim was not to make things happen, but to prevent things

---

[7] Hugo Hantsch, *Die Geschichte Österreichs*, II, 303–307; Näf, *Staat und Staatsgedanke*, 15–21; Constantin de Grünwald, *La Vie de Metternich*, 197–212; Rieben, *Metternichs Europapolitik*, 9–22; and Henry A. Kissinger, *A World Restored: Metternich, Castlereagh and the Problems of Peace, 1812–1822*.

[8] Srbik, *Metternich*, I, 88–93, 122–128, 324–327, 350–420, *et passim*.

from happening; not to meet problems in some positive way, but simply to restrain and prevent political action, change, innovation, and movement of all kinds. In Germany his aim was to hold down political movement by so organizing and directing the Confederation as to make such movement impossible, or nearly so. In Italy his goal was so to crush the Italian revolutions as to leave no spark which might set off future change and agitation, and to reorganize the Italian governments, strengthen the Austrian hegemony, and place the Italian states under great-power supervision—all in order to prevent change and movement. In the Russo-Turk crisis all his diplomatic activity was designed to prevent Russia from going to war because it opened up all sorts of possibilities for change and movement in Europe. With France and the Spanish revolution, again, his whole policy was designed to prevent French intervention if possible and to limit and control it if it could not be prevented, because it was vital to keep a restless nation like France from undertaking an active policy at home or abroad.

The same abhorrence of change governed Metternich's attitude and policy toward all the great powers. Prussia was for Austria a menace and a rival so long as she entertained plans for a constitution. Once persuaded by Metternich that she should make no change at all in her fundamental institutions, Prussia was accepted as a safe and loyal ally. Before 1820 Metternich feared Russia more than any other state, because she was a source of political movement and change; after 1820 the Tsarist government was Austria's strongest support, because Metternich had, as he liked to say, steered Alexander and Russia out of their vagaries and onto a fixed (unchanging) course. France was inherently changeable, and therefore inherently dangerous. So long as British policy remained thoroughly conservative at home and abroad, Metternich could accept everything about Great Britain—her constitution, her parliamentary system, even her civil liberties. Once, however, England adopted a policy of accepting and even encouraging political change, Metternich quickly discovered that the English government was based on thoroughly bad principles, and that her constitution, her parliamentary system, and her civil liberties were nothing but highroads toward the revolution in which England was doomed to disintegrate.

This tendency to deplore and restrain all political movement, evident not only in Metternich's major decisions and actions, but also in numerous lesser ones,[9] is so strong that it tempts one to the sweeping assertion that Metternich had no real foreign-policy goal in these years other than to prevent change. Every other goal which can legitimately be ascribed to him—preventing war, preserving the alliance, crushing revolutions, and "reforming" and strengthening governments—can be understood correctly, insofar as he actually pursued these goals, as a part of this general policy.

[9] The following is a partial list, arranged in rough chronological order, of various projects, not discussed in this study, which Metternich espoused and for which he solicited Allied support: supervising and controlling the policy of the French ministry in 1819; suppressing *The Friend of Liberty,* a periodical in Sweden, despite Swedish freedom of the press; suppressing the King of Württemberg's challenges to the Carlsbad and Vienna resolutions; rebuking King William of the Netherlands for recognizing the constitutional government at Naples; forcing King William to punish the Belgian editor of the periodical *Le Flambeau,* despite freedom of the press in the Netherlands, because *Le Flambeau* had attacked the Holy Alliance; repressing the activities of the leading German Philhellene, Professor Friedrich Thiersch of Munich; preventing the abdicated Victor Emmanuel of Sardinia from resuming residence in Piedmont; rebuking King Charles John of Sweden for his alleged defection from the monarchical cause; suppressing the liberal *Gazette* of Augsburg in Württemberg, despite freedom of the press in Württemberg; repressing the activities of English, French, and Russian agents in Italy; compelling Anstett, the Russian envoy at Frankfurt, to cease helping the opposition faction in the German Confederation; getting England to extradite, or at least to alienate, the Italian revolutionaries in exile there; forcing the Grand Duke of Tuscany to stop harboring Greek sailors at Pisa and Livorno and showing sympathy for them; making arrangements for the exchange of secret-police information with France, once France became safely Royalist; suppressing the Württemberg circular protesting against the secrecy of the Congress of Verona; and admonishing the Swiss not only to remove the Piedmontese refugees from the Italian border but also to keep watch over their movements in Switzerland. It would be difficult to say that any of the foregoing projects, to which Metternich devoted considerable attention, had something other than repressive purposes. See Metternich (Rome, April 23, 1819, and Vienna, February 14, 1820) to Esterhazy, Weisungen, Grossbritannien, Fasc. 210, No. 1, and Fasc. 213, No. 3; Lebzeltern (St. Petersburg, May 5, 1820) to Metternich, Berichte, Russland, Fasc. 29, No. 34A; Metternich (Vienna, September 29, 1820 [with supplement], June 23, July 18, October 14, December 6, 18, and 23, 1821) to Lebzeltern, Weisungen, Russland, Fasc. 44 and 45; Metternich (Vienna, January 26 and March 22, 1822) to Esterhazy, Weisungen, Grossbritannien, Fasc. 218, Nos. 1 and 4; Metternich (Vienna, March 31, 1822) to Lebzeltern, Weisungen, Russland, Fasc. 54, Nos. 4, 9, and 10; Metternich (Vienna, March 19, 1822) to Lützow (with supplements), Weisungen, Türkei, Fasc. 14; Metternich (Vienna, July 10, 1822) to Vincent, Weisungen, Frankreich, Fasc. 350, No. 4; Metternich (Vienna, January 30, February 8, and June 5, 1823) to Lebzeltern, Weisungen, Russland, Fasc. 60, Nos. 1, 2, and 4.

To argue, as I have, that Metternich's policy was one of repression and standstillism is not to imply that everything he did was wrong. His actions in the Russo-Turk crisis or the French-Spanish imbroglio, for example, might well be justified as the defense of a *status quo* which was better than any practicable change. It is quite arguable that Austria's internal weaknesses, together with the personality of her Emperor, made a policy of standstillism the only one possible. The only point here is that it is hard to see how such a purely negative policy can be labeled "constructive."

A further obstacle to such a label is the sheer inadequacy of the programs Metternich recommended to meet the fundamental problems of state in such areas as Naples, the rest of Italy, or Spain. Here a striking contrast between Metternich as diplomat and as statesman becomes evident. As a diplomat, Metternich possessed almost all the requisite talents. He was perceptive in his appraisal of the relevant factors in each situation, keenly analytical of his own and his opponent's positions, fertile in expedients, and readily adaptable to changed situations. His dealings with Alexander, Capodistrias, and Tatistchev demonstrate these abilities particularly well, but other examples could also be cited. Yet when Metternich came to devising programs and policies of government, these qualities of realism, farsightedness, flexibility, and skillful articulation of means to ends apparently abandoned him.

Here the Neapolitan example is instructive. Metternich certainly achieved some insight into the causes of the revolution—e.g., his rather tardy recognition of the effects of De Medicis' "blind fiscality" —but by and large his view of the revolution and its causes and consequences was quite defective. He continued to regard the sects and sectarian activity as the fundamental evil at Naples long after De Menz and even Ficquelmont had relegated them to a position of relative unimportance. He insisted that the constitutionalists and Muratists were Italian nationalists, although their whole program belied it. For a long time he refused to believe that Ferdinand I himself was behind the arbitrary and vengeful policies of his ministers, resorting to the palpable fiction that the King was only ill-advised. He blamed all the post-revolutionary troubles in the Neapolitan government and the ruinous deficits of the post-revolutionary regime on the chaos and wastefulness of the revolutionary re-

gime, despite overwhelming evidence given him by Ficquelmont
which disproved this contention.

If Metternich's appraisals of the existing situation were thus often
unrealistic (and more examples could be given), his proposals for
solving Naples' problems can fairly be described as superficial,
inadequate, and even at times irrelevant. The whole Laibach plan,
advanced as an answer to all the governmental troubles of the kingdom, called for nothing more than a limited amount of administrative reorganization. Whatever its merits—and these are open to dispute—it simply did not touch the basic social, economic, and cultural problems of Naples, or even its fundamental political problem
—the exclusion of the most intelligent and capable subjects from
any share in the government. Though De Menz repeatedly referred
to these problems, and Ficquelmont often touched upon them, Metternich seems to have paid no attention. De Menz, like Daiser in
Piedmont, urged education and reform of the clergy and the nobility
as a long-range answer to the problems of scarcity of good leaders
and administrators, the demoralization of public administration, and
the prevailing "spirit of buffoonery" in the Neapolitan regime. Ficquelmont suggested bringing back the Duke of Calabria and the
Muratists into the administration. De Menz's suggestions were ignored and Ficquelmont's proposal vetoed on political grounds. Metternich's uniform answer was that the King must solve his administrative problems by finding those men in his kingdom who were full
of loyalty, good will, and talents, and placing the functions of government in their hands—a solution which does nothing more than
restate the problem.

Other examples of the insufficiency of Metternich's proposed solutions could be adduced. It is, for instance, difficult to understand
how Metternich could be so long and so firmly confident that his
proposed *Consultas,* which were royally appointed, purely advisory
councils, could make of Naples a "tempered monarchy," free of
arbitrariness and despotism. His own experience richly proved that,
despite Ferdinand's complete dependence on Austria for military
and political support, all the diplomatic resources of Austria and
her Allies were not sufficient to bring the King under control. Similarly, his insistence that Naples could easily bear the costs of the
occupation if only it would make certain economies in its own ad-

ministration seems like a willful rejection of the facts. But enough
has perhaps been said to illustrate the point that a narrow and rigid
political philosophy prevented Metternich from appraising socio-
political situations with the same realism that he displayed in diplomatic situations, and from recognizing the weaknesses and inade-
quacies of his political and social ideas as he recognized the limitations of the diplomatic resources at his disposal.

Since Metternich's policy was negative, it is not surprising that
the results of it were mainly negative also. That Metternich scored
a noteworthy diplomatic victory in crushing the Neapolitan revolution goes without saying, and if one accepts the view that Austria
and Europe really could not endure the example of a successful
revolt and a constitutional regime in Italy, the intervention can be
justified as an Austrian and European necessity. There is no doubt,
however, that Naples paid for it in more ways than one. For after
the Austrian intervention, occupation, reorganization, and general
interference in Neapolitan affairs were over, only negative results
had been accomplished. The revolution was crushed, the constitution destroyed, Austrian hegemony secured. The old basic problems
of the kingdom, however, were worse than before, and some new
ones had been added. The monarch and his dynasty, formerly popular if not respected, were now hopelessly compromised. De Medicis'
taxes, which Metternich believed to be a chief cause of the revolution, were now of necessity more grinding and oppressive than ever.
The Austrian army had cost the kingdom of Naples a sum more than
twice as high as even the grossly exaggerated figure Metternich
gave as the cost of the revolution. The Neapolitan public debt grew
very sharply, while the national economy suffered correspondingly,[10]
and the problems of brigandage, Sicilian unrest and insurrection,
and sectarian activity persisted or grew worse.

Of course Metternich was not solely or even mainly responsible
for most of these ills, some of which were endemic in the Kingdom
of the Two Sicilies. Probably Austrian intervention was better than
Carbonaro rule. Certainly Metternich's moderating influence helped
to check some of the arbitrary excesses of the government in Naples,
which were distinctly embarrassing to Austria on the international
scene, and to forestall a repetition of the bloody and disgraceful

[10] Bianchini, *Storia delle finanze*, 455–460.

scenes of Ferdinand's restoration in 1799. Yet if the Austrian policy was not the worst possible, the question remains as to whether it was the wisest. In regard to Naples, it must be emphasized, the choice was not one between Austrian intervention and Carbonaro rule. No important power in Europe opposed an intervention led by Austria to suppress the Carbonari. Even the constitutional ministry at Naples would have welcomed it. Had Metternich's aims been confined to the suppression of the sects and the revision of the constitution, there would have been little or no problem; it was his other aims that caused all the difficulty and necessitated his diplomatic maneuverings. The choice lay really between an Austrian intervention to crush the revolution by force, occupy the kingdom, and restore absolute government under Austrian supervision, and some form of peaceful diplomatic intervention—as espoused by Capodistrias, Pasquier, Richelieu, A'Court, Castlereagh, and the Muratists—to moderate the revolution, alter the constitution, and ensure peace and order in Naples and Europe. Even if one may have grave doubts about the viability and political cohesion of the Neapolitan constitutional regime,[11] it does not seem unreasonable to believe that Zurlo, Campochiaro, and their colleagues, given a relatively modest amount of European diplomatic pressure and support, could have carried through the constitutional changes necessary for European security at Naples and have built a fairly orderly and stable regime. At least they were, unlike Ferdinand I, Circello, Canosa, Ruffo, and their ilk, decent and respectable men.[12] Contrast that type of intervention with the full-scale armed occupation of Naples, the sweeping reorganization and supervision of its government, and the wholesale Austrian interference in Neapolitan affairs which were necessary to force Ferdinand back upon his throne and to keep a government under him and his senile appointees in even a semblance of working order. One may doubt that this kind of intervention served even Austrian interests in the long run. For what the Austrian victory over the revolution served to discredit was not, as Metternich claimed,

---

[11] See Alberti, "Rivoluzione napoletana," *Atti del Parlamento*, IV, xxvii, xliii, xlviii, liv–lv, lvii, *et passim*.

[12] On the character of the revolutionists, see *ibid.*, lv, and Romani, *Neapolitan Revolution*, 81–83. In contrast, the sober and judicious historian Charles K. Webster calls Ferdinand "almost imbecile" and Ruffo "disreputable."—*Foreign Policy of Castlereagh*, 112, 337.

the spirit of revolution and the principle of unrest itself,[13] but rather
the moderate, conservative-constitutional liberalism of the Muratists,
who wanted only upper-bourgeois rule and the French *Charte* in
Naples. Ultimately Metternich succeeded in helping to prepare
Naples and Italy for the thoroughly radical and anti-Austrian nationalism of the 1840's and 1850's.

Were the Naples affair the only instance of a negative and repressive policy on the part of Metternich, it might plausibly be argued
that it alone is no sufficient gauge of his views—that Austrian interests of state and reasons of expediency compelled Metternich to
adopt measures that he otherwise would not have espoused. But this
is not the case. Not only does Metternich give every indication of
having genuinely believed that his program represented a real solution for all the ills of Naples, but also it fits in well, as has been
shown, with the policies he advocated all over Europe, even where
Austria's interests were minimal. The Spanish problem, for instance,
did not involve Metternich existentially, as Naples did. Such considerations as the remoteness of Spain, Metternich's relative lack of
concern over Spanish affairs, and the absence of important responsibility for the use which might be made of Austrian advice, all would
lead one to believe that a policy Metternich drew up for the King
of Spain ought to represent his genuine convictions and principles,
relatively uninfluenced by the exigencies of *Realpolitik*. The "Profession of Faith" which Metternich made for Ferdinand VII,[14]
however, shows exactly the same characteristics as his policy for
Naples. Once again, he ignores the most basic problems, analyzes
others only in a sterile and superficial manner, and answers them
with merely verbal and quite useless solutions—and all in a tone of
inflexible dogmatic certitude.

He ascribes, for example, all the ills of Spain, with their deep
political, economic, social, and cultural roots, to the fact that the

[13] Metternich apparently convinced himself that the blows delivered to
revolution at Carlsbad and Laibach had been mortal ones. "I assure you," he
wrote Alexander, "that the complication of the moment [the Russo-Turk crisis]
is the last great effort which the principle of evil will make. Be sure that the
evil will recede." Metternich (Vienna, December 3, 1821) to Alexander,
Weisungen, Russland, Fasc. 45.

[14] Metternich (Vienna, December 26, 1823) to Brunetti, Weisungen und
Varia, Spanien, Fasc. 191, Nos. 1 and 2.

forms of government maintained prior to 1807 had since been neglected and forgotten. Let these forms be restored, and Spain's political problems would be solved. He expects the ancient Cortes, appointed by the King and serving purely as an advisory body, to end the ferocious tyranny of Ferdinand VII. He concludes a long discussion of the present critical state of Spain's governmental finances with a single suggestion: Let Spain establish "a system of finances and public credit based on solid and practical foundations." Again, the problem is answered by restating it. Faced by the mediocrity, pettiness, and dearth of talent prevailing among all the parties contending for power in Spain, and, in addition, by the fanatically reactionary spirit of the King and his most loyal supporters, Brunetti, A'Court, and other observers on the scene in Spain had virtually given up hope for decent government. Metternich, however, had a simple solution to propose for the problem of finding good administrators: In Spain, as everywhere else after a revolution, there existed three classes of subjects—the wicked, to be punished; the weak, to be amnestied; and the men of loyalty, good principles, and talent, to be drawn into the King's service. Let Ferdinand make this classification and choice, and all would be well. Yet again one sees the very type of an answer which only restates the problem. In the whole long and turgid memoir, no mention is made of such problems as the backwardness of trade and industry, the decline of agriculture, the poverty of the masses, brigandage and crime, the unreformed state of Church and clergy, and the lack of education even among the nobility.

One need not judge Metternich by modern standards of the welfare state to arrive at an unfavorable verdict on his approach to fundamental problems of state. He lagged behind the better standards of his own time. His own emissaries—De Menz, Daiser, and Brunetti—showed insights and programs better than his. If enlightened despotism, as has been said, was the deathbed repentance of absolute monarchy, Metternich, in this period at least, never repented. He showed no great zeal for the aims of enlightened despotism— the promotion of industry and agriculture, the advancement of education and learning, the elevation of the physical lot of the worker and the peasant, and the development of the resources of the state— while he repudiated its fundamental premise—that the state and its monarch exist to promote the welfare of its subjects—as part of the false philosophy and philanthropy of the eighteenth century.[15]

It may be objected that this appraisal leaves out Metternich's most important contribution to statecraft, his contribution to the maintenance of European peace and order. His most vital insight was the recognition that liberalism and nationalism, left unchecked, would lead to the wars and anarchy of the twentieth century. A clear evidence of his statesmanship was his effort to meet this danger by attempting to preserve the unity of the great powers, by espousing a principle of intervention against revolution, and by promoting the beginnings of a confederation of Europe.[16] Whatever the shortcomings of Metternich's outlook on domestic issues, in other words, his program was genuinely and constructively European.

Certainly there is something to this thesis. That is, Metternich was undoubtedly "European" in a sense that Palmerston or Clemenceau was not. He valued five-power unity and international accord and could never bring himself, as Canning did, to rejoice that the era of congresses was over and that the old politics of national ambition and balance of power were back in vogue. It is, I feel, important to keep in mind the fact that Metternich was an early-nineteenth-century aristocratic internationalist in outlook, not a twentieth-century democratic one. There were definite limitations to Metternich's Europeanism; self-interest and class interest played a definite role in shaping it. By "Europe" he generally meant only the five great powers and their machinery of state.[17] The European society and civilization which he claimed to defend are hardly distinguishable from the narrow, highly aristocratic society within which he ruled and prospered. The dangers he foresaw were not those of totalitarian democracy and total war, but simply those of successful middle-class revolution, which represented for him the great abyss, beyond which all was dark and incalculable. The impending chaos,

---

[15] See Metternich's memoir titled "Napoleon Bonaparte. Écrit en l'année 1820," Varia, Frankreich, Fasc. 93. The works of Count Corti give ample evidence that not only Francis I, as Srbik would have it (*Metternich*, I, 438), but also Metternich regarded the state as patrimony. See, for example, Corti's *Rise of the House of Rothschild*, 349–363, and his *Metternich und die Frauen*, II, 283–284.

[16] Hantsch, *Geschichte Österreichs*, II, 307.

[17] On Metternich's purely rationalistic concept of the state, see Srbik, *Metternich*, I, 122–128.

anarchy, and dissolution of society against which he so incessantly warned meant simply the overthrow of absolute monarchy and aristocratic rule in favor of constitutions, representative government, and middle-class predominance. Yet all the limitations in Metternich's international outlook do not deny him the status of a genuine nineteenth-century European. No one could expect him, in his time, to be a Robert Schuman or a Paul-Henri Spaak. Certainly he saw clearly that the conservative ideals and social order he represented were European and international in character and scope, and had to be defended on an international basis. Too much importance has been attached, in my opinion, to Metternich's statement, "Europe has for a long time held for me the significance of a fatherland," [18] but it does contain a kernel of truth.

It is one thing to recognize that Metternich's outlook was European. It is quite another, however, to argue that his *policy in this period was also European*, i.e., that his chief aims were the maintenance of five-power unity and the promotion of European principles and institutions in the direction of a confederation of Europe. There is, in my opinion, no real evidence to sustain this latter contention, and a good deal of evidence pointing in the opposite direction. One can demonstrate quite clearly that Metternich consistently followed a policy of defending and advancing his country's interests (as, of course, any statesman must). That he was willing at any time to sacrifice, subordinate, or even de-emphasize Austrian interests to maintain European unity or advance European goals appears doubtful.

He was not, for instance, ready to make sacrifices to maintain the unity of the Concert of Powers. To picture Metternich as struggling in vain to hold the alliance together against the separatist tendencies of England and France is, in my view, a serious misconception. However much Metternich talked about allied harmony and exhorted England and France to adhere to the common cause, the fact is that he deliberately chose a policy which he knew would drive at least one of them, and possibly both, out of the alliance, because this policy would enable him to form a separate, intimate coalition with Russia and Prussia more suitable for Austrian interests.

[18] This statement is quoted by Bertier de Sauvigny in his *Metternich et son temps* (p. 91) with the comment that these are words "for which he doubtless can be forgiven a great deal."

This is the precise significance of Metternich's adoption of the
Russian intervention principle at Troppau. Metternich knew that
England could tolerate neither a change in the purpose of the existing alliance nor an extension of the commitments of existing treaties.
Both Metternich and Gentz agreed in principle with Castlereagh's
interpretation of the alliance, and used much the same arguments
as he in criticizing Capodistrias' memoir of November 2 at the
Congress. Yet once Metternich had succeeded in making Russian
policy thoroughly conservative instead of mildly liberal, he not only
was willing to accept the intervention principle he had formerly
repudiated, but even to propose a new general treaty which would
place all European governments under great-power supervision,
guaranteeing them, through the great-power right of intervention,
against any illegal change. This proposal of Metternich's represented
so drastic a change in the purpose of the alliance and so sweeping
an extension of alliance commitments that even the Russians were
here unwilling to follow him.

Such a policy meant, of course, breaking all ties with England.
It must be emphasized that this was a deliberate, conscious choice
on Metternich's part. He knew that he was separating Austria from
England and France and creating a separate coalition with aims
different from those of the general alliance, because a close union
with Russia and Prussia was worth far more to Austria than the
general alliance, with its mere outward show of great-power unity,
could possibly be. He therefore counted the achievement of this
union, despite its bad results for the alliance, as one of his greatest
achievements. He wrote to Bubna at the Congress of Laibach:

As long as we could not strike in the first four weeks [after the outbreak
of the Neapolitan revolution] we had to seek strong moral supports for
ourselves. These we have found. The close union with Russia—and in
this matter it is both intimate and impossible to doubt—is a blessing
which cannot be sufficiently valued. England is dead so far as the Continent is concerned; France, more than uncertain. If I have accomplished
anything, it is this: to have united [*verbruedert*] *all our neighbors* with
us. Once [they are] bound and *compromised* on a matter of this sort,
their retreat is no longer possible. Who would have believed that Austria
could march in a moral union with Russia and Prussia, with Germany

and all the Italian princes? Did not all the calculations of the liberals go against this? [19]

The breach with England which Metternich here accepted as a small price to pay for Russian support was, to be sure, partly healed when their common interests in the Russo-Turk crisis served to bring Austria and England together. A second rift split them again at Verona, however, this time for good, and for the same reason that had arisen at Troppau. Forced to choose between a close union with Russia on the basis of a general intervention principle and cooperation with England on the basis of the letter and intent of the original alliance, Metternich chose Russia.

As for France, in 1820–1821 she also repudiated the Austro-Russian intervention principle, though less vigorously than England. In 1822–1823, however, France discovered that she could adapt the intervention policy and the Austrian example in Italy to her own ends in Spain. Thus the effect of Metternich's policy was also to help launch France on a course independent of the alliance in foreign affairs.

Unquestionably, alliance unity would have broken down sooner or later anyway. The whole trend of the times was against it; Canning and Villèle would eventually have followed independent policies regardless of what Metternich said or did. Yet this does not

[19] Metternich (Laibach, March 10, 1821) to Bubna, Kongressakten, Laibach, Fasc. 41. Werner Markert's article, "Metternich und Alexander I. Die Rivalität der Mächte in der europäischen Allianz" (in *Schicksalswege deutscher Vergangenheit,* edited by Walter Hubatsch, 147–176), includes many perceptive comments on Austro-Russian relations in the decade after the Congress of Vienna. However, he overestimates Metternich's reluctance to break with England and to become involved in the Russian intervention principle, and attributes too much influence to the English failure to support Austria. He writes, for example (pp. 167–168) "Metternich saw himself forced for the sake of the 'matter' to recognize the Russian 'form.'" Again: "By his repudiation of continental ties Castlereagh had sacrificed Austria to the influence of Russia." Yet, as Metternich's letter to Bubna demonstrates, and the whole course of the conferences shows, Metternich actually went over to the Russian intervention principle quite willingly, even exceeding Alexander in his zeal for it, once he was assured that he could gain Russian support on his terms. Rather than to speak of Castlereagh's sacrificing Austria by cutting his ties to the Continent, it would be more accurate to speak of Metternich's sacrificing England as an ally by cutting his ties with Castlereagh.

alter the fact that, far from struggling to maintain the unity of the alliance at all costs, Metternich was the first to break away from it and to form a separate bloc of states to advance Austrian interests. The independent policies pursued by the western powers were in part reactions to the separatist policy already begun by Austria.[20] Nor can Metternich's espousal of the intervention principle be regarded as evidence of a policy of European social conservatism, as has sometimes been argued. Quite apart from the fact that the principle served to divide Europe into two opposed camps, it is plain that Metternich's attitude toward intervention, both in theory and application, was strictly opportunistic. He opposed the doctrine of intervention, both on theoretical and practical grounds, up to November 7, 1820; thereafter he defended it with arguments that were often directly contrary to those he had used before. As for the actual application of the principle, Metternich opposed intervention to suppress four of the six European revolutions which broke out in this period. Only in regard to Naples and Piedmont did he invoke the intervention principle to justify an Austrian intervention designed to protect strictly Austrian interests. The conclusion is unmistakable: Metternich tailored his principles on intervention to suit the political exigencies of the moment. As the friend of England, he opposed a principle of intervention; as the friend of Russia, he adopted it. Where Austrian interests were at stake, he used it; outside the sphere of Austrian hegemony, he tried to prevent its use.

It is equally difficult to see European principles or federative polity in the institutions which Metternich attempted to establish. Whatever the German Confederation and the abortive Italian League might conceivably have led to in the way of European confederation, they were assuredly not intended by Metternich as means

---

[20] Lest the impression be given that the policy followed by Metternich at Troppau was something new, it should be pointed out that this was only one of several occasions on which he set out to form secret agreements setting one group of powers within the alliance apart from or against one or more others. For instance, he tried several times in 1816 and 1817 to form a secret four-power alignment against Russia. (See Chapter I, note 16.) Even before the rift with England, he made secret arrangements with the Eastern Allies on their policy toward France in case of Louis' death and toward England in case of the accession of a Whig ministry. After Troppau, finally, he made all sorts of secret agreements with the Eastern Allies covering various diplomatic moves and policies too numerous to mention here. (See Chapter VIII, note 9.) It is hard to conceive of these as steps designed to maintain alliance unity.

to this end. Indeed, their purpose was just the opposite—to reinforce an exclusively Austrian hegemony in Central Europe, and to prevent German or Italian unification or federation.[21] Two other Metternichean ideas which might be construed as leading toward European confederation—his various proposals for great-power supervision of smaller states and his repeated attempts to establish a joint information center at Vienna—are equally devoid of real European sentiment. Whether the enlarging of the sovereignty of three autocratic states at the expense of numerous small ones or the erection of an international antirevolutionary secret-police and spy system represent steps toward European confederation, others may decide; certainly Metternich valued these devices solely as weapons against revolution and political change.[22] It is, moreover, important to realize that Metternich proposed these ideas knowing that they would not unite Europe but would split it even further into two contending camps. Not only England and France, but also other constitutional states—Sweden, the Netherlands, Switzerland, and possibly the South German states—would certainly have opposed an international antirevolutionary information center. As for Metternich's principle of intervention, no small state, constitutional or absolutist, could have been fully comfortable with it. Had either of these ideas ever really been effected, the result would have been a sharpening of the division of Europe into two spheres—the autocracies of the East and their satellites versus the constitutional West.

Nor do some of Metternich's diplomatic practices conform to the picture of the European statesman concerned to promote harmony among the powers. However much he proclaimed to France that

---

[21] The two outstanding authorities on the Italian League, Bettanini and Grossmann (see Chapter I, note 8), concur in their estimate of the purpose of the scheme, although they disagree rather sharply on its merits. Bettanini upholds the Piedmontese position in the Sardinian-Austrian dispute over the League, while Grossmann defends Austrian policy; yet both agree that the clash was not between Austrian federative polity and Sardinian nationalism, but between two egocentric policies, both motivated by interests of state.

[22] On the operations of the secret-police system within Austria, see Fritz von Reinöhl, "Die österreichische Informationsbüros des Vormärz, ihre Akten und Protokolle," *Archivalische Zeitschrift*, 3d Series, Vol. 5 (1929), 261–288. Although a rather dry, technical study, the article demonstrates clearly the persistent interest and energy with which Metternich promoted antirevolutionary secret-police activity at home and abroad—and the purely negative and repressive purposes behind all the plans for centers of information.

Austria had no intention of trying, in the old discredited manner, to create a sphere of influence in Italy, his persistent efforts to reinforce and extend Austrian hegemony in Italy were bound to produce the conviction in France that this was exactly what Austria was doing. Metternich's practice of sowing suspicion and distrust between different powers in the Concert in order to align one or the other power more closely with Austria was likewise hardly conducive to Allied unity. In 1819–1820 Metternich exerted himself to make the English government suspicious of Russia, supplying Castlereagh with copious information on alleged Russian intrigues in Europe, Persia, India, and the Ionian Isles, then under British rule.[23] In 1821–1823, however, he was equally zealous about informing Alexander of the revolutionary tendencies of British policy all over the world.[24] At the Congress of Verona, finally, he carried off the virtuosic feat of arousing and maintaining Russian suspicion of France, French suspicion of Russia, and English suspicion of both France and Russia, all at the same time.[25] In the same style, and of the same doubtful value to European solidarity, was Metternich's policy of attempting to unseat people he disliked from their posts within other governments. Some of the targets of his intrigues were, in England, Charles Stuart, Lord Burghersh, and Canning; in France, the Duke of Dalberg, La Tour du Pin, and Pasquier; in Prussia, Humboldt and Hardenberg; and in Russia, Tatistchev, Stroganov, Pozzo di Borgo, and Capodistrias.

One need not moralize about these practices. Only when Metternich is presented as the European statesman *par excellence* and the assertion is made and repeated that Europe and the unity of the alliance were uppermost in his thought and action do these aspects of his diplomacy become hard to understand. For they are precisely the sort of practices which Castlereagh, for one, sought to avoid because he believed they were detrimental to Allied unity.[26] When,

[23] See Metternich, (Rome, April 23, 1819, and Vienna, February 6 and 14 and April 17, 1820) to Esterhazy, Weisungen, Grossbritannien, Fasc. 210 and 213.

[24] See, for example, Metternich (Vienna, August 24, 1821, and March 31, 1822) to Lebzeltern, Weisungen, Russland, Fasc. 45, No. 3, with supplement, and Fasc. 54, No. 12, with supplements.

[25] See Chapter VII. Also see Lebzeltern (St. Petersburg, April 29, 1822) to Metternich, Berichte, Russland, Fasc. 29, No. 37C; Metternich (Vienna, April 4, 1823) to Vincent, Weisungen, Frankreich, Fasc. 354, Nos. 2 and 4.

[26] Webster, *Foreign Policy of Castlereagh*, 64–68.

however, Metternich is seen primarily as an Austrian diplomat with Austrian interests to defend, these practices become wholly understandable, if not admirable, tools of his trade. Indeed, there is not a single major aspect of his policy in this period which is not best and most simply understood as an effort to secure power, peace, and internal security for the fragile Austrian monarchy. In his correspondence with Stadion and others Metternich sometimes says as much. His remarkable success in achieving his goals under the guise of European principles, and not the validity or the sincerity of the principles themselves, constitutes his own particular brand of greatness.[27]

The third basic question, "Was Metternich a conservative?" is probably the most difficult to answer, precisely because of the wealth of definitions and connotations which the word "conservative" bears. If one defines as conservative any philosophy or policy which identifies itself with the existing order and seeks to maintain it, then Metternich was certainly a conservative, and indeed the outstand-

[27] Perhaps the best argument for Metternich's policy as "European" would be a frank admission that in its immediate goals it was Austrian-centered, coupled with the thesis that Austria was, owing to its multinational composition and supranational character, itself a Europe in microcosm, and that therefore an Austria-centered policy was by virtue of that fact also "European." Such an argument, based on the idea of Austria's European mission, must have some appeal to those who, like myself, regard the collapse of the Austrian monarchy in 1918 as a tragedy for Europe. The argument is really persuasive, however, only to the extent that one concedes that the existing Austrian Empire of 1820, which Metternich was defending, actually represented a Europe in microcosm, and that its political structure and nationalities policies presented a fruitful analogy and example for the ultimate solution of Europe's national rivalries. In other words, a reformed and transformed Austria, with some kind of federal structure and representative institutions for her various peoples, might very well have merited being preserved and defended, not merely on the usual grounds of *raison d'état*, but also as a European necessity and as an example and starting point for the confederation and transformation of Europe as a whole. That the bureaucratic-absolutist Austria of Francis I represented any such hopeful trend, however, is impossible to believe. While Metternich himself was doubtless desirous of going much further than Francis would go to assuage the feelings of the national groups through decentralized administration and cultural autonomy (see, for example, Arthur G. Haas's article, "Kaiser Franz, Metternich und die Stellung Illyriens," *Mitteilungen des österreichischen Staatsarchivs*, XI [1958], pp. 373–398), even he could never have been comfortable with the kind of reforms really needed. (On this latter point, see the stimulating essay on the Franciscan era and Metternich's system in Robert A. Kann's *A Study in Austrian Intellectual History: From Late Baroque to Romanticism*.)

ing representative of conservatism in his time. If, however, one tries
to distinguish between policies of conservatism, standstillism, and
reaction, the question becomes much more complicated. For according to the commonplace definitions of a liberal as one who welcomes
change in society and tries to promote it, a conservative as one who
accepts change and tries to restrain and guide it, a "stand-patter" as
one who resists change and tries to retain what exists unchanged,
and a reactionary as one who rejects change and tries to restore an
order already past, Metternich's policy appears in this period to be
occasionally one of reaction,[28] usually one of standstillism, and sel-
dom if ever one of conservatism. To use the German terms for which
there seem to be no precise English equivalents, his was a policy of
Beharren, not *Erhaltung.*

That Metternich's policy during this era was essentially a negative, repressive one of resistance to change has already been argued
at some length. The only point which might be added to that thesis
here is that this policy does not seem to have been only a temporary
expedient forced upon Metternich by the revolutionary events of the
time, but rather to have been coherent with his general outlook. It
is impossible to avoid the impression that Metternich equated change
and reform with subversion and revolution. He viewed the world
in Zoroastrian terms as an arena of perpetual struggle between two
world-governing principles, that of order and good versus that of
evil and anarchy. Every existing right was not merely legitimate but
holy (a favorite Metternichean phrase is "the sanctity of all existing
rights"); every call for change or attempt at change made by anyone except a legitimate sovereign was not merely illegitimate but
wickedly presumptuous. All the good men of right principles, sound
reasoning, loyalty, and courage were on Metternich's side; only
knaves, malcontents, and fools were on the other. All liberals, however moderate, were really revolutionaries; all demands for a constitution or for reforms, however limited, were really steps toward
anarchy and revolution; all attacks upon the existing order, whatever their nature, were plots fomented by the Central Revolutionary
Committee in Paris.[29] Now one may make many allowances in ap-

---

[28] While I believe Metternich's policy may on occasion be legitimately
termed "reactionary," the word bears such an ineradicable bad moral connotation that I intend to avoid its use where possible.

[29] As the *reductio ad absurdum* of Metternich's fears about the omnipresent

praising statements like this, encountered so frequently in Metternich's writings. One may attribute the moral fervor and the evangelistic ardor of his denunciations to the purposes of rhetoric and propaganda. One may account for the sweeping and dogmatic character of his assertions as the result of his tendency toward exaggeration, or of his propensity for clear-cut, rigid categories and classifications. Yet when every possible allowance has been made, it is only fair to Metternich to recognize that there is a substantial kernel of conviction beneath the husk of extravagant language. He was neither wholly cynical nor wholly self-deceived. Ultimately, he really believed that it was by preventing change and by preserving the *status quo* that he could do the most good in saving society.

Once again, one may readily grant that Metternich was not alone in this philosophy of state. He was doubtless the most distinguished of a whole host of sovereigns, ministers, and theorists who believed and argued as he did. His kind of thinking has persisted through revolutions and wars down to the present day. The only claim I am unwilling to grant is that Metternich's views represent any genuine conservative philosophy worthy of being compared with that of Edmund Burke, for example. His "system" was something else again —a wholehearted adherence to the *status quo* in principle, and a supple, stubborn, but ultimately hopeless defense of it in practice.

There are, to be sure, several considerations which appear to give the lie to this theory and to demonstrate in Metternich a greater flexibility in outlook than I have conceded. It might be argued that Metternich insisted he opposed not change *per se*, but only uncontrolled—hence revolutionary—change. He was no rigid absolutist, for he praised the British constitution and could at least tolerate constitutions in France and South Germany. Neither was he an inflexible legitimist, for he sometimes ignored or tampered with the principle of legitimacy, and nursed a secret admiration for the great usurper, Napoleon.

---

revolutionary conspiracy, one might cite his apparently serious contention that a speech by the American President, James Monroe, announcing diplomatic recognition of certain South American countries, coupled with a request by Colombia for such recognition from European powers, were evidence of a concerted plot hatched in Paris for the subversion of both worlds. Metternich (Vienna, June 5, 1822) to Lebzeltern, Weisungen, Russland, Fasc. 54, No. 3.

All these statements are true enough, and demonstrate that Metternich was not, in Grillparzer's phrase, "the Don Quixote of legitimacy," who spent his life fighting phantoms and tilting at windmills.
There is certainly a great gulf fixed between Metternich and the
monarchs with whom and with whose cause he was identified. But
the difference between himself and a Ferdinand I, a Charles X, a
Charles Felix, or a Francis I lay in Metternich's greater intelligence,
suppleness, and common sense, not in any fundamental difference
in outlook. Closely examined, the evidences for his flexibility prove
only that he knew when and how to yield to the power of circumstances—and he could never have been the great diplomat that he
was without a mastery of this art. Beyond this, these evidences
prove nothing.

The fact that Metternich sometimes conceded in principle the
admissibility of political change (as in the proposed Act of Guarantee at Troppau) does not bear great weight, first of all because, as
has already been argued, the whole role of principles in his policy
is a dubious one. He rode roughshod over several of what he claimed
were his most sacred principles in his dealings with Ferdinand I
and Naples,[30] while displaying on other occasions an ingenious but
logically questionable facility for drawing two exactly opposite
conclusions from one and the same principle to suit different needs.[31]

[30] The principles that Metternich violated most clearly were those of the
independence and integrity of sovereign states, noninterference in the internal
affairs of other states, and the unimpeachable authority and freedom of the
monarch's will within his domains.

[31] In October 1820, Metternich proved on the basis of monarchical principles
that only King Ferdinand I could decide what was good for his kingdom, and
that the Allies had to accept whatever he decreed; in November he proved on
the basis of the very same principles that the Allies had to decide what was
good for Naples, and that Ferdinand would have to accept this. In June 1820,
Metternich proved from history that no foreign material intervention had ever
served to crush a revolution or to cure its evils (this was when Russia wished
to intervene in Spain); in August, he argued, again from history, that only
material force would suffice to crush the hydra of revolution (this was when
Austria wished to intervene in Naples). Most capricious of all, perhaps, is the
logical sleight-of-hand by which Metternich at Laibach deduced from the
principle of the absolute sovereignty and independence of every state the sacred
right and duty of the Eastern powers to supervise the governments of lesser
states. Though Metternich, in my opinion, was no deep thinker, he was certainly intelligent enough to see through such legerdemain as this.

Not rancor or prejudice, then, but a prudent skepticism warns one against leaning heavily on a Metternichean statement of principle unless it has been translated into practice.

And precisely this did not happen. Theoretically, Metternich conceded the admissibility of change, provided that it was initiated from above by the legitimate sovereign (a right, incidentally, which a legitimist could hardly deny to a monarch). In practice, however, this theoretical admission played no role at all in Metternich's policy. His private counsel to every sovereign was to make no changes at all in fundamental institutions, and all other changes only in the interest of repressing agitation and revolution. He counted it a positive virtue of the Italian sovereigns, even before the 1820 revolutions, that they made no innovations at all, and he did his utmost at Laibach and Verona to take away their right to make innovations in the future. At best, Metternich's principle would have reserved the right to initiate changes solely to those least interested in making them; in actual practice he sought to reduce even these minimal chances of change to something approaching zero.

Metternich's theoretical admission of legitimate, peaceful change, therefore, does not really disprove the claim that his policy was one of standstillism; nor do his apparent concessions to constitutionalism make him less an absolutist. Certainly he accepted the British constitution so long as Great Britain and Austria were close partners— it would have been very foolish of him to attack it. The British constitution, he reasoned, was ancient and therefore real; all others were modern and hence artificial.[32] Once the split between England and Austria emerged at Laibach, however, a totally different appraisal of the British system appears in Metternich's dispatches, one consistent with the whole tenor of his other views and principles. Now he contended that England, because of her representative system and civil liberties, was on the road to becoming "the most dangerous enemy of repose and order which Europe will ever have faced."[33] An important evil which Austria had to fight against, he

---

[32] Metternich (Vienna, March 23, 1820) to Esterhazy, Weisungen, Grossbritannien, Fasc. 213.

[33] Metternich (Vienna, August 24, 1821) to Lebzeltern, Weisungen, Russland, Fasc. 45, No. 3, with supplement titled "Observations sur les discussions au Parlement Brittanique relativement à la question de Naples."

maintained, "is the essentially false position in which the English monarchy finds itself since the revolution of 1688." [34] The strain in Anglo-Austrian relations was simply the concomitant of a fundamental difference in system between a monarchy *de jure,* resting squarely on the right of prescription and legitimacy, and a monarchy which existed solely *de facto,* because it attempted to reconcile monarchical right with popular sovereignty. [35] The most signal proof of the degeneration of English statesmanship was that even Castlereagh and Liverpool repudiated the ideas of divine right and passive obedience and argued for the existence of that chimerical monster, a justified revolution. According to Metternich, the Revolution in 1688 was, in reality, no revolution at all, but solely a legal development of the existing system, and "the mere idea of a revolution founded upon any right whatsoever has never entered the head of any competent interpreter of the spirit and history of that [British] constitution." [36]

Much more could be said about these and other similarly startling assertions, as well as the Cassandralike prophecies of England's impending doom which Metternich up to the time of his death never tired of proclaiming. [37] But enough has been said to indicate that, whatever ideological kinship there may have existed between Metternich and a Lord Eldon or George IV, he was certainly at heart far from being a true disciple of Edmund Burke. [38]

As for the French *Charte,* during this period at least Metternich never approved of it in principle, but was reconciled to it only because any alternative to it (a Royalist *coup d'etat,* for example) was more dangerous than the *Charte* itself. [39] He regarded the

---

[34] Metternich (Vienna, June 30, 1821) to Esterhazy, Weisungen, Grossbritannien, Fasc. 217, No. 1.

[35] *Ibid.*

[36] Metternich (Vienna, July 16, 1821) to Esterhazy, *ibid.,* No. 3 (a secret letter) and another reserved letter. After the accession of Canning to power, Metternich and Francis denounced England and her system even more unreservedly. See various letters by Metternich in 1823 and 1825, in Metternich, *Nachgelassene Papiere,* IV, 11–12, 25, 156, 160–161, 212–220.

[37] A good critical study of Metternich's attitude toward England is Paul Anderegg, *Metternichs Urteil über die politischen Verhältnisse Englands.*

[38] As Srbik would have it (*Metternich,* I, 94–95).

[39] Gordon (with whom Metternich was on good terms) once commented, "There is little doubt that Prince Metternich's last and great object would be to destroy everything like a representative government in Europe, with the

French as innately unfit for constitutional rule, requiring despotic rule like that of Napoleon.[40] Far from breaking with the doctrine of legitimacy in regard to France, he argued that had the Allies not restored the Bourbon dynasty in France, all their glorious efforts would have been in vain, "for the first of all principles, . . . the foremost of all of society's interests [legitimacy], would not have been satisfied." [41]

Nor does Metternich's admiration for Napoleon (a highly equivocal admiration, incidentally) change the general picture of his outlook. For the Napoleon whom Metternich admired was a divine-right legitimist at heart, who regretted "not being able to invoke the principle of legitimacy as the basis of his power," and who hoped some day himself to assume the title of "Holy" which the Austrian Emperor had officially laid down.[42] What made Napoleon great in Metternich's eyes was his conquest of the revolution, his subjection of the masses, and his ability, while being himself indifferent to religious practices, to use and appreciate religion, particularly Catholicism, as the basis for government and the source of order.[43] In short, Metternich showed a leaning for neither the reformer nor the conqueror in Napoleon, but for the cynical and successful despot with a strong penchant for legitimacy and order—someone, that is, not far removed from Metternich himself.

No evidence, therefore, tells seriously against the view that Metternich's political theory in this period was that of absolutism, complete with divine right and passive obedience. However much he spoke of "tempered monarchy" and ancient forms, it altered in no way his insistence that all power in the state belonged indivisibly

---

exception of that of Great Britain." Memorandum by Gordon, September 22, 1822, in Wellington, *Correspondence*, I, 298.

[40] Metternich (Vienna, March 23, 1820) to Esterhazy, Weisungen, Grossbritannien, Fasc. 213.

[41] Metternich (Prague, June 5, 1820) to Lebzeltern, Weisungen, Russland, Fasc. 44, No. 2. The same attitude is confirmed by Metternich's displeasure even with good French Royalist political theorists like Vicomte Bonald for their failure to sufficiently stress the importance of legitimacy (Metternich [Vienna, October 6, 1821] to Lebzeltern, *ibid.*, Fasc. 45, No. 2), and his hearty approval of the principles, if not the tactics, of Charles X and Polignac.—Rieben, *Metternichs Europapolitik*, 94–97.

[42] Memoir by Metternich, "Napoleon Bonaparte. Écrit en l'année 1820," Varia, Frankreich, Fasc. 93.

[43] *Ibid.*

and inalienably to the king, the sole divinely-ordained source of all authority, against whose will there could be no possible justified resistance or revolt. No advisory bodies could exist, no ministers function in the state other than at the royal pleasure. Liberty meant simply the freedom of the king's will; autocratic governments were therefore free governments and constitutional regimes were *ipso facto* unfree. The national will was the will of the sovereign. Kings were made to govern, and people to be governed. Two things, to be ruled firmly and to enjoy material prosperity, represented the sum total of popular capabilities, needs, and aspirations. "The mass of the people," remarked Metternich, citing Napoleon as his authority, "is always inert; they suffer their burdens in silence; and material benefits are regarded and enjoyed by them as well-being." [44]

It bears repeating that no one need become exercised over this rather cynical but commonly-held doctrine of the early nineteenth century. It is so little surprising that Metternich shared it that the point would scarcely be worth making had not the rehabilitation of Metternich proceeded to the point where some would make of him a political philosopher with conservative principles of timeless validity.[45] Against this tendency, it may be useful to point out once more that Metternich was basically a rigid absolutist whose political outlook was tied to a system of government and society which may once have had its grandeur and fitness, but which even by Metternich's time was becoming outworn, and by our own is completely anachronistic. It does Metternich no good service to take very seriously his boastful claims to modernity. His famous lament that he was born in the wrong century and would have been better off seeing the light of day either a century earlier or later is only partly justified. In the seventeenth or eighteenth century, he would certainly have been at home. In his own age, he achieved undeniable stature, perhaps even greatness, as the outstanding representative

[44] *Ibid.*

[45] Among his biographers, this tendency is most noticeable in Helene du Coudray's *Metternich* and Algernon Cecil's *Metternich, 1773–1859: A Study of His Period and His Personality*. Such works as Peter Viereck's *Conservatism Revisited: The Revolt against Revolt*; the same writer's "New Views on Metternich," *Review of Politics*, XIII (April 1951), 211–228; Albert Garreau's *Saint Empire*; and Bela Menczer's "Metternich and Donoso Cortes," *Dublin Review*, No. 444 (1948), 19–51, go even further in this direction.

and defender of a dying order. But in the twentieth century, he could only have been a Von Papen.

To say all this is certainly not to return to Metternich as the blind monster sometimes portrayed in nineteenth-century historiography,[46] or even Viktor Bibl's more recent "demon of Austria," a Metternich without a single redeeming quality, responsible for everything that has gone wrong with Austria since 1809.[47] No one can deny to Metternich the virtues of moderation, caution, and love of peace, nor the qualities of courage (in his own way) and outstanding diplomatic skill. Often his diplomacy was very successful; sometimes his influence and policy worked for good, though on the whole their results for Austria and Europe were hardly good in the long run. Metternich also must bear only part of the responsibility for the standstill policy followed by Austria. Certainly the character of Francis I, the peculiar makeup of the Habsburg Empire, and possibly even the folk characteristics of the Austrian people were factors of equal or greater importance.[48] Finally, if it has any bearing, one may readily admit that the repressive policies of Metternich look very mild alongside the tyranny of a Hitler or Stalin.[49] Tyranny, like most things, is much more highly developed and organized in the twentieth century—and Metternich was never a tyrant in the real sense of the word.

The only view to which one must return if the interpretation set out here is correct is something like that of Charles Dupuis, who contended early in the twentieth century that Metternich led the Concert of Europe more as a good Austrian than as a good European, and that this was an important factor in the system's decline.[50]

---

[46] A particularly bad example of this is found in William Roscoe Thayer, *The Dawn of Italian Independence: Italy from the Congress of Vienna, 1814, to the Fall of Venice, 1849.*

[47] Viktor Bibl, *Metternich, der Dämon Österreichs,* 23–34, 354–367.

[48] On the causes of the breakdown of the pre-1848 order in Austria, see Josef Redlich, *Das österreichische Staats- und Reichsproblem. Geschichtliche Darstellung der inneren Politik der Habsburgischen Monarchie von 1848 bis zum Untergang des Reiches,* 67-79.

[49] Golo Mann, for example, writes of the Carlsbad decrees: "When their wording is carefully examined today one can only recall sadly and enviously the time when such decrees passed for the most monstrous example of despotism and reaction."—*Secretary of Europe,* 267.

[50] Dupuis, *Principe du équilibre,* 154–157.

My own interpretation involves simply seeing Metternich, for this period at least, as less statesman than diplomat; as less European than Austrian; as less a constructive conservative than a repressive "stand-patter"; as less profound and earnest than clever but essentially cynical and superficial; and also, perhaps, as less the philosopher-king and forerunner of European unity than the *grand seigneur*, outstanding in certain abilities but typical of his class in his general outlook, and dedicating his efforts to preserving and enjoying the old regime.

BIBLIOGRAPHY

PRIMARY SOURCES

A. Unpublished Documents (from the Haus- Hof- und Staatsarchiv in Vienna)

Staatskanzlei: Auswärtiges Amt:
Frankreich: Weisungen, Berichte, Varia, 1820–1823
Friedensakten, 1800–1840
Grossbritannien: Weisungen, Berichte, Varia, 1819–1823
Kongressakten: Troppau, Laibach, Florenz, Rom, Neapel, Verona
Neapel: Weisungen, Berichte, Varia, Korrespondenz,
  Hofkorrespondenz, 1820–1823
  Österreichische Armee in Neapel, 1815–1827
Russland: Weisungen, Berichte, Varia, 1820–1823
Sardinien: Weisungen, Berichte, Varia, 1820–1822
Spanien: Weisungen, Berichte, Varia, 1820–1823
Türkei: Weisungen, Berichte, Varia, 1821–1822
  Orientalische Angelegenheiten, 1810–1822
Verträge Betreffende Akten, 1800–1840
Staatskanzlei: Provinzen:
Lombardei-Venezien, 1819–1823
Staatskanzlei: Interiora:
Korrespondenz, Fascs. 81–82
Geheime Korrespondenz, Fasc. IV (not classified)

B. Published Documents, Memoirs, and Letters

Antioche, Adhémar Comte d'. *Chateaubriand Ambassadeur à Londres (1822) d'après ses dépêches inédites.* Paris: Perrin, 1912.
Atti del Parlamento delle Due Sicilie 1820–1821. Edited under the direction of Annibale Alberti. 6 vols. Bologna: Nicola Zanichelli, 1926–1941.
Atti relativi all'intervento di S. M. il Re delle Due Sicilie nel Congresso di Leybach. Naples: Luigi Nobile, 1820.

Bertier de Sauvigny, Guillaume de. *France and the European Alliance, 1816–1821: The Private Correspondence between Metternich and Richelieu.* Notre Dame, Ind.: University of Notre Dame Press, 1958.

British and Foreign State Papers. Vols. VII–XI (1819–1824). London: William Ridgway, 1826–1830.

Chateaubriand, François Vicomte de. *Congrès de Vérone; Guerre d'Espagne; Negociations; Colonies Espagnoles.* 2 vols. Paris: Bethune et Plon, 1838.

Consalvi, Hercule Cardinal. *Correspondance du Cardinal Hercule Consalvi avec le Prince Clement de Metternich 1815–1823.* Edited by Charles Van Duerm. Louvain: Polleunis and Centerick, 1899.

Gentz, Friedrich von. *Aus dem Nachlass Varnhagens von Ense: Tagebücher von Friedrich von Gentz.* Foreword by Ludmilla Assing. 4 vols. in 2 parts. Leipzig: F. A. Brockhaus, 1873–1874.

———. *Briefe von und an Friedrich von Gentz.* Edited by Friedrich Carl Wittichen and Ernst Salzer. 3 vols. in 4 parts. Munich and Berlin: R. Oldenbourg, 1909–1913.

———. *Dépêches inédites du chevalier de Gentz aux hospodars de Valachie pour servir à l'histoire de la politique européenne (1813 à 1828).* Published by Graf Anton Prokesch von Osten. 3 vols. Paris: E. Plon, 1876–1877.

Lebzeltern, Ludwig Graf. *Les rapports diplomatiques de Lebzeltern, ministre d'Autriche à la cour de Russie (1816–1826).* Edited by Grand Duc Nicolas Mikhailowitch. St. Petersburg: Manufacture des papiers de l'état, 1913.

———. *Un Collaborateur de Metternich: Mémoires et papiers de Lebzeltern.* Published by Emanuel de Lévis-Mirepoix. Paris: Plon, 1949.

Lieven, Daría Khristoforovna. *The Private Letters of Princess Lieven to Prince Metternich 1820–1826.* Edited with a biographical foreword by Peter Quennell. London: John Murray, 1937.

———. *The Unpublished Diary and Political Sketches of Princess Lieven together with Some of Her Letters.* Edited with elucidations by Harold Temperley. London: Jonathan Cape, 1925.

Londonderry, Robert Stewart, Second Marquess of. *Memoirs and Correspondence of Viscount Castlereagh, second Marquess of Londonderry.* Edited by his brother, Charles Vane, Third Marquess of Londonderry. 12 vols. London: H. Colburn, 1850–1853.

Metternich-Winneburg, Clemens Lothar Wenzel Fürst von. *Aus Metternichs nachgelassenen Papieren.* Edited by his son, Prince Richard Metternich-Winneburg. 8 vols. Vienna: W. Braumüller, 1880–1884.

———. *Briefe des Staatskanzlers Fürsten Metternich Winneburg an den österreichischen Minister des Allerhöchsten Hauses und des Äussern, Grafen Buol-Schauenstein, aus den Jahren 1852–1859.* Edited by Carl J. Burckhardt. Munich and Berlin: R. Oldenbourg, 1934.

————. *Geist und Herz Verbündet: Metternichs Briefe an die Gräfin Lieven.* Edited with a foreword by Emil Mika. Vienna: Wilhelm Andermann, 1942.

Moscati, Ruggero. *Il regno delle Due Sicilie e l'Austria: Documenti dal marzo 1821 al novembre 1830.* 2 vols. Naples: Presso la R. Deputazione, 1937.

Orloff, Grégoire Comte. *Mémoires historiques, politiques et littéraries sur le royaume de Naples.* Edited by Amaury Duval. 5 vols. Paris: Chasseriau, 1818–1821.

Pasquier, Étienne Denis Duc. *Histoire de mon temps. Mémoires du chancelier Pasquier.* Published by the Duke of Audiffret-Pasquier. 6 vols. Paris: E. Plon, Nourrit, 1893–1895.

Prokesch von Osten, Anton Graf. *Aus dem Nachlasse des Grafen Prokesch-Osten. Vol. II: Briefwechsel mit Herrn von Gentz und Fürsten Metternich.* Vienna: Gerold, 1881.

————. *Geschichte des Abfalls der Griechen vom türkischen Reiche in Jahre 1821 und der Gründung des hellenischen Königreiches. Aus diplomatischem Standpuncte.* 6 vols. Vienna: Gerold, 1867-1880.

Richelieu, Armand du Plessis, Duc de. "Le second ministère du duc de Richelieu. Fragment d'autobiographie," *Revue historique,* Vol. XXXVII (1888), 100–133.

Villèle, Jean Baptiste Comte de. *Mémoires et correspondance du Comte de Villèle.* 2d ed., 5 vols. Paris: Perrin, 1904.

Wellington, Arthur Wellesley, First Duke of, *Despatches, Correspondence, and Memoranda of Field Marshal Arthur Duke of Wellington, K. G.* Edited by his son, the Duke of Wellington, K.G. 8 vols. London: John Murray, 1867–1880.

SECONDARY WORKS

A. Books

Alberti, Annibale. "La rivoluzione Napoletana, il suo Parlamento e la reazione europea 1820–1821," in *Atti del Parlamento delle Due Sicilie 1820–1821,* edited under the direction of Annibale Alberti. Vol. IV, vii–cdx. Bologna: Nicola Zanichelli, 1935.

Anderegg, Paul. *Metternichs Urteil über die politischen Verhältnisse Englands.* Horn-Wien: F. Berger, 1954.

Artz, Frederick B. *Reaction and Revolution, 1814–1832.* Vol. XIII in the "Rise of Modern Europe Series," edited by William L. Langer. New York: Harper, 1934.

Berkeley, George F. H. *Italy in the Making, 1815–1848.* Vol. I, 1815–1846. Cambridge, England: University Press, 1932.

Bertier de Sauvigny, G. de. *Metternich et son Temps.* Paris: Hachette, 1959.

————. *La Restauration.* Paris: Flammarion, 1955.

Bianchi, Nicomede. *Storia documentata della diplomazia europea in Italia dall'anno 1814 all'anno 1861.* 8 vols. Turin: Unione Tipografico-Editrice, 1865–1872.

Bianchini, Lodovico. *Storia delle finanze del regno di Napoli.* 3d ed. Naples: Stamperia Reale, 1859.

Bianco, Giuseppe. *La rivoluzione Siciliana del 1820 con documenti e carteggi inediti.* Florence: Bernardo Seeber, 1905.

Bibl, Viktor. *Kaiser Franz, der letzte Römisch-Deutsche Kaiser.* Leipzig and Vienna: Günther, 1938.

————. *Metternich, der Dämon Österreichs.* 2d ed. Leipzig and Vienna: Günther, 1938.

————. *Metternich in neuer Beleuchtung: Sein geheimer Briefwechsel mit dem bayerischen Staatsminister Wrede nach unveröffentlichten Dokumenten aus den Archiven in Wien und München.* Vienna: L. W. Seidel, 1928.

————. *Der Zerfall Österreichs.* 2 vols. Leipzig, Vienna, Berlin, Munich: Rikola, 1922–1924.

Binder, Wilhelm. *Fürst Clemens von Metternich und sein Zeitalter, eine geschichtlich-biographische Darstellung.* Ludwigsburg: C. F. Nast, 1836.

Bourquin, Maurice. *Histoire de la Sainte-Alliance.* Geneva: Georg, 1954.

Brady, Joseph H. *Rome and the Neapolitan Revolution of 1820–1821: A Study in Papal Neutrality.* Columbia University Studies in History, Economics, and Public Law, No. 431. New York: Columbia University Press, 1937.

The Cambridge History of British Foreign Policy, 1783–1911. Edited by Sir A. W. Ward and George P. Gooch. 3 vols. New York: Macmillan, 1922–1923.

The Cambridge Modern History. Edited by Sir A. W. Ward, Sir G. W. Prothero, and Sir Stanley Leathes, K.C.B. Vol. X, *The Restoration.* Cambridge, England: University Press, 1934.

Capefigue, Jean Baptiste Honoré Raymond. *Histoire de la Restauration et des causes qui ont amené la chute de la branche ainée des Bourbons.* 10 vols. Paris: Dufey and Hezard, 1831–1833.

Cecil, Algernon. *Metternich, 1773–1859: A Study of His Period and His Personality.* London: Eyre and Spottiswoode, 1947.

Colletta, Pietro. *Storia del Reame di Napoli.* 2d ed. 2 vols. Florence: Le Monnier, 1848.

Corti, Egon Cäsar Conte. *Metternich und die Frauen.* 2 vols. Zurich: Europa-Verlag, 1948–1949.

————. *The Rise of the House of Rothschild.* Translated from the German by Brian and Beatrix Lunn. New York: Cosmopolitan, 1928.

Crawley, Charles William. *The Question of Greek Independence: A Study of British Policy in the Near East, 1821–1833.* Cambridge, England: University Press, 1930.

Cresson, W. P. *The Holy Alliance: The European Background of the Monroe Doctrine.* New York: Oxford University Press, 1922.

Debidour, Antonin. *Histoire diplomatique de l'Europe depuis l'ouverture du Congrès de Vienne jusqu'à la clôture du Congrès de Berlin, 1814–1878.* Paris: F. Alcan, 1891.

Demelitsch, Fedor von. *Metternich und seine auswärtige Politik.* Stuttgart: Cotta, 1898.

Driault, Edouard. *La question d'Orient depuis ses origines jusqu'à la paix de Sèvres* (1920). 8th ed. Paris: F. Alcan, 1921.

Du Coudray, Helene. *Metternich.* New Haven: Yale University Press, 1936.

Dupuis, Charles. *Le principe d'équilibre et le concert européen de la paix de Westphalie à l'acte d'Algésiras.* Paris: Perrin, 1909.

Finlay, George. *A History of Greece from its Conquest by the Romans to the Present Time, B.C. 146 to A.D. 1864.* Vol. VI, *The Greek Revolution, Part I, A.D. 1821–1827.* Oxford: Clarendon Press, 1887.

Garreau, Albert. *Saint Empire.* Paris: La Colombe, 1954.

Greenfield, Kent Roberts. *Economics and Liberalism in the Risorgimento: A Study of Nationalism in Lombardy.* Baltimore: Johns Hopkins University Press, 1934.

Griewank, Karl. *Der Wiener Kongress und die neue Ordnung Europas 1814–1815.* 2d ed. Leipzig: Koehler and Amelang, 1954.

Grünwald, Constantin de. *Alexandre Ier, le Tsar mystique.* Paris: Amiot-Dumont, 1955.

————. *La vie de Metternich.* Paris: Calmann-Lévy, 1939.

Gulick, Edward Vose. *Europe's Classical Balance of Power: A Case History of the Theory and Practice of One of the Great Concepts of European Statecraft.* Ithaca: Cornell University Press, 1955.

Hantsch, Hugo. *Die Geschichte Österreichs.* 2d ed. 2 vols. Graz and Vienna: Styria Steirische Verlagsanstalt, 1937, 1951.

Herman, Arthur. *Metternich.* London: G. Allen and Unwin, 1932.

Hudal, Alois. *Die österreichische Vatikanbotschaft (1806–1918).* Munich: Pohl, 1952.

Hudson, Nora E. *Ultra-Royalism and the French Restoration.* Cambridge, England: University Press, 1936.

Kann, Robert A. *A Study in Austrian Intellectual History: From Late Baroque to Romanticism.* New York: Praeger, 1960.

Kissinger, Henry A. *A World Restored: Metternich, Castlereagh and the Problems of Peace, 1812–1822.* Boston: Houghton Mifflin, 1957.

Lamprecht, Karl. *Deutsche Geschichte.* 13 vols. Berlin: R. Gaertner, 1894–1909.

Lauber, Emil. *Metternichs Kampf um die europäische Mitte: Struktur seiner Politik von 1809 bis 1815.* Vienna and Leipzig: A. Luser, 1939.

Lemmi, Francesco, *et al. La rivoluzione Piemontese dell'anno 1821.* Vols.

XI and XII of *Bibliotecà di storia italiana recente* (1800–1870). Turin: Bocca, 1923.

Luzio, Alessandro. *Carlo Alberto e Giuseppe Mazzini: Studi e ricerche di storia del Risorgimento.* Turin: Bocca, 1923.

Mann, Golo. *Secretary of Europe: The Life of Friedrich von Gentz, Enemy of Napoleon.* Translated from the German by William H. Woglom. New Haven: Yale University Press, 1946.

Maturi, Walter. *Il Principe di Canosa.* Florence: Le Monnier, 1944.

May, Arthur. *The Age of Metternich, 1814–1848.* New York: Henry Holt, 1933.

Mayr, Josef Karl. *Geschichte der österreichischen Staatskanzlei im Zeitalter des Fürsten Metternich.* Vienna: Haus- Hof- und Staatsarchiv Verlag, 1935.

——. *Metternichs Geheimer Briefdienst. Postlogen und Postkurse.* Vienna: Haus- Hof- und Staatsarchiv Verlag, 1935.

Meyer, Werner. *Vormärz. Die Ara Metternichs 1815 bis 1848.* Potsdam: Potsdamer Verlagsgesellschaft, 1948.

Monti, Antonio. *Il Risorgimento.* Vol. I (1814–1860) in *Storia politica d'Italia dalle origini ai giorni nostri.* Milan: Francesco Vallardi, 1948.

Näf, Werner. *Staat und Staatsgedanke. Vorträge zur neueren Geschichte.* Berne: Lang, 1935.

——. *Zur Geschichte der Heiligen Allianz.* Vol. 1 in *Berner Untersuchungen zur allgemeinen Geschichte,* edited by Werner Näf. Berne: Haupt, 1928.

Nettement, Alfred. *Histoire de la Restauration.* 8 vols. Paris: J. LeCoffre, 1860–1872.

Nicolson, Harold G. *The Congress of Vienna: A Study in Allied Unity, 1812–1822.* New York: Harcourt, Brace, 1946.

Paleologue, Georges Maurice. *The Romantic Diplomat: Talleyrand, Metternich, Chateaubriand.* Translated from the French by Arthur Chambers. London: Hutchinson, 1926.

Phillips, Walter Alison. *The Confederation of Europe: A Study of the European Alliance, 1813–1823, as an Experiment in the International Organization of Peace.* London: Longmans, 1913.

——. *The War of Greek Independence, 1821 to 1833.* London: Smith, Elder, 1897.

Pirenne, Jacques-Henri. *La Sainte-Alliance: Organisation européenne de la paix mondiale.* 2 vols. Neuchâtel, Switzerland: Boudry, 1946–1949.

Pouqueville, F. C. H. L. *Histoire de la régénération de la Grèce, comprénant le précis des événements depuis 1740 jusqu'en 1824.* 4 vols. Paris: F. Didot, 1824.

Puryear, Vernon J. *France and the Levant from the Bourbon Restoration to the Peace of Kutiah.* Vol. 27, University of California Publications in History. Berkeley and Los Angeles: University of California Press, 1941.

Redlich, Josef. *Das österreichische Staats- und Reichs-problem. Geschichtliche Darstellung der inneren Politik der Habsburgischen Monarchie von 1848 bis zum Untergang des Reiches.* Leipzig: Neue Geist, 1920.

Rieben, Hans. *Prinzipiengrundlage und Diplomatie in Metternichs Europapolitik, 1815–1848.* Vol. 12 in *Berner Untersuchungen zur allgemeinen Geschichte,* edited by Werner Näf. Aarau, Switzerland: H. Sauerländer, 1942.

Rohden, Peter Richard. *Die klassische Diplomatie von Kaunitz bis Metternich.* Leipzig: Koehler and Amelang, 1939.

Romani, George T. *The Neapolitan Revolution of 1820–1821.* Evanston, Ill.: Northwestern University Press, 1950.

Sandonà, Augusto. *Il regno Lombardo Veneto 1814–1859: La costituzione e l'amministrazione.* Milan: L. F. Cogliati, 1912.

Schenk, Hans G. *The Aftermath of the Napoleonic Wars: The Concept of Europe—an Experiment.* New York: Oxford University Press, 1947.

Schiemann, Theodor. *Geschichte Russlands unter Kaiser Nikolaus I.* 4 vols. Berlin: G. Reimer, 1904–1919.

Schlitter, Heinrich. *Aus Österreichs Vormärz.* 4 vols. in 2. Zurich, Leipzig, Vienna: Amalthea, 1920.

Schmalz, Hans W. *Versuche einer gesamteuropäischen Organisation 1815–1820, mit besonderer Berücksichtigung der Troppauer Interventionspolitik.* Vol. 10 in *Berner Untersuchungen zur allgemeinen Geschichte,* edited by Werner Näf. Aarau, Switzerland: H. Sauerländer, 1940.

Schnabel, Franz. *Deutsche Geschichte im Neunzehnten Jahrhundert.* 4 vols. Freiburg im Breisgau: Herder, 1929–1936.

Schwarz, Wilhelm. *Die Heilige Allianz: Tragik eines europäischen Friedensbundes.* Stuttgart: Cotta, 1935.

Schweizer, Paul. *Geschichte der schweizerischen Neutralität.* Frauenfeld: Huber, 1895.

Seignobos, Charles. *Histoire politique de l'Europe contemporaine: evolution des partis et des formes politiques, 1814–1914.* 7th ed. 2 vols. Paris: A. Colin, 1924–1926.

Soutzo, Alexandre. *Histoire de la révolution grècque.* Paris: F. Didot, 1829.

Spellanzon, Cesare. *Storia del Risorgimento e dell'Unità d'Italia.* 5 vols. Milan: Rizzoli, 1933–1951.

Srbik, Heinrich Ritter von. *Deutsche Einheit. Idee und Wirklichkeit vom Heiligen Reich bis Königgrätz.* 4 vols. Munich: F. Bruckmann, 1935–1943.

———. *Geist und Geschichte vom deutschen Humanismus bis zur Gegenwart.* 2 vols. Munich: F. Bruckmann, 1950–1951.

———. "Metternich," in Vol. 3, *Meister der Politik,* edited by Erich Marcks. Stuttgart and Berlin: Deutsche Verlag, 1924.

————. *Metternich: Der Staatsmann und der Mensch.* 3 vols. Munich: F. Bruckmann, 1925, 1954.

Stählin, Karl. *Geschichte Russlands von den Anfängen bis zur Gegenwart.* 4 vols. in 5. Königsberg and Berlin: Ost-Europa Verlag, 1923–1939.

Stern, Alfred. *Geschichte Europas seit den Verträgen von 1815 bis zum Frankfurter Frieden von 1871.* 2d ed. 10 vols. Stuttgart and Berlin: Cotta, 1913–1925.

Stewart, H. F., and Paul Desjardins. *French Patriotism in the Nineteenth Century (1814–1833) Traced in Contemporary Texts.* Cambridge, England: University Press, 1923.

Strakhovsky, Leonid I. *Alexander I of Russia: The Man Who Defeated Napoleon.* New York: W. W. Norton, 1947.

Sweet, Paul R. *Friedrich von Gentz: Defender of the Old Order.* Madison: University of Wisconsin Press, 1941.

Temperley, Harold W. V. *The Foreign Policy of Canning, 1822–1827: England, the Neo-Holy Alliance, and the New World.* London: G. Bell, 1925.

Thayer, William Roscoe. *The Dawn of Italian Independence: Italy from the Congress of Vienna, 1814, to the Fall of Venice, 1849.* 2 vols. Boston: Houghton Mifflin, 1892.

Tritsch, Walther. *Metternich und sein Monarch: Biographie eines seltsamen Doppelgestirns.* Darmstadt: Halle, 1952.

Viereck, Peter. *Conservatism from John Adams to Churchill.* New York: D. Van Nostrand, 1956.

————. *Conservatism Revisited: The Revolt against Revolt.* New York: Scribner's, 1949.

Ward, Sir Adolphus W. *The Period of Congresses.* London and New York: Macmillan, 1919.

Webster, Charles K. *The Congress of Vienna, 1814–1815.* London: H. M. Stationery Office, 1919.

————. *The Foreign Policy of Castlereagh, 1815–1822: Britain and the European Alliance.* London: G. Bell, 1925.

Woodhouse, Christopher Montague. *The Greek War of Independence, its Historical Setting.* London: Hutchinson's University Library, 1952.

Woodward, E. L. *Three Studies in European Conservatism. Metternich: Guizot: The Catholic Church in the Nineteenth Century.* London: Constable, 1929.

B. ARTICLES

Avetta, Maria. "Al Congresso di Lubiano coi ministri di Re Vittorio Emanuele I," *Il Risorgimento italiano,* XVI (1923), 1-50, and XVII (1924), 212–250.

Bertier de Sauvigny, Guillaume de. "Metternich et Decazes, d'après leur correspondance inédite (1816–1820)," *Études d'histoire moderne et contemporaine,* V (1953), 60–115.

————. "Sainte-Alliance et Alliance dans les conceptions de Metternich," *Revue historique*, CCXXIII, No. 2 (April-June 1960), 249–274.

Bettanini, Antonio Maria. "Un disegno di Confederazione italiana nella politica internazionale della restaurazione," in *Studi di storia dei trattati e politica internazionale*. Padua: A. Milani, 1939, pp. 3–50.

Bittner, Ludwig. "Ein neues Werk über Metternich," *Mitteilungen des Instituts für österreichische Geschichtsforschung*, XLI (1926), 302–319.

Brinkmann, Karl. "Metternich der Staatsmann und der Mensch von Heinrich von Srbik," *Historische Zeitschrift*, CXXXIV (1926), 576–584.

Cessi Drudi, Maria. "Metternich in un giudizio del Hübner," *Nuova rivista storica*, XLII, No. 1 (January-April 1958), 78–86.

Dupuis, Charles. "La Sainte-Alliance et le Directoire européen de 1815–1818," *Revue d'histoire diplomatique*, XLVIII (1934), 265–292, 436–469.

Egidi, Pietro. "I moti studenteschi di Torino," in *La Rivoluzione Piemontese dell'anno 1821*. Vol. XI of *Biblioteca di storia Italiana recente (1800–1870)*. Turin: Bocca, 1923, 103–165.

Filipuzzi, Angelo. "La restaurazione nel Regno delle Due Sicilie dopo il Congresso di Lubiana," *Annali Triestini di diritto, economia e politica*, XI (1940), 161–206, 230–282.

————. "La rivoluzione di Grecia e la diplomazia europea fino al Congresso di Verona," *ibid.*, IX (1937–1938), 90–143.

Furlani, Silvio. "La questione postale italiana al Congresso di Verona," *Nuova rivista storica*, XXXII (1948), 36–49.

————. "La Santa Sede e il Congresso di Verona," *ibid.*, XXXIX (1955), 465–491, XL (1956), 14–47.

Green, John Eric Sidney. "Castlereagh's Instructions for the Conferences at Vienna," *Transactions of the Royal Historical Society*, 3d Series, VII (1913), 103–128.

————. "Wellington, Bois-Le-Comte, and Verona," *ibid.*, 4th Series, I (1918), 59–76.

————. "Wellington and the Congress of Verona, 1822," *English Historical Review*, CXXXVII (1920), 200–211.

Grossmann, Karl. "Metternichs Plan eines italienischen Bundes," *Historische Blätter*, No. 4 (1931), 37–76.

Grünwald, Constantin de. "Metternich et Alexandre Ier," *Le Monde Slave*, XV, No. 1 (January 1938), 29–61.

Haas, Arthur G. "Kaiser Franz, Metternich und die Stellung Illyriens," *Mitteilungen des österreichischen Staatsarchivs*, XI (1958), 373–398.

Kann, Robert A. "Metternich: a Reappraisal of his Impact on International Relations," *Journal of Modern History*, XXXII, No. 4 (December 1960), 333–339.

Kittel, E. "Metternichs Politische Grundanschauungen," *Historische Vierteljahrschrift*, XXXIV, No. 3 (1927), 443–483.

Markert, Werner. "Metternich und Alexander I. Die Rivalität der Mächte in der europäischen Allianz," in *Schicksalswege deutscher Vergangenheit*, edited by Walther Hubatsch. Düsseldorf: Droste-Verlag, 1950, 147–176.

Maturi, Walter. "Il Congresso di Vienna e la restaurazione dei Borboni a Napoli," *Rivista storica italiana*, New Series, III (1938), 32–72; IV (1939), 1–61.

Menczer, Bela. "Metternich and Donoso Cortes," *Dublin Review*, No. 444 (1948), 19–41.

Mendelssohn-Bartholdy, Karl. "Die orientalische Politik Metternichs," *Historische Zeitschrift*, XVIII (1867), 41–76.

Meyer, Arnold O. "Der Streit um Metternich," *Historische Zeitschrift*, CLVII (1938), 75–84.

Nichols, Irby C., Jr. "The Eastern Question and the Vienna Conference, September 1822," *Journal of Central European Affairs*, XXI, No. 1 (April 1961), 53–66.

Rantzau, Johann Albrecht von. "Friedrich von Gentz und die Politik," *Mitteilungen des Instituts für österreichische Geschichtsforschung*, XLIII (1929), 77–112.

Reinöhl, Fritz von. "Die österreichische Informationsbüros des Vormärz, ihre Akten und Protokolle," *Archivalische Zeitschrift*, 3d Series, V (1929), 261–288.

Schieder, Theodor. "Das Problem der Revolution im 19ten Jahrhundert," *Historische Zeitschrift*, CLXX (1950), 233–271.

Srbik, Heinrich Ritter von. "Entgegnung auf Wertheimers 'Gibt es einen neuen Metternich!'" *Forschungen zur Brandenburgischen und Preussischen Geschichte*, XXXIX (1927), 134–138.

———. "Erklärung zu Viktor Bibls 'Metternich der Dämon Österreichs,'" *Mitteilungen des Instituts für österreichische Geschichtsforschung*, L (1936), 505–507.

———. "Der Ideengehalt des Metternichschen Systems," *Historische Zeitschrift*, CXXXI (1925), 240–262.

———. "Der Kampf um Metternich," *Preussische Jahrbücher*, CCXV (1929), 118–120.

———. "Metternichs Plan der Neuordnung Europas 1814–1815," *Mitteilungen des Instituts für österreichische Geschichtsforschung*, XL (1927), 109–126.

———. "Viktor Bibls 'Metternich in neuer Beleuchtung,'" *ibid.*, XLII (1929), 397–409.

———. "Der Zerfall Österreichs. I Bd. Kaiser Franz und sein Erbe. Von Viktor Bibl," *Historische Zeitschrift*, CXXX (1924), 128–133.

Stählin, Karl. "Ideal und Wirklichkeit im letzten Jahrzehnt Alexanders I," *Historische Zeitschrift*, CXLV (1931), 90–105.

Tamborra, Angelo. "I Congressi della Santa Alleanza di Lubiana e di Verona e la politica della Santa Sede (1821–1822)," *Archivio storico italiano*, CXVIII (1960), 190–211.

Viereck, Peter. "New Views on Metternich," *Review of Politics,* XIII (April 1951), 211–228.

Wahl, Adalbert. "Metternich in neuer Beleuchtung von V. Bibl," *ibid.,* CXXXVIII (1928), 584–589.

Wertheimer, Eduard von. "Gibt es einen neuen Metternich! " *Forschungen zur Brandenburgischen und Preussischen Geschichte,* XXXVIII (1926), 339–367.

———. "Schlusswort an Prof. Heinrich von Srbik," *Preussische Jahrbücher,* CCXV (1929), 208–210.

C. UNPUBLISHED STUDIES

Nichols, Irby C., Jr. "Great Britain and the Congress of Verona." Doctoral dissertation, University of Michigan, 1955.

Skokan, Josefine Selma. "Die Korrespondenz des Fürsten Metternich mit dem Staatsrat Hudelist." Doctoral dissertation, University of Vienna, 1946.

Tarnawski, Ferdinand Franz. "Der Kongress von Verona." Doctoral dissertation, University of Vienna, 1925.

INDEX

of

SUBJECTS

and

PERSONS

INDEX of SUBJECTS

INDEX of PERSONS